Sources for
America's History

Volume 2: Since 1865

Sources for
America's History

Volume 2: Since 1865
Tenth Edition

Kevin B. Sheets
State University of New York, College at Cortland

bedford/st.martin's
Macmillan Learning
Boston | New York

Vice President: Leasa Burton
Senior Program Director: Michael Rosenberg
Senior Executive Program Manager: William J. Lombardo
Director of Content Development: Jane Knetzger
Senior Development Editor: Heidi Hood
Assistant Editor: Carly Lewis
Director of Media Editorial: Adam Whitehurst
Media Editor: Mollie Chandler
Senior Marketing Manager: Melissa Rodriguez
Senior Director, Content Management Enhancement: Tracey Kuehn
Senior Managing Editor: Michael Granger
Assistant Content Project Manager: Natalie Jones
Senior Workflow Project Manager: Lisa McDowell
Production Supervisor: Robin Besofsky
Director of Design, Content Management: Diana Blume
Interior Design: Lumina Datamatics, Inc.
Cover Design: William Boardman
Text Permissions Editor: Michael McCarty
Text Permissions Researcher: Udayakumar Kannadasan
Photo Permissions Editors: Christine Buese and Jirarut Anderson
Photo Researcher: Bruce Carson
Director of Digital Production: Keri deManigold
Executive Media Project Manager: Michelle Camisa
Copyeditor: Harold Johnson
Composition: Lumina Datamatics, Inc.
Cover Image: Study for 'Swing Your Partner,' c. 1945 (oil & ink on paper laid down on board)/Benton, Thomas Hart (1889–1975)/CHRISTIES IMAGES/Private Collection /Bridgeman Images/© 2020 T.H. and R.P. Benton Testamentary Trusts/UMB Bank Trustee/Licensed by VAGA at Artists Rights Society (ARS), NY
Printing and Binding: LSC Communications

Library of Congress Control Number: 2020938153

ISBN: 978-1-319-27484-9

Printed in the United States of America.

1 2 3 4 5 6   25 24 23 22 21 20

Acknowledgments
Text acknowledgments and copyrights appear at the back of the book on pages 656–57, which constitute an extension of the copyright page. Art acknowledgments and copyrights appear on the same page as the art selections they cover.

For information, write: Bedford/St. Martin's, 75 Arlington Street, Boston, MA 02116

PREFACE

My goal in compiling the tenth edition of *Sources for America's History* is to help students encounter the past in its most raw and visceral form. Designed to accompany the tenth edition of *America's History, America's History, Concise Edition,* and *America's History, Value Edition,* the sources collected here put students in unmediated contact with those whose experiences shaped our past. Historians are fond of quoting L. P. Hartley's famous line: "The past is a foreign country; they do things differently there." It is a helpful image that emphasizes the distance, remoteness, and inscrutability of the past. Visiting a country whose language you do not speak can be disorienting until you start deciphering the gestures, unlocking the meaning behind facial expressions, and picking apart the cultural practices natives take for granted. For many students, the past is equally disorienting, and to seek safe harbor they ignore differences to emphasize commonalities. "Those people in the past are just like me, except they wear funny clothes." Stripped down, they do resemble us, but more often they encountered their world in radically different ways. Understanding these differences is what makes the study of history so compelling.

Textbook authors present an argument about the past, something historians refer to as a "narrative." Those arguments, of course, are based on historians' interpretation and assessment of primary sources. This document collection makes its own argument based on the specific sources selected for inclusion, but invites debate by encouraging the reader to interpret sources in different ways. *Sources for America's History* is designed to encourage a productive intellectual give-and-take, enabling students of history to offer their own perspective on the past. In this way, students join the ongoing discussion among the community of scholars seeking to understand the long and complex history of what became the United States.

Each chapter in *Sources for America's History* includes a variety of both obscure and well-known voices, whose testimony highlights key themes of the period. The sources in each chapter give competing perspectives on leading events and ideas. This purposeful tension between sources is not intended to frustrate the reader. Instead, the differing viewpoints introduce students to the challenge that historians face in sifting through the evidence left to us. How do we make sense of the large body of primary sources that we have related to America's half millennium of recorded lived experience?

To facilitate this effort, *Sources for America's History* includes a number of key features. Each chapter in the collection includes five or six documents that support the periodization and themes of the corresponding parent text chapter. Every chapter begins with an introduction that situates the documents within their wider historical context. Individual documents follow, each accompanied by its own headnote and a set of Reading and Discussion Questions designed to help students practice historical thinking skills. The variety of readings, ranging from political cartoons and speeches by celebrated historical figures to personal letters and diary entries by ordinary people, offers students the opportunity to compare and contrast different types of documents. Each chapter concludes with Comparative Questions designed to encourage students to recognize connections between documents and relate the sources to larger historical themes. To further support the structure of the parent text, unique Part Document Sets at the end of every part section present five or six sources chosen specifically to illustrate the major themes and developments covered in each of the parent text's nine thematic parts, allowing students to make even broader comparisons and connections across time and place.

New to This Edition

In response to reviewers' comments, we have included even more visual sources than in previous editions and also trimmed the length of some of the primary source texts to focus on key ideas, themes, and arguments. This edition features over thirty new image sources, including more political cartoons from both American and British sources. Several photographs capture moments of political mobilization, including women's rights marches and anti-tax protests. We bring the collection up to the present moment with a photograph of protesters rallying against President Trump's 2017 immigration policies. We also added a collection of immigration-related tweets from President Trump, both to highlight immigration as a national issue and to showcase the power of social media.

We have continued to emphasize the first-person experience. In this edition, we hear from African Americans whose poignant letters written to Abraham Lincoln and former masters in the wake of the Emancipation Proclamation demonstrate the agency and determination of the formerly enslaved as they fought for recognition in a hostile, rebellious South. Several sources invite consideration of the Native American experience. Two new sources give voice to Native American protest against federally imposed land and citizenship policies. This edition also includes more LGBTQ sources, including congressional investigations into homosexuality in the federal workforce, an account of the now-famous Stonewall riot, and a photograph of protestors demanding resources for AIDS research.

Acknowledgments

As with any big undertaking, many hands helped craft the book you are holding. Thanks go to Rebecca Edwards from Vassar College, one of the lead authors of *America's History*, for her confidence in me. Several instructors at the college, community college, and high school levels offered insightful suggestions based on their teaching experiences. They will see here many of the suggestions they recommended, though I could not accommodate all of the excellent ideas they shared. Particular thanks go to Paul Rubinson, Bridgewater State University; Matthew D. McDonough, Coastal Carolina University; Michael H. Kim, Schurr High School; and Colette A. Hyman, Winona State University.

My editor for this edition, Carly Lewis, perfected the art of the gentle reminder, while also giving insightful feedback on sources. The following colleagues at Bedford/St. Martin's helped in innumerable ways, most of which occurred silently and behind the scenes: Bill Lombardo, Heidi Hood, and Michael Rosenberg. Thanks also to Natalie Jones, who managed the production process.

My colleagues in the history department at the State University of New York, College at Cortland, have always provided an intellectually enriching environment in which to work and live. Special thanks go to my wife, Laura Gathagan, a medieval historian, and my two boys, William and Alexander, who excused my many exits from the room, announced with my refrain: "I'm going to work on Bedford." Family: Bedford is done. What should we do?

INTRODUCTION FOR STUDENTS

I was this close to wearing Eisenhower's pajamas. During my junior year in college, I interned at the Smithsonian's National Museum of American History in Washington, D.C. Every now and again, when I had a few minutes of free time, I poked around the collection of artifacts in storage. There was Lincoln's top hat. On a high shelf was the table where Lee surrendered to Grant. A pullout metal rack filled with paintings also housed a disturbing framed collection of hair from the first sixteen presidents. One day I spied a box containing President Dwight D. Eisenhower's pajamas. These were the PJs Ike wore while recovering in Denver from his 1955 heart attack. Oh, the temptation to slip them on, but reason and self-preservation prevailed. Back on the shelf they went.

Those whom the past enchants were often first beguiled by the stuff of history. Touching those objects helps collapse time, putting us in the immediate presence of someone else at some other time. I once held John Brown's gun and while peering down the long barrel wondered who or what he was aiming at. His trigger finger and mine overlapped and briefly spirited me back to 1850s Pottawatomie, Kansas, where Brown waged his own civil war against slavery. The past is contained in those leavings, the letters and diaries, the political cartoons and music, the paintings and the guns and pajamas. Primary sources bring alive the past and help us to understand its significance and meaning.

This collection of primary sources aims to engage you in a conversation with the past. There will be times when you burst out laughing. Some sources will make you so mad you'll want to throw the book across the room. (Please don't. I spent a lot of time writing it, but I share your frustration.) Other times, you'll shake your head in disbelief. (Yes, they really thought that back then!) You are about to enter an amazing world of difference populated with people some of whom you will admire, many of whom you won't like, and others whom you will despair of ever really knowing or understanding. Good. I hope you laugh. I hope you get mad. I even hope you get confused at times and scratch your head wondering what on earth these people were talking about. Out of your responses to these texts comes insight.

My advice? Read these texts with a fist full of questions. Historians do something called "sourcing" when they first encounter a primary text, and it is a good practice for you, too. Start with the author. *Who wrote or created the source?* What do you know about this person? Was he rich, poor, or middling? Was she educated? Where was he or she born and to what sort of family?

You might know the answers to some of these questions, but even if you do not, keeping the questions in mind might help you understand where the author is coming from. ***When was this source created?*** While it is important to know the date, it can also be revealing to know when in the person's life he or she created the source. Was she a young girl or an older woman raising children? Was he at the beginning of his career or already famous? ***What was happening when the source was created?*** We call this "context," and it is an important element in making sense of the source you are reading. (You will encounter the word *context* often in the Reading and Discussion Questions and Comparative Questions following the sources and at the end of each chapter.) In addition to author and context, consider audience and purpose. ***Who was this source for, and why was it created?*** Was the source intended for a public or private audience? Was the source created to persuade or to inform? Was the author talking to allies or foes? What did he or she assume about their audience? A final and related point touches upon the format of the source. ***What type of source is it?*** Historians think about and interpret sources differently. You might be more honest in a private letter to your spouse than you would be in a letter to a political opponent, for example. Similarly, a campaign poster for a particular candidate has a different purpose than a portrait of a politician commissioned for a private residence. As these examples show, the format of a source is often linked to audience and purpose.

What a source tells a historian is not always self-evident. Very few of the sources that historians use were created *for* historians. (No one writes letters that begin: "Dear Historian of a hundred years from now, here is what I am thinking about the Obama presidency.") Historians need to "read between the lines" to derive meaning. As you read the documents in this book, you can unearth the meaning in these sources by asking questions, thinking about context, paying attention to vocabulary and cultural references, and comparing them to other sources related to the same topic or event.

This form of active reading takes a bit more time than it would if you were to simply read starting at the first word and running through to the end. To truly think like a historian, be an active reader. Engage the texts. Ask them questions. If this is your own copy of the book, don't be afraid to write in it. Draw circles around important words or phrases. Write "key point" in the margins where you think the author is hitting his mark. Don't be afraid to throw in a few question marks where you get confused. If you have a furrowed brow, chances are someone else in class is confused, too. Bring it up in discussion and you'll be the class superhero. Take advantage of the questions I pose at the end of each source and chapter. I wrote them to inspire you to go back to the texts and think about what you read. The end-of-chapter Comparative Questions encourage you to see connections between and among multiple texts.

Remember, the past is about having a conversation. These texts speak to one another. It is OK to eavesdrop on their discussions. In fact (here's me being bold), I think you have an obligation to listen in on their chatter. Many of the issues these sources address, though sometimes distant to us in time, remain relevant: What is just? What kind of society do we want to live in? How should we treat each other? How do we balance rights and responsibilities? The authors included in this book do not solve these enduring questions. But they all have a perspective that helps to clarify our own responses.

My hope is that you will engage these texts to understand how different people, in different places and different times, constructed the specific world they inhabited. I hope, too, that you find your voice and come to know that you have an opportunity and a responsibility to engage in the conversation. The thrill of history is to know that you are part of a very long conversation about meaning. So, the next time you are wearing Ike's PJs while shouldering John Brown's gun, think about the contribution to that conversation you want others to remember you by. What will you say?

CONTENTS

PART 8	THE MODERN STATE AND THE AGE OF LIBERALISM (1945–1980)	507

Sources for
America's History

Volume 2: Since 1865

14

Reconstruction

1865–1877

The Civil War sparked more questions than it settled. While the Thirteenth Amendment to the Constitution unambiguously decided the question of slavery, practical issues concerning freedmen's rights persisted. In the face of white southern resistance and northern fatigue, the national government created federal agencies to help freedmen transition from slavery to freedom, a journey that was burdened by persistent racism. Opposition came from those who continued to believe African Americans were either incapable of self-government—much less governing the state—or were susceptible to the political manipulation of northern opportunists. Policymakers faced other perplexing questions regarding the relationship of the former Confederate states to the Union and the social, economic, and political challenges facing a defeated South. Though this political turmoil led to a presidential impeachment, exacerbated strained relationships between the North and South, and gave birth to white-hooded violence, one undeniable truth stood out: African Americans were free.

14-1 | President Focuses on Work of Reconstruction

ABRAHAM LINCOLN, *Last Public Address* (1865)

On the night of April 11, 1865, Abraham Lincoln spoke to a joy-filled crowd gathered at the White House to celebrate the surrender of Robert E. Lee's Confederate army, a sign of the war's imminent end. Lincoln took the occasion to address the work ahead. In this speech, Lincoln discussed Louisiana's recent legislative efforts and, by doing so, signaled his approach to Reconstruction. John Wilkes Booth was in the audience that night and heard Lincoln speak. Three days later, at Ford's Theatre, he aimed a pistol at the back of Lincoln's head and pulled the trigger.

We meet this evening, not in sorrow, but in gladness of heart. The evacuation of Petersburg and Richmond, and the surrender of the principal insurgent army, give hope of a righteous and speedy peace whose joyous expression can not be restrained. In the midst of this, however, He from whom all blessings flow, must not be forgotten. A call for a national thanksgiving is being prepared, and will be duly promulgated. Nor must those whose harder part gives us the cause of rejoicing, be overlooked. Their honors must not be parcelled out with others. I myself was near the front, and had the high pleasure of transmitting much of the good news to you; but no part of the honor, for plan or execution, is mine. To Gen. Grant, his skilful officers, and brave men, all belongs. The gallant Navy stood ready, but was not in reach to take active part.

By these recent successes the re-inauguration of the national authority—reconstruction—which has had a large share of thought from the first, is pressed much more closely upon our attention. It is fraught with great difficulty. Unlike a case of a war between independent nations, there is no authorized organ for us to treat with. No one man has authority to give up the rebellion for any other man. We simply must begin with, and mould from, disorganized and discordant elements. Nor is it a small additional embarrassment that we, the loyal people, differ among ourselves as to the mode, manner, and means of reconstruction.

As a general rule, I abstain from reading the reports of attacks upon myself, wishing not to be provoked by that to which I can not properly offer an answer. In spite of this precaution, however, it comes to my knowledge that I am much censured for some supposed agency in setting up, and seeking to sustain, the new State government of Louisiana. In this I have done just so much as, and no more than, the public knows. In the Annual Message of Dec. 1863 and accompanying Proclamation, I presented a plan of re-construction (as the phrase goes) which, I promised, if adopted by any State, should be acceptable to, and sustained by, the Executive government of the nation. I distinctly stated that this was not the only plan which might possibly be acceptable; and I also distinctly protested that the Executive claimed no right to say when, or whether members should be admitted to seats in Congress from such States. This plan was, in advance, submitted to the then Cabinet, and distinctly approved by every member of it. One of them suggested that I should then, and in that connection, apply

Abraham Lincoln Online (www.abrahamlincolnonline.org/lincoln/speeches/last.htm).

the Emancipation Proclamation to the theretofore excepted parts of Virginia and Louisiana; that I should drop the suggestion about apprenticeship for freed-people, and that I should omit the protest against my own power, in regard to the admission of members to Congress; but even he approved every part and parcel of the plan which has since been employed or touched by the action of Louisiana. The new constitution of Louisiana, declaring emancipation for the whole State, practically applies the Proclamation to the part previously excepted. It does not adopt apprenticeship for freed-people; and it is silent, as it could not well be otherwise, about the admission of members to Congress. So that, as it applies to Louisiana, every member of the Cabinet fully approved the plan. The message went to Congress, and I received many commendations of the plan, written and verbal; and not a single objection to it, from any professed emancipationist, came to my knowledge, until after the news reached Washington that the people of Louisiana had begun to move in accordance with it. From about July 1862, I had corresponded with different persons, supposed to be interested, seeking a reconstruction of a State government for Louisiana. When the message of 1863, with the plan before mentioned, reached New-Orleans, Gen. Banks wrote me that he was confident the people, with his military co-operation, would reconstruct, substantially on that plan. I wrote him, and some of them to try it; they tried it, and the result is known. Such only has been my agency in getting up the Louisiana government. As to sustaining it, my promise is out, as before stated. But, as bad promises are better broken than kept, I shall treat this as a bad promise, and break it, whenever I shall be convinced that keeping it is adverse to the public interest. But I have not yet been so convinced.

I have been shown a letter on this subject, supposed to be an able one, in which the writer expresses regret that my mind has not seemed to be definitely fixed on the question whether the seceding States, so called, are in the Union or out of it. It would perhaps, add astonishment to his regret, were he to learn that since I have found professed Union men endeavoring to make that question, I have purposely forborne any public expression upon it. As appears to me that question has not been, nor yet is, a practically material one, and that any discussion of it, while it thus remains practically immaterial, could have no effect other than the mischievous one of dividing our friends. As yet, whatever it may hereafter become, that question is bad, as the basis of a controversy, and good for nothing at all—a merely pernicious abstraction.

We all agree that the seceded States, so called, are out of their proper relation with the Union; and that the sole object of the government, civil and military, in regard to those States is to again get them into that proper practical relation. I believe it is not only possible, but in fact, easier to do this, without deciding, or even considering, whether these States have ever been out of the Union, than with it. Finding themselves safely at home, it would be utterly immaterial whether they had ever been abroad. Let us all join in doing the acts necessary to restoring the proper practical relations between these States and the Union; and each forever after, innocently indulge his own opinion whether, in doing the acts, he brought the States from without, into the Union, or only gave them proper assistance, they never having been out of it.

The amount of constituency, so to speak, on which the new Louisiana government rests, would be more satisfactory to all, if it contained fifty, thirty, or even twenty thousand, instead of only about twelve thousand, as it does. It is also unsatisfactory to some that the elective franchise is not given to the colored man. I would myself prefer that it were now conferred on the very intelligent, and on those who serve our cause as soldiers. Still the question is not whether the Louisiana government, as it stands, is quite all that is desirable. The question is, "Will it be wiser to take it as it is, and help to improve it; or to reject, and disperse it?" "Can Louisiana be brought into proper practical relation with the Union sooner by sustaining, or by discarding her new State government?"

Some twelve thousand voters in the heretofore slave-state of Louisiana have sworn allegiance to the Union, assumed to be the rightful political power of the State, held elections, organized a State government, adopted a free-state constitution, giving the benefit of public schools equally to black and white, and empowering the Legislature to confer the elective franchise upon the colored man. Their Legislature has already voted to ratify the constitutional amendment recently passed by Congress, abolishing slavery throughout the nation. These twelve thousand persons are thus fully committed to the Union, and to perpetual freedom in the state—committed to the very things, and nearly all the things the nation wants—and they ask the nation[']s recognition and it's [*sic*] assistance to make good their committal. Now, if we reject, and spurn them, we do our utmost to disorganize and disperse them. We in effect say to the white men "You are worthless, or worse—we will neither help you, nor be helped by you." To the blacks we say "This cup of liberty which these, your old masters, hold to your lips, we will dash from you, and leave you to the chances of gathering the spilled and scattered contents in some vague and undefined when, where, and how." If this course, discouraging and paralyzing both white and black, has any tendency to bring Louisiana into proper practical relations with the Union, I have, so far, been unable to perceive it. If, on the contrary, we recognize, and sustain the new government of Louisiana the converse of all this is made true. We encourage the hearts, and nerve the arms of the twelve thousand to adhere to their work, and argue for it, and proselyte for it, and fight for it, and feed it, and grow it, and ripen it to a complete success. The colored man too, in seeing all united for him, is inspired with vigilance, and energy, and daring, to the same end. Grant that he desires the elective franchise, will he not attain it sooner by saving the already advanced steps toward it, than by running backward over them? Concede that the new government of Louisiana is only to what it should be as the egg is to the fowl, we shall sooner have the fowl by hatching the egg than by smashing it? Again, if we reject Louisiana, we also reject one vote in favor of the proposed amendment to the national Constitution. To meet this proposition, it has been argued that no more than three fourths of those States which have not attempted secession are necessary to validly ratify the amendment. I do not commit myself against this, further than to say that such a ratification would be questionable, and sure to be persistently questioned; while a ratification by three-fourths of all the States would be unquestioned and unquestionable.

I repeat the question, "Can Louisiana be brought into proper practical relation with the Union *sooner* by *sustaining* or by *discarding* her new State Government?"

What has been said of Louisiana will apply generally to other States. And yet so great peculiarities pertain to each state, and such important and sudden changes occur in the same state; and withal, so new and unprecedented is the whole case, that no exclusive, and inflexible plan can be safely prescribed as to details and colatterals [*sic*]. Such exclusive, and inflexible plan, would surely become a new entanglement. Important principles may, and must, be inflexible.

In the present "*situation*" as the phrase goes, it may be my duty to make some new announcement to the people of the South. I am considering, and shall not fail to act, when satisfied that action will be proper.

READING AND DISCUSSION QUESTIONS

1. How would you characterize Lincoln's policy toward Reconstruction? Does Lincoln come across as an idealist, like Radical Republicans, or a pragmatist who accepted compromise for the sake of progress?

2. What can you infer about Louisiana's recent experience that angered some, encouraged others, and led to Lincoln's support and approval?

3. What about his speech do you think provoked John Wilkes Booth, a southerner and Confederate sympathizer, to murder Lincoln?

14-2 | A Freed Family's Dream of Landownership

BETTY POWERS, *Federal Writers' Project Interview* (c. 1936)

Betty Powers was eight or nine years old when the Civil War ended. She was born a slave on a Texas plantation and shared in her family's jubilation when slavery ended. Seventy years later, she was interviewed by the New Deal's Federal Writers' Project, which conducted oral histories with former slaves. Despite her "head mis'ry," which she claimed impaired her memory, she recalled poignant details of her family's life in slavery and their transition to freedom with a farm of their own.

What for you wants dis old nigger's story 'bout de old slavery days? 'Tain't worth anythin'. I's jus' a hard workin' person all my life and raised de family and done right by 'em as best I knowed. To tell de truf 'bout my age, I don't know 'zactly. I 'members de war time and de surrender time. O's old 'nough to fan flies off de white folks and de tables when surrender come. If you come 'bout five year ago, I could telt you lots more, but I's had de head mis'ry.

Library of Congress, *Born in Slavery: Slave Narratives from the Federal Writers' Project, 1936–1938,* Texas Narratives, vol. 16, part 3, 190–192.

I's born in Harrison County, 'bout twenty-five miles from Marshall. Mass's name am Dr. Howard Perry and next he house am a li'l buildin' for he office. De plantation an awful big one, and miles long, and more'n two hundred slaves was dere. Each cabin have one family and dere am three rows of cabins 'bout half a mile long.

Mammy and pappy and us twelve chillen live in one cabin, so mammy has to cook for fourteen people, 'sides her field work. She am up way befo' daylight fixin' breakfast and supper after dark, with de pine knot torch to make de light. She cook on de fireplace in winter and in de yard in summer. All de rations measure out Sunday mornin' and it have to do for de week. It am not 'nough for heavy eaters and we has to be real careful or we goes hungry. We has meat and cornmeal and 'lasses and 'taters and peas and beans and milk. Dem short rations causes plenty trouble, 'cause de niggers has to steal food and it am de whippin' if dey gets cotched. Dey am in a fix if dey can't work for bein' hungry, 'cause it am de whippin' den, sho', so dey has to steal, and most of 'em did and takes de whippin'. Dey has de full stomach, anyway.

De babies has plenty food, so dey grow up into strong, portly men and women. Dey stays in de nursery whilst dey mammies works in de fields, and has plenty milk with cornbread crumble up in it, and potlicker, too, and honey and 'lasses on bread.

De massa and he wife am fine, but de overseer am tough, and he wife, too. Dat woman have no mercy. You see dem long ears I has? Dat's from de pullin' dey gits from her. De field hands works early and late and often all night. Pappy makes de shoes and mammy weaves, and you could hear de bump, bump of dat loom at night, when she done work in de field all day.

Missy know everything what go on, 'cause she have de spies 'mongst de slaves. She purty good, though. Sometimes de overseer tie de nigger to a log and lash him with de whip. If de lash cut de skin, dey puts salt on it. We ain't 'low to go to church and has 'bout two parties a year, so dere ain't much fun. Lawd, Lawd, most dem slaves too tired to have fun noway. When all dat work am finish, dey's glad to git in de bed and sleep.

Did we'uns have weddin's? White man, you knows better'n dat. Dem times, cullud folks am jus' put together. De massa say, "Jim and Nancy, you go live together," and when dat order give, it better be done. Dey thinks nothin' on de plantation 'bout de feelin's of de women and dere ain't no 'spect for dem. De overseer and white mens took 'vantage of de women like dey wants to. De woman better not make no fuss 'bout sich. If she do, it am de whippin' for her. I sho' thanks the Lawd surrender done come befo' I's old 'nough to have to stand for sich. Yes, sar, surrender saves dis nigger from sich.

When de war am over, thousands of sojers passes our place. Some camps nearby, and massa doctors dem. When massa call us to say we's free, dere am a yardful of niggers. He give every nigger de age statement and say dey could work on halves or for wages. He 'vises dem to stay till dey git de foothold and larn how to do. Lots stays and lots goes. My folks stays 'bout four years and works on shares. Den pappy buys de piece of land 'bout five miles from dere.

De land ain't clear, so we'uns al pitches in and clears it and builds de cabin. Was we'uns proud? There 'twas, our place to do as we pleases, after bein' slaves.

Dat sho' am de good feelin'. We works live beavers puttin' de crop in, and my folks stays dere till dey dies. I leaves to git married de next year and I's only thirteen years old, and marries Boss Powers.

We'uns lives on rent land nearby for six years and has three chillen and den he dies. After two years I marries Henry Ruffins and has three more chillen, and he dies in 1911. I's livin' with two of dem now. I never took de name of Ruffins, 'cause I's dearly love Powers and can't stand to give up he name. Powers done make de will and wrote on de paper, "To my beloved wife, I gives all I has." Wasn't dat sweet of him?

I comes to Fort Worth after Ruffin dies and does housework till I's too old. Now I gits de $12.00 pension every month and dat help me git by.

READING AND DISCUSSION QUESTIONS

1. How does Powers's account help historians understand the period of Reconstruction from the perspective of social history, or the history of ordinary people?

2. Analyze and evaluate the details Powers recalls about her fellow slaves' experiences to understand the contrast she draws with her life in the era after slavery. How do those details help you understand the meaning of freedom as former enslaved people experienced it?

3. How does the context of this historical source, an oral history recorded decades after the events it describes, impact your assessment of its utility as evidence for the Civil War and Reconstruction eras?

14-3 | A Former Slave Owner Complains of "Negro Problem"

FRANCES BUTLER LEIGH, *Letter to a Friend in England* (1867)

While Betty Powers experienced the era of Reconstruction with the optimism of the newly freed, Frances Butler Leigh wrote defiant and discouraging letters from her father's Sea Island plantation on St. Simon's Island, Georgia. She and her father, divorced years earlier from Leigh's mother, the British actress and antislavery advocate Frances Kemble, moved from Philadelphia to the plantation just after the war ended in a failed effort to keep the family's estate afloat. Within a few years, she sold the plantation and moved to England, where in 1883 she wrote *Ten Years on a Georgia Plantation Since the War*, a memoir defending the Old South.

S. Simon's Island: June 23, 1867

Dearest S ——, We are, I am afraid, going to have terrible trouble by-and-by with the Negroes, and I see nothing but gloomy prospects for us ahead. The unlimited power that the war has put into the hands of the present government at Washington seems to have turned the heads of the party now in office, and they don't know where to stop. The whole South is settled and quiet, and the

Frances Butler Leigh, *Ten Years on a Georgia Plantation Since the War* (London: Richard Bentley & Son, Publishers in Ordinary to her Majesty the Queen, 1883), 66–71.

people too ruined and crushed to do anything against the government, even if they felt so inclined, and all are returning to their former pursuits, trying to rebuild their fortunes and thinking of nothing else. Yet the treatment we receive from the government becomes more and more severe every day, the last act being to divide the whole South into five military districts, putting each under the command of a United States general, doing away with all civil courts and law. Even D —— who you know is a Northern republican, says it is most unjustifiable, not being in any way authorised by the existing state of things, which he confesses he finds very different from what he expected before he came. If they would frankly say they intend to keep us down, it would be fairer than making a pretence of readmitting us to equal rights, and then trumping up stories of violence to give a show of justice to treating us as the conquered foes of the most despotic Government on earth, and by exciting the negroes to every kind of insolent lawlessness, to goad the people into acts of rebellion and resistance.

The other day in Charleston, which is under the command of that respectable creature General S —— , they had a firemen's parade, and took the occasion to hoist a United States flag, to which this modern Gesler[1] insisted on everyone raising his cap as he passed underneath. And by a hundred other such petty tyrannies are the people, bruised and sore, being roused to desperation; and had this been done directly after the war it would have been bad enough, but it was done the other day, three years [sic] after the close of the war.

The true reason is the desire and intention of the Government to control the elections of the South, which under the constitution of the country they could not legally do. So they have determined to make an excuse for setting aside the laws, and in order to accomplish this more fully, each commander in his separate district has issued an order declaring that unless a man can take an oath that he had not voluntarily borne arms against the United States Government, nor in any way aided or abetted the rebellion, he cannot vote. This simply disqualifies every white man at the South from voting, disfranchising the whole white population, while the negroes are allowed to vote *en masse*.

This is particularly unjust, as the question of negro voting was introduced and passed in Congress as an amendment to the constitution, but in order to become a law a majority of two-thirds of the State Legislatures must ratify it, and so to them it was submitted, and rejected by all the Northern States with two exceptions, where the number of negro voters would be so small as to be harmless. Our Legislatures are not allowed to meet, but this law, which the North has rejected, is to be forced upon us, whose very heart it pierces and prosperity it kills. Meanwhile, in order to prepare the negroes to vote properly, stump speakers from the North are going all through the South, holding political meetings for the negroes, saying things like this to them: "My friends, you will have your rights, won't you?" ("Yes," from the negroes.) "Shall I not go back to

---

[1] **Gesler:** Gessler, the legendary tyrant in the fifteenth-century folktale William Tell who made the people bow to his hat, placed on a pole; Tell refused and was forced to shoot an arrow through an apple resting atop the head of his son.

Massachusetts and tell your brothers there that you are going to ride in the street cars with white ladies if you please?" ("Yes, yes," from the crowd.) "That if you pay your money to go to the theatre you will sit where you please, in the best boxes if you like?" ("Yes," and applause.) This I copy verbatim from a speech made at Richmond the other day, since which there have been two serious negro riots there, and the General commanding had to call out the military to suppress them.

These men are making a tour through the South, speaking in the same way to the negroes everywhere. Do you wonder we are frightened? I have been so forcibly struck lately while reading Baker's "Travels in Africa," and some of Du Chaillu's lectures,[2] at finding how exactly the same characteristics show themselves among the negroes there, in their own native country, where no outside influences have ever affected them, as with ours here. Forced to work, they improve and are useful; left to themselves they become idle and useless, and never improve. Hard ethnological facts for the abolitionists to swallow, but facts nevertheless.

It seems foolish to fill my letter to you with such matters, but all this comes home to us with such vital force that it is hard to write, or speak, or think of anything else, and the one subject that Southerners discuss whenever they meet is, "What is to become of us?"

Affectionately yours,
F——

READING AND DISCUSSION QUESTIONS

1. Compare Leigh's point of view concerning slaves and slavery with the perspective of Susan Dabney Smedes (Document 11-1). How might you account for the differences you see in their assessments of the Old South? What factors might have shaped each viewpoint?

2. From Leigh's letter, what conclusions can you draw regarding the challenges facing the national government in mending the political divisions between northern and southern states and between the federal and state or local governments in the South?

14-4 | Challenges of Southern Reconstruction
Three Photographs of Richmond, Virginia (1864–1865)

The Civil War was a human tragedy. Historians now think the Civil War death toll topped 750,000 people. A comparable percentage today would be approximately 6.5 million deaths. That staggering human cost was compounded by the physical destruction of those places that witnessed many of the war's decisive battles, and nearly all of them were in the South. In the three-part photo essay included here, we see several scenes from Richmond, Virginia, the Confederate capital and one of the South's important manufacturing cities. Though photographs show only what a photographer chooses to highlight and thus capture just part of the story, these images give us a sense of the immense physical toll caused by the war.

---

[2] **Baker's . . . lectures:** Leigh may be referring to Samuel White Baker's 1855 book *Eight Years' Wandering in Ceylon* and to Paul du Chaillu's 1861 *Explorations and Adventures in Equatorial Africa*.

Aerial view of Richmond, 1864
Hulton Archive/Getty Images

Crippled Locomotive, Richmond & Petersburg Railroad Depot, American Civil War, Richmond, Virginia, USA, 1865 (b/w photo)/American Photographer (19th century)/GLASSHOUSE IMAGES/Private Collection/Bridgeman Images

Ruined Buildings in Burnt District, Richmond, Virginia, USA, 1865 (b/w photo)
/American Photographer (19th century)/GLASSHOUSE IMAGES/Bridgeman Images

READING AND DISCUSSION QUESTIONS

1. Describe the scenes captured by these photographers. What story of the Civil War do they tell?

2. Who do you imagine these photographs were intended for? Do you think the photographers were sympathetic to southerners?

3. Given the destruction recorded in these images, what challenges did the South face in its effort to recover from the Civil War? How do images like these help us understand the history of the Reconstruction period?

14-5 | Nast Lampoons Freedmen's Government

THOMAS NAST, *Colored Rule in a Reconstructed State* (1874)

Political cartoons developed sophistication in the years after the Civil War largely through the talents of the influential artist Thomas Nast (1840–1902), whose compositions effectively captured a frustrated electorate's disgust. In this image, Nast plays on then-common stereotypes and foregrounds the pervasive assumptions northern and southern whites held about black political incompetence and corruption. Many white South Carolinians popularized these beliefs in their effort to redeem state government from the African American majority that controlled the legislature.

Library of Congress, LC-USZ62-102256

READING AND DISCUSSION QUESTIONS

1. Analyze and evaluate Nast's image to identify the racial stereotypes it conveys. Whose view of black political abilities does it express?

2. What is the significance of the Columbia figure standing at the speaker's platform, and what is she trying to accomplish?

3. To what extent do the stereotypes Nast employed reflect the historical context of race relations during the Reconstruction period?

14-6 | African American Congressman Urges Support of Civil Rights Bill

ROBERT BROWNE ELLIOTT, *Speech to Congress* (1874)

While planters and their former slaves negotiated a new relationship in the wake of slavery's abolition, Congress was abuzz with legislative activity to secure the rights of citizenship freedmen had so recently won. The Civil Rights Act of 1875, which the African American member of Congress Robert Elliott supported in a speech to Congress, guaranteed to African Americans equal treatment in public accommodations. In 1873, the U.S. Supreme Court decided in the *Slaughterhouse Cases* to construe the Fourteenth Amendment protections narrowly, arguing that states properly retained the exercise of power over domestic and civil rights. Here Elliott is attempting to counter anti–civil rights efforts to use these cases to frustrate federal legislative action on behalf of freedmen.

Mr. Speaker: While I am sincerely grateful for this high mark of courtesy that has been accorded to me by this House, it is a matter of regret to me that it is necessary at this day that I should rise in the presence of an American Congress to advocate a bill which simply asserts equal rights and equal public privileges for all classes of American citizens. I regret, sir, that the dark hue of my skin may lend a color to the imputation that I am controlled by motives personal to myself in my advocacy of this great measure of national justice. Sir, the motive that impels me is restricted by no such narrow boundary, but is as broad as your Constitution. I advocate it, sir, because it is right. The bill, however, not only appeals to your justice, but it demands a response from your gratitude. . . .

[S]ir, we are told by the distinguished gentleman from Georgia (Mr. Stephens[3]) that Congress has no power under the Constitution to pass such a law, and that the passage of such an act is in direct contravention of the rights of the states.

Lift Every Voice: African American Oratory, 1787–1900, eds. Philip S. Foner and Robert James Branham (Tuscaloosa and London: The University of Alabama Press, 1998), 521–524, 527–528, 532–533, 535–536.

[3] **Mr. Stephens**: Alexander Stephens, senator from Georgia who was elected vice president of the Confederate States of America during the Civil War.

I cannot assent to any such proposition. The Constitution of a free government ought always to be construed in favor of human rights. Indeed, the thirteenth, fourteenth, and fifteenth amendments, in positive words, invest Congress with the power to protect the citizen in his civil and political rights. Now, sir, what are civil rights? Rights natural, modified by civil society. Mr. Lieber says: "By civil liberty is meant, not only the absence of individual restraint, but liberty within the social system and political organism—a combination of principles and laws which acknowledge, protect and favor the dignity of man . . . civil liberty is the result of man's twofold character as an individual and social being, so soon as both are equally respected." . . .

Are we then, sir, with the amendments to our Constitution staring us in the face; with these grand truths of history before our eyes; with innumerable wrongs daily inflicted upon five million citizens demanding redress, to commit this question to the diversity of legislation? In the words of Hamilton, "Is it the interest of the government to sacrifice individual rights to the preservation of the rights of an artificial being called the states? There can be no truer principle than this, that every individual of the community at large has an equal right to the protection of government. Can this be a free government if partial distinctions are tolerated or maintained?"

The rights contended for in this bill are among "the sacred rights of mankind, which are not to be rummaged for among old parchments or musty records; they are written as with a sunbeam in the whole volume of human nature, by the hand of the divinity itself, and can never be erased or obscured by mortal power."

But the Slaughterhouse cases!—The Slaughterhouse cases!

The honorable gentleman from Kentucky, always swift to sustain the failing and dishonored cause of proscription, rushes forward and flaunts in our faces the decision of the Supreme Court of the United States in the Slaughterhouse cases, and in that act he has been willingly aided by the gentleman from Georgia. Hitherto, in the contests which have marked the progress of the cause of equal civil rights, our opponents have appealed sometimes to custom, sometimes to prejudice, more often to pride of race, but they have never sought to shield themselves behind the Supreme Court. But now, for the first time, we are told that we are barred by a decision of that court, from which there is no appeal. If this be true we must stay our hands. The cause of equal civil rights must pause at the command of a power whose edicts must be obeyed till the fundamental law of our country is changed.

Has the honorable gentleman from Kentucky considered well the claim he now advances? If it were not disrespectful I would ask, has he ever read the decision which he now tells us is an insuperable barrier to the adoption of this great measure of justice?

In the consideration of this subject, has not the judgment of the gentleman from Georgia been warped by the ghost of the dead doctrines of states' rights?

Has he been altogether free from prejudices engendered by long training in that school of politics that well-nigh destroyed this government?

Mr. Speaker, I venture to say here . . . that there is not a line or word, not a thought or dictum even, in the decision of the Supreme Court in the great Slaughterhouse cases, which casts a shadow of doubt on the right of Congress to pass the pending bill, or to adopt such other legislation as it may judge proper and necessary to secure perfect equality before the law to every citizen of the Republic. . . .

These [Civil War] amendments[4] . . . are thus declared to have as their all-pervading design and ends the security of the recently enslaved race, not only their nominal freedom, but their complete protection from those who had formerly exercised unlimited dominion over them. It is in this broad light that all these amendments must be read, the purpose to secure the perfect equality before the law of all citizens of the United States. What you give to one class you must give to all, what you deny to one class you shall deny to all, unless in the exercise of the common and universal police power of the state, you find it needful to confer exclusive privileges on certain citizens, to be held and exercised still for the common good of all. . . .

Sir, it is scarcely twelve years since that gentleman [Senator Stephens] shocked the civilized world by announcing the birth of a government which rested on human slavery as its cornerstone.[5] The progress of events has swept away that pseudo government which rested on greed, pride and tyranny, and the race whom he then ruthlessly spurned and trampled on is here to meet him in debate, and to demand that the rights which are enjoyed by its former oppressors—who vainly sought to overthrow a government which they could not prostitute to the base uses of slavery—shall be accorded to those who even in the darkness of slavery kept their allegiance true to freedom and the Union. Sir, the gentleman from Georgia has learned much since 1861, but he is still a laggard. Let him put away entirely the false and fatal theories which have so greatly marred an otherwise enviable record. Let him accept, in its fullness and beneficence, the great doctrine that American citizenship carries with it every civil and political right which manhood can confer. . . .

Sir, equality before the law is now the broad, universal, glorious rule and mandate of the Republic. No state can violate that. Kentucky and Georgia may crowd their statute books with retrograde and barbarous legislation; they may rejoice in the odious eminence of their consistent hostility to all the great steps of human progress which have marked our national history since slavery

---

[4] **Amendments**: Elliott is referring to the Thirteenth, Fourteenth, and Fifteenth Amendments, which, respectively, prohibited slavery, guaranteed due process and defined citizenship, and forbade the denial of the vote on the basis of race.

[5] **Gentleman . . . cornerstone**: See Document P5-4.

tore down the Stars and Stripes on Fort Sumter; but, if Congress shall do its duty, if Congress shall enforce the great guarantees which the Supreme Court has declared to be the one pervading purpose of all the recent amendments, then their unwise and unenlightened conduct will fall with the same weight upon the gentlemen from those states who now lend their influence to defeat this bill, as upon the poorest slave who once had no rights which the honorable gentlemen were bound to respect. . . .

The results of the [Civil] war, as seen in reconstruction, have settled forever the political status of my race. The passage of this bill will determine the civil status, not only of the Negro, but of any other class of citizens who may feel themselves discriminated against. It will form the capstone of that temple of liberty, begun on this continent under discouraging circumstances, carried on in spite of the sneers of monarchists and the cavils of pretended friends of freedom, until at last it stands, in all its beautiful symmetry and proportions, a building the grandest which the world has ever seen, realizing the most sanguine expectations and the highest hopes of those who, in the name of equal, impartial and universal liberty, laid the foundation stone.

The Holy Scriptures tell us of an humble handmaiden who long, faithfully and patiently gleaned in the rich fields of her wealthy kinsman, and we are told further that at last, in spite of her humble antecedents she found favor in his sight. For over two centuries our race has "reaped down your fields," the cries and woes which we have uttered have "entered into the ears of the Lord of Sabaoth" and we are at last politically free. The last vestiture only is needed—civil rights. Having gained this, we may, with hearts overflowing with gratitude and thankful that our prayer has been answered, repeat the prayer of Ruth: "Entreat me not to leave thee, or to return from following after thee, for whither thou goest, I will go; and where thou lodgest, I will lodge; thy people shall be my people, and thy God my God; where thou diest I will die, and there will I be buried; the Lord do so to me, and more also, if ought but death part thee and me." [Great applause.]

READING AND DISCUSSION QUESTIONS

1. Summarize and evaluate the argument Elliott makes in support of the civil rights bill. What can you infer about the opposition from his argument?

2. What does it suggest to you about the nature of politics in the Reconstruction-era South that an African American member of Congress from South Carolina was able to speak in support of a civil rights bill on the floor of the House of Representatives in 1874? How does this document help you to understand the historical context of the period?

▪ COMPARATIVE QUESTIONS ▪

1. Explain whether you see the era of Reconstruction as the end or the beginning of a distinctive period in American history. What evidence from the documents in this chapter can you provide to prove your thesis?

2. What challenges did the nation face during the Reconstruction period? Based on the sources provided in this chapter, how were the challenges the North and South faced similar and different?

3. To what extent was the Jeffersonian regard for land as a source of one's independence (Document 7-2) an enduring ideal in the era of Reconstruction?

4. Historians have debated whether Reconstruction was a success, a failure, or an incomplete fulfillment of the American promise. How do the multiple perspectives represented by the sources in this chapter help you develop your own argument about the historical significance of Reconstruction?

15

Conquering a Continent
1860–1890

The Civil War is a pivotal point in American history, but the focused attention it receives sometimes obscures significant continuities. Such is the
case with Americans' drive to expand the bounds of their country. The
earlier period of Manifest Destiny in the 1840s led to the U.S.-Mexico War
(1846–1848) and the political crises over the extension of slavery that precipitated the Civil War. In the postwar years, however, the itch to move
was no less powerful a motive than it had been decades earlier. This continuing historical pattern of expansion shaped the latter decades of the
nineteenth century. Railroads became the means of realizing continental
dreams. The political muscle required to push them west both reflected
the economic goals of the Republican Party and jeopardized the lives of
Native Americans whose territorial claims became obstacles to industrialists' expansionist efforts. Western boosters convinced others that the
cost to American Indians served the broader aims of integrating the West
into the national economy, tapping the vast mineral, timber, and animal
resources the continent offered. The costs were indeed high, and not only
to Native Americans. Chinese laborers were hired to lay the tracks for
railroads that hauled away the West's natural resources and changed its
geography forever.

15-1 | Opening the West

Indian Territory, That Garden of the World (c. 1880)

The Manifest Destiny spirit of the 1830s and 1840s continued into the latter nineteenth century, aided by federal policies like the 1862 Homestead Act, which granted parcels of federal territory to adult citizens who resided on and improved the land for five years. Most of this federal territory had once been Native American land but was now set aside for settlement, the result of policies that forced Native Americans onto reservations. This advertisement encourages homesteaders to take advantage of federal policy opening Indian territory. The map shows in white those portions of land (in present-day Oklahoma) now opened to homesteaders.

Courtesy The National Archives

READING AND DISCUSSION QUESTIONS

1. Who was responsible for creating this advertisement? If the land was free to homesteaders, what motivation lay behind the ad's creation?

2. What can you infer about federal Indian policy during the 1870s and 1880s by looking at the map and text included in this advertisement?

3. How did homesteaders in the 1860s get to the Oklahoma Territory? What does the advertisement suggest about the potential for migrating and settling this region?

15-2 | Railroad Transforms the Nation

CURRIER & IVES, *Across the Continent* (1868)

For better or worse, the railroad altered the geography of America and ushered in economic, social, and political changes that touched the lives of nearly all Americans. Like the canal era before it, the period of rapid railroad development promised market expansions as goods and resources crossed the continent and local economies integrated with national and global trade networks. Once-isolated communities found themselves connected to consumer and communication webs hardly imagined in the horse-and-wagon days. This image, produced by the printmaking firm Currier & Ives and captioned "Across the Continent: 'Westward the Course of Empire Takes Its Way,'" captures this expansion at its beginning, with the anticipation and foreboding it inspired.

Across the Continent: 'Westward the Course of Empire Takes Its Way', 1868 (litho)/Currier, N. (1813–88) and Ives, J.M (1824–95)/SARAH ROBERTSON/Private Collection/Bridgeman Images

READING AND DISCUSSION QUESTIONS

1. Analyze and evaluate the elements of this print for evidence of the artist's point of view with respect to the railroad and western development. What does the artist suggest about the effect the railroad had on Americans and their communities?

2. How might you explain the popularity of this Currier & Ives print? Why do you think this image resonated with those who purchased it to decorate their homes?

15-3 | Romanticizing the Western Landscape

JOHN MUIR, *Letters to Asa Gray* (1870s)

While the first two sources in the chapter present images of the West as newly commercialized spaces, John Muir's letters offer a different perspective. Muir was one of the era's leading naturalists and his voluminous writings applied nineteenth-century romanticism to America's vast western landscapes. His romanticism contrasted with earlier views of wilderness as an obstacle to overcome or subdue. Here we see Muir write about nature's spiritual dimension, though his careful observation of the region's plants and physical features no doubt appealed to his scientist friend, the Harvard botanist Asa Gray. Though Muir spent his career exploring the western landscape, here he is describing what he sees and experiences in Yosemite in northern California. President Lincoln signed the Yosemite Valley Grant Act in 1864, which gave the land to California for public recreational use. That act inspired the creation of Yellowstone National Park eight years later, an important turning point in the history of America's conservation and preservation efforts.

Yosemite Valley, December 18, 1872

My Dear Gray:

I received the last of your notes two days ago, announcing the arrival of the ferns. You speak of three boxes of Primula.[1] I sent seven or eight.

I had some measurements to make about the throat of the South Dome, so yesterday I climbed there, and then ran up to Clouds' Rest for your Primulas, and as I stuffed them in big sods into a sack, I said, "Now I wonder what mouthfuls this size will accomplish for the Doctor's primrose hunger." Before filling your sack I witnessed one of the most glorious of our mountain sunsets; not one of the assembled mountains seemed remote—all had ceased their labor of beauty and gathered around their parent sun to receive the evening blessing, and waiting angels could not be more solemnly hushed. The sun himself seemed to have reached a higher life as if he had died and only his soul were glowing with rayless, bodiless *Light,* and as Christ to his disciples, so this departing sun soul said to every precious beast, to every pine and weed, to every stream and mountain, "My peace I give unto you."

The Life and Letters of John Muir, William Frederick Bade, ed., vol. 1 (Boston: Houghton Mifflin Company, 1923), 369–371, 379–381.

[1] **Primula:** Genus of flowering plants that include the primrose.

I ran home in the moonlight with your sack of roses slung on my shoulder by a buckskin string—down through the junipers, down through the first, now in black shadow, now in white light, past great South Dome white as the moon, past spirit-like Nevada, past Pywiack, through the groves of Illilouette[2] and spiry pines of the open valley, star crystals sparkling above, frost crystals beneath, and rays of spirit beaming everywhere.

I reached home a trifle weary, but could have wished so Godful a walk some miles and hours longer, and as I slid your roses off my shoulder I said, "This is one of the big round ripe days that so fatten our lives—so much of sun on one side, so much of moon on the other."

I am very cordially
Your friend
John Muir

Yosemite Valley, February 22, 1873

Dear Dr. Gray:

Our winter is very glorious. January was a block of solid sun-gold, not of the thin frosty kind, but of a quality that called forth butterflies and tingled the fern coils and filled the noontide with a dreamy hum of insect wings. On the 15th of January I found one big *Phacelia*[3] in full bloom on the north side of the Valley about one thousand feet above the bottom or five thousand above the sea. Also at the same sunny nook several bushes of *Arctostaphylos glauca* were in full flower, and many other plants were swelling their buds and breathing fragrance, showing that they were full of the thoughts and intentions of spring. Our Laurel was in flower a month ago; so was our winter wheat (*Libocedrus*).

This month up to present date has been profusely filled with snow. About ten feet has fallen on the bottom of the Valley since the 30th of January. Your primulas on Clouds' Rest must be covered to a depth of at least twelve or fifteen feet. I wish you could see our pines in full bloom of soft snow, or waving in storm. They know little of the character of a pine tree who see it only when swaying drowsily in a summer breeze or when balanced motionless and fast asleep in hushed sunshine.

We are grandly snowbound and have all this winter glory of sunlight and storm-shade to ourselves. Our outside doors are locked, and who will disturb us?

I call your attention to the two large yellow and purple plants from the top of Mount Lyell, above all of the pinched and blinking dwarfs that almost justify Darwin's mean ungodly word "struggle."[4] They form a rounded expansion upon the wedge of plant life that slants up into the thin lean sky. They are the

---

[2] Muir is referring to specific geographical features of Yosemite including South and Pywiack Domes, which are granite elevations created by glaciers, and the Nevada and Illilouette waterfalls.

[3] *Phacelia, Arctostaphylos glauca, Libocedrus*: Scientific names of plants, which would have been familiar to Gray.

[4] Muir is referring to naturalist Charles Darwin whose 1859 book *On the Origin of Species* argues that evolution proceeded through a process of natural selection.

noblest plant mountaineers I ever saw, climbing above the glaciers into the frosty azure, and flowering in purple and gold, rich and abundant as ever responded to the thick, creamy sun-gold of the tropics.

Ever very cordially yours

John Muir

READING AND DISCUSSION QUESTIONS

1. How does Muir describe the Yosemite landscape to Gray? Think about the details he chooses to include and the language he uses. What does it suggest to you about his attitude toward nature?

2. Why do you think Muir's view of nature may have appealed to readers in the latter nineteenth century?

3. What impact on policy and on Americans' ideas toward nature do you think Muir had?

15-4 | Harvesting the Bison Herds

J. WRIGHT MOOAR, *Buffalo Days* (1933)

Railroads helped integrate the West into the national and global economy. The Great Plains, in particular, developed as a key region for America's economic growth, a development that would have surprised an earlier generation accustomed to thinking of the vast interior as a worthless desert. Commercialized buffalo hunting drove the economic transformation while also working to eliminate American Indians as obstacles to westward expansion. J. Wright Mooar, whose stories of his buffalo-hunting days were first published in 1933, claimed to have killed twenty thousand buffalo, selling the meat to feed the proliferating numbers of railroad workers, and the hides to East Coast tanneries. The destruction of the herds opened the plains to cattle ranching and sealed the fate of Plains Indians whose lives were organized around the buffalo.

Curing Buffalo Meat

It was in October, 1877, while I was killing buffalo on Deep Creek, that John returned from a trip to Fort Griffin after the mail, and reported that a large herd of cattle was coming into the country, and that the John Hum outfit was then only twenty miles east of our hunting grounds.

It was immediately determined to move camp seventy miles north, to Double Lake in Lynn County. Here headquarters were maintained and the meat was hauled to the old Deep Creek camp, where the smokehouse for curing the meat was located.

As soon as the hide was stripped from the fallen bison, the meat was cut from the hams in four large pieces, the bone being cut out. When from one thousand to twelve hundred pounds of meat was thus collected, it was piled in a vat

Buffalo Days (1933). From J. Wright Mooar, "The Killing of the White Buffalo." *In Buffalo Days: Stories from J. Wright Mooar As told to James Winford Hunt,* edited by Robert F. Pace, pp. 76–81. Copyright © 2005 by State House Press. Buffalo Days provided by State House Press.

constructed by driving four stakes into the ground in a square four by four feet, the stakes standing four feet high. To these four corner stakes, a hide, hair side out, was tied by its corners, and let sag in the middle to form a sack or sort of vat. Into this the meat was thrown, and salted as it was thrown in. A brine was then poured over this until the meat was covered. A hide was stretched over the whole for a lid, thus keeping out sun and dirt. Four days later, sugar and saltpeter were added in precise measure to the brine. This was left for two weeks. The thoroughly medicated meat was then taken out and placed in the smokehouse for final seasoning.

The smokehouse was constructed by stretching buffalo hides over a framework of hackberry poles, put together with eightpenny nails, one hundred pounds of which had been hauled from Fort Worth. The house thus constructed was one hundred and ten feet long and twenty feet wide. Along the center of the floor space were ten square pits for the fire. For wood, hackberry and chinaberry logs were used, and the smoking process required ten or twelve days. This prepared meat was hauled to Fort Griffin and sold.

During this winter of '77, we took three thousand seven hundred hides, which were hauled to Fort Worth, and twenty-five thousand pounds of meat, which were sold locally.

Cattle were now being driven into the country very rapidly, and the Mooar Brothers bought the John Goff cattle in Fisher County and changed the brand from XTS to SXT. This brand was kept up in Fisher County for ten years, and then moved to the old buffalo camp on Deep Creek, where my ranch is today.

Passing of the Buffalo

By the arrival of 1879, the hunters were leaving for the mining states, or seeking other lines of business, as they realized the great hunting days were over. Mooar Brothers, however, continued pursuit of the dwindling herds to the great plains country, and during the year of 1878 secured two thousand eight hundred hides and twenty thousand pounds of meat. The last of the buffalo, save a few scattered bands of young animals too young for the hunters to bother with, fell to my big guns in March, 1879. Loading seven thousand pounds of cured meat on two wagons drawn by six good mules, and accompanied by a seventeen-year-old boy, [we] headed west on a fifty-two day trip to Prescott and Phoenix, Arizona, where the meat was sold to the miners. I did not return to Texas until October, 1880.

In the meantime, John had moved the Deep Creek camp to the Fisher County cattle camp. The last of the buffalo hides were sold to Charley Rath, who had bought all interest in the Reynolds store in Stonewall County. As the buffalo days ended, he moved the goods remaining in this store to Camp Supply, in Indian Territory. John did the hauling for Rath on this move, making the long journey with his ox teams. From Camp Supply, he made one trip for Rath to Dodge City, and returned to Texas in December, 1879, loaded with corn from the Red River Country. This he sold to the Texas Ranger camp at Big Spring, Texas.

R.C. Ware was in charge of the Ranger camp. He became a noted citizen of the changing Southwest.

Thus ended eight full years of continuous and eventful hunting of the great American bison.

The Indians realized very keenly that the work of the buffalo hunters was the real menace to the wild, free life they wished to lead, and never lost an opportunity to wreak vengeance. This made the life of the hunter one of constant peril. He was always under observation, wild eyes from some covert watching his every move. It is past comprehension to people of today how, under such circumstances, a lone hunter could wander at will and escape ambush or sudden assault in overwhelming numbers. Two things alone protected him: his rifle and his marksmanship. Perhaps one might also add that, while seemingly wandering at will, he was as alert as an Indian and seldom caught off his guard.

The Half-Inch Rifle

His rifle was one made at the request of his guild at the very outset, and was manufactured by the Sharps Rifle Manufacturing Company to meet the requirements for the biggest game on the North American continent — the buffalo. The weapon was a gun weighing from twelve to sixteen pounds, and the caliber was .50-110. One hundred and ten grains of powder, in a long brass shell, hurled from the beautifully rifled muzzle of the great gun a heavy leaden missle that in its impact and its tearing, shattering qualities would instantly bring down the biggest bison, if properly aimed, and that reached out to incredible distances for rifles of that period.

In the account of our trek to Deep Creek, a strip of country like the plains country is mentioned. This plain was evidently once a part of the great Central Plain, but this was at some distant period cut off to itself by upheavals in the general level. In extent it is thirty or forty miles long and from five to fifteen miles wide. Deep Creek marks its western boundary.

Riding eastward across this level, open stretch, and with a wagon and mule team following, I came one afternoon to the broken country east of the tableland. A sunken country rolled away to the east, and the terrain was marked by deep draws, mesquite flats, and small knolls and mesas called the Sugar Loaf Hills. The country looked to be a good place for hunting, with plenty of wood and water at hand, but somewhat dangerous because furnishing plenty of covert for Indian ambuscades. No Indians had been seen in that part, however, and I was about to select a place for a camp and indicate it to my wagoner, when a slight movement at the head of a brushy draw caught my attention. Watching closely I was rewarded in a moment by seeing an Indian rush his pony down into the draw, and in a few moments another stealthily followed him. I had been just alert enough to see the last two Indians of what turned out to be a large band.

Concealing myself, I became the eyewitness of Indian travel tactics. When the band reappeared it had reached the mouth of the draw, and dashed one at a time across to the mouth of another draw breaking down from the plain. They traveled back up this, concealed from all observers, until they would be forced to rush across to the head of another draw and so down it, approaching in this stealthy and devious manner the objective sought.

We drove quickly back to the camp on Deep Creek, content to hunt in more open country.

READING AND DISCUSSION QUESTIONS

1. What evidence do Mooar's stories provide for understanding the historical patterns of change transforming the Great Plains into a commercialized region of economic activity?

2. What can you infer about the historical interpretation, or meaning, Mooar gave to his 1870s Great Plains adventures? Do you think he saw himself participating in a historically significant moment?

15-5 | Addressing the Indian Question

FRANCIS A. WALKER, *Annual Report of the Commissioner of Indian Affairs* (1872)

Another war raged during the 1860s, but unlike the Civil War, the war with the Plains Indians persisted for decades. Following policies established by Andrew Jackson in the 1830s, the federal government in the 1860s and 1870s attempted to open western settlement by corralling American Indians onto reservations. Native resistance to these efforts inevitably resulted in a military response from the federal government, leading to notorious conflicts at such places as Sand Creek, Colorado; Fort Phil Kearny, Wyoming; Little Big Horn in the Montana Territory; and Wounded Knee, South Dakota. These clashes stirred debate about the long-term effectiveness of U.S. policy, which Francis Walker, commissioner of Indian affairs in the early 1870s, attempts to describe and justify.

The Indian policy, so called, of the Government, is a policy, and it is not a policy, or rather it consists of two policies, entirely distinct, seeming, indeed, to be mutually inconsistent and to reflect each upon the other: the one regulating the treatment of the tribes which are potentially hostile, that is, whose hostility is only repressed just so long as, and so far as, they are supported in idleness by the Government; the other regulating the treatment of those tribes which, from traditional friendship, from numerical weakness, or by the force of their location, are either indisposed toward, or incapable of, resistance to the demands of the Government. . . . This want of completeness and consistency in the treatment of the Indian tribes by the Government has been made the occasion of much

Francis A. Walker, "Annual Report of the Commissioner of Indian Affairs, November 1, 1872," in *Documents of United States Indian Policy*, 3rd ed., ed. Francis Paul Prucha (Lincoln: University of Nebraska Press, 2000), 135–140.

ridicule and partisan abuse; and it is indeed calculated to provoke criticism and to afford scope for satire; but it is none the less compatible with the highest expediency of the situation. . . . And yet, for all this, the Government is right and its critics wrong; and the "Indian policy" is sound, sensible, and beneficent, because it reduces to the minimum the loss of life and property upon our frontier, and allows the freest development of our settlements and railways possible under the circumstances. . . .

The Use of the Military Arm

The system now pursued in dealing with the roving tribes dangerous to our frontier population and obstructing our industrial progress, is entirely consistent with, and, indeed, requires the occasional use of the military arm, in restraining or chastising refractory individuals and bands. Such a use of the military constitutes no abandonment of the "peace policy," and involves no disparagement of it. It was not to be expected — it was not in the nature of things — that the entire body of wild Indians should submit to be restrained in their Ishmaelitish proclivities without a struggle on the part of the more audacious to maintain their traditional freedom. In the first announcement made of the reservation system, it was expressly declared that the Indians should be made as comfortable on, and as uncomfortable off, their reservations as it was in the power of the Government to make them; that such of them as went right should be protected and fed, and such as went wrong should be harassed and scourged without intermission. It was not anticipated that the first proclamation of this policy to the tribes concerned would effect the entire cessation of existing evils; but it was believed that persistence in the course marked out would steadily reduce the number of the refractory, both by the losses sustained in actual conflict and by the desertion of individuals as they should become weary of a profitless and hopeless struggle, until, in the near result, the system adopted should apply without exception to all the then roving and hostile tribes. Such a use of the strong arm of the Government is not war, but discipline. . . .

The Forbearance of the Government

It is unquestionably true that the Government has seemed somewhat tardy in proceeding under the second half of the reservation policy, and in applying the scourge to individuals and bands leaving their prescribed limits without authority, or for hostile purposes. This has been partly from a legitimate deference to the conviction of the great body of citizens that the Indians have been in the past unjustly and cruelly treated, and that great patience and long forbearance ought to be exercised in bringing them around to submission to the present reasonable requirements of the Government, and partly from the knowledge on the part of the officers of the Government charged with administering Indian affairs, that, from the natural jealously [sic] of these people, their sense of wrongs suffered in the past, and their suspiciousness arising from repeated acts of treachery on the part of the whites; from the great distance of many bands and individuals from points of personal communication with the agents of the Government, and the absence of all means of written communication with them; from the efforts of abandoned and degraded whites, living among the Indians and exerting much influence over them, to misrepresent the policy of the Government, and to keep alive the hostility and suspicion of the savages; and, lastly, from the extreme untrustworthiness of many of the interpreters on whom the Government is obliged to rely for bringing its intentions to the knowledge of the Indians: that by the joint effect of all these obstacles, many tribes and bands could come very slowly to hear, comprehend, and trust the professions and promises of the Government. . . .

The patience and forbearance exercised have been fully justified in their fruits. The main body of the roving Indians have, with good grace or with ill grace, submitted to the reservation system. Of those who still remain away from the assigned limits, by far the greater part are careful to do so with as little offense as possible; and when their range is such as for the present not to bring them into annoying or dangerous contact with the whites, this Office, has, from the motive of economy, generally been disposed to allow them to pick up their own living still by hunting and fishing, in preference to tying them up at agencies where they would require to be fed mainly or wholly at the expense of the Government. . . .

The Beginning of the End

It belongs not to a sanguine, but to a sober view of the situation, that three years will see the alternative of war eliminated from the Indian question, and the most powerful and hostile bands of to-day thrown in entire helplessness on the mercy of the Government. Indeed, the progress of two years more, if not of another summer, on the Northern Pacific Railroad will of itself completely solve the great Sioux problem, and leave the ninety thousand Indians ranging between the two trans-continental lines as incapable of resisting the Government as are the Indians of New York or Massachusetts. Columns moving north from the Union Pacific, and south from the Northern Pacific, would crush the Sioux and their confederates as between the upper and the nether millstone; while the rapid movement of troops along the northern line would prevent the escape of the savages, when hard pressed, into the British Possessions, which have heretofore afforded a convenient refuge on the approach of a military expedition.

Toward the south the day of deliverance from the fear of Indian hostility is more distant, yet it is not too much to expect that three summers of peaceful progress will forever put it out of the power of the tribes and bands which at present disturb Colorado, Utah, Arizona, and New Mexico to claim consideration of the country in any other attitude than as pensioners upon the national bounty. The railroads now under construction, or projected with a reasonable assurance of early completion, will multiply fourfold the striking force of the Army in that section; the little rifts of mining settlement, now found all through the mountains of the southern Territories will have become self-protecting communities; the feeble, wavering line of agricultural occupation, now sensitive to the faintest breath of Indian hostility, will then have grown to be the powerful "reserve" to lines still more closely advanced upon the last range of the intractable tribes.

Submission the Only Hope of the Indians

No one certainly will rejoice more heartily than the present Commissioner when the Indians of this county cease to be in a position to dictate, in any form or degree, to the Government; when, in fact, the last hostile tribe becomes reduced to the condition of suppliants for charity. This is, indeed, the only hope of salvation for the aborigines of the continent. If they stand up against the progress of civilization and industry, they must be relentlessly crushed. The westward course of population is neither to be denied nor delayed for the sake of all the Indians that ever called this country their home. They must yield or perish; and there is something that savors of providential mercy in the rapidity with which their fate advances upon them, leaving them scarcely the chance to resist before they shall be surrounded and disarmed. It is not feebly and futilely to attempt to stay this tide, whose depth and strength can hardly be measured, but to snatch the remnants of the Indian race from destruction from before it, that the friends of humanity should exert themselves in this juncture, and lose no time. And it is because the present system allows the freest extension of settlement and industry possible under the circumstances, while affording space and time for humane endeavors to rescue the Indian tribes from a position altogether barbarous and incompatible with civilization and social progress, that this system must be approved by all enlightened citizens. . . .

The Claims of the Indian

The people of the United States can never without dishonor refuse to respect these two considerations: 1st. That this continent was originally owned and occupied by the Indians, who have on this account a claim somewhat larger than the privilege of one hundred and sixty acres of land, and "find himself" in tools and stock, which is granted as a matter of course to any newly-arrived foreigner who declares his intention to become a citizen; that something in the nature of an endowment, either capitalized or in the form of annual expenditures for a series of years for the benefit of the Indians, though at the discretion of the Government as to the specific objects, should be provided for every tribe or band which is deprived of its roaming privilege and confined to a diminished reservation: such an endowment being not in the nature of a gratuity, but in common honesty the right of the Indian on account of his original interest in the soil. 2d. That inasmuch as the progress of our industrial enterprise has cut these people off from modes of livelihood entirely sufficient for their wants, and for which they were qualified, in a degree which has been the wonder of more civilized races, by inherited aptitudes and by long pursuit, and has left them utterly without resource, they have a claim on this account again to temporary support and to such assistance as may be necessary to place them in a position to obtain a livelihood by means which shall be compatible with civilization.

Had the settlements of the United States not been extended beyond the frontier of 1867, all the Indians of the continent would to the end of time have found upon the plains an inexhaustible supply of food and clothing. Were the westward course of population to be stayed at the barriers of to-day, notwithstanding the tremendous inroads made upon their hunting-grounds since 1867, the Indians would still have hope of life. But another such five years will see the Indians of Dakota and Montana as poor as the Indians of Nevada and Southern California; that is, reduced to an habitual condition of suffering from want of food.

The freedom of expansion which is working these results is to us of incalculable value. To the Indian it is of incalculable cost. Every year's advance of our frontier takes in a territory as large as some of the kingdoms of Europe. We are richer by hundreds of millions; the Indian is poorer by a large part of the little that he has. This growth is bringing imperial greatness to the nation; to the Indian it brings wretchedness, destitution, beggary. Surely there is obligation found in considerations like these, requiring us in some way, and in the best way, to make good to these original owners of the soil the loss by which we so greatly gain.

Can any principle of national morality be clearer than that, when the expansion and development of a civilized race involve the rapid destruction of the only means of subsistence possessed by the members of a less fortunate race, the higher is bound as a simple right to provide for the lower some substitute for the means of subsistence which it has destroyed? That substitute is, of course, best realized, not by systematic gratuities of food and clothing continued beyond a present emergency, but by directing these people to new pursuits which shall be consistent with the progress of civilization upon the continent; helping them over the first rough places on "the white man's road," and, meanwhile, supplying such subsistence as is absolutely necessary during the period of initiation and experiment.

READING AND DISCUSSION QUESTIONS

1. Analyze and evaluate the policy recommendations Walker endorses with respect to Native American tribes facing the expansion of white commerce and settlement. To what extent is he sympathetic to their plight?

2. What does Walker see as the ultimate fate of American Indians?

3. What conclusions about the political culture of the 1870s can you draw from Walker's annual report as commissioner of Indian affairs?

15-6 | Remembering Indian Boarding School Days

MOURNING DOVE, *A Salishan Autobiography* (1990)

Okanogan Indian Christine Quintasket, or Mourning Dove, experienced the effects of America's Native American policies in the late nineteenth century, a period she writes about in her autobiography, published half a century after her death. By the time of her birth in the mid-1880s, those policies rejected earlier efforts to concentrate Native Americans onto reservations. With the passage of the Dawes Severalty Act in 1887, the federal government's new aim was to eradicate "the Indian" within Native Americans. By discouraging reservations, where tribes had been able to maintain native languages and customs, the new policy hoped to "Americanize" them. Part of that effort led to an Indian boarding school movement whose adherents recommended that Native Americans be taught English, forced to adopt nonnative clothes and customs, and made to live apart from their extended families.

Although Mother continued persistently to give me my ancient education with the help of my native teacher, she was also a fanatically religious Catholic. We never missed mass or church unless it was absolutely necessary. If church was not scheduled at the little mission below our cabin, then we "pilgrimed" to Goodwin Mission to attend church. Winter and summer, she never failed to make her confession and communion on the first Friday of every month. To her mind, and that of many of the early converts, the word of the priest was law. She strictly observed anything that the pioneer Father De Rouge so much as hinted at. On the other hand, my father was considered a "slacker" or a black sheep of the flock. He attended church only occasionally and without the devotion of my mother. . . .

During one of our monthly trips to Goodwin for the first Friday service, we met Father De Rouge on the big steps of the church, where he had come outside to mingle with his beloved Indian congregation.

The good [Jesuit] priest came forward and shook hands with Mother, spying me behind her wide skirts. He looked right at me and asked if I had made my first communion. He had a way of jumbling up words from several Indian languages he had learned so that his words sounded childish, but I dared not chuckle at his comment. Instead, I shook my head in answer to his question. He looked at mother reproachfully and, shaking his head, said, "Tut, Tut, Lucy. You must let your child go to school with the good sisters to learn her religion so that she can make her first communion like other children of her age." Mother tried to make a protest, saying she needed me at home to care for the babies. But Father De Rouge could seldom be enticed to change his mind. He always had a very strict, ruling hand with the Indians. His word was much respected by the natives of the Colville Reservation.

He shook his finger at Mother and said, "Tut, Tut, Lucy. I command you." Then, pointing at the cross atop the bell tower of the church, he continued, "Your church commands that your child must go to school to learn her religion and the laws of the church." In obedience, Mother promised to send me to the mission for the fall term of 1898.

I had known Father De Rouge all my life. He had been a stationary superior at the Goodwin Mission until the arrival of Father Carnia [Caruana], whom the Indians called T-quit-na-wiss (Large Stomach), since the new priest had plenty of abdominal carriage. After that De Rouge became a traveling priest, covering all the territory of the Colville Reservation and beyond. He taught the Indians their prayers and erected the first little cabins that served as chapels until they were later remodeled into larger frame churches. These early church locations included Ellisford, St. Mary's Mission on Omak Creek, Nespelem, Keller, and Inchelium. These last four compose the modern districts of the Colville Reservation. Earlier these districts all had their share of the faithful work of the self-sacrificing Father Etienne (Stephen) De Rouge.

He was the descendant of a rich and influential French count, but he rejected his claim to this title to fulfill his mission among his beloved Colville. Many times he would stop by our cabin home at Pia to visit with the family. He traveled astride his cayuse leading a pack animal loaded with the sacred belongings needed to say mass. This gave him the convenience of holding services in any Indian tipi or cabin where night would overtake him. He was never too busy to answer a call for help, rushing in the night to visit the sick or administer the last sacraments to poor, dying natives. His life was thoroughly wrapped up in his chosen work. He spent every penny he could get from his rich family and from small Indian contributions to aid the needy.

It was through his influence and encouragement that the Indians gradually discontinued their ancient customs and were more willing to send their children to school at Goodwin. He later erected a fine and roomy school at St. Mary's Mission, after he had permanently established other churches that were maintained either by traveling priests or by one permanently settled in the location to teach the Indians and provide an example. This boarding school, built with his own money and contributions from Catholic whites in the East, remains a successful monument to his life's work. . . .

When my father told me I had better start at school, I was scared. It took much coaxing, and buying me candy and nuts along with other luxuries at the log store at Marcus, before I consented to go.

Father was holding my hand when we went through the big white gates into the clean yard of the school. A high whitewashed fence enclosed all the huge buildings, which looked so uninviting. I hated to stay but promised Father I would not get lonesome. I walked at his side as he briskly entered a building to meet a woman in a long black skirt, with a roll of stiff white, oval cloth around her pale face. I looked away from her lovely, tapered fingers. I loved my mother's careworn hands better.

Since I could not understand English, I could not comprehend the conversation between Father and the kind woman in black. Later I learned she was the superior at the school. When my father was ready to leave, I screamed, kicked, and clung to him, begging to go home. This had always worked before, but now his eyes grew dim and he gently handed me to the sister and shamelessly ran out the door. When the sister tried to calm me, I screamed all the louder and kicked her. She picked me up off the floor and marched me into a dark closet under the long stairway to scream as loud as I could. She left me to sob myself to sleep. This cured my temper.

I was too young to understand. I did not know English, and the other girls were forbidden to speak any native language. I was very much alone. Most of the time I played with wooden blocks and the youngest girls. I did not attend much school.

Each morning the children got up and dressed to attend church before breakfast. We walked in a double row along the path that climbed the slope to the large church, where my parents came for feast days. We entered the church from the west side door as the boys entered from the east one. The few adults came through the front double doors. There was also a small school chapel that we used when the weather was too bad to march outside.

Our dormitory had three rows of single iron beds, covered every day with white spreads and stiff-starched pillow shams that we folded each night and laid on a small stand beside the bed. Every Sunday night we were issued spotlessly clean nighties. This was the first nightgown I ever wore. Previously, I had slept in all my clothes.

Our dining hall, called the refectory, looked big to me, perhaps because I was used to eating in a cramped space. I was afraid of falling off the chair and always waited for others to sit first. The tables were lined up close to the walls, and the sister in charge had her table in the center, where she served our food on white enamel plates. We brought them up to her empty and carried them back full. Then we all waited until she rang the bell to begin eating.

The school ran strictly. We never talked during meals without permission, given only on Sunday or special holidays. Otherwise there was silence—a terrible silent silence. I was used to the freedom of the forest, and it was hard to learn this strict discipline. I was punished many times before I learned.

I stayed at the mission for less than a year because I took ill and father had to come and take me to the family camp at Kettle Falls. People were catching late salmon and eel. I returned to the mission again until my mother died in 1902 and I went home to care for my siblings. . . .

My second stay at the school was less traumatic. I was anxious to learn more English and read. The school had been enlarged, with much larger buildings adjoining the old ones. The old chicken yard was moved farther away from the hospital windows. There was a fine white modern building, with a full veranda along the front, for the white students who paid fifteen dollars a month to board there. Although they were next door, we never met them; it was as if we lived in different worlds. They had their own playroom, refectory, classrooms, and dormitory. We only saw them in church, when they filed in ahead of us and sat in front of the guardian sisters. Our own teachers sat on long benches behind our rows. The only white girls we got to know were the charity orphans who boarded with us.

The paying boarders got school tuition, books, meals, and free music lessons for their money. This price was so low that many white families around Marcus, Meyers Falls, Colville, and Chewelah sent their children to Goodwin. Native children only went as far as the lower grades, but some had the privilege of attending more academic grades in the classroom of the white girls. Only two girls ever did this, and they were both white charity cases. Some Indian children studied music free, learning piano and organ. We all learned to sing church hymns. Eva, the chunky little daughter of Bridgett Lemere, became a fine organist and choir leader at the Pia Mission. She had a beautiful voice, and her fingers flew over the keys so lightly that the sacred music would ring through the building. Her sister Annie was a few years older than I and became my chum. I stayed away from the girls my own age because my whole life was spent around older people, except for my sisters. . . .

I was very interested in my work. With the knowledge Jimmy Ryan[5] had taught me from his yellowback novels, I passed first grade during the first semester. After my promotion the sisters had no second reader, so I had to study out of the third-year one. My marks were so good in all classes but grammar, which I never could understand, that I graduated at third level. I worked hard on catechism, which Mother had taught me in the native language. When I passed, I made my first communion in the big church, with many younger girls, including Eva and Annie Lemere. Our white dresses and shoes were supplied by the sisters. We wore flowing veils with flowered wreaths to hold them in place. It was Easter morning of 1899. We filed back to the convent, and the sisters gave us a big banquet with many goodies. It was a memorable day, and I thoroughly believed in the Catholic creed. I honored it as much as my native tutor had taught me to revere the ancient traditions of my forebears. I saw no difference between them and never questioned the priest.

I was so enthusiastic that I promised the sisters and girls I would come back in the fall. We were dismissed in June on the feast of Corpus Christi, always a big event in our year.

I never got back to Goodwin, however. Mother had a son, christened Johnny, whom I had to take care of because the duties of the ranch took much of her time. I began secretly to read Jimmy's books. My parents scolded and rebuked me many times because they thought reading was an excuse for being idle. There was much work to be done around the cabin and in the fields.

One day I heard about the Tonasket Indian School, where the Pierre children went to school. I begged Mother to go, but she replied in agitated tones, "Do you

---

[5] **Jimmy Ryan:** A young Irish boy adopted by Mourning Dove's parents. He shared his collection of cheap dime novels, from which she learned to read.

want to know too much, and be like the other schoolgirls around here? They come home from school and have no shame for their good character. That is all girls learn in government schools—running around and exposing their bodies." I ran outside into the rosebushes and cried in bitter humiliation. I wanted to go to school and learn the Mysteries of books. My meager education was just enough to make out the simplest words. Jimmy Ryan was only a little better, but he could speak English well.

READING AND DISCUSSION QUESTIONS

1. Describe Mourning Dove's experiences at school. What can you infer about the school's educational goals, practices, and policies with respect to Native American children?

2. What conclusions can you draw about Mourning Dove's attitude toward the education she received at the boarding school? To what extent did her native traditions exist alongside the culture of whites she was expected to embrace?

■ COMPARATIVE QUESTIONS ■

1. How do the decades following the Civil War compare to the 1840s as two periods of expansionism? Were the motivations similar or different?

2. Compare the history of white–American Indian relations during the 1870s to the point of view expressed by Thomas Hariot (Document 1-1) and the Reverend Father Louis Cellot (Document 2-6). How do these documents show continuity or change in attitudes toward Native Americans?

3. To what extent do the multiple perspectives in this chapter support or challenge the argument that railroads and western expansion represented positive developments in the history of the United States?

4. Compare the image of the West that emerges from these sources with earlier sources such as the selection from *The Panoplist and Missionary Herald* (Document 7-4), Lansford Hastings's *Emigrants' Guide* (Document 11-3), and George Caleb Bingham's painting (Document 11-4). Explain how these documents reveal a diversity of perspective about the region as a land of opportunity, a hazard to life and limb, or a bit of both depending on one's experience.

5. Compare the artist's perspective in *Across the Continent* (Document 15-2) with the point of view expressed by the artist depicting the Erie Canal (Document 8-1). What historical patterns of continuity and change are suggested by these two images?

Consolidating a Continental Union
1844–1877

CHAPTER 12
Sectional Conflict and Crisis, 1844–1860

CHAPTER 13
Bloody Ground: The Civil War, 1861–1865

CHAPTER 14
Reconstruction, 1865–1877

CHAPTER 15
Conquering a Continent, 1860–1890

The Civil War era was driven by themes of politics and power. The political crisis over slavery and territorial expansion that surfaced in the wake
of the war with Mexico engaged reformers, politicians, and ordinary
Americans in heated debates over the true meaning of the Constitution,
the relationship between federal and state government, and the definition
of citizenship. The outbreak of war in 1861 was evidence of the failure of
those debates to reach agreement. While many no doubt harbored a hope
that the Union victory had settled accounts, fundamental disagreements
persisted into the Reconstruction era and linger even today. Different political and social groups during these years competed for influence, shaped
political institutions and values, and contested the meaning of citizenship.
The status of enslaved African Americans was, of course, central to these
debates, but so, too, were the rights of women and Native Americans
and the participation of immigrant groups who diversified the nation's
growing population. In the boisterous democracy of the mid-nineteenth

century, all those who called America home were caught up in the deafening argument over the values shaping the political system and the part they were to play in strengthening the political process.

P5-1 | Women Reformers Demand Citizenship Rights

ELIZABETH CADY STANTON, *Declaration of Rights and Sentiments* (1848)

In 1848, the basic rights of citizenship guaranteed in the Constitution were denied to half of the population on account of their sex. Women could not exercise the right to vote, and they enjoyed limited legal rights to property. They were excluded by custom and barred by law from certain professions and suffered discrimination in wages. Elizabeth Cady Stanton and other reformers convened a meeting in Seneca Falls, New York, in 1848 to organize a protest of society's narrow interpretation of female citizenship under the Constitution. Using the model of Jefferson's Declaration of Independence, Stanton and ninety-nine others signed the Declaration of Rights and Sentiments, thereby focusing the debate on the meaning of citizenship for women.

When, in the course of human events, it becomes necessary for one portion of the family of man to assume among the people of the earth a position different from that which they have hitherto occupied, but one to which the laws of nature and of nature's God entitle them, a decent respect to the opinions of mankind requires that they should declare the causes that impel them to such a course.

We hold these truths to be self-evident: that all men and women are created equal; that they are endowed by their Creator with certain inalienable rights; that among these are life, liberty, and the pursuit of happiness; that to secure these rights governments are instituted, deriving their just powers from the consent of the governed. Whenever any form of government becomes destructive of these ends, it is the right of those who suffer from it to refuse allegiance to it, and to insist upon the institution of a new government, laying its foundation on such principles, and organizing its powers in such form, as to them shall seem most likely to effect their safety and happiness. Prudence, indeed, will dictate that governments long established should not be changed for light and transient causes; and accordingly all experience hath shown that mankind are more disposed to suffer while evils are sufferable, than to right themselves by abolishing the forms to which they are accustomed. But when a long train of abuses and usurpations, pursuing invariably the same object, evinces a design to reduce them under absolute despotism, it is their duty to throw off such government, and to provide new guards for their future security. Such has been the patient sufferance of the women under this government, and such is now the necessity which constrains them to demand the equal station to which they are entitled. The history of mankind is a history of repeated injuries and usurpations on the

Elizabeth Cady Stanton, *A History of Woman Suffrage*, vol. 1 (Rochester, NY: Fowler and Wells, 1889), 70–71.

part of man toward woman, having in direct object the establishment of an absolute tyranny over her. To prove this, let facts be submitted to a candid world.

He has never permitted her to exercise her inalienable right to the elective franchise.

He has compelled her to submit to laws, in the formation of which she had no voice.

He has withheld from her rights which are given to the most ignorant and degraded men—both natives and foreigners.

Having deprived her of this first right of a citizen, the elective franchise, thereby leaving her without representation in the halls of legislation, he has oppressed her on all sides.

He has made her, if married, in the eye of the law, civilly dead.

He has taken from her all right in property, even to the wages she earns.

He has made her, morally, an irresponsible being, as she can commit many crimes with impunity, provided they be done in the presence of her husband. In the covenant of marriage, she is compelled to promise obedience to her husband, he becoming, to all intents and purposes, her master—the law giving him power to deprive her of her liberty, and to administer chastisement.

He has so framed the laws of divorce, as to what shall be the proper causes of divorce; in case of separation, to whom the guardianship of the children shall be given; as to be wholly regardless of the happiness of women—the law, in all cases, going upon a false supposition of the supremacy of man, and giving all power into his hands.

After depriving her of all rights as a married woman, if single, and the owner of property, he has taxed her to support a government which recognizes her only when her property can be made profitable to it.

He has monopolized nearly all the profitable employments, and from those she is permitted to follow, she receives but a scanty remuneration.

He closes against her all the avenues to wealth and distinction which he considers most honorable to himself. As a teacher of theology, medicine, or law, she is not known.

He has denied her the facilities for obtaining a thorough education—all colleges being closed against her.

He allows her in Church, as well as State, but a subordinate position, claiming Apostolic authority for her exclusion from the ministry, and, with some exceptions, from any public participation in the affairs of the Church.

He has created a false sentiment, by giving to the world a different code of morals for men and women, by which moral delinquencies which exclude women from society, are not only tolerated, but deemed of little public account in man.

He has usurped the prerogative of Jehovah himself, claiming it as his right to assign for her a sphere of action, when that belongs to her conscience and to her God.

He has endeavored, in every way that he could, to destroy her confidence in her own powers, to lessen her self-respect, and to make her willing to lead a dependent and abject life.

Now, in view of this entire disfranchisement of one-half the people of this country, their social and religious degradation, — in view of the unjust laws above mentioned, and because women do feel themselves aggrieved, oppressed, and fraudulently deprived of their most sacred rights, we insist that they have immediate admission to all the rights and privileges which belong to them as citizens of the United States.

In entering upon the great work before us, we anticipate no small amount of misconception, misrepresentation, and ridicule; but we shall use every instrumentality within our power to effect our object. We shall employ agents, circulate tracts, petition the state and national legislatures, and endeavor to enlist the pulpit and the press in our behalf. We hope this Convention will be followed by a series of Conventions, embracing every part of the country. . . .

Resolutions

Whereas the great precept of nature is conceded to be, "that man shall pursue his own true and substantial happiness." Blackstone,[1] in his Commentaries, remarks, that this law of Nature being coeval with mankind, and dictated by God himself, is of course superior in obligation to any other. It is binding over all the globe, in all countries, and at all times; no human laws are of any validity if contrary to this, and such of them as are valid, derive all their force, and all their validity, and all their authority, mediately and immediately, from this original; therefore,

Resolved, That such laws as conflict, in any way, with the true and substantial happiness of woman, are contrary to the great precept of nature, and of no validity; for this is "superior in obligation to any other."

Resolved, That all laws which prevent woman from occupying such a station in society as her conscience shall dictate, or which place her in a position inferior to that of man, are contrary to the great precept of nature, and therefore of no force or authority.

Resolved, That woman is man's equal—was intended to be so by the Creator— and the highest good of the race demands that she should be recognized as such.

Resolved, That the women of this country ought to be enlightened in regard to the laws under which they live, that they may no longer publish their degradation, by declaring themselves satisfied with their present position, nor their ignorance, by asserting that they have all the rights they want.

Resolved, That inasmuch as man, while claiming for himself intellectual superiority, does accord to woman moral superiority, it is pre-eminently his duty to encourage her to speak, and teach, as she has an opportunity, in all religious assemblies.

Resolved, That the same amount of virtue, delicacy, and refinement of behavior, that is required of woman in the social state, should also be required of man, and the same transgressions should be visited with equal severity on both man and woman.

---

[1] **Blackstone**: Sir William Blackstone, English jurist, published volume 1 of his *Commentaries on the Laws of England* in 1766, which became the most authoritative scholarly overview of English common law, influencing American legal thinkers through the nineteenth century.

Resolved, That the objection of indelicacy and impropriety, which is so often brought against woman when she addresses a public audience, comes with a very ill-grace from those who encourage, by their attendance, her appearance on the stage, in the concert, or in the feats of the circus.

Resolved, That woman has too long rested satisfied in the circumscribed limits which corrupt customs and a perverted application of the Scriptures have marked out for her, and that it is time she should move in the enlarged sphere which her great Creator has assigned her.

Resolved, That it is the duty of the women of this country to secure to themselves their sacred right to the elective franchise.

Resolved, That the equality of human rights results necessarily from the fact of the identity of the race in capabilities and responsibilities.

Resolved, therefore, That, being invested by the Creator with the same capabilities, and the same consciousness of responsibility for their exercise, it is demonstrably the right and duty of woman, equally with man, to promote every righteous cause, by every righteous means; and especially in regard to the great subjects of morals and religion, it is self-evidently her right to participate with her brother in teaching them, both in private and in public, by writing and by speaking, by any instrumentalities proper to be used, and in any assemblies proper to be held; and this being a self-evident truth, growing out of the divinely implanted principles of human nature, any custom or authority adverse to it, whether modern or wearing the hoary sanction of antiquity, is to be regarded as self-evident falsehood, and at war with the interests of mankind.

READING AND DISCUSSION QUESTIONS

1. Analyze the efforts of the Seneca Falls delegates to define and gain access to individual rights and citizenship for women. What definition of citizenship did they embrace for women?

2. What impact on the interpretation of constitutional rights do you think these women expected their reforms to provoke?

P5-2 | The Catholic Threat to American Politics

SAMUEL F. B. MORSE, *Foreign Conspiracy Against the Liberties of the United States* (1855)

European immigration was on the rise in the 1830s, when Samuel Morse published in book form his editorials first serialized in the *New York Observer*. By the time the seventh edition was published in the mid-1850s, immigration had increased even more, spurred on by the revolutions in Europe in 1848. Morse, who is better known for the telegraphic code he invented, was a nativist who justified his opposition to Catholic immigration as a defense of

Samuel F. B. Morse, *Foreign Conspiracy Against the Liberties of the United States* (New York: American and Foreign Christian Union, 1855), 89–96, 98–99.

constitutional liberties and republican government against papal conspiracies directed from Rome. His understanding of the Constitution powered such antebellum political movements as the Nativist or Know-Nothing Party of the 1840s and 1850s.

[S]ome of my readers . . . may be inclined to ask in what manner can the despots of Europe effect, by means of Popish emissaries, any thing in this country to counteract the influence of our liberal institutions? In what way can they operate here?

With the *necessity existing of doing something, from the instinct of self-preservation*, to check the influence of our free institutions on Europe, with the *funds* provided, and *agents* on the spot interested in their plans, one would think it needed but little sagacity to find modes and opportunities of operating; especially, too, when such *vulnerable points* as I have exposed (and there are many more which I have not brought forward) invite attack.

To any such inquirers, let me say there are many ways in which a body organized as are the Catholics, and moving in concert, might *disturb* (to use the mildest term) the good order of the republic, and thus compel us to present to observing Europe the spectacle of republican anarchy. Who is not aware that a great portion of that stuff which composes a mob, ripe for riot or excess of any kind, and of which we have every week or two a fresh example in some part of the country, is a Catholic population? And what makes it turbulent? Ignorance — an ignorance which it is for the interest of its leaders not to enlighten; for, enlighten a man, and he will think for himself, and have some self-respect; he will understand the laws, and know his interest in obeying them. Keep him in ignorance, and he is the slave of the man who will flatter his passions and appetites, or awe him by superstitious fears. Against the outbreakings of such men, society, as it is constituted on our free system, can protect itself only in one of two ways: it must either bring these men under the influence and control of a sound republican and religious education, or it must call in the aid of *the priests* who govern them, and who may *permit* and *direct*, or *restrain* their turbulence, in accordance with what they may judge at any particular time to be the *interest of the church*. Yes, be it well remarked, the same hands that can, whenever it suits their interest, *restrain*, can also, at the proper time, "*let slip the dogs of war.*" In this mode of restraint by a *police of priests*, by substituting the *ecclesiastical* for the *civil* power, the *priest-led* mobs of Portugal and Spain, and South America, are instructive examples. And start not, American reader, *this kind of police is already established in our country!* We have had mobs again and again, which neither the civil nor military power have availed any thing to quell, until the magic "*peace, be still,*" of the *Catholic priest* has hushed the winds, and calmed the waves of popular tumult. . . .

And what now prevents the interference of Catholics, as a sect, directly in the *political elections* of the country? They are organized under their priests: is there any thing in their religious principles to restrain them? Do not Catholics of the present day use the bonds of religious union to effect political objects in other countries? . . .

It is not true that Popery meddles not with the politics of the country. The cloven foot has already shown itself. *Popery is organized at the elections!* For example: in Michigan, the Bishop Richard, a Jesuit (since deceased), was several times chosen delegate to Congress from the territory, the majority of the people being Catholics. As Protestants became more numerous, the contest between the bishop and his Protestant rival was more and more close, until at length, by the increase of Protestant emigration, the latter triumphed. The bishop, in order to detect any delinquency in his flock at the polls, *had his ticket printed on colored paper*! . . . Does it not show that Popery, with all its speciousness, is the same here as elsewhere? It manifests, when it has the opportunity, its genuine disposition to use *spiritual* power for the promotion of its *temporal* ambition. It uses its ecclesiastical weapons to control an election. . . .

It is unnecessary to multiply facts of this nature. . . . Surely American Protestants . . . will see that Popery is now, what it has ever been, a system of the darkest *political* intrigue and despotism, cloaking itself, to avoid attack, under the sacred name of religion. They will be deeply impressed with the truth, that Popery is a political as well as a religious system; that in this respect it differs totally from all other sects, from all other forms of religion in the country. *Popery imbodies in itself* THE CLOSEST UNION OF CHURCH AND STATE. . . .

Can we not discern the *political* character of Popery? Shall the name of *Religion*, artfully connected with it, still blind our eyes? Let us suppose a body of men to combine together, and claim as their right, that *all public and private property, of whatever kind, is held at their disposal; that they alone are to judge of their own right to dispose of it*; that they alone are authorized *to think or speak on the subject; that they who speak or write in opposition to them are traitors*, and must *be put to death; that all temporal power is secondary to theirs, and amenable to their superior and infallible judgment*; and the better to hide the presumption of these tyrannical claims, suppose that these men should pretend to *divine right*, and call their system *Religion*, and so claim the protection of our laws, and pleading *conscience*, demand to be tolerated. Would the name of *Religion* be a cloak sufficiently thick to hide such absurdity, and shield it from public indignation? Take, then, from *Popery* its name of *Religion*; strip its *officers* of their pompous titles of *sacredness*, and its *decrees* of the nauseous cant of piety, and what have you remaining? Is it not a *naked, odious Despotism*, depending for its strength on the observance of the strictest military discipline in its ranks, from the Pope, through his Cardinals, Archbishops, Bishops, &c. down to the lowest priest of his dominions? And is not this despotism acting *politically* in this country?

READING AND DISCUSSION QUESTIONS

1. How does Morse's argument about the Catholic threat to America provide evidence for the impact of anti-immigrant ideas on the political system? What social effect might his efforts to limit participation by Catholics have had on antebellum American politics?

2. Why do you think his ideas about the Constitution's vulnerabilities toward Catholic influence found a receptive audience?

P5-3 | Debating the Meaning of the Constitution
ABRAHAM LINCOLN, *Cooper Union Address* (1860)

In 1860, the clear point of contention between Republicans and Democrats was the authority of Congress to regulate slavery within the territories. Illinois senator Stephen Douglas, whom Lincoln had famously debated in 1858, promoted the idea of "popular sovereignty," whereby voters would decide the fate of slavery in a territory, claiming the founding fathers had endorsed such a policy in the Constitution. Lincoln's meticulous rejoinder in his Cooper Union address in New York City argued instead that the founders had acknowledged Congress's duty to regulate slavery in the territories. Though Lincoln was a minor political figure before the speech, his New York triumph propelled him to the front ranks of Republican Party politics, leading later that year to his nomination for president.

In his speech last autumn, at Columbus, Ohio, as reported in "The New-York Times," Senator Douglas said:

"Our fathers, when they framed the Government under which we live, understood this question just as well, and even better, than we do now."

I fully indorse this, and I adopt it as a text for this discourse. I so adopt it because it furnishes a precise and an agreed starting point for a discussion between Republicans and that wing of the Democracy headed by Senator Douglas. It simply leaves the inquiry: "What was the understanding those fathers had of the question mentioned?"

What is the frame of government under which we live?

The answer must be: "The Constitution of the United States." That Constitution consists of the original, framed in 1787 (and under which the present government first went into operation), and twelve subsequently framed amendments, the first ten of which were framed in 1789.

Who were our fathers that framed the Constitution? I suppose the "thirty-nine" who signed the original instrument may be fairly called our fathers who framed that part of the present Government. It is almost exactly true to say they framed it, and it is altogether true to say they fairly represented the opinion and sentiment of the whole nation at that time. . . .

I take these "thirty-nine," for the present, as being "our fathers who framed the Government under which we live."

What is the question which, according to the text, those fathers understood "just as well, and even better than we do now"?

It is this: Does the proper division of local from federal authority, or anything in the Constitution, forbid our *Federal Government* to control as to slavery in *our Federal Territories*?

Upon this, Senator Douglas holds the affirmative, and Republicans the negative. This affirmation and denial form an issue; and this issue — this question — is precisely what the text declares our fathers understood "better than we."

Let us now inquire whether the "thirty-nine," or any of them, ever acted upon this question; and if they did, how they acted upon it — how they expressed that better understanding?

Abraham Lincoln Online (www.abrahamlincolnonline.org/lincoln/speeches/cooper.htm).

In 1784, three years before the Constitution—the United States then owning the Northwestern Territory, and no other, the Congress of the Confederation had before them the question of prohibiting slavery in that Territory; and four of the "thirty-nine" who afterward framed the Constitution, were in that Congress, and voted . . . for the prohibition, thus showing that, in their understanding, no line dividing local from federal authority, nor anything else, properly forbade the Federal Government to control as to slavery in federal territory. . . .

In 1787, still before the Constitution . . . the same question of prohibiting slavery in the territory again came before the Congress of the Confederation; and two more of the "thirty-nine" who afterward signed the Constitution . . . both voted for the prohibition—thus showing that, in their understanding, no line dividing local from federal authority, nor anything else, properly forbids the Federal Government to control as to slavery in Federal territory. . . .

In 1789, by the first Congress which sat under the Constitution, an act was passed to enforce the Ordinance of '87, including the prohibition of slavery in the Northwestern Territory. The bill . . . passed both branches without yeas and nays, which is equivalent to a unanimous passage. In this Congress there were sixteen of the thirty-nine fathers who framed the original Constitution. . . .

This shows that, in their understanding, no line dividing local from federal authority, nor anything in the Constitution, properly forbade Congress to prohibit slavery in the federal territory; else both their fidelity to correct principle, and their oath to support the Constitution, would have constrained them to oppose the prohibition.

Again, George Washington, another of the "thirty-nine," was then President of the United States, and, as such approved and signed the bill; thus completing its validity as a law, and thus showing that, in his understanding, no line dividing local from federal authority, nor anything in the Constitution, forbade the Federal Government, to control as to slavery in federal territory. . . .

In 1803, the Federal Government purchased the Louisiana country. . . . Congress did not, in the Territorial Act, prohibit slavery; but they did interfere with it—take control of it—in a more marked and extensive way than they did in the case of Mississippi. The substance of the provision therein made, in relation to slaves, was:

First. That no slave should be imported into the territory from foreign parts.

Second. That no slave should be carried into it who had been imported into the United States since the first day of May, 1798.

Third. That no slave should be carried into it, except by the owner, and for his own use as a settler; the penalty in all the cases being a fine upon the violator of the law, and freedom to the slave. . . .

In the Congress which passed it, there were two of the "thirty-nine." . . . They would not have allowed it to pass without recording their opposition to it, if, in their understanding, it violated either the line properly dividing local from federal authority, or any provision of the Constitution. . . .

The cases I have mentioned are the only acts of the "thirty-nine," or of any of them, upon the direct issue, which I have been able to discover. . . .

The sum of the whole is, that of our thirty-nine fathers who framed the original Constitution, twenty-one—a clear majority of the whole—certainly understood that no proper division of local from federal authority, nor any part of the Constitution, forbade the Federal Government to control slavery in the federal territories. . . .

But enough! *Let all who believe that "our fathers, who framed the Government under which we live, understood this question just as well, and even better, than we do now," speak as they spoke, and act as they acted upon it. This is all Republicans ask — all Republicans desire — in relation to slavery. As those fathers marked it, so let it be again marked, as an evil not to be extended, but to be tolerated and protected only because of and so far as its actual presence among us makes that toleration and protection a necessity. Let all the guarantees those fathers gave it, be, not grudgingly, but fully and fairly, maintained.* For this Republicans contend, and with this, so far as I know or believe, they will be content.

And now, if they would listen — as I suppose they will not — I would address a few words to the Southern people. . . .

You say we are sectional. We deny it. That makes an issue; and the burden of proof is upon you. You produce your proof; and what is it? Why, that our party has no existence in your section — gets no votes in your section. The fact is substantially true; but does it prove the issue? . . . The fact that we get no votes in your section, is a fact of your making, and not of ours. And if there be fault in that fact, that fault is primarily yours, and remains until you show that we repel you by some wrong principle or practice. . . . Do you accept the challenge? No! Then you really believe that the principle which "our fathers who framed the Government under which we live" thought so clearly right as to adopt it, and indorse it again and again, upon their official oaths, is in fact so clearly wrong as to demand your condemnation without a moment's consideration.

Some of you delight to flaunt in our faces the warning against sectional parties given by Washington in his Farewell Address. Less than eight years before Washington gave that warning, he had, as President of the United States, approved and signed an act of Congress, enforcing the prohibition of slavery in the Northwestern Territory, which act embodied the policy of the Government upon that subject up to and at the very moment he penned that warning; and about one year after he penned it, he wrote LaFayette[2] that he considered that prohibition a wise measure, expressing in the same connection his hope that we should at some time have a confederacy of free States. . . .

Again, you say we have made the slavery question more prominent than it formerly was. We deny it. We admit that it is more prominent, but we deny that we made it so. It was not we, but you, who discarded the old policy of the fathers. We resisted, and still resist, your innovation; and thence comes the greater prominence of the question. . . .

You charge that we stir up insurrections among your slaves. We deny it; and what is your proof? Harper's Ferry! John Brown!! John Brown was no Republican; and you have failed to implicate a single Republican in his Harper's Ferry enterprise. . . .

---

[2] **LaFayette:** The Marquis de Lafayette was a French aristocrat who served with Washington as a major general in the Continental army during the American Revolution.

Under all these circumstances, do you really feel yourselves justified to break up this Government unless such a court decision as yours is, shall be at once submitted to as a conclusive and final rule of political action? But you will not abide the election of a Republican president! In that supposed event, you say, you will destroy the Union; and then, you say, the great crime of having destroyed it will be upon us! That is cool. A highwayman holds a pistol to my ear, and mutters through his teeth, "Stand and deliver, or I shall kill you, and then you will be a murderer!" . . .

A few words now to Republicans. . . .

Wrong as we think slavery is, we can yet afford to let it alone where it is, because that much is due to the necessity arising from its actual presence in the nation; but can we, while our votes will prevent it, allow it to spread into the National Territories, and to overrun us here in these Free States? If our sense of duty forbids this, then let us stand by our duty, fearlessly and effectively. Let us be diverted by none of those sophistical contrivances wherewith we are so industriously plied and belabored — contrivances such as groping for some middle ground between the right and the wrong, vain as the search for a man who should be neither a living man nor a dead man — such as a policy of "don't care" on a question about which all true men do care — such as Union appeals beseeching true Union men to yield to Disunionists, reversing the divine rule, and calling, not the sinners, but the righteous to repentance — such as invocations to Washington, imploring men to unsay what Washington said, and undo what Washington did.

Neither let us be slandered from our duty by false accusations against us, nor frightened from it by menaces of destruction to the Government nor of dungeons to ourselves. LET US HAVE FAITH THAT RIGHT MAKES MIGHT, AND IN THAT FAITH, LET US, TO THE END, DARE TO DO OUR DUTY AS WE UNDERSTAND IT.

READING AND DISCUSSION QUESTIONS

1. Summarize Lincoln's interpretation of the Constitution with respect to the issue of slavery's expansion within federal territories. What impact do you think his views had on southerners in the historical context of the 1850s and 1860s?

2. What argument does Lincoln make about the role of the federal government and its potential as an agent of political change in the context of the slavery issue?

P5-4 | Southern Leader Contrasts Union and Confederate Constitutions

ALEXANDER STEPHENS, *"Cornerstone" Speech* (1861)

The federal and Confederate constitutions that Alexander Stephens described during the secession crisis in March 1861 were a study in contrasts. Whereas Lincoln at Cooper Union had claimed that the Constitution granted Congress the authority to regulate slavery in the territories, Stephens emphasized instead its guarantee of slavery. Regardless, Stephens declared that the federal Constitution rested on flawed assumptions concerning the equality of the races. He therefore championed the new Confederate Constitution for its attachment to what he called "this great physical, philosophical, and moral truth." This truth, which he labeled the cornerstone of the Confederacy, was the inflexible belief in "the Negro's" inferiority.

This new constitution . . . amply secures all our ancient rights, franchises, and liberties. All the great principles of Magna Charta are retained in it. No citizen is deprived of life, liberty, or property, but by the judgment of his peers under the laws of the land. The great principle of religious liberty, which was the honor and pride of the old constitution, is still maintained and secured. All the essentials of the old constitution, which have endeared it to the hearts of the American people, have been preserved and perpetuated. [Applause.] . . .

The new constitution has put at rest, *forever,* all the agitating questions relating to our peculiar institution—African slavery as it exists amongst us—the proper *status* of the negro in our form of civilization. This was the immediate cause of the late rupture and present revolution. Jefferson in his forecast, had anticipated this, as the "rock upon which the old Union would split." He was right. What was conjecture with him, is now a realized fact. But whether he fully comprehended the great truth upon which that rock *stood* and *stands,* may be doubted. The prevailing ideas entertained by him and most of the leading statesmen at the time of the formation of the old constitution, were that the enslavement of the African was in violation of the laws of nature; that it was wrong in *principle,* socially, morally, and politically. It was an evil they knew not well how to deal with, but the general opinion of the men of that day was that, somehow or other in the order of Providence, the institution would be evanescent and pass away. This idea, though not incorporated in the constitution, was the prevailing idea at that time. The constitution, it is true, secured every essential guarantee to the institution while it should last, and hence no argument can be justly urged against the constitutional guarantees thus secured, because of the common sentiment of the day. Those ideas, however, were fundamentally wrong. They rested upon the assumption of the equality of races. This was an error. It was a sandy foundation, and the government built upon it fell when the "storm came and the wind blew."

Our new government is founded upon exactly the opposite idea; its foundations are laid, its corner-stone rests upon the great truth, that the negro is not equal to the white man; that slavery—subordination to the superior race—is his natural and normal condition. [Applause.]

This, our new government, is the first, in the history of the world, based upon this great physical, philosophical, and moral truth. This truth has been slow in the process of its development, like all other truths in the various departments of science. It has been so even amongst us. Many who hear me, perhaps, can recollect well, that this truth was not generally admitted, even within their day. The errors of the past generation still clung to many as late as twenty years

Alexander H. Stephens, in Public and Private. With Letters and Speeches, Before, During, and Since the War, ed. Henry Cleveland (Philadelphia: National Publishing Company, 1866), 718–723.

ago. Those at the North, who still cling to these errors, with a zeal above knowledge, we justly denominate fanatics. All fanaticism springs from an aberration of the mind—from a defect in reasoning. It is a species of insanity. One of the most striking characteristics of insanity, in many instances, is forming correct conclusions from fancied or erroneous premises; so with the anti-slavery fanatics; their conclusions are right if their premises were. They assume that the negro is equal, and hence conclude that he is entitled to equal privileges and rights with the white man. If their premises were- correct, their conclusions would be logical and just—but their premise being wrong, their whole argument fails. . . .

May we not, therefore, look with confidence to the ultimate universal acknowledgment of the truths upon which our system rests? It is the first government ever instituted upon the principles in strict conformity to nature, and the ordination of Providence, in furnishing the materials of human society. Many governments have been founded upon the principle of the subordination and serfdom of certain classes of the same race; such were and are in violation of the laws of nature. Our system commits no such violation of nature's laws. With us, all of the white race, however high or low, rich or poor, are equal in the eye of the law. Not so with the negro. Subordination is his place. He, by nature, or by the curse against Canaan, is fitted for that condition which he occupies in our system. The architect, in the construction of buildings, lays the foundation with the proper material—the granite; then comes the brick or the marble. The substratum of our society is made of the material fitted by nature for it, and by experience we know that it is best, not only for the superior, but for the inferior race, that it should be so. It is, indeed, in conformity with the ordinance of the Creator. It is not for us to inquire into the wisdom of his ordinances, or to question them. For his own purposes, he has made one race to differ from another, as he has made "one star to differ from another star in glory."

The great objects of humanity are best attained when there is conformity to his laws and decrees, in the formation of governments as well as in all things else. Our confederacy is founded upon principles in strict conformity with these laws. This stone which was rejected by the first builders "is become the chief of the corner"—the real "corner-stone"—in our new edifice. [Applause.]

READING AND DISCUSSION QUESTIONS

1. Summarize the differences in interpretation that separated Stephens from Lincoln (Document P5-3) on the question of the federal Constitution's position on slavery and the slavery extension issue. How did these arguments over the meaning of the Constitution affect American politics in the 1850s and 1860s?

2. To what extent do these interpretive differences represent short- or long-term causes of the Civil War?

3. How did the Confederate interpretation of constitutional values, as reflected in Stephens's speech, help southern politicians distinguish their Constitution from the federal Constitution they rejected?

P5-5 | Contesting African American Citizenship

THOMAS NAST, *"This Is a White Man's Government" Cartoon* (1868)

Many who supported the ratification of the Fifteenth Amendment (1870) saw its defense of black (male) suffrage as payment for the sin of slavery and a reward for African American service during the Civil War. In this September 1868 cartoon, Thomas Nast criticizes those on the other side of the argument. Here Nast comments on the efforts of the Democratic Party to trample on the rights of African Americans. The figure on the left is a common Nast caricature of a Catholic Irish American. Nast depicts him holding hands with Nathan Bedford Forrest, a Confederate officer and a founder of the Ku Klux Klan and, on the right, August Belmont, a wealthy party leader shown holding a packet of money to purchase votes.

Library of Congress, LC-USZ62-121735

READING AND DISCUSSION QUESTIONS

1. What interpretation of the Democratic Party is Nast expecting his viewers to share?

2. Why do you think Nast includes an Irish Catholic character in this cartoon? What is he suggesting about the relationship between Irish Americans (many of whom were immigrants or naturalized citizens) and African Americans?

3. What does this cartoon suggest about the struggle African Americans faced in securing the rights of citizenship? To what extent did the Fifteenth Amendment, ratified two years after the publication of Nast's cartoon, make a difference?

P5-6 | Standing Bear Aggrieves Federal Government's Indian Policy
Standing Bear's Odyssey (c. 1870s)

The women Elizabeth Cady Stanton spoke for, like freedmen after the Civil War, sought rights of citizenship conferred by the Constitution. For them, the Constitution was a guarantor of rights, what Frederick Douglass called the "glorious liberty document." The same was not true of Native Americans who were excluded from the provisions of the Fourteenth Amendment ratified in 1868 that defined citizenship. Native Americans were not considered U.S. citizens, yet they frequently found themselves at the mercy of federal policies that disrupted their lives and trampled on their rights. During the post-Civil War years, many Native Americans were displaced by federal policies that aided westward expansion. The experience of the Ponca tribe in 1877 was a poignant example, as told by one of the tribe's chiefs, Standing Bear. As he tells the story, the federal government pushed his people off of their land in northeastern Nebraska and forced them onto reservations in the Indian Territory in Oklahoma. Standing Bear was put on trial when he left the reservation without federal permission. In 1879, a U.S. District Court ruled in *Standing Bear vs. Crook* that Native Americans were "'persons' within the meaning of the laws of the United States" and were to be accorded the same Constitutional protections as whites. The court's ruling was a vindication for Standing Bear and for Native Americans more generally, but the price of victory was steep.

We lived on our land as long as we can remember. No one knows how long ago we came there. The land was owned by our tribe as far back as memory of men goes. We were living quietly on our farms. All of a sudden one white man came. We had no idea what for. This was the inspector. He came to our tribe with Rev. Mr. Hinman. These two, with the agent, James Lawrence, they made our trouble.

"Standing Bear's Odyssey," in *Native American Testimony: Indian-White Relations From Prophecy to the Present*, 1492–1992, ed. Peter Nabokov (New York: Viking Penguin, 1991), pp. 165–169.

They said the President[3] told us to pack up — that we must move to the Indian Territory.

The inspector said to us: "The President says you must sell this land. He will buy it and pay you the money, and give you new land in the Indian Territory."

We said to him: "We do not know your authority. You have no right to move us till we have had council with the President."

We said to him: "When two persons wish to make a bargain, they can talk together and find out what each wants, and then make their agreement."

We said to him: "We do not wish to go. When a man owns anything, he does not let it go till he has received payment for it."

We said to him: "We will see the President first."

He said to us: "I will take you to see the new land. If you like it, then you can see the President, and tell him so. If not, then you can see him and tell him so." And he took all ten of our chiefs down. I went, and Bright Eyes' uncle went. He took us to look at three different pieces of land. He said we must take one of the three pieces, so the President said. After he took us down there, he said: "No pay for the land you left."

We said to him: "You have forgotten what you said before we started. You said we should have pay for our land. Now you say not. You told us then you were speaking truth."

All these three men took us down there. The man got very angry. He tried to compel us to take one of the three pieces of land. He told us to be brave. He said to us: "If you do not accept these, I will leave you here alone.

You are one thousand miles from home. You have no money. You have no interpreter, and you cannot speak the language." And he went out and slammed the door. The man talked to us from long before sundown till it was nine o'clock at night.

We said to him: "We do not like this land. We could not support ourselves. The water is bad. Now send us to Washington, to tell the President, as you promised."

He said to us: "The President did not tell me to take you to Washington; neither did he tell me to take you home."

We said to him: "You have the Indian money you took to bring us down here. That money belongs to us. We would like to have some of it. People do not give away food for nothing. We must have money to buy food on the road."

He said to us: "I will not give you a cent."

---

[3] **President:** Ulysses S. Grant was president when the removal policy began. Standing Bear and other Ponca chiefs later met with a sympathetic President Rutherford B. Hayes to protest their forced removal, but they were ultimately told to remain in Indian Territory.

We said to him: "We are in a strange country. We cannot find our way home. Give us a pass, that people may show us our way."

He said: "I will not give you any."

We said to him: "This interpreter is ours. We pay him. Let him go with us."

He said: "You shall not have the interpreter. He is mine, and not yours."

We said to him: "Take us at least to the railroad; show us the way to that."

And he would not. He left us right there. It was winter. We started for home on foot. At night we slept in haystacks. We barely lived till morning, it was so cold. We had nothing but our blankets. We took the ears of corn that had dried in the fields; we ate it raw. The soles of our moccasins wore out. We went barefoot in the snow. We were nearly dead when we reached the Otoe Reserve. It had been fifty days. We stayed there ten days to strengthen up, and the Otoes gave each of us a pony. The agent of the Otoes told us he had received a telegram from the inspector, saying that the Indian chiefs had run away; not to give us food or shelter, or help in any way. The agent said: "I would like to understand. Tell me all that has happened. Tell me the truth. . . ."

Then we told our story to the agent and to the Otoe chiefs—how we had been left down there to find our way.

The agent said: "I can hardly believe it possible that anyone could have treated you so. The inspector was a poor man to have done this. If I had taken chiefs in this way, I would have brought them home; I could not have left them there."

In seven days we reached the Omaha Reservation. Then we sent a telegram to the President; asked him if he had authorized this thing. We waited three days for the answer. No answer came.

In four days we reached our own home. We found the inspector there. While we were gone, he had come to our people and told them to move.

Our people said: "Where are our chiefs? What have you done with them? Why have you not brought them back? We will not move till our chiefs come back."

Then the inspector told them: "Tomorrow you must be ready to move. If you are not ready you will be shot." Then the soldiers came to the doors with their bayonets, and ten families were frightened. The soldiers brought wagons, they put their things in and were carried away. The rest of the tribe would not move. . . .

Then, when he found that we would not go, he wrote for more soldiers to come.

Then the soldiers came, and we locked our doors, and the women and children hid in the woods. Then the soldiers drove all the people [to] the other side of the river, all but my brother Big Snake and I. We did not go; and the soldiers took us and carried us away to a fort and put us in jail. There were eight officers who held council with us after we got there. The commanding officer said:

"I have received four messages telling me to send my soldiers after you. Now, what have you done?"

Then we told him the whole story. Then the officer said: "You have done no wrong. The land is yours; they had no right to take it from you. Your title is good. I am here to protect the weak, and I have no right to take you; but I am a soldier, and I have to obey orders."

He said: "I will telegraph to the President, and ask him what I shall do. We do not think these three men had any authority to treat you as they have done. When we own a piece of land, it belongs to us till we sell it and pocket the money."

Then he brought a telegram, and said he had received answer from the President. The President said he knew nothing about it.

They kept us in jail ten days. Then they carried us back to our home. The soldiers collected all the women and children together; then they called all the chiefs together in council; and then they took wagons and went round and broke open the houses. When we came back from the council, we found the women and children surrounded by a guard of soldiers.

They took our reapers, mowers, hay rakes, spades, ploughs, bedsteads, stoves, cupboards, everything we had on our farms, and put them in one large building. Then they put into the wagons such things as they could carry. We told them that we would rather die than leave our lands; but we could not help ourselves. They took us down. Many died on the road. Two of my children died. After we reached the new land, all my horses died. The water was very bad. All our cattle died; not one was left. I stayed till one hundred and fifty-eight of my people had died. Then I ran away with thirty of my people, men and women and children. Some of the children were orphans. We were three months on the road. We were weak and sick and starved. When we reached the Omaha Reserve the Omahas gave us a piece of land, and we were in a hurry to plough it and put in wheat. While we were working, the soldiers came and arrested us. Half of us were sick. We would rather have died than have been carried back; but we could not help ourselves.

STANDING BEAR, Ponca

READING AND DISCUSSION QUESTIONS

1. How does Standing Bear describe his people's relationship to the federal government?

2. Why do you think Standing Bear shared his story? What do you think he hoped would come from it?

▪ COMPARATIVE QUESTIONS ▪

1. How would you examine and evaluate the multiple perspectives on American politics for evidence of the values guiding the political system during the Civil War era?

2. How did arguments over the meaning and interpretation of the nation's founding documents, such as the Declaration of Independence and the Constitution, affect American politics in the period from the U.S.-Mexico War through Reconstruction?

3. What do you discover when you compare the interpretation of federal power as defined by Lincoln (Document P5-3) and Stephens (Document P5-4) with earlier appraisals from Alexander Hamilton (Document 7-1), the Hartford Convention (Document 7-6), and Andrew Jackson (Document 9-3)?

4. How would you assess the long-term legacy of the constitutional debates from the mid-nineteenth century? Are the underlying issues that those who took part in the debates struggled to define relevant to contemporary political discussion?

16

Industrial America: Corporations and Conflicts
1877–1911

The deafening roar of America's industrial era ushered in epic changes that affected the lives of workers, immigrants, and the entrepreneurs who employed them. In this period, the scope, scale, and meaning of work underwent radical transformations, brought about by innovations in manufacturing, corporate structure, and labor management. These changes resulted in conflict between capital and labor, a theme that drives historical interpretations of the period. The rise of big business was heralded by some as evidence of ingenuity and pluck, leading to efficiencies never before imagined. Those who labored in the shops and factories of this industrializing economy saw the trend of consolidation differently, as a threat to their autonomy and skill and a menace to America's democratic institutions. Immigrants, whose increasing numbers in these years enabled industrial gains, found themselves in the crosshairs, victims of native-born resentments and capitalist manipulations as they tried to catch for themselves a slender piece of America's promise.

16-1 | Industrialist Justifies Fortunes Used for the Common Good

ANDREW CARNEGIE, *Wealth* (1889)

Andrew Carnegie was a Scottish immigrant whose life reflected the American Dream that inspired many poor boys in nineteenth-century America, though few ever came close to matching his phenomenal success. A tenacious self-starter, Carnegie worked hard and took advantage of key opportunities to invest in the telegraphic, railroad, oil, and steel industries, ultimately amassing an enormous fortune as head of Carnegie Steel Company, which he later sold for a staggering profit to J. Pierpont Morgan. In this 1889 essay, Carnegie justifies such colossal capital accumulation, not as an end in itself, but as a means to advance the common good.

The problem of our age is the proper administration of wealth, so that the ties of brotherhood may still bind together the rich and poor in harmonious relationship. The conditions of human life have not only been changed, but revolutionized, within the past few hundred years. In former days there was little difference between the dwelling, dress, food, and environment of the chief and those of his retainers. The Indians are to-day where civilized man then was. When visiting the Sioux, I was led to the wigwam of the chief. It was just like the others in external appearance, and even within the difference was trifling between it and those of the poorest of his braves. The contrast between the palace of the millionaire and the cottage of the laborer with us to-day measures the change which has come with civilization.

This change, however, is not to be deplored, but welcomed as highly beneficial. It is well, nay, essential for the progress of the race, that the houses of some should be homes for all that is highest and best in literature and the arts, and for all the refinements of civilization, rather than that none should be so. Much better this great irregularity than universal squalor. Without wealth there can be no Mæcenas.[1] The "good old times" were not good old times. Neither master nor servant was as well situated then as to-day. A relapse to old conditions would be disastrous to both—not the least so to him who serves—and would sweep away civilization with it. But whether the change be for good or ill, it is upon us, beyond our power to alter, and therefore to be accepted and made the best of. It is a waste of time to criticise the inevitable.

It is easy to see how the change has come. One illustration will serve for almost every phase of the cause. In the manufacture of products we have the whole story. It applies to all combinations of human industry, as stimulated and enlarged by the inventions of this scientific age. Formerly articles were manufactured at the domestic hearth or in small shops which formed part of the household. The master and his apprentices worked side by side, the latter living with

---

Andrew Carnegie, "Wealth," *North American Review* 148, no. 391 (June 1889): 653–664.

[1] **Mæcenas:** First-century B.C. Roman patron of the arts.

the master, and therefore subject to the same conditions. When these apprentices rose to be masters, there was little or no change in their mode of life, and they, in turn, educated in the same routine succeeding apprentices. There was, substantially social equality, and even political equality, for those engaged in industrial pursuits had then little or no political voice in the State.

But the inevitable result of such a mode of manufacture was crude articles at high prices. To-day the world obtains commodities of excellent quality at prices which even the generation preceding this would have deemed incredible. In the commercial world similar causes have produced similar results, and the race is benefited thereby. The poor enjoy what the rich could not before afford. What were the luxuries have become the necessaries of life. The laborer has now more comforts than the landlord had a few generations ago. The farmer has more luxuries than the landlord had, and is more richly clad and better housed. The landlord has books and pictures rarer, and appointments more artistic, than the King could then obtain.

The price we pay for this salutary change is, no doubt, great. We assemble thousands of operatives in the factory, in the mine, and in the counting-house, of whom the employer can know little or nothing, and to whom the employer is little better than a myth. All intercourse between them is at an end. Rigid Castes are formed, and, as usual, mutual ignorance breeds mutual distrust. Each Caste is without sympathy for the other, and ready to credit anything disparaging in regard to it. Under the law of competition, the employer of thousands is forced into the strictest economies, among which the rates paid to labor figure prominently, and often there is friction between the employer and the employed, between capital and labor, between rich and poor. Human society loses homogeneity.

The price which society pays for the law of competition, like the price it pays for cheap comforts and luxuries, is also great; but the advantages of this law are also greater still, for it is to this law that we owe our wonderful material development, which brings improved conditions in its train. . . .

Objections to the foundations upon which society is based are not in order, because the condition of the race is better with these than it has been with any others which have been tried. Of the effect of any new substitutes proposed we cannot be sure. The Socialist or Anarchist who seeks to overturn present conditions is to be regarded as attacking the foundation upon which civilization itself rests, for civilization took its start from the day that the capable, industrious workman said to his incompetent and lazy fellow, "If thou dost not sow, thou shalt not reap," and thus ended primitive Communism by separating the drones from the bees. . . .

The question then arises, — What is the proper mode of administering wealth after the laws upon which civilization is founded have thrown it into the hands of the few? And it is of this great question that I believe I offer the true solution. . . .

There are but three modes in which surplus wealth can be disposed of. It can be left to the families of the decedents; or it can be bequeathed for public purposes; or, finally, it can be administered during their lives by its possessors. . . .

There are instances of millionaires' sons unspoiled by wealth, who, being rich, still perform great services in the community. Such are the very salt of the earth, as valuable as, unfortunately, they are rare; still it is not the exception, but the rule, that men must regard, and, looking at the usual result of enormous sums conferred upon legatees, the thoughtful man must shortly say, "I would as soon leave to my son a curse as the almighty dollar," and admit to himself that it is not the welfare of the children, but family pride, which inspires these enormous legacies.

As to the second mode, that of leaving wealth at death for public uses, it may be said that this is only a means for the disposal of wealth, provided a man is content to wait until he is dead before it becomes of much good in the world. Knowledge of the results of legacies bequeathed is not calculated to inspire the brightest hopes of much posthumous good being accomplished. The cases are not few in which the real object sought by the testator is not attained, nor are they few in which his real wishes are thwarted. In many cases the bequests are so used as to become only monuments of his folly. It is well to remember that it requires the exercise of not less ability than that which acquired the wealth to use it so as to be really beneficial to the community. . . .

There remains, then, only one mode of using great fortunes; but in this we have the true antidote for the temporary unequal distribution of wealth, the reconciliation of the rich and the poor—a reign of harmony—another ideal, differing, indeed, from that of the Communist in requiring only the further evolution of existing conditions, not the total overthrow of our civilization. It is founded upon the present most intense individualism, and the race is projected to put it in practice by degree whenever it pleases. Under its sway we shall have an ideal state, in which the surplus wealth of the few will become, in the best sense the property of the many, because administered for the common good, and this wealth, passing through the hands of the few, can be made a much more potent force for the elevation of our race than if it had been distributed in small sums to the people themselves. Even the poorest can be made to see this, and to agree that great sums gathered by some of their fellow-citizens and spent for public purposes, from which the masses reap the principal benefit, are more valuable to them than if scattered among them through the course of many years in trifling amounts. . . .

This, then, is held to be the duty of the man of Wealth: First, to set an example of modest, unostentatious living, shunning display or extravagance; to provide moderately for the legitimate wants of those dependent upon him; and after doing so to consider all surplus revenues which come to him simply as trust funds, which he is called upon to administer, and strictly bound as a matter of duty to administer in the manner which, in his judgment, is best calculated to produce the most beneficial results for the community—the man of wealth thus becoming the mere agent and trustee for his poorer brethren, bringing to their service his superior wisdom, experience and ability to administer, doing for them better than they would or could do for themselves. . . .

Thus is the problem of Rich and Poor to be solved. The laws of accumulation will be left free; the laws of distribution free. Individualism will continue, but the millionaire will be but a trustee for the poor; intrusted for a season with a great part of the increased wealth of the community, but administering it for the community far better than it could or would have done for itself. The best minds will thus have reached a stage in the development of the race in which it is clearly seen that there is no mode of disposing of surplus wealth creditable to thoughtful and earnest men into whose hands it flows save by using it year by year for the general good. This day already dawns. But a little while, and although, without incurring the pity of their fellows, men may die sharers in great business enterprises from which their capital cannot be or has not been withdrawn, and is left chiefly at death for public uses, yet the man who dies leaving behind many millions of available wealth, which was his to administer during life, will pass away "unwept, unhonored, and unsung," no matter to what uses he leaves the dross which he cannot take with him. Of such as these the public verdict will then be: "The man who dies thus rich dies disgraced."

Such, in my opinion, is the true Gospel concerning Wealth, obedience to which is destined some day to solve the problem of the Rich and the Poor, and to bring "Peace on earth, among men Good-Will."

READING AND DISCUSSION QUESTIONS

1. What argument does Carnegie make about the uses to which the great fortunes of industrialists should be devoted?

2. What factors might have motivated Carnegie to write his essay on wealth, and for whom do you think he wrote it? What inferences can you draw about the social and political context during which Carnegie wrote, which may have inspired his essay?

3. Why does Carnegie insist that his "gospel of wealth" was founded "upon the present most intense individualism"? What can you conclude about the cultural significance of that term as Carnegie used it?

16-2 | Industrial Brotherhood Counters Excesses of Capitalist Power

TERENCE POWDERLY, *Thirty Years of Labor* (1889)

The Knights of Labor emerged in the 1880s as a major labor organization. Knights were dedicated to the idea of uniting the "producing" classes in cooperative efforts to advance workers' interests and counter the power of capitalists, whose outsized wealth they saw as a threat to America's republican traditions. Terence Powderly, the national leader of the Knights of Labor, tried to unite skilled and unskilled workers and opened membership to women and African Americans. The group's inclusive vision, expressed here in its platform, was quickly eclipsed by craft-based unionism promoted by the American Federation of Labor.

T. V. Powderly, *Thirty Years of Labor, 1859 to 1889* (Columbus, OH: Excelsior Publishing House, 1889), 116–120.

The recent alarming development and aggression of aggregated wealth, which, unless checked, will inevitably lead to the pauperization and hopeless degradation of the toiling masses, render it imperative, if we desire to enjoy the blessings of the government bequeathed to us by the founders of the republic, that a check should be placed upon its power and unjust accumulation, and a system adopted which will secure to the laborer the fruits of his toil; and as this much desired object can only be accomplished by the thorough unification of labor, and the united efforts of those who obey the divine injunction, that "in the sweat of thy face thou shalt eat bread," we have formed the INDUSTRIAL BROTHERHOOD, with a view of securing the organization and direction, by co-operative effort of the power of the industrial classes, and we submit to the people of the United States the objects sought to be accomplished by our organization, calling upon all who believe in securing "the greatest good to the greatest number," to aid and assist us:

I. To bring within the folds of organization every department of productive industry, making knowledge a standpoint for action, and industrial, moral, and social worth—not wealth—the true standard of individual and national greatness.

II. To secure to the toilers a proper share of the wealth that they create; more of the leisure that rightfully belongs to them; more societary advantages; more of the benefits, privileges and emoluments of the world; in a word, all those rights and privileges necessary to make them capable of enjoying, appreciating, defending and perpetuating the blessings of republican institutions.

III. To arrive at the true condition of the producing masses in their educational, moral, and financial condition, we demand from the several States and from the national government the establishment of bureaus of labor statistics.

IV. The establishment of co-operative institutions, productive and distributive.

V. The reserving of the public lands, the heritage of the people, for the actual settler—not another acre for railroads or speculators.

VI. The abrogation of all laws that do not bear equally upon capital and labor, the removal of unjust technicalities, delays, and discriminations in the administration of justice, and the adoption of measures providing for the health and safety of those engaged in mining, manufacturing or building pursuits.

VII. The enactment of a law to compel chartered corporations to pay their employes [sic] at least once in every month in full for labor performed during the preceding month in the lawful money of the country.

VIII. The enactment of a law giving mechanics and other laborers a first lien on their work.

IX. The abolishment of the contract system on national, state, and municipal work.

   X. To inaugurate a system of public markets, to facilitate the exchange of the productions of farmers and mechanics, tending to do away with middlemen and speculators.

  XI. To inaugurate systems of cheap transportation to facilitate the exchange of commodities.

 XII. The substitution of arbitration for strikes, whenever and wherever employers and employees are willing to meet on equitable grounds.

XIII. The prohibition of the importation of all servile races, the discontinuance of all subsidies granted to national vessels bringing them to our shores, and the abrogation of the Burlingame treaty.[2]

XIV. To advance the standard of American mechanics by the enactment and enforcement of equitable apprentice laws.

 XV. To abolish the system of contracting the labor of convicts in our prisons and reformatory institutions.

XVI. To secure for both sexes equal pay for equal work.

XVII. The reduction of the hours of labor to eight per day, so that laborers may have more time for social enjoyment and intellectual improvement, and be enabled to reap the advantages conferred by labor-saving machinery, which their brains have created.

XVIII. To prevail upon the government to establish a just standard of distribution between capital and labor by providing a purely national circulating medium based upon the faith and resources of the nation, issued directly to the people, without the intervention of any system of banking corporations, which money shall be a legal tender in the payment of all debts, public or private, and interchangeable at the option of the holder for government bonds, bearing a rate of interest not to exceed three and sixty-five hundredths per cent., subject to future legislation of Congress.

READING AND DISCUSSION QUESTIONS

1. Analyze and evaluate the Knights' platform for evidence of the union's point of view toward the federal government. What role does it see for the state in regulating the relationship between workers and employers?

2. Imagine the reaction of Andrew Carnegie (Document 16-1) to the reforms advocated by the Knights of Labor in their statement of principles. Which specific statements might have elicited the strongest reaction and why?

3. From the union's platform, what conclusion can you draw about the status of labor in industrial America? What obstacles and challenges do Powderly and his fellow Knights identify as stumbling blocks to the equitable society they sought?

---

[2] **Burlingame treaty:** The Burlingame-Seward Treaty (1868) granted most-favored-nation trading status to China; it was abrogated by the Chinese Exclusion Act (1882).

16-3 | Worker Finds His Way on the Shop Floor

ANTANAS KAZTAUSKIS, *Life Story of a Lithuanian* (c. 1906)

America's industrial engine ran on the fuel of immigrant labor. Workers hailed from all parts of Europe, Asia, and the Americas, resulting in a diverse workforce with distinctive cultural, linguistic, and religious customs. What united them was the hope that had inspired Antanas Kaztauskis's migration from Lithuania: the prospect of a life better than the one back home. Though the reality dimmed his initial optimism, Kaztauskis found stability in the company of others.

Summer was over and Election Day was coming. The Republican boss in our district, Jonidas, was a saloon keeper. A friend took me there. Jonidas shook hands and treated me fine. He taught me to sign my name, and the next week I went with him to an office and signed some paper, and then I could vote. I voted as I was told, and then they got me back into the yards to work, because one big politician owns stock in one of those houses. Then I felt that I was getting in beside the game. I was in a combine like other sharp men. Even when work was slack I was all right, because they got me a job in the street cleaning department. I felt proud, and I went to the back room in Jonidas's saloon and got him to write a letter to Alexandria to tell her she must come soon and be my wife.

But this was just the trouble. All of us were telling our friends to come soon. Soon they came—even thousands. The employers in the yard liked this, because those sharp foremen are inventing new machines and the work is easier to learn, and so these slow Lithuanians and even green girls can learn to do it, and then the Americans and Germans and Irish are put out and the employer saves money, because the Lithuanians work cheaper. This was why the American labor unions began to organize us all just the same as they had organized the Bohemians and Poles before us.

Well, we were glad to be organized. We had learned that in Chicago every man must push himself always, and Jonidas had taught us how much better we could push ourselves by getting into a combine. Now, we saw that this union was the best combine for us, because it was the only combine that could say, "It is our business to raise your wages."

But that Jonidas—he spoilt our first union. He was sharp. First he got us to hire the room over his saloon. He used to come in at our meetings and sit in the back seat and grin. There was an Irishman there from the union headquarters, and he was trying to teach us to run ourselves. He talked to a Lithuanian, and the Lithuanian said it to us, but we were slow to do things, and we were jealous and were always jumping up to shout and fight. So the Irishman used to wipe his hot red face and call us bad names. He told the Lithuanian not to say these names to us, but Jonidas heard them, and in his saloon, where we all went down

The Life Stories of Undistinguished Americans, As Told by Themselves, ed. Hamilton Holt, intr. Edwin E. Slosson (New York: James Pott & Company, 1906), 24–33.

after the meeting when the Irishman was gone, Jonidas gave us free drinks and then told us the names. I will not write them here.

One night that Irishman did not come and Jonidas saw his chance and took the chair. He talked very fine and we elected him President. We made him Treasurer, too. Down in the saloon he gave us free drinks and told us we must break away from the Irish grafters. The next week he made us strike, all by himself. We met twice a day in his saloon and spent all of our money on drinks and then the strike was over. I got out of this union after that. I had been working hard in the cattle killing room and I had a better job. I was called a cattle butcher now and I joined the Cattle Butchers' Union. This union is honest and it has done me a great deal of good.

It has raised my wages. The man who worked at my job before the union came was getting through the year an average of $9 a week. I am getting $11. In my first job I got $5 a week. The man who works there now gets $5.75.

It has given me more time to learn to read and speak and enjoy life like an American. I never work now from 6 A.M. to 9 P.M. and then be idle the next day. I work now from 7 A.M. to 5.30 P.M., and there are not so many idle days. The work is evened up.

With more time and more money I live much better and I am very happy. So is Alexandria. She came a year ago and has learned to speak English already. Some of the women go to the big store the day they get here, when they have not enough sense to pick out the clothes that look right, but Alexandria waited three weeks till she knew, and so now she looks the finest of any woman in the district. We have four nice rooms, which she keeps very clean, and she has flowers growing in boxes in the two front windows. We do not go much to church, because the church seems to be too slow. But we belong to a Lithuanian society that gives two picnics in summer and two big balls in winter, where we have a fine time. I go one night a week to the Lithuanian Concertina Club. On Sundays we go on the trolley out into the country.

But we like to stay at home more now because we have a baby. When he grows up I will not send him to the Lithuanian Catholic school. They have only two bad rooms and two priests, who teach only in Lithuanian from prayer books. I will send him to the American school, which is very big and good. The teachers there are Americans and they belong to the Teachers' Labor Union, which has three thousand teachers and belongs to our Chicago Federation of Labor. I am sure that such teachers will give him a good chance.

Our union sent a committee to Springfield last year and they passed a law which prevents boys and girls below sixteen from working in the stockyards.

We are trying to make the employers pay on Saturday night in cash. Now they pay in checks and the men have to get money the same night to buy things for Sunday, and the saloons cash checks by thousands. You have to take one drink to have the check cashed. It is hard to take one drink.

The union is doing another good thing. It is combining all the nationalities. The night I joined the Cattle Butchers' Union I was led into the room by a negro member. With me were Bohemians, Germans and Poles, and Mike Donnelly, the

President, is an Irishman. He spoke to us in English and then three interpreters told us what he said. We swore to be loyal to our union above everything else except the country, the city and the State—to be faithful to each other—to protect the women-workers—to do our best to understand the history of the labor movement, and to do all we could to help it on. Since then I have gone there every two weeks and I help the movement by being an interpreter for the other Lithuanians who come in. That is why I have learned to speak and write good English. The others do not need me long. They soon learn English, too, and when they have done that they are quickly becoming Americans.

But the best thing the union does is to make me feel more independent. I do not have to pay to get a job and I cannot be discharged unless I am no good. For almost the whole 30,000 men and women are organized now in some one of our unions and they all are directed by our central council. No man knows what it means to be sure of his job unless he has been fired like I was once without any reason being given.

So this is why I joined the labor union. There are many better stories than mine, for my story is very common. There are thousands of immigrants like me. Over 300,000 immigrants have been organized in the last three years by the American Federation of Labor. The immigrants are glad to be organized if the leaders are as honest as Mike Donnelly is. You must get money to live well, and to get money you must combine. I cannot bargain alone with the Meat Trust. I tried it and it does not work.

READING AND DISCUSSION QUESTIONS

1. What evidence of unions' effectiveness can you discover in the story Kaztauskis tells of his experiences working in the Chicago stockyards? What advantages does he attribute to his membership in the union?

2. How does Kaztauskis's point of view toward industrialization compare with the views expressed by Carnegie in his essay on wealth?

16-4 | Women in the Workplace
Mail Order Office with Women Typists (c. 1900)

Antanas Kaztauskis's experience of work on the factory floor reflects the changes industrialization brought to late nineteenth-century workers. The increasing scale of nineteenth-century business enterprises required an elaborate corporate structure and a bureaucracy to manage the flow of information these organizations generated. Clerical work became a critical component of the modern corporation. Earlier in the nineteenth century, male clerks did much of this work as a form of preparation for their rise into the managerial ranks. But by the end of the century, as corporate bureaucracy expanded and the processing of paperwork became routine, most of this labor was re-gendered as women's work. Such labor was no longer seen as a necessary stepping stone to managerial status; instead, clerical work was a fixed position within an expansive corporate hierarchy. Thus, white, working-class women became secretaries staffing the business offices that sustained modern American capitalism.

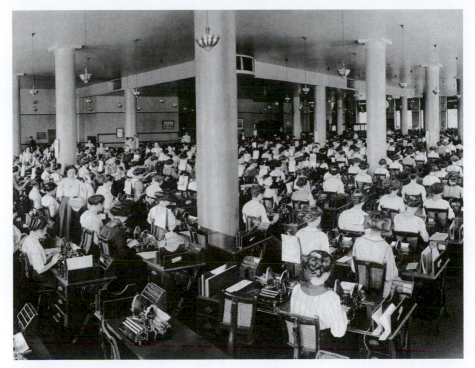

Bettmann/Getty Images

READING AND DISCUSSION QUESTIONS

1. What does this photograph tell us about the work environment these women experienced? Why might white, working-class women have been drawn to the type of work depicted here? How did this work compare to work in a factory, for example?

2. The photographer's vantage point above the women suggests he or she was on a ladder, so we can assume this was not a candid photograph, but instead, a staged shot. Why do you think this photograph was taken? What story do you think the photographer wanted to tell?

16-5 | Border Wall Against Immigration

THE SATURDAY GLOBE, *A Crying Need for General Repairs. American Labor Calls Uncle Sam's Attention to the Inefficiency of His Immigration Restriction Wall* (1904)

Anti-immigration walls, both real and metaphorical, have been part of American political discourse since at least the 1840s when the Know-Nothing (or American) Party gained traction. In the latter nineteenth century, as immigration expanded significantly and included people from Asia as well as southern and eastern Europe, anti-immigrant Americans pushed for political reform that ultimately led to the 1924 National Origins Act, which drastically limited the number of people who could legally enter the United States. Earlier, the 1882 Chinese Exclusion Act closed the border to additional Chinese immigrants, whose numbers had grown steadily since the 1840s with the California Gold Rush and the building of the transcontinental railroad. Advocates of immigration restriction frequently claimed that immigrants threatened America's social, political, and economic institutions. In this cartoon, a wall of immigration restriction has been erected, but it seems not to be working.

The Ohio State University, Billy Ireland Cartoon Library and Museum

READING AND DISCUSSION QUESTIONS

1. What is the cartoonist's viewpoint regarding immigration policies at the turn of the century?

2. In this cartoon, we see an "American Laborer" speaking with Uncle Sam. The caption reads, "American Labor Calls Uncle Sam's Attention to the Inefficiency of His Immigration Restriction Wall." What is the argument American Labor is making to Uncle Sam?

3. The gentleman in the top hat and checkered pants is an "Employer of Labor" and he is helping an immigrant down the ladder. Why? What does this cartoon suggest about the tension between the American Employer and the American Laborer?

16-6 | Economist Scores the Costs and Benefits of Monopoly

ARTHUR TWINING HADLEY, *The Good and the Evil of Industrial Combination* (1897)

The polarized assessment of big business in America often reflected perceptions of the good or evil of monopolies, as Yale economist and president Arthur Twining Hadley underscored in an 1897 article for *The Atlantic Monthly,* a New England–based journal of culture and ideas. No foe of capitalism, Hadley highlighted the economic benefits of the emerging corporate structure, emphasizing the lower costs of goods and the general trend of rising wages, a view disputed by labor's advocates. Still, Hadley did acknowledge the limitations of monopoly, or what he called combinations, and offered an economist's view of how best to control them without undermining the advantages he identified.

The tendency of monopoly to retard the introduction of industrial improvements is, in the opinion of the present writer, a more serious thing than its tendency to allow unfair rates. This aspect of the matter has hardly received proper attention. We have been so accustomed to think of competition as a regulator of prices that we have lost sight of its equally important function as a stimulus to efficiency. Wherever competition is absent, there is a disposition to rest content with old methods, not to say slack ones. . . .

Enough has been said on both sides to show the difficulty of passing judgment on the absolute merits or demerits of modern industrial monopoly. It is a somewhat easier as well as a much more important task to examine the relative merits of the different methods of control which have been suggested.

These methods may be grouped under five heads: (1) Direct Prohibition, (2) State Ownership, (3) Limitation of Profits, (4) Control of Prices, (5) Enforced Publicity.

Of direct prohibition, it is enough to say that it has been persistently tried, and has had very little success. . . . The Interstate Commerce Law has prohibited railroad pools; in so doing it has simply driven the railroads to adopt other devices for securing the end to which pooling was a means. The legislation of the years 1891 and 1892 led to the dissolution of the Standard Oil Trust; but the Standard Oil Companies have continued to be managed with undiminished unity of aim and centralization of power. . . .

State ownership of industry is urged on such a variety of grounds that it would require a separate article, or series of articles, to discuss them all. But on the ground of industrial efficiency and public service, it has not, on the whole, shown itself equal to private ownership. . . . All the great inventions of modern times — the steam-engine, the steamship, the railroad, the telegraph, the telephone — have been developed and introduced by private enterprise. . . .

Arthur Twining Hadley, "The Good and the Evil of Industrial Combination," *The Atlantic Monthly* 79, no. 479 (March 1897): 377, 383–385.

Limitation of profits has not proved a successful method of dealing with monopolies. It is easy for a company to reduce its profits to the prescribed minimum by diminishing its efficiency and economy instead of by reducing its rates. We have seen how great is the danger of slack service when the stimulus of competition is removed. . . .

Control of prices has worked better than limitation of profits. In fact, it sometimes seems like a necessity. . . . But it is by no means a satisfactory one. In the first place, such rates are very often made too low; and the reduction of service that follows proves a worse evil than the extortion in charge that preceded. . . .

Where this responsibility for the future can be brought home to the managers of corporate enterprise, it furnishes a better means of control than any of the methods hitherto considered. If, as was indicated at the outset, the permanent interests of the capitalist coincide pretty closely with those of his customers or employers, any agency which shall give force to those permanent interests points the way to a solution desirable for all parties. Where the short-sighted policy is due to corrupt interests within the corporation, which knowingly antagonize the real interests of the investors, it may be restricted by enforced publicity of accounts or by better laws governing responsibility of directors. The former lessens the opportunity for abuse, the latter lessens the motive. Where the short-sighted policy is pursued in good faith, a better understanding may be promoted by commissions like those in whose development Massachusetts has taken the lead, or perhaps still more effectively by the highest class of judicial decisions. Such agencies serve to create an intelligent public sentiment on matters of business, and one that can be developed in no other way.

It is a slow process to educate a community to the point where we can rely on rational egoism to subserve public good; but the community which has attained that result, in any department of life, possesses an inestimable advantage. Thanks to the decisions of the courts, supplemented by the influence of a few great writers like Adam Smith, we have pretty nearly reached this stage of development in competitive business. In monopolized business we have not done so. Our capitalists have learned to look a day or a month ahead, but not always a year or a decade. It is when we take it in this connection that we see the full significance of the problem of industrial combination at the present day. It marks a critical phase in the education which a community must undergo to fit itself for the increasingly difficult problems of industrial freedom. If we resort to systems of prescribed rates, we defer this education to a day when it may be a harder process than it is now. If we resort to state ownership, we abandon the hope of such education altogether, and pass from the traditional lines of development of England and America to those of France or Germany. But if we can meet the evils of the present crisis by the creation of a more enlightened public sentiment, we shall be handling the problems of our day as our fathers handled those of their day, and shall leave our children the legacy of a freedom enlarged rather than impaired by the magnitude of the burdens imposed upon it.

READING AND DISCUSSION QUESTIONS

1. How does Hadley summarize the arguments for and against monopoly? Whereas some attributed rising prices to the power of monopolies, what did Hadley see as their "more serious" problem? Why do you think he identifies that problem as his leading concern?

2. Analyze the methods for controlling monopolies that Hadley describes for evidence of the political conflict between the interests of capital and labor that existed during this period. What reformers does he allude to in discussing the popular methods of control, which he criticizes as ineffective and counterproductive?

■ COMPARATIVE QUESTIONS ■

1. What do the sources in this chapter reveal about the historical patterns of nativist thought over time? What similarities do you see continuing into the twenty-first century?

2. How would you evaluate and synthesize the conflicting evidence in this chapter to construct a convincing historical argument about immigration during the latter nineteenth century?

3. In thinking about the period from 1877 to 1911, what theme or themes emerge from the sources that serve to unify these years as a coherent block of time for historical analysis and interpretation?

4. Evaluate monopoly as a source of political conflict by considering the multiple views in this chapter. What similarities and conflicts do you see?

5. How does this period of industrialization compare with the period of rapid economic development during the early national period? Explain and evaluate the similarities and differences that you see across time and place.

6. Compare the experience of work revealed in the sources from this chapter, including Antanas Kaztauskis's memoir (Document 16-3) and the photograph of women typists (Document 16-4). How did industrialization and the rise of corporations shape the working lives of Americans?

17

Making Modern American Culture

1880–1917

The turn of the twentieth century witnessed clashing paradigms, as Victorian sentimentality based on genteel ideas of refinement and religion bumped uneasily into modern notions of hard-nosed progress and science. These caricatures, of course, simplify the complexity of cultural conflict during these years, but they aptly summarize what many considered the stakes as an industrializing economy and society transformed before their eyes. Darwinism provided a frame of reference for understanding these changes, justifying as it did the endemic competition and struggle witnessed over these years. This theme was highlighted in the thinking of some, like Theodore Roosevelt, who praised the effects on self and society of a life "strenuously" lived. For others, it lurked in the recesses, shaping perceptions about society that helped them challenge Victorian domesticity. This was true for women and their advocates whose spirited claims on their behalf opened educational and career possibilities previously closed to them. African Americans continued to face discrimination, now cloaked in scientific interpretation, but they, too, pushed an agenda for change, though the means to realize in full the freedoms they sought remained a point of dispute within reform circles. As new ideas eclipsed American Victorianism, old certainties passed away, making room for a modern American culture.

17-1 | Pursuing the Manly Sports for Self and Society

THEODORE ROOSEVELT, *Professionalism in Sports* (1890)

Industrialization brought luxury within reach of the managerial classes, providing them with leisure, vacations, and a work life defined by the desk and office, not the machine or plough. This white-collar world alarmed some, including Theodore Roosevelt, who championed physical activity as an antidote to what many termed "overcivilization." Roosevelt's advocacy, eleven years before becoming president, reflects a late-nineteenth-century drive to ensure America's emerging position in the world by encouraging what he described as "manly, healthy, vigorous pastimes." This muscular citizenship would benefit the individual and through him the nation.

It is hardly necessary at the present day to enter a plea for athletic exercise and manly out-door sports. During the last twenty-five years there has been a wonderful growth of interest in and appreciation of healthy muscular amusements; and this growth can best be promoted by stimulating, within proper bounds, the spirit of rivalry on which all our games are based. The effect upon the physique of the sedentary classes, especially in the towns and cities, has already been very marked. We are much less liable than we were to reproaches on the score of our national ill health, of the bad constitutions of our men, and of the fragility and early decay of our women.

There are still plenty of people who look down on, as of little moment, the proper development of the body; but the men of good sense sympathize as little with these as they do with the even more noxious extremists who regard physical development as an end instead of a means. As a nation we have many tremendous problems to work out, and we need to bring every ounce of vital power possible to their solution. No people has ever yet done great and lasting work if its physical type was infirm and weak. Goodness and strength must go hand in hand if the Republic is to be preserved. The good man who is ready and able to strike a blow for the right, and to put down evil with the strong arm, is the citizen who deserves our most hearty respect. There is a certain tendency in the civilization of our time to underestimate or overlook the need of the virile, masterful qualities of the heart and mind which have built up and alone can maintain and defend this very civilization, and which generally go hand in hand with good health and the capacity to get the utmost possible use out of the body. There is no better way of counteracting this tendency than by encouraging bodily exercise, and especially the sports which develop such qualities as courage, resolution, and endurance.

Theodore Roosevelt, " 'Professionalism' in Sports," *The North American Review* 151, no. 405 (August 1890): 187–191.

The best of all sports for this purpose are those which follow the Macedonian rather than the Greek model: big-game hunting, mountaineering, the chase with horse and hound, all wilderness life with all its keen, hardy pleasures. The hunter and mountaineer lead healthier lives — in time of need they would make better soldiers — than the trained athlete. Nor need these pleasures be confined to the rich. The trouble with our men of small means is quite as often that they do not know how to enjoy pleasures lying at their doors as that they cannot afford them. From New York to Minneapolis, from Boston to San Francisco, there is no large city from which it is impossible to reach a tract of perfectly wild, wooded or mountainous land within forty-eight hours; and any two young men who can get a month's holiday in August or September cannot use it to better advantage than by tramping on foot, pack on back, over such a tract. Let them go alone; a season or two will teach them much woodcraft, and will enormously increase their stock of health, hardihood, and self-reliance. . . .

However, most of our people, whether from lack of means, time, or inclination, do not take to feats of this kind, and must get their fun and exercise in athletics proper. The years of late boyhood and early manhood — say from twelve or fourteen to twenty-eight or thirty, and often until much later — are those in which athletic sports prove not only most attractive, but also most beneficial to the individual and the race. In college — and in most of the schools which are preparatory for college — rowing, foot-ball, base-ball, running, jumping, sparring, and the like have assumed a constantly increasing prominence. Nor is this in any way a matter for regret. Of course any good is accompanied by some evil; and a small number of college boys, who would probably turn out badly anyhow, neglect everything for their sports, and so become of little use to themselves or any one else. But as a whole college life has been greatly the gainer by the change. Only a small proportion of college boys are going to become real students and do original work in literature, science, or art; and these are certain to study their best in any event. The others are going into business or law or some kindred occupation; and these, of course, can study but little that will be directly of use to them in after-life. The college education of such men should be largely devoted to making them good citizens, and able to hold their own in the world; and character is far more important than intellect in making a man a good citizen or successful in his calling — meaning by character not only such qualities as honesty and truthfulness, but courage, perseverance, and self-reliance.

Now, athletic sports, if followed properly, and not elevated into a fetish, are admirable for developing character, besides bestowing on the participants an invaluable fund of health and strength. . . .

The colleges contain but a small proportion of the men interested in amateur athletics, as can be seen by the immense number of ball clubs, rowing clubs, polo clubs, hunt clubs, bicycle clubs, snow-shoe clubs, lacrosse clubs, and athletic clubs proper which are to be found scattered among our cities and towns. Almost any man of sedentary life who wishes to get exercise enough to keep him in vigorous health can readily do so at one of these clubs; and an increasing proportion of our young men are finding this out and acting accordingly. . . .

Already this awakening of interest in manly sports, this proper care of the body, have had a good effect upon our young men; but there are, of course, accompanying dangers in any such movement. With very few exceptions the man who makes some athletic pursuit his main business, instead of turning to it as a health-giving pastime, ceases to be a particularly useful citizen. Of course I do not refer to the men who act as trainers and instructors at the different colleges and clubs; these perform a most useful and honorable function, and among them several could be named who have rendered as high service as any men in the community.

But the amateur athlete who thinks of nothing but athletics, and makes it the serious business of his life, becomes a bore, if nothing worse. A young man who has broken a running or jumping record, who has stroked a winning club crew, or played on his college nine or eleven, has a distinct claim to our respect; but if, when middle-aged, he has still done nothing more in the world, he forfeits even this claim which he originally had.

It is so in an even more marked degree with the "professional" athlete. In America the difference between amateurs and professionals is in one way almost the reverse of what it is in England, and accords better with the ways of life of our democratic community. In England the average professional is a man who works for his living, and the average amateur is one who does not; whereas with us the amateur usually is, and always ought to be, a man who, like other American citizens, works hard at some regular calling,—it matters not what, so long as it is respectable,—while the professional is very apt to be a gentleman of more or less elegant leisure, aside from his special pursuit.

The mere statement of the difference is enough to show that the amateur, and not the professional, is the desirable citizen, the man who should be encouraged. Our object is to get as many of our people as possible to take part in manly, healthy, vigorous pastimes, which will benefit the whole nation; it is not to produce a limited class of athletes who shall make it the business of their lives to do battle with one another for the popular amusement. Most masterful nations have shown a strong taste for manly sports. In the old days, when we ourselves were still a people of backwoodsmen, at every merrymaking there were sure to be trials of skill and strength, at running, wrestling, and rifle-shooting, among the young men. We should encourage by every method the spirit which makes such trials popular; it is a very excellent revival of old-time American ways. But the existence of a caste of gladiators in the midst of a population which does not itself participate in any manly sports is usually, as it was at Rome, a symptom of national decadence.

The Romans who, when the stern and simple strength of Rome was departing, flocked to the gladiatorial shows, were influenced only by a ferocious craving for bloody excitement; not by any sympathy with men of stout heart and tough sinew. So it is, to a lesser extent, today. In baseball alone, the professional teams, from a number of causes, have preserved a fairly close connection with non-professional players, and have done good work in popularizing a most admirable and characteristic American game; but even here the outlook is now less favorable, and, aside from this one pastime, professionalism is the curse of many an athletic sport, and the chief obstacle to its healthy development. Professional rowing is under a dark cloud of suspicion because of the crooked practices which have disgraced it. Horse-racing is certainly not in an ideal condition. A prize-fight is simply brutal and degrading. The people who attend it, and make a hero of the prizefighter, are,—excepting boys who go for fun and don't know any better,—to a very great extent, men who hover on the border-line of criminality; and those who are not are speedily brutalized, and are never rendered more manly. They form as ignoble a body as do the kindred frequenters of rat-pit and cock-pit. The prizefighter and his fellow professional athletes of the same ilk are, together with their patrons in every rank of life, the very worst foes with whom the cause of general athletic development has to contend.

READING AND DISCUSSION QUESTIONS

1. What distinction does Roosevelt make between the amateur and the professional in sport? Which does he value more and why?

2. What conclusions about audience can you draw from Roosevelt's essay published in *The North American Review*? How might you describe the sort of individuals who subscribed to the magazine? What can you infer about Roosevelt's perspective on class?

3. How does Roosevelt's argument about sport reflect the broader historical context of late-nineteenth-century culture?

17-2 | Healthy Girls

FRANCES BENJAMIN JOHNSTON, *Children Doing Calisthenics While Sitting at Their Desks* (c. 1890s)

Roosevelt's masculine view of citizenship ignored girls and women, but Frances Johnston's 1890s photograph of elementary school girls brought them into focus. Johnston was a pioneering female photographer whose career spanned decades. She enjoyed unusual access to the White House, and she made special studies of girls' schools and African American schools. In this image from a Washington, D.C. school, girls take a break from their lessons to exercise. Many progressive educators shared Roosevelt's belief in physical culture, a departure from earlier nineteenth-century views that cautioned against strenuous efforts by women and girls.

Universal History Archive/Getty Images

READING AND DISCUSSION QUESTIONS

1. Johnston was a photojournalist and used her images to tell stories. What story do you think she was telling with this image?

2. What conclusions regarding girls' education during the 1890s can you draw from this photograph? What do the details from the classroom and the girls themselves reveal?

3. Explain whether you see this photograph as "Victorian" or "modern."

17-3 | Arguing the Merits of College for Women

ELIZABETH SHEPLEY SERGEANT, *Educated for What?* (1916)

The imagined fireside conversation Elizabeth Shepley Sergeant drew for readers of *The New Republic* highlights the ambivalence with which early-twentieth-century Americans considered the subject of women's higher education. By the time Sergeant was writing in 1916, colleges, both women's and coeducational, had welcomed young women to the point that some complained about the "feminization" of the university. Still, doubt lingered as to the purpose of women's education. The Victorian sentimentality describing women as better

Elizabeth Shepley Sergeant, "Educated for What?" *The New Republic* 5, no. 61 (January 1, 1916): 219–220.

fitted to the roles of mother and wife came into conflict with the modern, which embraced new opportunities for women's personal and professional fulfillment. Sergeant herself blazed trails, graduating from Bryn Mawr in 1903 and pursuing a career in journalism, including a stint as war correspondent in 1917 Paris, where she sustained a battlefield injury.

"Why are women in the professions so halfhearted?" asked Tom suddenly. The question fell like a bomb into the group of five that sat lazily drinking tea by his farmhouse fire. Both Jane and Mary—one an unmarried social investigator, the other a doctor as well as a wife—sat up argumentatively in their chairs. But Felicia, the hostess, pointing out that men were in a minority, asked Mary's husband, Dr. Jim, to speak his mind first.

"Of course we are all feminists here," he began. "I have given the best proof of it a man can. My own experience of professional women is limited—the only set I've known well were Mary's fellow students at the medical school. But I'm sorry to say I agree with Tom: the first thing that struck me about them was that nine-tenths of them didn't seem to know why they were there. They weren't single-minded about their work as men are. You felt a sort of hesitation, a sort of sag in them. The difference in the spirit—well, it was startling." He shook his head. "Those poor girls seemed sort of haunted."

"Nagged at," suggested Mary.

"That's it. It was as if they had been so nagged at all their lives by non-essentials that they had lost the faculty of keeping their eye on one goal as we two were doing."

Mary returned his look. Their goal was biological research, and they had been pursuing it together through their young twenties with complete unity and an almost dedicated aloofness.

"These are burning questions to Tom and me," said Felicia. "Here we are with three girls to educate. We passionately believe that they must all do some self-supporting work in the world. In fact, even if we could afford not to, we should turn them out of the house at the age of eighteen on principle. But where are we going to direct them? So far they themselves show no interest in the subject."

"Well, it's up to you," said Dr. Jim. "I believe it comes back to home training. Girls have never had a profession kept before them as boys have. Till they do, we won't get anything but amateur professional women."

"Heaven knows," broke out his wife, "why girls do well even in college. It's in spite of their families. Now most of my friends' parents, like my own, were kind, intelligent people, tolerant of college education for girls. You could go if you wanted, and you could probably go on to something else afterward if you insisted. But nobody cared. What I studied, the marks I got—it was all a matter of course, of indifference. They never asked me or themselves what I was being educated for. It happened by miracle that Jim and my career coincided very early in the game."

"Aha!" exclaimed Tom, "now we are getting to the point. Where does matrimony come into woman's education? That is the real question, isn't it?"

"Rot," retorted the doctor briskly. "Don't you go worrying about the mating instinct, Tom. It's quite strong enough to take care of itself. It comes in anywhere and everywhere, because it has to. What we need to cultivate is the professional instinct. Now take my lovely sisters—can't do a blessed thing but sit around and wait to get married. I was never allowed to forget for a day that I had to earn a living and 'make good.' But nothing was expected of the dear girls but domestic accomplishments."

"Now, Jim," protested Felicia, "domestic accomplishments can't be dismissed so easily. Wait till you have a home and children. You're speaking as an interne. I want my daughters to have occupations but I also frankly want them to have husbands, so I believe they should be educated also for domesticity. Indeed, I go farther—I think they must have the sort of occupation that makes the two compatible. You scorn 'odd jobs,' but who's going to do them if not women? The men simply haven't time in the midst of the economic struggle. Of course there are cases where the woman is more creative or a better wage-earner than the man—then he should fill in. But generally speaking, a woman, I don't care what her profession, has got to be willing and able, well—not only to do the marketing, but to go and see a sick grandmother at the end of a hard day, or sit up with the baby."

"Look here," protested Jane, "I claim the right to speak at last, and I object strenuously to sex distinctions in the matter of patchwork—as I do to Felicia's assumption that the professional woman is not in the economic struggle. She *is* there. That's the crux of the matter, and the odd job has got to be either eliminated or shared. Even now we are so handicapped by the necessity of doing our so-called 'woman's work' as well as the other, that it's no wonder the Mme. Curies are unique. Give us five hundred years of really equal opportunity, and, as Jim says, equal psychological expectancy and see what happens. Give us co-education in the professional school and you won't find the sag he noted. I don't believe the women at Johns Hopkins are half-hearted."

"You are trying to evade the issue, Jane," objected Tom. "The handicap, as I see it, is chiefly nature. Surely you don't deny woman's instinct for service? Even in your case, if there's a choice between your work and a human being the work suffers. I myself have seen you wobble."

"You haven't," protested Jane indignantly. "Or if you have it's only because the odd job is there to do, not because I want to do it. And I assure you that if I had been what Felicia calls educated for domesticity I shouldn't have got anywhere at all. It was my academic training that kept me going and made me cherish my small spark."

"You talk, my dear," objected Felicia, "as if you were being less creative when you help to make beautiful human relations than when you write your sociological treatises.

"Can't you understand why the college graduate of my generation takes it hard when radicals like you and Tom turn on her? We had just barely achieved the right to our opportunity against those who claimed it would injure our chances of matrimony. It had even been conceded that we might be old maids if we chose. And now we are wept over because we wither on the tree, and asked to revert to domestic science. What if I prefer a book to a husband? Jim is right: a little mental discipline, a little objectivity of purpose, *will do more* for us, *married or single*, than any lessons in dusting."

"Dusting, nothing!" said Tom. "We are speaking scientifically, I hope. Go on and marry your old book, though the state needs your children, also, and the real problem before feminists to-day is whether it can or can't have both. It's positively ostrich-like to go on assuming that you are training women to be just doctors and sociologists. The college professor knows it isn't so and is bothered, and the modern father, hang it, does insist on knowing what his daughter is being educated for. Can't he pretty well assume it is half for motherhood?"

"So that's what you're driving at, Tom?" remarked Jim. "But reflect that if the lack of outlet for the maternal instinct were the only difficulty, trained nurses—I forgot to mention them before—would be perfectly happy. They are satisfying their instinctive motherhood every hour of the day, yet it is the very exceptional nurse, as I see her, who gets much out of her job but filthy lucre."

"And who isn't ready to cut it all to hook on to the first available man?" added Tom. "Just so. Having chosen to earn her living by satisfying her strongest need, she follows the need through to its logical conclusion."

"The nurse's case is a little outside of our argument," commented Felicia, "but there must be something significant in the enormous proportion of college graduates who go in for teaching and social work—the so to speak maternal professions."

"Nonsense," said Jane. "Those callings attract many besides the born mothers; first because they are obvious, traditional; second because they are cheap and easy so far as higher training goes—by comparison, I mean, with law or medicine."

"But are social workers whole-hearted?" insisted Tom. "Only the exceptional again. And the Lord knows we all complain of the way school teachers dry up. What America needs is more mixing up of work and matrimony, instead of the present artificial separation."

"What women need," said Mary, "is, I insist, professional training. Now science has given me all the weapons I need for life if I can only use them; clearness of sight, economy and honesty of mind, straightness of emotion. It doesn't allow any side tracks or any falterings. So when I have children I shall not hang broodingly over them as you do, Felicia; I shall firmly engage a competent nurse and firmly send them off to a good school later. They will be expected to get more out of my biological discoveries than from my constant attention. But even if I should give up research to-morrow," she added reflectively, "it *would* be worth the grind and the sacrifice of these last years."

Tom burst into a delighted laugh. "There's where I score," he exclaimed. "Six years of medicine in order to be a good wife!"

"Not at all," said Mary, stiffly. "It is true that my profession helps me to stand behind Jim, prevents me from quarrelling with his inevitable detachment as most scientists' wives do. What I personally get out of medicine is a sense of having a share in the independent world of impersonal truth. Half-hearted? Not if I never have children."

"The answer to that is, wait till you do have them, Mary," said Felicia. "Then we shall really be able to judge whether—excuse my pompous language—you can serve both science and the race."

READING AND DISCUSSION QUESTIONS

1. Consider the multiple perspectives on women's education, which Sergeant highlights in her *New Republic* article. What conclusions can you draw about the reasons why some supported and others questioned the usefulness of women's education?

2. How does Sergeant's article reflect the broader historical context of the period? To what extent does the discussion over women's education echo other debates between traditionalists and those pushing new ways of thinking?

17-4 | The Lure of the Department Store

THEODORE DREISER, *Sister Carrie* (1900)

Dreiser was a novelist associated with the naturalist school, which meant he wrote fiction with a journalist's eye toward the gritty realities of America's cities. His novel *Sister Carrie* tells the story of eighteen-year-old Caroline (Carrie) Meeber, who flees a drab farm life for the urban enchantments of turn-of-the-century Chicago. To survive, Carrie exchanges her virtue for vice, a choice presented without judgment by Dreiser in a break with literary norms that held characters accountable for their morally compromised actions. In this scene, Carrie seeks employment at one of Chicago's elegant department stores, where she is bewitched by the consumer fantasies on display.

At that time the department store was in its earliest form of successful operation, and there were not many. The first three in the United States, established about 1884, were in Chicago. Carrie was familiar with the names of several through the advertisements in the "Daily News," and now proceeded to seek them. . . . Some time she spent in wandering up and down, thinking to encounter the buildings by chance, so readily is the mind, bent upon prosecuting a hard but needful errand, eased by that self-deception which the semblance of search, without the reality, gives. At last she inquired of a police officer, and was directed to proceed "two blocks up," where she would find "The Fair."

The nature of these vast retail combinations, should they ever permanently disappear, will form an interesting chapter in the commercial history of our nation. Such a flowering out of a modest trade principle the world had never witnessed up to that time. They were along the line of the most effective retail organisation, with hundreds of stores cöordinated into one and laid out upon the

Theodore Dreiser, Sister Carrie (1900)

most imposing and economic basis. They were handsome, bustling, successful affairs, with a host of clerks and a swarm of patrons. Carrie passed along the busy aisles, much affected by the remarkable displays of trinkets, dress goods, stationery, and jewelry. Each separate counter was a show place of dazzling interest and attraction. She could not help feeling the claim of each trinket and valuable upon her personally, and yet she did not stop. There was nothing there which she could not have used—nothing which she did not long to own. The dainty slippers and stockings, the delicately frilled skirts and petticoats, the laces, ribbons, hair-combs, purses, all touched her with individual desire, and she felt keenly the fact that not any of these things were in the range of her purchase. She was a work-seeker, an outcast without employment, one whom the average employee could tell at a glance was poor and in need of a situation.

It must not be thought that any one could have mistaken her for a nervous, sensitive, high-strung nature, cast unduly upon a cold, calculating, and unpoetic world. Such certainly she was not. But women are peculiarly sensitive to their adornment.

Not only did Carrie feel the drag of desire for all which was new and pleasing in apparel for women, but she noticed too, with a touch at the heart, the fine ladies who elbowed and ignored her, brushing past in utter disregard of her presence, themselves eagerly enlisted in the materials which the store contained. Carrie was not familiar with the appearance of her more fortunate sisters of the city. Neither had she before known the nature and appearance of the shop girls with whom she now compared poorly. They were pretty in the main, some even handsome, with an air of independence and indifference which added, in the case of the more favoured, a certain piquancy. Their clothes were neat, in many instances fine, and wherever she encountered the eye of one it was only to recognise in it a keen analysts of her own position—her individual shortcomings of dress and that shadow of *manner* which she thought must hang about her and make clear to all who and what she was. A flame of envy lighted in her heart. She realised in a dim way how much the city held—wealth, fashion, ease—every adornment for women, and she longed for dress and beauty with a whole heart.

On the second floor were the managerial offices, to which, after some inquiry, she was now directed. There she found other girls ahead of her, applicants like herself, but with more of that self-satisfied and independent air which experience of the city lends; girls who scrutinised her in a painful manner. After a wait of perhaps three-quarters of an hour, she was called in turn.

"Now," said a sharp, quick-mannered Jew, who was sitting at a roll-top desk near the window, "have you ever worked in any other store?"

"No, sir," said Carrie.

"Oh, you haven't," he said, eyeing, her keenly.

"No, sir," she replied.

"Well, we prefer young women just now with some experience. I guess we can't use you."

Carrie stood waiting a moment, hardly certain whether the interview had terminated.

"Don't wait!" he exclaimed. "Remember we are very busy here."

Carrie began to move quickly to the door.

"Hold on," he said, calling her back. "Give me your name and address. We want girls occasionally."

When she had gotten safely into the street, she could scarcely restrain the tears. It was not so much the particular rebuff which she had just experienced, but the whole abashing trend of the day. She was tired and nervous. She abandoned the thought of appealing to the other department stores and now wandered on, feeling a certain safety and relief in mingling with the crowd.

READING AND DISCUSSION QUESTIONS

1. What do Dreiser's observations suggest about women's participation in turn-of-the-century consumer society? To what extent was class a factor in shaping a woman's participation?

2. What conclusion can you draw regarding the appeal of the city in the late nine-teenth century? From Carrie's perspective, what did the city offer that her rural Wisconsin home could not?

3. Why do you think Victorians might have rejected the detailed and graphic depictions of characters, settings, and plots naturalist writers like Dreiser included in their novels? What Victorian sensibilities were upset by these more modern approaches to fiction?

17-5 | A Black Leader's Compromise for Racial Opportunity

BOOKER T. WASHINGTON, *Atlanta Cotton States and International Exposition Speech* (1895)

Few speeches in American history have elicited the same attention and controversy as Booker T. Washington's address before the mostly white audience at the Cotton States and International Exposition held in Atlanta, Georgia, in 1895. Born a slave, Washington worked and pursued schooling in the Reconstruction era, ultimately becoming president of Tuskegee Normal and Industrial Institute, the all-black college in Alabama. His speech was well received by many whites, but it infuriated some blacks, including W. E. B. Du Bois, who labeled Washington's ideas for racial advance a compromise to white prejudice.

Ignorant and inexperienced, it is not strange that in the first years of our new life we began at the top instead of at the bottom; that a seat in Congress or the state legislature was more sought than real estate or industrial skill; that the political convention or stump speaking had more attractions than starting a dairy farm or truck garden.

Louis R. Harlan, ed., *The Booker T. Washington Papers*, vol. 3 (Urbana: University of Illinois Press, 1974), 583–587.

A ship lost at sea for many days suddenly sighted a friendly vessel. From the mast of the unfortunate vessel was seen a signal, "Water, water; we die of thirst!" The answer from the friendly vessel at once came back, "Cast down your bucket where you are." A second time the signal, "Water, water; send us water!" ran up from the distressed vessel, and was answered, "Cast down your bucket where you are." And a third and fourth signal for water was answered, "Cast down your bucket where you are." The captain of the distressed vessel, at last heeding the injunction, cast down his bucket, and it came up full of fresh, sparkling water from the mouth of the Amazon River. To those of my race who depend on bettering their condition in a foreign land or who underestimate the importance of cultivating friendly relations with the Southern white man, who is their next-door neighbor, I would say: "Cast down your bucket where you are" — cast it down in making friends in every manly way of the people of all races by whom we are surrounded.

Cast it down in agriculture, mechanics, in commerce, in domestic service, and in the professions. . . . Our greatest danger is that in the great leap from slavery to freedom we may overlook the fact that the masses of us are to live by the productions of our hands, and fail to keep in mind that we shall prosper in proportion as we learn to dignify and glorify common labour, and put brains and skill into the common occupations of life; shall prosper in proportion as we learn to draw the line between the superficial and the substantial, the ornamental gewgaws of life and the useful. No race can prosper till it learns that there is as much dignity in tilling a field as in writing a poem. It is at the bottom of life we must begin, and not at the top. Nor should we permit our grievances to overshadow our opportunities.

To those of the white race who look to the incoming of those of foreign birth and strange tongue and habits for the prosperity of the South, were I permitted I would repeat what I say to my own race, "Cast down your bucket where you are." Cast it down among the eight millions of Negroes whose habits you know, whose fidelity and love you have tested in days when to have proved treacherous meant the ruin of your firesides. Cast down your bucket among these people who have, without strikes and labour wars, tilled your fields, cleared your forests, builded [*sic*] your railroads and cities, and brought forth treasures from the bowels of the earth, and helped make possible this magnificent representation of the progress of the South. Casting down your bucket among my people, helping and encouraging them as you are doing on these grounds, and to education of head, hand, and heart, you will find that they will buy your surplus land, make blossom the waste places in your fields, and run your factories. While doing this, you can be sure in the future, as in the past, that you and your families will be surrounded by the most patient, faithful, law-abiding, and un-resentful people that the world has seen. As we have proved our loyalty to you in the past, in nursing your children, watching by the sick-bed of your mothers and fathers, and often following them with tear-dimmed eyes to their graves, so in the future, in our humble way, we shall stand by you with a devotion that no foreigner can approach, ready to lay down our lives, if need be, in defense of yours, interlacing our industrial, commercial, civil, and religious life with yours in a way that shall make the interests of both races one. In all things that are purely social we can be as separate as the fingers, yet one as the hand in all things essential to mutual progress. . . .

The wisest among my race understand that the agitation of questions of social equality is the extremest folly, and that progress in the enjoyment of all the privileges that will come to us must be the result of severe and constant struggle rather than of artificial forcing. No race that has anything to contribute to the markets of the world is long in any degree ostracized. It is important and right that all privileges of the law be ours, but it is vastly more important that we be prepared for the exercise of these privileges. The opportunity to earn a dollar in a factory just now is worth infinitely more than the opportunity to spend a dollar in an opera-house.

READING AND DISCUSSION QUESTIONS

1. What inferences about Washington's audience can you make from the tone and message of his Atlanta speech? How does his argument reflect the historical context of race relations at the time?

2. To what extent did the context of American industrialization shape the reform program Washington advocated for African Americans?

17-6 | Women Progressives Champion Reform

MINNIE U. RUTHERFORD, *The Conservation of the Health of Mothers, a Primary Responsibility of the State* (1915)

The disruptions and unrest industrialization brought as the price for cheap goods and enormous profits inspired women reformers to define and study social problems. Long before they achieved the right to vote, women pushed into the public sphere and advocated for policies. They staffed the clubs and agencies that generated the research and data that convinced many local, state, and national legislators to act. Women progressives, like Minnie U. Rutherford, advocated for health, education, and temperance. Rutherford's speech, excerpted here, was delivered before the Southern Sociological Congress held in Houston, Texas in 1915. The fact that this conference was held in Texas is a reminder that progressivism was not exclusively a northern urban reform movement. Rutherford's casual reference to eugenics, however, is another reminder that progressivism had its dark side. Many progressives promoted eugenics, a science advocating for selective human breeding to prevent "feeble-minded" individuals from reproducing. Here Rutherford links alcoholism to mental disease and urges state action to ensure the health of the nation. The way she frames her argument for reform reveals the extent to which a Darwinian worldview, with its emphasis on the "survival of the fittest," existed alongside her appeal for state intervention.

Minnie U. Rutherford, "The Conservation of the Health of Mothers, a Primary Responsibility of the State," in *The New Chivalry-Health* ed. James E. McCulloch (Southern Sociological Congress, 1915), 153–159.

The word "efficiency" is said to be the most overworked word in the English language to-day, and yet the army of the unemployed grows and those who are employed continue to ask higher wages which they are too often utterly incapable of earning. Meanwhile the world's most important work is relatively neglected and the social spirit is so warped that the United States troops are called upon to quell riot and bloodshed in my State [Arkansas] and others and the fundamental reason is "inefficiency" – mental, manual, and spiritual.

Upon women has developed the chief care of the feeble-minded, the undeveloped, the socially incompetent; and this demand has given her comparatively little time for performing her real function of teaching and developing the normal and "super-excellent" specimens of the race. The consequence has been an inevitable lowering of the average standard of human quality, not below that which it was necessarily, but below that which it should be at this time in human evolution.

The primary duty of the State would certainly seem to be the preservation of that health which is necessary basis of efficiency at its source — in motherhood, here considered solely as the strongest link in the evolution of the race.

But health is physical, mental, political, social, and moral, and so closely related are they that one is relatively useless without the others. . . .

Recently commercial greed, in the guise of canners, forced through the New York Legislature a bill annulling a more enlightened one passed by the 1913 Legislature. It permits women to work as many as one hundred hours per week, according to the report of the New York Factory Commission, in clattering rooms in which there are either no seats at all, or benches without backs, where the floors are constantly wet and nineteen per cent of the women cannot keep their feet dry. The commission selected fifty of these workers at random and found that they earned an average wage of $4.53 per week. In sharp contrast the Legislature of an equal suffrage State (California) enacts an eight-hour-day law and the Supreme Court of the United States sustains the law and quotes: "Woman is properly placed in a class by herself and legislation designed for her protection may be sustained when like legislation is not necessary for men and could not be sustained. Her physical structure and a proper discharge of her maternal functions — having in view not merely her own health, but the well-being of the race — justify legislation to protect her from the greed as well as the passion of man. . . . The two sexes differ in the influence of vigorous health upon the future well-being of the race, the self-reliance which enables one to assert full rights and in the capacity to maintain the struggle for subsistence. . ."

Mothers' Pensions

In a large majority of [juvenile court] cases a home is found that does not function. The mother spirit is inoperative, usually because of poverty in the wake of vice and crime. About half of the States have, therefore, attempted to provide mothers' pensions. The mother, trying to do double duty, amid all the discriminations of the industrial world, cannot preserve, unaided, that physical and mental health necessary to the task of developing the normal and super-excellent specimens of the race, much less the greater task of bringing up the subnormal results of diseased conditions. The very least that the State can do, in self-defense, is to provide some sort of fund that will help unable the mother to preserve not only her own health, but the health of the home that will make of it, in some sense, a haven of refuge from forced neglect and resultant crime for the children.

Prohibition of the Liquor Traffic

It is conceded that the feeble-minded mother is a great menace to the race, bearing more children than the normal woman, as she does, and a prey to every evil-minded, uncontrolled man in her vicinity. Science says that the greatest contributing cause of this form of mental disease is alcoholic heredity. Dr. Leppich observed ninety-seven children conceived at the time one or both parents were intoxicated and found only seventeen of them normal, and Dr. Bezzola found that of seventy idiots thirty-five were conceived during the wine harvest when the Swiss peasant carouses. Many other investigations of scientists reveal the close connection between alcohol and the various forms of mental disease, as well as the physical degeneracy that causes fifty-five per cent of the children of alcoholic mothers to be stillborn, or to die within the first year or two of life. The drunkard's children are the despair of the child welfare worker, the drunkard's family the insoluble problem of organized charity. The eugenics movement finds its most implacable enemy in the liquor traffic, with its dens of iniquity and disease and its inflamed lust which demands the while slave and further threatens the race through all the forms of venereal disease. The abolition of the liquor traffic would do more to keep women from the operating table of our hospitals than all the policies of segregation or non-segregation of vice. No long hours of toil, no poverty, unmixed with the alcohol problem, ever matched in menace to the health of our women, as well as our people at large, that of the legalized liquor traffic.

Education and Equal Suffrage

. . .On our farms, in this section, are growing up thousands of round-shouldered, narrow-chested, narrow-horizoned, future mothers, incapable of giving to future generations health of either mind of body, because they do not possess either themselves. They are as much a menace to the race as the shopgirls, the mill or factory girls, because of their numbers. Often the only thing they know is how to hoe and pick cotton, and that has, in their minds, no connection with an agricultural education. The schools which we maintain in the rural districts, or elsewhere for that matter, generally fail to furnish the needed efficiency to these girls, even if they attended throughout the entire term and all the grades. . . .

I do not know that the ideal school for the purpose has yet been brought into existence, but certainly some of our States have, in part, made great improvement. If I might be allowed to attempt to express . . . something of my idea of a really educating school, I should say that it is a well-equipped and highly glorified democratic club, intelligently guided, instead of disciplined, the students of which use and enjoy the rights that are theirs and become citizens by practice. In this school there will be textbooks, of course, but there will be also playground, gymnasium, field, shop, a wage, law-making, and self-government.

The chemistry class will make soap and the violation of the pure food law impossible, and the political science class will make the grafting street commissioner a rare thing under the sun; and all this for girls who will, thus educated, be a very difficult commodity in the handling for the white slaver, who will know what their own health means to the race and how to preserve it with that of the entire family as they take their proper place in the government which has become more and more the organization of woman's "sphere" and from participation in which it is the blindest of folly to exclude her if the race is to grow and wax strong with that health which is the only basis of efficiency.

READING AND DISCUSSION QUESTIONS

1. What role does Rutherford see the state playing in conserving the health of women?

2. What do you think Rutherford means when she describes the primary duty of women as the development of the "'super-excellent' specimens of the race?"

3. What does Rutherford's advocacy of both health and education reforms and eugenics tell us about early-twentieth-century progressivism?

▪ COMPARATIVE QUESTIONS ▪

1. Analyze the role gender played in shaping the cultural meaning of terms like *Victorian* and *modern*. How does gender as a lens for interpreting the world show up in the sources in this chapter?

2. In thinking about the effort by historians to interpret particular periods of time, how would you assess the usefulness of the terms *Victorian* and *modern* as descriptors of cultural norms during the years between 1880 and 1917?

3. Analyze the multiple perspectives from this period to offer a coherent interpretation of turn-of-the-century American culture. What conclusions can you draw from the sources to support your argument?

4. To what extent are the cultural changes of these years a cause or consequence of America's industrialization in the late nineteenth century?

5. Compare Booker T. Washington's advocacy for African Americans (Document 17-5) with Robert Elliott's speech to Congress (Document 14-6). How did each define the challenges facing African Americans, and what solutions did they propose?

18

"Civilization's Inferno": The Rise and Reform of Industrial Cities

1880–1917

Urban America was full of Dickensian contrasts. The industrial city made possible the enormous wealth that enriched an elite class, built the infrastructure, and endowed the cultural institutions and entertainments that marked America's urban renaissance. At the same time, many immigrant and working-class families struggled to survive. Factories and sweatshops provided jobs but dangers, too. Few workplace health and safety policies existed until tragedies forced legislators to heed the calls of reformers. Living conditions in the ethnically defined neighborhoods inspired social settlement work and a style of journalism exposing the seedy underbelly of America's urban sprawl. African Americans faced their own challenges, including lynching and mob violence for crimes committed and alleged. In the face of mounting urban challenges, labor and reform activists, including many women who pioneered and led these movements, targeted local, state, and national legislatures, pressuring them to institute reforms to make city living a decent and healthy possibility for the millions squeezed into the small spaces within the very large and bruising world of urban America.

18-1 | Escaping the City for a Fantasy World of Pleasure
Luna Park at Night (c. 1913)

This postcard of Coney Island's Luna Park captures the thrill and wonder that enchanted city dwellers as they escaped, however briefly, the mundane and hard-knock lives they endured as part of New York's working class. Amusement parks like this one treated their customers to dazzling displays, exhilarating rides, and attractions such as Luna Park's famous "Trip to the Moon." This postcard image shows the incandescent main entrance to the park, radiant from the million electric lights beguiling visitors into the nighttime revelry.

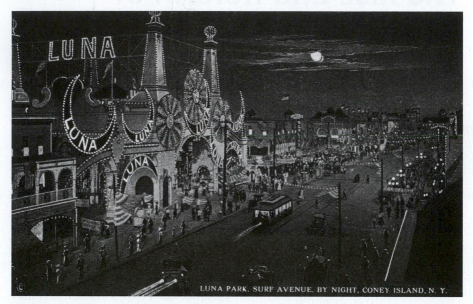

Everett Collection, Inc.

READING AND DISCUSSION QUESTIONS

1. This image was the front of a postcard. What conclusions might the historian draw from this artifact, considering its function as a postcard and its depiction of Luna Park? What might have motivated visitors to Luna Park to purchase and use the postcard? What sorts of comments do you imagine senders of these cards wrote?

2. Examine and analyze the details of the image for evidence of early-twentieth-century ideas about work and leisure. What role did amusements play among the middle and working classes?

18-2 | Competing Against the Party Machine

JANE ADDAMS, *Why the Ward Boss Rules* (1898)

Jane Addams, the pioneering social reformer and founder of Chicago's Hull House, knew political corruption when she saw it. She also understood its power to seduce the poor who depended on the largesse of party bosses dispensing jobs and food to the hungry and unemployed. She intended for the settlement house she established in a poor immigrant neighborhood in Chicago to counter those seductions through educational programs for mothers, classes for children, and activities to uplift, improve, and better both the poor she served and the middle-class women reformers who sought a useful outlet for their time and talents.

Primitive people, such as the South Italian peasants who live in the Nineteenth Ward, deep down in their hearts admire nothing so much as the good man. The successful candidate [for Alderman] must be a good man according to the standards of his constituents. He must not attempt to hold up a morality beyond them, nor must he attempt to reform or change the standard. If he believes what they believe, and does what they are all cherishing a secret ambition to do, he will dazzle them by his success and win their confidence. . . . A man stands by his friend when he gets too drunk to take care of himself, when he loses his wife or child, when he is evicted for non-payment of rent, when he is arrested for a petty crime. It seems to such a man entirely fitting that his Alderman should do the same thing on a larger scale. . . .

The Alderman, therefore, bails out his constituents when they are arrested, or says a good word to the police justice when they appear before him for trial; uses his "pull" with the magistrate when they are likely to be fined for a civil misdemeanor, or sees what he can do to "fix up matters" with the State's attorney when the charge is really a serious one.

Because of simple friendliness, the Alderman is expected to pay rent for the hard-pressed tenant when no rent is forthcoming, to find jobs when work is hard to get, to procure and divide among his constituents all the places which he can seize from the City Hall. The Alderman of the Nineteenth Ward at one time made the proud boast that he had two thousand six hundred people in his ward upon the public pay-roll. . . . [E]ach one felt under distinct obligations to him for getting the job. . . .

The Alderman gives presents at weddings and christenings. He seizes these days of family festivities for making friends. . . . The Alderman procures passes from the railroads when his constituents wish to visit friends or to attend the funerals of distant relatives; he buys tickets galore for benefit entertainments given for a widow or a consumptive in peculiar distress; he contributes to prizes which are awarded to the handsomest lady or the most popular man. At a church bazaar, for instance, the Alderman finds the stage all set for his dramatic performance. When others are spending pennies he is spending dollars. Where anxious relatives are canvassing to secure votes for the two most beautiful children who are being voted upon, he recklessly buys votes from both sides, and laughingly declines to say which one he likes the best, buying off the young lady who is persistently determined to find out, with five dollars for the flower bazaar, the posies, of course, to be sent to the sick of the parish. The moral atmosphere of a bazaar suits him exactly. He murmurs many times, "Never mind: the money all goes to the poor" or, "It is all straight enough if the church gets it." . . . .

Indeed, what headway can the notion of civic purity, of honesty of administration, make against this big manifestation of human friendliness, this stalking survival of village kindness? . . . .

The question does, of course, occur to many minds. Where does the money come from with which to dramatize so successfully? The more primitive people accept the truthful statement of its sources without any shock to their moral sense. To their simple minds he gets it "from the rich," and so long as he again gives it out to the poor, as a true Robin Hood, with open hand, they have no objections to offer. Their ethics are quite honestly those of the merry making foresters. The next less primitive people of the vicinage are quite willing to admit that he leads "the gang" in the City Council, and sells out the city franchises; that he makes deals with the franchise-seeking companies; that he guarantees to steer dubious measures through the Council, for which he demands liberal pay: that he is, in short, a successful boodler.[1] But when there is intellect enough to get this point of view, there is also enough to make the contention that this is universally done: that all the Aldermen do it more or less successfully, but that the Alderman of the Nineteenth Ward is unique in being so generous: that such a state of affairs is to be deplored of course, but that that is the way business is run, and we are fortunate when a kind-hearted man who is close to the people gets a large share of the boodle; that he serves these franchised companies who employ men in the building and construction of their enterprises, and that they are bound in return to give jobs to his constituency. Even when they are intelligent enough to complete the circle, and to see that the money comes, not from the pockets of the companies' agents, but from the street-car fares of people like themselves, it almost seems as if they would rather pay two cents more each time they ride than give up the consciousness that they have a big, warm-hearted friend at court who will stand by them in an emergency. The sense of just dealing comes apparently much later than the desire for protection and kindness. The Alderman is really elected because he is a good friend and neighbor. . . .

If we would hold to our political democracy, some pains must be taken to keep on common ground in our human experiences, and to some solidarity in our ethical conceptions. And if we discover that men of low ideals and corrupt practice are forming popular political standards simply because such men stand by and for and with the people, then nothing remains but to obtain a like sense of identification before we can hope to modify ethical standards.

---

[1] **Boodler**: Corrupt politician who gives or accepts bribes.

READING AND DISCUSSION QUESTIONS

1. What challenge does Addams see blocking the efforts of urban reformers trying to improve the lives of the working class in Chicago? How did the reform aid she provided differ from the work of party bosses?

2. To what extent might issues of class and gender have helped or hindered the reform work Addams undertook at Hull House? What conclusions about women's role in reform can you draw from Addams's essay?

18-3 | American Dream Meets Tenement Reality

MARIE GANZ AND NAT J. FERBER, *Rebels: Into Anarchy—and Out Again* (1920)

Five-year-old Marie Ganz emigrated with her mother from the central European region of Galicia to join her father, Lazarus, in New York City in 1896. Like millions of other immigrants, Marie and her family left the world they knew for the unknown but promising opportunities in America. Her memoir, published in 1920 when she was thirty, evokes the dreams and disappointments immigrant families faced in their early years. Ganz's early experiences inspired her labor reform efforts and anarchism.

It was a home of two tiny rooms. The room in the rear was not much larger than a good-sized clothes closet, and not the stuffiest of closets could be more lacking in sunlight and air. The walls were as blank as an underground dungeon's. There was neither window nor ventilating shaft. The room in front, almost twice as large, though half a dozen steps would have brought anybody with full-grown legs across its entire length, was a kitchen and living-room by day, a bedroom by night. Its two little windows gave a view of a narrow, stone-paved court and, not ten feet away, the rear wall of another tenement. The sunlight never found its way into that little court. By day it was dim and damp, by night a fearsome place, black and sepulchral.

In this little bit of a home lived five persons, my father and mother, myself, my baby brother, and Schmeel, our boarder. What squalid home in New York's crowded ghetto is without its boarder? How can that ever-present bogy, the rent, be met without him? He must be wedged in somehow, no matter how little space there may be.

My father had established this home, our first in the New World, through God knows how much toil and worry and self-sacrifice. It took him two years to do it, and he must have haggled with all the bartering instinct of his race over the price of many a banana in the stock on his pushcart in Hester Street before his little hoard of savings had grown large enough to hire and furnish those two miserable rooms and to send tickets to his family in Galicia.

Marie Ganz, in collaboration with Nat J. Ferber, *Rebels: Into Anarchy—and Out Again* (New York: Dodd, Mead and Company, 1920), 1–5.

I was only five years old when in the summer of 1896 we joined him in America, but I remember well the day when he met us at Ellis Island. He was like a stranger to me, for I had been not much more than a baby when he left us on our Galician farm, but no child could be on distant terms with him long. Children took to him at once. He understood them, and was never so happy as when joining in their play. A quiet, unobtrusive man was my father, tall and slender, with a short yellow beard and mild blue eyes, and I have not forgotten the childlike glow of happiness that was in his face as he welcomed us.

I suppose it is the experience of most people that among the little scraps of our past lives that we carry with us the most insignificant things are apt to stand out more clearly than others of greater moment. I have found it so. I like to go groping into the past now and then, stirred by curiosity as to how far memory will carry me. It is a fascinating game, this of peering into the dim vistas of the long ago, where the mists of time are shifting as if blown by the wind. Now against the far horizon one scene stands out clearly, then another, as the mists fall apart and close again. Now the perfume of flowers comes to me, and I see our garden in front of the old Galician home — the bright little spot which is all I remember of the Old World. Now a breath of salt air is in my face, and I see a rolling sea and a distant, low-lying shore — my one memory of our journey to America.

But however disconnected and far apart the few scenes that still come back to me from the first years of my life, I have glimpses of our arrival in New York that are as vivid as if it had been only yesterday. In a quiet hour alone I wave the years away, and I am a child again, trudging along beside my father, who, weighted down with the great rolls of bedding we had brought with us from the old home, is guiding us through strange, noisy streets. I am staring in wonder at the great buildings and the never-ending crowds of people. I am frightened, bewildered, ready to cry. I keep a tiny hand twisted in the tail of my father's coat, fearing to lose him.

At last we turn into a dark, dirty alley, which runs like a tunnel under a tenement house and leads us to our future home in the building in the rear.

Oh, how hot and stuffy were those two little rooms that we entered! The city was scorching under one of the hot waves that bring such untold misery to the tenements. Not a breath of air stirred. The place was an oven. But, flushed with heat and perspiring though he was, my father ushered us in with a great show of joy and enthusiasm. Suddenly his smile gave way to an expression that reflected bitter disappointment and injured pride as he became aware of the disgust which my mother could not conceal.

"So we have crossed half the world for this!" she cried, thinking bitterly of the comfortable farmhouse we had left behind us. I can see her now as she stood that moment facing my father, her eyes full of reproach — a pretty, slender woman with thick, black hair and a face as fresh and smooth as a girl's.

I am sure it had never occurred to poor, dreamy, impractical Lazarus Ganz that his wife might be disappointed with the new home he had provided for her, or that he had ever fully realized how squalid it was. He was one of the most sensitive of men, and the look of pain in his face as he saw the impression the place made on her filled me with pity for him, young as I was. A five-year-old child is not apt to carry many distinct memories from that age through life, but that scene I have never forgotten.

When at last it grows dark we creep up flight after flight of narrow stairs, lighted by only a tiny gas flame at each landing, to the roof. Long rows of men, women and children are lying there under the stars. We look off over miles and miles of housetops to where they disappear in a blue haze. We spread the bedding we have carried from below, and we lie down to sleep. All the stars of heaven are winking roguishly down at me as I slip away into dreamland.

Beginning with that first night our housetop had a wonderful fascination for me—the cool breezes, the far vistas over the city's roofs, the mysteries of the night sky, the magic moonlight—a fairyland, a place of romance after the dreary day in the stuffy little rooms below or in the crowded, noisy streets.

READING AND DISCUSSION QUESTIONS

1. Evaluate Ganz's impressions of the city upon her arrival in New York. What conclusions can you draw that help you understand the impact of the urban environment on the lives of immigrants?

2. Ganz's story was a child's experience filtered through the memory of her older self. How did her point of view differ from her mother's, and what evidence of her changing perspective does her memoir provide?

3. How does Ganz's experience connect to the broader national and global history of turn-of-the-century migration? Assess whether her experience was determined by her Eastern European roots or if her experience was more a reflection of the general experiences of the immigrant poor.

18-4 | Persistent and Violent Racism Against African Americans

NEW YORK WORLD, *New York Negroes Stage Silent Parade of Protest* (1917)

African Americans had begun to move away from the rural South into more urban areas, including northern cities, by the second decade of the twentieth century, an exodus that would peak during the Great Migration of World War I. They continued to suffer persistent racism, bearing the disdain of many whites who never reconciled with emancipation's legacy. Sometimes this hostility erupted into fatal violence. Lynching became epidemic during the late nineteenth and early twentieth centuries, provoking an anti-lynching campaign among reformers. A silent parade in New York City in 1917 focused attention on this crisis in the African American community, as described in this article from the *New York World*.

Ralph Ginzburg, *100 Years of Lynchings* (Baltimore: Black Classic Press, 1988), 104–106.

Leaders among the negroes of New York City decided that a silent parade would be the most dramatic and effective way to make felt the protest of their race against injustice and inhumanity growing out of lynch law.

And this silent parade was staged with real impressiveness and dignity and with an indefinable appeal to the heart in Fifth Avenue yesterday afternoon.

From the time that the 3,500 or 4,000 men, women, and children marchers left Fifty-sixth Street shortly after 1 o'clock until they were completing their dispersal in Twenty-fourth Street about 3[,] no note of discord was struck.

Police Inspector Morris, who, with upward of one hundred policemen, was in charge of the arrangement down to Forty-second Street, expressed his warm admiration for those in the silent lines.

"They have done everything just right," he said to a reporter for *The World*. "They have been lovely."

And it might be mentioned that this was the first time that the reporter, who has observed many parades in the past few years in New York, ever heard a police official use the adjective "lovely" to describe those whom it is his task to keep in order.

Of the many printed signs prepared by the marchers, Inspector Morris doubted the good taste of only one. It showed a colored mother crouching protectively over two cowering children with the caption, "East St. Louis." And then it showed a photograph of President Wilson and his assertion that the world must be made safe for democracy.

"I asked them if they did not think it was in bad taste too," the Inspector said. "And they agreed that it was and put it aside. They made every effort to have this parade exactly what it was planned to be."

The only sound as the marchers passed down the avenue was the slow tum, tum, tum-tum-tum. And except for little cries of sympathy and admiration from women when they saw a tiny, bright-eyed, kinky-haired baby peeping solemnly over the moist neck of its marching mother, the silence of the parade spread to and enveloped the watchers on the sidewalk too.

There must have been as many colored men and women and babies on the sidewalk as there were in the parade. Probably there were more. And they too showed the same restraint and sense of decorum that governed the marchers.

The parade was led by a drum corps of boys in khaki. Then there were fourteen lines of young girls. After them were six rows of boys, eighty-five rows of women, many of them mothers with babies in their arms, and fifty-five lines of men. The lines appeared to average twenty persons.

In the line of march were doctors, lawyers, ministers, school teachers and trained nurses. Many veterans of the Spanish-American War were there too. The Grand Marshal, Capt. Hubert Jackson, served in Cuba and the Philippines as Captain of Company L of the Sixth Massachusetts. Clifton G. A. French, a lawyer, was in the Twenty-third Kansas. He explained the purpose of the parade this way:

"We love our Government. And we want our Government to love us too."
The banners carried aloft bore the following inscriptions:

"Thou shalt not kill."

"Unto the least of these, my brethren."

"Mother, do lynchers go to heaven?"

"Suffer little children and forbid them not."

"Give me a chance to live."

"Mr. President, why not make America safe for democracy."

"The first blood for American independence was shed by a negro, Crispus Attucks."[2]

"Put the spirit of Christ in the making and the execution of laws."

"Your hands are full of blood."

"We have 30,000 teachers."

"Race prejudice is the offspring of ignorance and the mother of lynching."

"Ten thousand of us fought in the Spanish-American War."

"Three thousand negroes fought for American independence under George Washington."

"No negro has ever betrayed his country or attempted to assassinate a President or any official of the Government."

"Patriotism and loyalty presuppose protection and liberty."

"America has lynched without trial 2,867 negroes in thirty-one years. Not a single murderer has suffered."

"Memphis and Waco, centres of American culture?"

"Twenty thousand black men fought for your liberty in the Civil War."

"The world owes no man a living, but every man an opportunity to earn a living."

"Thirty-four negroes have received Carnegie hero medals."

"Our music is the only American music."

"A square deal for every man."

And there was another one to the effect that if there is any fault to be found with color, either white people or God is responsible.

READING AND DISCUSSION QUESTIONS

1. Interpret the tone of this newspaper article. To what extent is the author sympathetic to the plight of African Americans? What residue of racism remains? Consider, for instance, the author's attention to the orderliness of the parade.

2. Analyze the inscriptions on the banners African Americans carried in the parade. What message(s) do you think they intended to send and to whom? Who was the audience for their signs and for the silent parade itself?

---

[2] **Crispus Attucks:** African American killed during the Boston Massacre in 1770.

18-5 | The Need for Play

CHARLES FREDERICK WELLER, *Camp Good Will. And Other Summer Outings Conducted by the Chicago Bureau of Charities* (1900)

Like Jane Addams, Charles Weller was a Chicago social worker who was active in municipal reform aimed at improving the lives of the city's working class. In 1900, Weller was the superintendent of the West Side district of the Chicago Bureau of Charities, a private philanthropic organization. Later, he and his wife Eugenia Winston Weller founded the first playground in Washington, D.C. and became leaders in the Playground and Recreation Association. In this article, published in *The Commons*, a monthly social settlement magazine, Weller reports on the summer experience of Camp Good Will, a program that provided weeklong camping excursions for Chicago's poor families. His advocacy for outdoor recreation was part of a broader Progressive Era initiative to integrate natural play spaces within America's sprawling cities, providing healthy alternatives to the crowded tenement streets, fire escapes, and rooftops where the children of the working poor typically played.

"This here milk," said a lad at Evanston Camp Good Will this summer, "ain't very good, because it isn't blue."

Another suggestive story is that of a tired mother, thirty-seven years old, who confessed that she had never in her entire lifetime been outside Chicago. "I never realized there were such trees and grass and bathing places. And I never imagined, even, that there were such people as you folks here who spend all this money and do all these kind things for poor people who have no claim upon you and are not at all important." She actually believed she had discovered, in the Evanstonians who supported Camp Good Will, an unfamiliar, new species of human beings. "I tell you," she said, on the return trip to Chicago, "it has been a great lesson to me and I am going back to do all the little acts of kindness I can around my own neighborhood. For," she added, somewhat diffidently, "I'd like myself to be you kind of folks."

One hundred and twenty children and mothers from among Chicago's "reconcentrados"[3] were taken to Evanston every Wednesday afternoon for five weeks during last July and August. Each party remained for seven days, privileged guests of the entire town, whose every citizen was zealous to lend a helping hand. There were seventeen living tents, each having four cots, two double-deckers; this made each tent accommodate six children and one adult, with a baby sometimes added, sleeping in the cot bed with its mother.

Charles F. Weller, "Camp Good Will. And Other Summer Outings Conducted by the Chicago Bureau of Charities," *The Commons* No. 50 (September 15, 1900): 9–12.

[3] **Reconcentrados**: a term for rural noncombatants during the Cuban and Philippine wars in the latter nineteenth century who were placed for their protection in small fortified towns.

These sleeping tents had raised wooden floors, curtains before the beds, camp stools and canvas flies which became awnings, fore and aft, in daytime, and doors at night. There were two mammoth tents for a kitchen and dining-room, respectively, and other tents providing a wash room, two toilet rooms with modern plumbing, and a superintendent's quarters where a long-distance telephone had been provided. A large "assembly tent" seemed to the boys like a circus of their very own, and here the best amateur talent of Evanston and of the Northwestern University contributed to frequent programs, music, recitations, stories and stereopticon[4] views. Upon the lake shore, beneath the wooded bluff on which the camp stood, there was bathing daily in suits provided by some anonymous friend of the children and there was a great bonfire also every Saturday evening, when young men and ladies brought out their mandolins and guitars, told stories and distributed fresh-roasted peanuts. "Goodness!" said one of the Chicago guests, who worried about her family's fuel for the winter, "I wish't I had that pile of kindling at my house . . ." The Bureau's General Office took charge of a private residence near Plano, Ill., and sent thirty children there each week. The groups remained two weeks each, and one entire party was composed exclusively of crippled children who dragged misshapen limbs about among the trees and flowers and got some warm, brown color from the sun into their waxen faces . . .

Over 4,000 children and mothers altogether have been afforded outings this summer thro the Chicago Bureau of Charities. This involved a great deal of labor and expense, for pains were taken to search out, thro hidden corners of the entire city, the neediest, most friendless little folk, and no family was recommended for an outing anywhere until one of the Bureau's workers visited the home and made tactful inquiries into each family's circumstances. As one indirect result of these investigations, medical service, employment, material alms, the continued service of a Friendly Visitor, or some other permanent benefit was made to follow, in the case of especially destitute families, the week or two of country life.

READING AND DISCUSSION QUESTIONS

1. How does Weller describe the benefits of Camp Good Will on those who participated? Why does he think these activities are important to working-class urban families?

2. What does Weller's article suggest about the ways turn-of-the-century Americans contrasted "country" and "city"?

3. Who is the audience for this article? What affect do you think Weller wants to have on readers? How does he make his appeal?

---

[4] **Stereopticon**: a slide projector with two lenses. In the era before moving pictures, the stereopticon was a popular form of entertainment.

18-6 | Muckraker Exposes Chicago's Meat-Packing Industry
UPTON SINCLAIR, *The Jungle* (1906)

Social reformers exposed the evils of the industrial economy through a new form of investigative journalism caricatured by some as "muckraking" for the filth they stirred while peering into the unhealthy and dehumanizing conditions then existing in the nation's factories. With a journalist's eye for detail, author Upton Sinclair investigated Chicago's meat-packing industry, expecting to shock readers of his novel *The Jungle* with scenes of a workplace dystopia, where laborers were abused to the point of mental and physical collapse. In the end, the novel's graphic depictions of the "disassembly" line, where pigs were butchered into the nation's packaged meat industry, captured the most attention, resulting in a public outcry and passage of the Meat Inspection Act and the Pure Food and Drug Act.

There is over a square mile of space in the yards, and more than half of it is occupied by cattle-pens; north and south as far as the eye can reach there stretches a sea of pens. And they were all filled—so many cattle no one had ever dreamed existed in the world. Red cattle, black, white, and yellow cattle; old cattle and young cattle; great bellowing bulls and little calves not an hour born; meek-eyed milch cows and fierce, long-horned Texas steers. The sound of them here was as of all the barnyards of the universe; and as for counting them—it would have taken all day simply to count the pens. Here and there ran long alleys, blocked at intervals by gates; and Jokubas told them that the number of these gates was twenty-five thousand. Jokubas had recently been reading a newspaper article which was full of statistics such as that, and he was very proud as he repeated them and made his guests cry out with wonder. Jurgis[5] too had a little of this sense of pride. Had he not just gotten a job, and become a sharer in all this activity, a cog in this marvellous machine?

Here and there about the alleys galloped men upon horseback, booted, and carrying long whips; they were very busy, calling to each other, and to those who were driving the cattle. They were drovers and stock-raisers, who had come from far states, and brokers and commission-merchants, and buyers for all the big packing-houses. Here and there they would stop to inspect a bunch of cattle, and there would be a parley, brief and businesslike. The buyer would nod or drop his whip, and that would mean a bargain; and he would note it in his little book, along with hundreds of others he had made that morning. Then Jokubas pointed out the place where the cattle were driven to be weighed, upon a great scale that would weigh a hundred thousand pounds at once and record it automatically. It was near to the east entrance that they stood, and all

---

Upton Sinclair, *The Jungle* (New York: Doubleday, Page & Company, 1906), 37–41.

[5] **Jokubas . . . Jurgis**: Jokubas Szedvilas and Jurgis Rudkus, two characters in the novel, are both Lithuanian immigrants who ultimately succumb to what Sinclair describes as the brutalities of capitalism.

along this east side of the yards ran the railroad tracks, into which the cars were run, loaded with cattle. All night long this had been going on, and now the pens were full; by to-night they would all be empty, and the same thing would be done again.

"And what will become of all these creatures?" cried Teta Elzbieta.

"By to-night," Jokubas answered, "they will all be killed and cut up; and over there on the other side of the packing-houses are more railroad tracks, where the cars come to take them away."

There were two hundred and fifty miles of track within the yards, their guide went on to tell them. They brought about ten thousand head of cattle every day, and as many hogs, and half as many sheep — which meant some eight or ten million live creatures turned into food every year. One stood and watched, and little by little caught the drift of the tide, as it set in the direction of the packing-houses. There were groups of cattle being driven to the chutes, which were roadways about fifteen feet wide, raised high above the pens. In these chutes the stream of animals was continuous; it was quite uncanny to watch them, pressing on to their fate, all unsuspicious — a very river of death. Our friends were not poetical, and the sight suggested to them no metaphors of human destiny; they thought only of the wonderful efficiency of it all. The chutes into which the hogs went climbed high up — to the very top of the distant buildings; and Jokubas explained that the hogs went up by the power of their own legs, and then their weight carried them back through all the processes necessary to make them into pork.

"They don't waste anything here," said the guide, and then he laughed and added a witticism, which he was pleased that his unsophisticated friends should take to be his own: "They use everything about the hog except the squeal." In front of Brown's General Office building there grows a tiny plot of grass, and this, you may learn, is the only bit of green thing in Packingtown; likewise this jest about the hog and his squeal, the stock in trade of all the guides, is the one gleam of humor that you will find there.

After they had seen enough of the pens, the party went up the street, to the mass of buildings which occupy the centre of the yards. These buildings, made of brick and stained with innumerable layers of Packingtown smoke, were painted all over with advertising signs, from which the visitor realized suddenly that he had come to the home of many of the torments of his life. It was here that they made those products with the wonders of which they pestered him so — by placards that defaced the landscape when he travelled, and by staring advertisements in the newspapers and magazines — by silly little jingles that he could not get out of his mind, and gaudy pictures that lurked for him around every street corner. Here was where they made Brown's Imperial Hams and Bacon, Brown's Dressed Beef, Brown's Excelsior Sausages! Here was the headquarters of Durham's Pure Leaf Lard, of Durham's Breakfast Bacon, Durham's Canned Beef, Potted Ham, Devilled Chicken, Peerless Fertilizer!

Entering one of the Durham buildings, they found a number of other visitors waiting; and before long there came a guide, to escort them through the place. They make a great feature of showing strangers through the packing-plants, for it is a good advertisement. But ponas [Mr.] Jokubas whispered maliciously that the visitors did not see any more than the packers wanted them to.

They climbed a long series of stairways outside of the building, to the top of its five or six stories. Here were the chute, with its river of hogs, all patiently toiling upward; there was a place for them to rest to cool off, and then through another passageway they went into a room from which there is no returning for hogs.

It was a long, narrow room, with a gallery along it for visitors. At the head there was a great iron wheel, about twenty feet in circumference, with rings here and there along its edge. Upon both sides of this wheel there was a narrow space, into which came the hogs at the end of their journey; in the midst of them stood a great burly negro, bare-armed and bare-chested. He was resting for the moment, for the wheel had stopped while men were cleaning up. In a minute or two, however, it began slowly to revolve, and then the men upon each side of it sprang to work. They had chains which they fastened about the leg of the nearest hog, and the other end of the chain they hooked into one of the rings upon the wheel. So, as the wheel turned, a hog was suddenly jerked off his feet and borne aloft.

At the same instant the ear was assailed by a most terrifying shriek; the visitors started in alarm, the women turned pale and shrank back. The shriek was followed by another, louder and yet more agonizing — for once started upon that journey, the hog never came back; at the top of the wheel he was shunted off upon a trolley, and went sailing down the room. And meantime another was swung up, and then another, and another, until there was a double line of them, each dangling by a foot and kicking in frenzy — and squealing. The uproar was appalling, perilous to the ear-drums; one feared there was too much sound for the room to hold — that the walls must give way or the ceiling crack. There were high squeals and low squeals, grunts, and wails of agony; there would come a momentary lull, and then a fresh outburst, louder than ever, surging up to a deafening climax. It was too much for some of the visitors — the men would look at each other, laughing nervously, and the women would stand with hands clenched, and the blood rushing to their faces, and the tears starting in their eyes.

Meantime, heedless of all these things, the men upon the floor were going about their work. Neither squeals of hogs nor tears of visitors made any difference to them; one by one they hooked up the hogs, and one by one with a swift stroke they slit their throats. There was a long line of hogs, with squeals and life-blood ebbing away together; until at last each started again, and vanished with a splash into a huge vat of boiling water.

It was all so very businesslike that one watched it fascinated. It was pork-making by machinery, pork-making by applied mathematics. And yet somehow the most matter-of-fact person could not help thinking of the hogs; they were so innocent, they came so very trustingly; and they were so very human in their protests—and so perfectly within their rights! They had done nothing to deserve it; and it was adding insult to injury, as the thing was done here, swinging them up in this cold-blooded, impersonal way, without a pretence at apology, without the homage of a tear. Now and then a visitor wept, to be sure; but this slaughtering-machine ran on, visitors or no visitors. It was like some horrible crime committed in a dungeon, all unseen and unheeded, buried out of sight and of memory.

One could not stand and watch very long without becoming philosophical, without beginning to deal in symbols and similes, and to hear the hog-squeal of the universe. Was it permitted to believe that there was nowhere upon the earth, or above the earth, a heaven for hogs, where they were requited for all this suffering? Each one of these hogs was a separate creature. Some were white hogs, some were black; some were brown, some were spotted; some were old, some were young; some were long and lean, some were monstrous. And each of them had an individuality of his own, a will of his own, a hope and a heart's desire; each was full of self-confidence, of self-importance, and a sense of dignity. And trusting and strong in faith he had gone about his business, the while a black shadow hung over him and a horrid Fate waited in his pathway. Now suddenly it had swooped upon him, and had seized him by the leg. Relentless, remorseless, it was; all his protests, his screams, were nothing to it—it did its cruel will with him, as if his wishes, his feelings, had simply no existence at all; it cut his throat and watched him gasp out his life. And how was one to believe that there was nowhere a god of hogs, to whom this hog-personality was precious, to whom these hog-squeals and agonies had a meaning? Who would take this hog into his arms and comfort him, reward him for his work well done, and show him the meaning of his sacrifice? Perhaps some glimpse of all this was in the thoughts of our humble-minded Jurgis, as he turned to go on with the rest of the party, and muttered: "Dieve [God]—but I'm glad I'm not a hog!"

READING AND DISCUSSION QUESTIONS

1. How do you assess *The Jungle* as a cause of Progressive Era legislation? Distinguish between short-term or immediate causes, like the publication of Sinclair's novel, and longer-term causes of reform legislation, such as unsanitary working conditions.

2. Analyze and explain Sinclair's point of view toward workplace conditions. To what extent does his depiction of the Chicago meat-packing industry reflect Progressive Era concerns about social democracy or the ability of individuals to live and participate fully in civil society?

■ COMPARATIVE QUESTIONS ■

1. Compare the perspectives on the city offered in this chapter with the views offered in *Sister Carrie* (Document 17-4). What did "city" and "country" mean to different people?

2. What response do you think *The Jungle* (Document 18-6) would have elicited from such different reformers as Jane Addams and Marie Ganz? How might each have interpreted the evidence of workplace abuse Sinclair presented in novel form?

3. Why do you think Progressive Era reformers adopted the strategies they did? What methods did they believe would achieve the most lasting effect? Were their methods successful? Did they have in mind similar audiences?

4. After having read and analyzed the multiple perspectives presented in this chapter, describe the ways in which working-class Americans responded to the challenges of the industrial city. Which tactics seemed to work best, and which hindered or did not have much effect on their struggle?

5. Compare Theodore Roosevelt's ideas on professionalism in sports (Document 17-1), Frances Benjamin Johnston's photo of children doing calisthenics in school (Document 17-2), and Charles Weller's article in *The Commons* (Document 18-5). What shared values informed these approaches to urban reform?

19

Whose Government? Politics, Populists, and Progressives
1880–1917

Turn-of-the-century reformers had plenty of targets. The industrial economy and urban development created opportunities and problems. The problems kept both Populists and Progressives busy but in different ways. Both groups pointed to failures in the laissez-faire capitalist system as it had matured in the context of industrialization, spawning monopolies and political manipulation and corruption that threatened the fabric of democratic self-governance. These reform groups, irritated by the indifference of the two major parties controlled by political bosses and Wall Street manipulators, forged new movements designed to wrest control from vested interests and return power to the people. Of course, specific issues divided reformers, rendering any coherence within progressive ranks all but impossible to achieve. Still, the era accomplished a great deal, mobilizing efforts to reform civic government, introducing workplace health and safety regulations, and addressing persistent racism and discrimination against African Americans. Despite an unfinished agenda, this period of reform helped create the modern state, whose architecture survives into the twenty-first century.

19-1 | Populist Manifesto for a Reformed America
Omaha Platform (1892)

The People's Party crested then fell in the 1890s, but at the time it was the only viable alternative to the entrenched political interests represented by Republicans and Democrats. Formed
largely from local and regional Farmers' Alliances and the Granger movement in the 1880s,
populism represented a broad spectrum of disgruntled Americans critical of concentrated
wealth and corporate power. Their agenda, clarified in the party's 1892 platform, pushed a
series of political reforms. More broadly, they offered an alternative vision for government's
role in modern America, one whose details alarmed corporate interests and the more affluent
Americans profiting from the status quo.

Assembled upon the 116th anniversary of the Declaration of Independence, the
People's Party of America, in their first national convention, invoking upon their
action the blessing of Almighty God, put forth in the name and on behalf of the
people of this country, the following preamble and declaration of principles:

Preamble

The conditions which surround us best justify our co-operation; we meet in the
midst of a nation brought to the verge of moral, political, and material ruin. Corruption dominates the ballot-box, the Legislatures, the Congress, and touches
even the ermine of the bench. The people are demoralized; most of the States
have been compelled to isolate the voters at the polling places to prevent universal intimidation and bribery. The newspapers are largely subsidized or muzzled,
public opinion silenced, business prostrated, homes covered with mortgages,
labor impoverished, and the land concentrating in the hands of capitalists. The
urban workmen are denied the right to organize for self-protection, imported
pauperized labor beats down their wages, a hireling standing army, unrecog-
nized by our laws, is established to shoot them down, and they are rapidly
degenerating into European conditions. The fruits of the toil of millions are
boldly stolen to build up colossal fortunes for a few, unprecedented in the history of mankind; and the possessors of those, in turn, despise the republic and
endanger liberty. From the same prolific womb of governmental injustice we
breed the two great classes—tramps and millionaires.

 The national power to create money is appropriated to enrich bondhold-
ers; a vast public debt payable in legal tender currency has been funded into
gold-bearing bonds, thereby adding millions to the burdens of the people.

 Silver, which has been accepted as coin since the dawn of history, has been
demonetized to add to the purchasing power of gold by decreasing the value of
all forms of property as well as human labor, and the supply of currency is purposely abridged to fatten usurers, bankrupt enterprise, and enslave industry. . . .

The World Almanac, 1893 (New York: 1893), 83–85. Reprinted in George Brown Tindall, ed.,
A Populist Reader, Selections from the Works of American Populist Leaders (New York: Harper &
Row, 1966), 90–96.

We have witnessed for more than a quarter of a century the struggles of the two great political parties for power and plunder, while grievous wrongs have been inflicted upon the suffering people. We charge that the controlling influences dominating both these parties have permitted the existing dreadful conditions to develop without serious effort to prevent or restrain them. Neither do they now promise us any substantial reform. They have agreed together to ignore, in the coming campaign, every issue but one. They propose to drown the outcries of a plundered people with the uproar of a sham battle over the tariff, so that capitalists, corporations, national banks, rings, trusts, watered stock, the demonetization of silver and the oppressions of the usurers may all be lost sight of. They propose to sacrifice our homes, lives, and children on the altar of mammon;[1] to destroy the multitude in order to secure corruption funds from the millionaires.

Assembled on the anniversary of the birthday of the nation, and filled with the spirit of the grand general and chief who established our independence, we seek to restore the government of the Republic to the hands of "the plain people," with which class it originated. We assert our purposes to be identical with the purposes of the National Constitution; to form a more perfect union and establish justice, insure domestic tranquillity, provide for the common defence, promote the general welfare, and secure the blessings of liberty for ourselves and our posterity.

We declare that this Republic can only endure as a free government while built upon the love of the whole people for each other and for the nation; that it cannot be pinned together by bayonets; that the civil war is over, and that every passion and resentment which grew out of it must die with it, and that we must be in fact, as we are in name, one united brotherhood of free men.

Our country finds itself confronted by conditions for which there is no precedent in the history of the world; our annual agricultural productions amount to billions of dollars in value, which must, within a few weeks or months, be exchanged for billions of dollars' worth of commodities consumed in their production; the existing currency supply is wholly inadequate to make this exchange; the results are falling prices, the formation of combines and rings, the impoverishment of the producing class. We pledge ourselves that if given power we will labor to correct these evils by wise and reasonable legislation, in accordance with the terms of our platform. . . .

Platform

We declare, therefore—

First.—That the union of the labor forces of the United States this day consummated shall be permanent and perpetual; may its spirit enter into all hearts for the salvation of the Republic and the uplifting of mankind.

Second.—Wealth belongs to him who creates it, and every dollar taken from industry without an equivalent is robbery. "If any will not work, neither shall he eat." The interests of rural and civic labor are the same; their enemies are identical.

---

[1] **Mammon**: Riches, or material wealth.

Third.—We believe that the time has come when the railroad corporations will either own the people or the people must own the railroads, and should the government enter upon the work of owning and managing all railroads, we should favor an amendment to the Constitution by which all persons engaged in the government service shall be placed under a civil-service regulation of the most rigid character, so as to prevent the increase of the power of the national administration by the use of such additional government employes.

FINANCE.—We demand a national currency, safe, sound, and flexible, issued by the general government only, a full legal tender for all debts, public and private, and that without the use of banking corporations, a just, equitable, and efficient means of distribution direct to the people, at a tax not to exceed 2 per cent. per annum, to be provided as set forth in the sub-treasury plan of the Farmers' Alliance, or a better system; also by payments in discharge of its obligations for public improvements.

1. We demand free and unlimited coinage of silver and gold at the present legal ratio of 16 to 1.
2. We demand that the amount of circulating medium be speedily increased to not less than $50 per capita.
3. We demand a graduated income tax.
4. We believe that the money of the country should be kept as much as possible in the hands of the people, and hence we demand that all State and national revenues shall be limited to the necessary expenses of the government, economically and honestly administered.
5. We demand that postal savings banks be established by the government for the safe deposit of the earnings of the people and to facilitate exchange.

TRANSPORTATION.—Transportation being a means of exchange and a public necessity, the government should own and operate the railroads in the interest of the people. The telegraph, telephone, like the post-office system, being a necessity for the transmission of news, should be owned and operated by the government in the interest of the people.

LAND.—The land, including all the natural sources of wealth, is the heritage of the people, and should not be monopolized for speculative purposes, and alien ownership of land should be prohibited. All land now held by railroads and other corporations in excess of their actual needs, and all lands now owned by aliens should be reclaimed by the government and held for actual settlers only.

Expression of Sentiments

Your Committee on Platform and Resolutions beg leave unanimously to report the following:

Whereas, Other questions have been presented for our consideration, we hereby submit the following, not as a part of the Platform of the People's Party, but as resolutions expressive of the sentiment of this Convention.

1. RESOLVED, That we demand a free ballot and a fair count in all elections and pledge ourselves to secure it to every legal voter without Federal Intervention, through the adoption by the States of the unperverted Australian or secret ballot system.

2. RESOLVED, That the revenue derived from a graduated income tax should be applied to the reduction of the burden of taxation now levied upon the domestic industries of this country.

3. RESOLVED, That we pledge our support to fair and liberal pensions to ex-Union soldiers and sailors.

4. RESOLVED, That we condemn the fallacy of protecting American labor under the present system, which opens our ports to the pauper and criminal classes of the world and crowds out our wage-earners; and we denounce the present ineffective laws against contract labor, and demand the further restriction of undesirable emigration.

5. RESOLVED, That we cordially sympathize with the efforts of organized workingmen to shorten the hours of labor, and demand a rigid enforcement of the existing eight-hour law on Government work, and ask that a penalty clause be added to the said law.

6. RESOLVED, That we regard the maintenance of a large standing army of mercenaries, known as the Pinkerton system, as a menace to our liberties, and we demand its abolition. . . .

7. RESOLVED, That we commend to the favorable consideration of the people and the reform press the legislative system known as the initiative and referendum.

8. RESOLVED, That we favor a constitutional provision limiting the office of President and Vice-President to one term, and providing for the election of Senators of the United States by a direct vote of the people.

9. RESOLVED, That we oppose any subsidy or national aid to any private corporation for any purpose.

10. RESOLVED, That this convention sympathizes with the Knights of Labor and their righteous contest with the tyrannical combine of clothing manufacturers of Rochester, and declare it to be a duty of all who hate tyranny and oppression to refuse to purchase the goods made by the said manufacturers, or to patronize any merchants who sell such goods.

READING AND DISCUSSION QUESTIONS

1. Analyze the party's platform for evidence of Populists' diagnosis of society's ills. What specifically did they see wrong with the national economy, and what measures did they suggest as part of their reform agenda?

2. In reading the Populists' platform, what conclusions can you draw about the constituencies they hoped to win? Do their proposals appeal to specific demographics? Consider such factors as race, class, gender, region, and occupational types.

19-2 | Progressive Leader Identifies the Problem with Cities

FREDERIC HOWE, *The City: The Hope of Democracy* (1909)

Frederic Howe fits the description of a progressive reformer. Though born in a small town, he spent most of his life in cities (Cleveland and New York), earned a college degree (and a PhD), and became active in local civic reform associations, including settlement house work and urban government. Howe was the author of many books, and his text on the city became a classic, defining the progressives' interest in municipal reform and diagnosing the systemic problems facing urban America.

The literature on the city deals almost exclusively with the machinery, the personnel, the charter, the legal limitations and relations. Either this or the corruption of the officials. It is a literature of forms and functions. Its point of view is ethical, personal, political. The economic foundations have been passed by as incidental, as a subject of administrative detail. In like manner, municipal reform has been viewed as a thing of conventional morals, of improving the individual citizen, and stimulating his patriotism.

This volume is a reversal of method. It is an attempt at the Economic Interpretation of the City. It holds that the corruption, the indifference, the incompetence of the official and the apathy of the citizen, the disparity of wealth, the poverty, vice, crime, and disease, are due to causes economic and industrial. They are traceable to our Institutions, rather than to the depravity of human nature. Their correction is not a matter of education or of the penal code. It is a matter of industrial democracy. The incidental conditions are personal and ethical. Whether we adopt the personal or the economic interpretation will determine our attitude towards the problems of modern city life.

The convictions of this volume are the result of several years of actual political experience in the administration of the city of Cleveland, Ohio, as well as of personal study of municipal conditions in the leading cities of America and Great Britain. They represent a drift away from what I have termed the personnel, which is the orthodox view of politics. Instead of the city being controlled by the charter, the suffrage, or by purely political institutions, I have become convinced that it is the economic environment which creates and controls man's activities as well as his attitude of mind. This arouses his civic or his self interest; this underlies the poverty and the social problems with which the city is confronted. This explains contemporary politics. . . .

We do not question this motive in the saloon keeper, who organizes his precinct for a liberal Sunday. His politics are not ethical, they are due to self-interest. The same instinct is reflected, consciously or unconsciously, in the leaders of finance, the franchise-seekers, the banker, and the broker, the lawyer, and the

Frederic C. Howe, *The City: The Hope of Democracy* (New York: Charles Scribner's Sons, 1909), vii–xi.

Press; all are fearful of democracy, when democracy dares to believe in itself. We all know that economic self-interest determines the politics of the saloon. We are beginning to realize that the same self-interest is the politics of big business. This realization explains the awakening of democracy, which is taking place in city and state all over the land.

The same is true of the social problems of city life. The worst of the distressing poverty, as well as the irresponsible wealth, is traceable to economic institutions, to franchise privileges and unwise taxation; to laws which are open to correction as they were to creation. Conditions in the tenement are not ethical, not personal, they are traceable to laws of our own enactment. There is no other possible explanation of the fact that destitution is greatest where wealth is most abundant and industry most highly developed.

Almost without question we have accepted the other, the personal explanation of these things. Our programme has been to improve the individual man by education, by charity; not to improve the city by a change in our industrial policy. We have been bailing water with a sieve. The reformatory sends forth one offender only to find two others at the gate. The big business man may grow disgusted with his traffic in privilege, only to see another man less critical of means take his place. Only by exiling privileges shall we exile corruption. Only by offering opportunity to labor shall we close the doors of our hospitals, almshouses, and prisons. Only by taxing monopoly, will monopoly be forced to let go its hold on the resources of the earth and the means for a livelihood.

My own mind has passed through the evolution here suggested. Starting with the conviction that our evils were traceable to personal causes, to the absence of educational or property qualifications in our suffrage; to the activity of the spoilsman and the saloon keeper in alliance with the foreign voter; to the indifference of our best citizens to politics because it was politics, I have been forced by experience to a changed point of view, to a belief that democracy has not failed by its own inherent weakness so much as by virtue of the privileged interests which have taken possession of our institutions for their own enrichment. From a belief in a business man's government I have come to a belief in a people's government; from a conviction that we had too much democracy I have come to the conviction that we have too little democracy; from a study of history I have been forced to the realization that the progress of civilization has been a constant struggle of liberty against privilege; that wherever privilege has been dominant liberty has passed away and national life has decayed, and that our democratic forms are no more immune from the same dominion than were the nations of antiquity or of modern Europe. It is privilege of an industrial rather than a personal sort that has given birth to the boss, created the machine, and made of the party an agency for the control of our cities, states, and nation, rather than for the advancement of political ideals.

It is the economic motive that makes municipal reform a class struggle; on the one hand are the few who enjoy privileges which they are seeking to retain; on the other hand are millions awakening to the conviction of industrial democracy.

Two facts must be faced. First, the motive of those who control our politics and whose chief interest in the city lies in the direction of their own advantage. Second, the economic environment of those who are compelled to a lifelong struggle for the barest necessities of existence. It is only by facing these facts that the problems of the city may be solved and its possibilities achieved.

READING AND DISCUSSION QUESTIONS

1. Define the transformation Howe says he experienced in his understanding of the problems cities faced. How had reformers been accustomed to thinking about urban problems?

2. How might Howe's argument about the root of urban problems have influenced the reform methods progressives pursued? What connections can you make between Howe's ideology and some of the actions taken by progressive reformers and lawmakers in the first two decades of the twentieth century?

3. Consider the title of his book. What do you think he means by the "hope of democracy"? Is democracy a solution or a problem for urban reformers like Howe?

19-3 | Radical Reformer Appeals to Chicago's Voters

JOSEPHINE CONGER-KANEKO, *What a Socialist Alderman Would Do* (1914)

While progressive reformers like Frederic Howe lamented the economic disparities driving the wealthy and poorer classes apart, he did not go so far as Josephine Conger-Kaneko in calling for the collective ownership of factories, railroads, and utilities. Conger-Kaneko was active in socialist circles in the early twentieth century, emphasizing issues important to working women, which she promoted in *The Socialist Woman*, a small newspaper she edited based in Chicago. Her 1914 campaign speech for alderman of Chicago's Sixth Ward lays out her vision for an improved America.

I WAS BORN A DEMOCRAT. I was raised a Democrat. I am a Democrat today. I hope I shall die a DEMOCRAT.

And yet, in spite of the fact that I got my first lessons of real life in the office of a country Democratic newspaper, and in spite of the fact that I have followed the Bryan[2] band wagon, and sung in a Bryan glee club, I am today a dues-paying member of the Socialist party.

I am a Socialist because I believe that Socialism is more democratic than the Democratic party.

Josephine Conger-Kaneko, "What a Socialist Alderman Would Do," *The Coming Nation: A Magazine for the Creators of the New Social Order* 1, no. 5 (March 1914): 10, 13.

[2] **Bryan**: William Jennings Bryan represented the populist wing of the Democratic Party and ran unsuccessfully for president three times.

Soon after I left the little Democratic paper, upon which I had been working, I became associated editorially with the largest Socialist weekly in the world. Here I learned many things. It was like standing on a high hill and watching the activities of the peoples of a great nation. For we were connected with every nook and corner of this country, and in communication with numerous places outside. Formerly I had not believed in suffrage for women. I, a working woman, was not interested in using the ballot in my own behalf. My family were the dyed-in-the-wool Democrats of the old South, suh. They were of that next to impenetrable combination, Democratic from both principle and prejudice, and they stood right where our present Democratic Congress stands on the woman question.

Therefore, I realized for the first time, while working on this great Socialist journal, that women are a part of our social order, that they help to bear its burdens, and that they should share its privileges with the rest of mankind. I learned that I was not a consistent Socialist unless I was an active advocate of woman suffrage. So I joined a suffrage club. And thus I became, through Socialism, a suffragist.

I found further, that while the Democratic party stands for the welfare of the middle class under the present system, that the Socialist party stands for the welfare of all the people through its advocacy of the abolition of our present insane system of production and distribution of the necessities of life. For instance, our present system is driving the middle class out of existence, and forcing its members into the ranks of the working class, through the monopolization of the industries. The little business man, once respectable in his small line, today sees his business devoured by the great trust, while he is left to seek employment at so much a week wherever he can get it, and his children, instead of inheriting his business as was the process in former years, become employes of some big concern for the rest of their days. Then big business lowers wages to the lowest possible point, and raises the price of its goods to the highest possible point, and thus both the worker and the consumer fare badly.

Socialism would have the big industries owned by the people and controlled by the people for the benefit of the people, instead of the benefit of private owners, and thus would be the ally, or friend, of ALL the people.

These are, briefly, some of the things I found out about Socialism.

When I began to look into the woman movement of this country I found that the women were also looking out for the interests of the people, rather than the interests of the private corporations. The women did not get as far as the Socialists, and yet their demands were almost identical with what we call the immediate demands of the Socialist party.

The annual reports of the women's federated clubs are interesting commentaries on the ideals and outlook of the women. They show committees organized for the abolition of child labor; for the eight-hour day for working women; for the extension of play grounds; for sanitation; for good housing ordinances; for food inspection; pure milk; for mother's pensions; for juvenile courts; for reduction of the cost of living, and for many things that are essential to the welfare of the whole people. That the old political parties did not stand for these things is proven in the fact that women have had to fight for every reform they have gone after. . . .

In the South child labor is a splendid profit-maker for the factory owner, who, by the way, is often a Northerner. For this reason the legislators will not abolish child labor. They are owned body and soul by the big factory interests. The women, however, are not worrying about the interests of the factory owners. I believe the women would be willing to see the government own the factories if this would abolish child labor.

Socialism says the government should own the factories. And that it should pay men and women living wages, and keep the children in the schools where they belong.

The program of the Socialist party calls for the following, among other things:

"The collective ownership and democratic management of railroads, wire and wireless telegraphs and telephones, express services, steamboat lines and all other social means of transportation and communication and of large-scale industries.

"The extension of the public domain to include mines, quarries, oil wells, forests and water power.

"The further conservation and development of natural resources for the use and benefit of all the people.

"The collective ownership of land wherever practicable, and in such cases where such ownership is impracticable, the appropriation by taxation of the annual rental of all land held for speculation or exploitation." . . .

The Socialists would further establish—

"The immediate government relief of the unemployed by the extension of all useful public works. All persons employed on such works to be engaged directly by the government under a workday of not more than eight hours and at not less than the prevailing wages. The government also to establish employment bureaus, to lend money to states and municipalities without interest for the purpose of carrying on public works, and to take such other measures within its power as will lessen the widespread misery of the workers caused by the misrule of the capitalist class."

These are typical of the entire policy of the Socialist party.

What a Socialist woman alderman would do if elected to office in Chicago ought to be clear in your minds. . . . The Socialists stand for progress, the women stand for progress. As a Socialist I could not do one thing that would be against the interests of the masses of the people, as a woman I would not want to do any such thing. As a member of the city council from your ward it would be my duty and my pleasure to see that our streets are kept in good repair; that sanitary conditions exist throughout the ward; that the housing and other existing ordinances are enforced; that all new laws making for the betterment of the general comfort are enacted.

Co-operating with the entire council for the city at large, I would insist upon municipal ownership of public utilities wherever possible, such as telephone, gas and electric light, rail traffic, etc.; upon the inauguration of municipal markets where food and clothing could be sold direct from the producer to the consumer, thus cutting out the cost of middlemen; upon the erection of municipal lodging houses for working women and girls; upon a minimum wage for workers of both sexes; upon relief of the unemployed by the extension of useful public works; upon the extension of the playgrounds system to the public parks, and the opening of the schools for social centers. I would do what I could toward the alleviation and abolition of the white slave traffic by providing employment for working girls, and by paying both men and women a living wage, and opening respectable places of amusement for the city's great army of young people who today resort to the nickel shows without guardianship for their only pleasure. I believe that women in plain clothes, or ordinary dress, should be added to the police force as watchers in the amusement centers, to prevent young girls from being led into wrong paths.

It is impossible to point out in a brief talk like this what might be done for the betterment of a city like Chicago. But there is one fundamental point upon which we can agree — that is, we cannot expect much from a home in which children are hungry and ragged and dirty. Neither can we expect the best results from a city whose workers are underpaid, poorly fed, badly housed. Crime and ignorance and big police costs will inevitably result from such conditions. The wisest and safest plan is first to give our multitudes employment at a living wage; feed and clothe them at the lowest possible cost to themselves, and furnish them with wholesome, satisfying amusements. If, as a city we can do this, every other good thing will be added unto us. For then we shall have the REAL democracy.

I do not believe there is a woman here who can criticise this program, and if you are true to yourselves you will try and see that it is put into effect as soon as possible.

READING AND DISCUSSION QUESTIONS

1. Describe the appeal of socialism, compared to the Democratic Party, for someone like Conger-Kaneko. How did she distinguish between the two?

2. What connection did Conger-Kaneko draw between socialism and "the woman movement"? How did they support each other as reform movements?

19-4 | Supreme Court Ruling on Women's Rights

U.S. SUPREME COURT, *Muller v. Oregon* (1908)

In the Supreme Court's 1905 *Lochner v. New York* decision, the justices struck down a New York law that had capped at ten the number of hours a bakery employee could work each day. Citing the Fourteenth Amendment, the Court ruled that employees enjoyed a constitutionally protected "freedom of contract." The state's limit on work hours, the justices argued, violated a worker's rights. Three years later, the Court faced a similar issue, this time involving an Oregon law prohibiting women from working more than ten hours a day. In rendering its decision, the Court cited a legal brief submitted by Louis Brandeis, who presented social science evidence related to industrial labor conditions and women's health.

It is undoubtedly true, as more than once declared by this Court, that the general right to contract in relation to one's business is part of the liberty of the individual, protected by the Fourteenth Amendment to the Federal Constitution; yet it is equally well settled that this liberty is not absolute, and extending to all contracts, and that a State may, without conflicting with the provisions of the Fourteenth Amendment, restrict in many respects the individual's power of contract. . . .

That woman's physical structure and the performance of maternal functions place her at a disadvantage in the struggle for subsistence is obvious. This is especially true when the burdens of motherhood are upon her. Even when they are not, by abundant testimony of the medical fraternity, continuance for a long time on her feet at work, repeating this from day to day, tends to injurious effects upon the body, and, as healthy mothers are essential to vigorous offspring, the physical wellbeing of woman becomes an object of public interest and care in order to preserve the strength and vigor of the race.

Still again, history discloses the fact that woman has always been dependent upon man. He established his control at the outset by superior physical strength, and this control in various forms, with diminishing intensity, has continued to the present. As minors, though not to the same extent, she has been looked upon in the courts as needing especial care that her rights may be preserved. Education was long denied her, and while now the doors of the schoolroom are opened and her opportunities for acquiring knowledge are great, yet, even with that and the consequent increase of capacity for business affairs, it is still true that, in the struggle for subsistence, she is not an equal competitor with her brother. Though limitations upon personal and contractual rights may be removed by legislation, there is that in her disposition and habits of life which will operate against a full assertion of those rights. She will still be where some legislation to protect her seems necessary to secure a real equality of right. Doubtless there are individual exceptions, and there are many respects in which she has an advantage over him; but, looking at it from the viewpoint of the effort to maintain an

Muller v. Oregon 208 U.S. 412 (1908).

independent position in life, she is not upon an equality. Differentiated by these matters from the other sex, she is properly placed in a class by herself, and legislation designed for her protection may be sustained even when like legislation is not necessary for men, and could not be sustained. It is impossible to close one's eyes to the fact that she still looks to her brother, and depends upon him. Even though all restrictions on political, personal, and contractual rights were taken away, and she stood, so far as statutes are concerned, upon an absolutely equal plane with him, it would still be true that she is so constituted that she will rest upon and look to him for protection; that her physical structure and a proper discharge of her maternal functions — having in view not merely her own health, but the wellbeing of the race — justify legislation to protect her from the greed, as well as the passion, of man. The limitations which this statute places upon her contractual powers, upon her right to agree with her employer as to the time she shall labor, are not imposed solely for her benefit, but also largely for the benefit of all. Many words cannot make this plainer. The two sexes differ in structure of body, in the functions to be performed by each, in the amount of physical strength, in the capacity for long-continued labor, particularly when done standing, the influence of vigorous health upon the future wellbeing of the race, the self-reliance which enables one to assert full rights, and in the capacity to maintain the struggle for subsistence. This difference justifies a difference in legislation, and upholds that which is designed to compensate for some of the burdens which rest upon her. . . .

For these reasons, and without questioning in any respect the decision in *Lochner v. New York*, we are of the opinion that it cannot be adjudged that the act in question is in conflict with the Federal Constitution so far as it respects the work of a female in a laundry, and the judgment of the Supreme Court of Oregon is affirmed.

READING AND DISCUSSION QUESTIONS

1. How did the Supreme Court rule in *Muller v. Oregon*? How does the Court's decision differ from its ruling in *Lochner v. New York*?

2. To what extent did the justices' understanding of gender shape the Court's ruling?

3. Was this decision a victory for women?

19-5 | Women Take Up Progressive-Era Environmentalism

MINNIE MOORE WILSON, *Bird Preservation* (1912)

In George Perkins Marsh's 1864 book *Man and Nature* he argues, "All Nature is linked together by invisible bonds and every organic creature, however low, however feeble, however dependent, is necessary to the well-being of some other among the myriad forms of life." In the decades following, many reformers embraced Marsh's view concerning the interdependency of humankind and the natural world. Such thinking inspired preservationists who fought to protect wild landscapes like Yellowstone National Park and the Adirondacks. It also shaped conservationists, like Gifford Pinchot and Theodore Roosevelt who worked to safeguard natural resources. Minnie Moore Wilson's 1912 *Forest and Stream* article incorporates both a preservationist and conservationist approach to reform. Here, she advocates for the preservation of birds, some species of which were endangered. Fashionable women had for decades outfitted themselves in couture hats festooned with the feathers of exotic birds. The demand for feathers led to the slaughter of thousands of birds and roused some women, like Wilson, to act. Their advocacy, in a period before ratification of women's suffrage, led to state and federal legislation, including the Weeks-McLean Act (1913) and the subsequent Migratory Bird Treaty Act (1918) that protected migrating bird species.

It is a bright and glorious morning. The scene is in a Florida yard. Mockingbirds are singing with all the abandon of happiness; redbirds of the most scarlet hue feed complacently along with the dove, breakfasting on the seeds of the now dying grass. Laybirds in numbers herald their presence as they beg for crumbs. Central in the scene are two large white birds, the great white heron or American egret—all happy and contented because man with his gun is not in pursuit.

These egrets, among the shyest of wild birds, are found in domestication to be as gentle as chickens. The more one studies these creatures, less God-like than ourselves, the more one feels an indulgent care and kindly sympathy for them. If the American women could know the wild bird, its native confidence in man and how quickly it responds to kindness, saying nothing of its economic value, surely the wearing of feathers and wings would soon be relegated to the past. . . .

As we picture these beautiful birds watching over their nestlings with as much gentleness as the human parents, who shall say God will not call to account every plume hunter and every woman who wears the aigrette[3] and wings of the wild bird? The slaughter of the wild bird life of the world is almost too sad to dwell upon, and yet to illustrate truths we must see the picture. What the guillotine was to the French nobles during the bloody revolution, the millinery trade[4] is to the birds of to-day. Slaughter, starving nestlings and blood-stained aigrettes belong to the tragic picture. The parental instinct of the birds is so strong that they will not leave their young, no matter what the danger, a great convenience to the hunter, for it permits him to shoot almost every bird

---

Minnie Moore Wilson, "Bird Preservation," *Forest and Stream*, 78 (April 27, 1912): 531–532.

[3] **Aigrette:** an ornamental headdress made with feathers of a heron.

[4] **Millinery trade:** business of making and selling women's hats.

in the colony, and yet this tragic epoch of the nation's history must be laid at the door of woman. Woman, tender, true and a heroine in time of distress and disaster, who is ever in the front ranks for the prevention of cruelty to children and animals, and whose love for humanity has made civilized America the great nation that it is. No chain is stronger than its weakest link. To what then must we ascribe the barbarous slaughter of the exquisite bird life of the world? Woman's weak point must be vanity. Rich women of the world set the fashion and poor women foolishly follow. Unfortunately, it is something that is expensive and hard to acquire that the wealthy seek after. To their credit be it said that many leaders of fashion would like to be something better than parasites and idlers if they could, and why not help protect the birds?

If all the well-to-do women in America would absolutely stop wearing feathers in their hats to-morrow, if they would realize the cruel, brutal fashion of tearing the wings from living birds for the purpose of putting on to hats to stick up into the air like a foolish looking Valkyrie,[5] they certainly could not be happy at the thought that the wings on their hates may mean that half a dozen young birds starved to death in their nests. Another thought: These dust and germ-collecting feathers on the heads of women are far from a standard of refined cleanliness.

What fashionable leader will start the idea of hats without feathers? Aside from the humanity and the fact that the earth suffers because the birds are killed off by millions, it rests with leaders of fashion to bring fame to themselves and glory to their country and to make the world kinder and life sacred to our feathered kin. Just as human life would be impossible without earth, air and water, so it would be impossible without birds. These flitting beautiful creatures are the patrols of the earth, air and water, and unlike the policeman on his beat they never lag and are on duty day and night.

Fighting for the preservation of the gentle, beautiful and helpless feathered creatures is the work of the great Audubon Societies, and equally is the National Government doing all in its power to arrest the extermination of the valuable plumage birds of America. The feminine devotee of fashion has for years been demanding the delicate aigrette from the snowy heron. The milliner has supplied it, and man has broken the law, but at last a stronger power has come that will save the lives of the beautiful egrets in the future, and this is the terrible calumny.[6] "Out of style," and for this reason:

When the New York milliners were compelled to close out every single egret feather, because of the New York law prohibiting their sale of possession, then it was that the shop girls and chambermaids were able to purchase for a song what they had been envying my lady of Fifth avenue so many years, until now the well dressed woman or the fashion dealer would scorn the one-time $30 to $50 egret plumes because Mary, the chambermaid, may be seen on a Sunday

---

[5] **Valkyrie**: from Norse mythology, a female figure sent to the battlefield by the god Odin to choose from among the fallen those who deserved a place in Valhalla, a place of honor like heaven.

[6] **Calumny**: a malicious comment intended to cause harm to a person's reputation.

afternoon flaunting her enormous egret plumes, which she no doubt bought for a song, and my lady who rides in her liveried Victoria much prefers a feather plucked from the crowing chanticleer of the farmer's back yard.

Fashion has a strong hold on us all. Having watched the waving aigrettes on the cheap hats of New York mads all summer, on reaching Florida the first hat observed was at a fashionable hotel and worn by a well-gowned woman, but it looked passé; enough aigrettes were heaped on it to represent the lives of half a dozen beautiful birds, bought, no doubt, at a marked-down sale. Fashion follows a decree very quickly, and before spring the death warrant of the beautiful Florida heron will be stayed, for the fashionable woman will not wear bargain counter goods, and as each woman follows the other blindly, like sheep jumping one after the other into the field where the wolves are, the day of the aigrette is over, but this will apply only to the silken plume of the heron. Wings and birds on hats will continue until fashion puts her ban on them; that fashion must be declared by woman strong in financial and social circles. . . .

Birds of economic and agricultural value are each year getting better known, and this through our Audubon and Government experts. When we reflect that the annual loss through insect and rodent ravages is now estimated to be $800,000,000 in the United States alone, and this loss is because of the extinction of bird life, is it not time that the women of America should step in and assist the authorities in stopping one of the most serious forms of agricultural waste and also one of the worst barbarities.

At present a strong movement is uppermost to preserve those effectual little farm hands, robin redbreast and the turtle doves. They ask no wages and do much toward saving the Southern crops. Especially is their value untold to the cotton belt. These wild birds, flying South each fall to escape the cold, have been killed by countless thousands by negroes and other hunters. The wild dove, which lives largely upon seeds, destroys more weeds than the quickest human paid worker the farmer can employ, and if the wholesale slaughter is not stopped, this bird, like the wild pigeon, will become extinct and the loss to the South will be beyond computation. Florida with her statute books rich in decrees still permits the senseless slaughter of these valuable birds. When will a Florida campaign be inaugurated that will enforce laws, and not only protect our own bird life, but feel it a bounden duty to give protection to the visitors from Northern States?

READING AND DISCUSSION QUESTIONS

1. What arguments does Wilson use in making the case for bird preservation? Why is this reform important to her?

2. Whom do you think Wilson was trying to reach with this article in *Forest and Stream* magazine? How does consideration of audience shape an author's approach?

3. What can we learn about society's affluent women from Wilson's article? How does she depict the relationship between different classes of women?

19-6 | Negro Problem Solved Through Education of Leadership Class

W. E. B. DU BOIS, *The Talented Tenth* (1903)

Progressives invested enormous faith in education as a lever for social progress, an idea not lost on the leading black intellectual of the early twentieth century, W. E. B. Du Bois. Born and raised in New England, Du Bois attended Fisk University (a historically black college in Nashville), then Harvard, where in 1895 he became the first African American to earn the PhD degree. As a sociologist, he was active in black civil rights and cofounded the National Association for the Advancement of Colored People (NAACP) in 1909. Du Bois challenged Booker T. Washington's approach to advancing black interests in his "Talented Tenth" essay published in 1903.

The Negro race, like all races, is going to be saved by its exceptional men. The problem of education, then, among Negroes must first of all deal with the Talented Tenth; it is the problem of developing the Best of this race that they may guide the Mass away from the contamination and death of the Worst, in their own and other races.

From the very first it has been the educated and intelligent of the Negro people that have led and elevated the mass, and the sole obstacles that nullified and retarded their efforts were slavery and race prejudice; for what is slavery but the legalized survival of the unfit and the nullification of the work of natural internal leadership? Negro leadership, therefore, sought from the first to rid the race of this awful incubus that it might make way for natural selection and the survival of the fittest. . . .

[F]or three long centuries this people lynched Negroes who dared to be brave, raped black women who dared to be virtuous, crushed dark-hued youth who dared to be ambitious, and encouraged and made to flourish servility and lewdness and apathy. But not even this was able to crush all manhood and chastity and aspiration from black folk. A saving remnant continually survives and persists, continually aspires, continually shows itself in thrift and ability and character. Exceptional it is to be sure, but this is its chiefest promise; it shows the capability of Negro blood, the promise of black men. . . .

How then shall the leaders of a struggling people be trained and the hands of the risen few strengthened? There can be but one answer: The best and most capable of their youth must be schooled in the colleges and universities of the land. . . .

Where ought they to have begun to build? At the bottom, of course, quibbles the mole with his eyes in the earth. Aye! truly at the bottom, at the very bottom; at the bottom of knowledge, down in the very depths of knowledge there where

W. E. B. Du Bois, "The Talented Tenth," in *The Negro Problem: A Series of Articles by Representative American Negroes of To-Day*, contributions by Booker T. Washington, Principal of Tuskegee Institute, W. E. Burghardt Du Bois, Paul Laurence Dunbar, Charles W. Chestnutt, and others (New York: James Pott & Company, 1903), 33–35, 43–48, 57–63, 73–75.

the roots of justice strike into the lowest soil of Truth. And so they did begin; they founded colleges, and up from the colleges shot normal schools, and out from the normal schools went teachers, and around the normal teachers clustered other teachers to teach the public schools; the college trained in Greek and Latin and mathematics, 2,000 men; and these men trained full 50,000 others in morals and manners, and they in turn taught thrift and the alphabet to nine millions of men, who to-day hold $300,000,000 of property. It was a miracle — the most wonderful peace-battle of the 19th century, and yet to-day men smile at it, and in fine superiority tell us that it was all a strange mistake; that a proper way to found a system of education is first to gather the children and buy them spelling books and hoes; afterward men may look about for teachers, if haply they may find them; or again they would teach men Work, but as for Life — why, what has Work to do with Life, they ask vacantly. . . .

I would not deny, or for a moment seem to deny, the paramount necessity of teaching the Negro to work, and to work steadily and skillfully; or seem to depreciate in the slightest degree the important part industrial schools must play in the accomplishment of these ends, but I *do* say, and insist upon it, that it is industrialism drunk with its vision of success, to imagine that its own work can be accomplished without providing for the training of broadly cultured men and women to teach its own teachers, and to teach the teachers of the public schools. . . .

I am an earnest advocate of manual training and trade teaching for black boys, and for white boys, too. I believe that next to the founding of Negro colleges the most valuable addition to Negro education since the war, has been industrial training for black boys. Nevertheless, I insist that the object of all true education is not to make men carpenters, it is to make carpenters men. . . .

Men of America, the problem is plain before you. Here is a race transplanted through the criminal foolishness of your fathers. Whether you like it or not the millions are here, and here they will remain. If you do not lift them up, they will pull you down. Education and work are the levers to uplift a people. Work alone will not do it unless inspired by the right ideals and guided by intelligence. Education must not simply teach work — it must teach Life. The Talented Tenth of the Negro race must be made leaders of thought and missionaries of culture among their people. No others can do this work and Negro colleges must train men for it. The Negro race, like all other races, is going to be saved by its exceptional men.

READING AND DISCUSSION QUESTIONS

1. How radical do you think readers in 1903 considered Du Bois's reform message? What from his own experiences or from the recent history of his time gave him confidence in his solution to the "Negro problem"?

2. Examine Du Bois's argument as a reflection of the historical context of progressivism and race relations in the early twentieth century. Are his ideas relevant to the discussion of race relations today? Explain.

■ COMPARATIVE QUESTIONS ■

1. Compare populism, progressivism, and socialism by identifying similarities in the ways they diagnosed society's problems and the reforms they championed. In what ways did their ideologies differ?

2. What change in the form and function of government did reformers in this period advocate? How did their ideas of government's proper role differ from earlier conceptions of government's power and responsibilities?

3. Assess populism by comparing its reforms (Document 19-1) with the views expressed by Terence Powderly and the Knights of Labor (Document 16-2). What common cause do you see between them? Why do you think both failed as reform movements?

4. To what extent did questions of race and ethnicity help or hurt reform movements? Compare W. E. B. Du Bois (Document 19-6) with Antanas Kaztauskis (Document 16-3), Booker T. Washington (Document 17-5), Marie Ganz (Document 18-3), and the account of the Negro parade (Document 18-4).

5. Compare Du Bois's approach to reform for African Americans (Document 19-6) to the proposal Booker T. Washington advanced in his Atlanta speech (Document 17-5). How might you explain their different emphases? What role did class and geography play in shaping their divergent ideas?

Industrializing America: Upheavals and Experiments

1877–1917

CHAPTER 16
Industrial America: Corporations and Conflicts, 1877–1911

CHAPTER 17
Making Modern American Culture, 1880–1917

CHAPTER 18
"Civilization's Inferno": The Rise and Reform of Industrial Cities, 1880–1917

CHAPTER 19
Whose Government? Politics, Populists, and Progressives, 1880–1917

A critic for the *New York Times* warned readers attending the 1913 Armory Show of international modern art that they would be entering "a stark region of abstractions" with paintings "hideous to our unaccustomed eyes" and "revolting in their inhumanity." The bold experimentation that Cubists and postimpressionists showcased in 1913 rejected prevailing cultural norms of the nineteenth century, overturning convention in favor of "modern" cultural values. The clash of realism with modern art symbolized but one cultural revolution witnessed during these years. The conflicting ideas, beliefs, and creative expressions of the period affected not only art and literature but also broader philosophical, moral, and scientific ideas touching on gender, race, and ethnicity. Shaped by the growing influence of Charles Darwin's theory of natural selection, philosophers and social scientists adapted his insights related to biology and the natural world to promote a sociology that exalted struggle as the means to achieve progress. This strict and exacting philosophy rewarded the victor with assurances of his superiority while justifying the fate of those at the bottom. The period's changing cultural values defined the era, as individuals sought to understand the implications both for themselves and for society as a whole. The sources in this chapter are united by their participation in a turn-of-the-century debate over the clash between two worldviews: Victorianism and modernism. In these sources, we see some people holding on to traditional ideas while others reject old ways for new ones. Together, they show the breadth of this debate and the stakes that made it meaningful to so many.

P6-1 | Social Darwinist Explains Relationship Between Classes

WILLIAM GRAHAM SUMNER, *What Social Classes Owe to Each Other* (1883)

William Graham Sumner, Yale sociologist and devotee of English philosopher Herbert Spencer, embraced Social Darwinism as a philosophy that structured and framed his understanding of society's development and progress over time. Inspired by Charles Darwin's theories of natural selection, Sumner spoke for many latter-nineteenth-century champions of laissez-faire capitalism, who saw the race of life as a struggle that rewarded only those "fittest" to survive. When considering the question of what the social classes owed to one another, the short answer, according to Sumner, was nothing.

"The poor," "the weak," "the laborers," are expressions which are used as if they had exact and well-understood definition. Discussions are made to bear upon the assumed rights, wrongs, and misfortunes of certain social classes; and all public speaking and writing consists, in a large measure, of the discussion of general plans for meeting the wishes of classes of people who have not been able to satisfy their own desires. These classes are sometimes discontented, and sometimes not. Sometimes they do not know that anything is amiss with them until the "friends of humanity" come to them with offers of aid. Sometimes they are discontented and envious. They do not take their achievements as a fair measure of their rights. They do not blame themselves or their parents for their lot, as compared with that of other people. Sometimes they claim that they have a right to everything of which they feel the need for their happiness on earth. To make such a claim against God or Nature would, of course, be only to say that we claim a right to live on earth if we can. But God and Nature have ordained the chances and conditions of life on

---

William Graham Sumner, *What Social Classes Owe to Each Other* (New York and London: Harper & Brothers Publishers, 1883), 13–16, 21–24.

earth once for all. The case cannot be reopened. We cannot get a revision of the laws of human life. We are absolutely shut up to the need and duty, if we would learn how to live happily, of investigating the laws of Nature, and deducing the rules of right living in the world as it is. These are very wearisome and commonplace tasks. They consist in labor and self-denial repeated over and over again in learning and doing. When the people whose claims we are considering are told to apply themselves to these tasks they become irritated and feel almost insulted. They formulate their claims as rights against society—that is, against some other men. In their view they have a right, not only to pursue happiness, but to get it; and if they fail to get it, they think they have a claim to the aid of other men—that is, to the labor and self-denial of other men—to get it for them. They find orators and poets who tell them that they have grievances, so long as they have unsatisfied desires.

Now, if there are groups of people who have a claim to other people's labor and self-denial, and if there are other people whose labor and self-denial are liable to be claimed by the first groups, then there certainly are "classes," and classes of the oldest and most vicious type. For a man who can command another man's labor and self-denial for the support of his own existence is a privileged person of the highest species conceivable on earth. Princes and paupers meet on this plane, and no other men are on it at all. On the other hand, a man whose labor and self-denial may be diverted from his maintenance to that of some other man is not a free man, and approaches more or less toward the position of a slave. Therefore we shall find that, in all the notions which we are to discuss, this elementary contradiction, that there are classes and that there are not classes, will produce repeated confusion and absurdity. We shall find that, in our efforts to eliminate the old vices of class government, we are impeded and defeated by new products of the worst class theory. We shall find that all the schemes for producing equality and obliterating the organization of society produce a new differentiation based on the worst possible distinction—the right to claim and the duty to give one man's effort for another man's satisfaction. We shall find that every effort to realize equality necessitates a sacrifice of liberty. . . .

The humanitarians, philanthropists, and reformers, looking at the facts of life as they present themselves, find enough which is sad and unpromising in the condition of many members of society. They see wealth and poverty side by side. They note great inequality of social position and social chances. They eagerly set about the attempt to account for what they see, and to devise schemes for remedying what they do not like. In their eagerness to recommend the less fortunate classes to pity and consideration they forget all about the rights of other classes; they gloss over all the faults of the classes in question, and they exaggerate their misfortunes and their virtues. They invent new theories of property, distorting rights and perpetrating injustice, as any one is sure to do who sets about the re-adjustment of social relations with the interests of one group distinctly before his mind, and the interests of all other groups thrown into the background. When I have read certain of these discussions I have thought that it must be quite disreputable to be respectable, quite dishonest to own property, quite unjust to go one's own way and earn one's own living, and that the only really admirable person was the good-for-nothing. The man who by his own effort raises himself above poverty appears, in these discussions, to be of no account. The man who has done nothing to raise himself above poverty finds that the social doctors flock about him, bringing the capital which they have collected from the other class, and promising him the aid of the State to give him what the other had to work for. In all these schemes and projects the organized intervention of society through the State is either planned or hoped for, and the State is thus made to become the protector and guardian of certain classes. The agents who are to direct the State action are, of course, the reformers and philanthropists. Their schemes, therefore, may always be reduced to this type—that A and B decide what C shall do for D. It will be interesting to inquire, at a later period of our discussion, who C is, and what the effect is upon him of all these arrangements. In all the discussions attention is concentrated on A and B, the noble social reformers, and on D, the "poor man." I call C the Forgotten Man, because I have never seen that any notice was taken of him in any of the discussions. When we have disposed of A, B, and D we can better appreciate the case of C, and I think that we shall find that he deserves our attention, for the worth of his character and the magnitude of his unmerited burdens. Here it may suffice to observe that, on the theories of the social philosophers to whom I have referred, we should get a new maxim of judicious living: Poverty is the best policy. If you get wealth, you will have to support other people; if you do not get wealth, it will be the duty of other people to support you.

READING AND DISCUSSION QUESTIONS

1. How were Sumner's philosophical ideas of Social Darwinism used to defend the dominant economic and social order of the latter nineteenth century?

2. Who is Sumner targeting for criticism as a "school of writers" heralding "the coming duty and the coming woe"? How might these people have responded to Sumner's analysis of the relationship between social classes?

P6-2 | Promoting the Social Gospel

WALTER RAUSCHENBUSCH, *Christianity and the Social Crisis* (1907)

As a New York City minister during the late nineteenth century, Rauschenbusch witnessed the consequences on the poor of America's industrialization. Economic uncertainties, low wages, poor living conditions, unsafe work environments, and a prevailing ideology favoring limited government intervention regulating the market produced hardships Rauschenbusch hoped to remedy through a revitalized Christian mission. The Social Gospel Movement called on the Christian Church to address the social crisis by making the kingdom of God a reality for the working poor.

Walter Rauschenbusch, *Christianity and the Social Crisis* (New York: The Macmillan Company, 1907), 350–352, 369–372, 375, 414.

We are assured that the poor are poor through their own fault; that rent and profits are the just dues of foresight and ability; that the immigrants are the cause of corruption in our city politics; that we cannot compete with foreign countries unless our working class will descend to the wages paid abroad. These are all very plausible assertions, but they are lies dressed up in truth.

But in the main these misleading theories are the complacent self-deception of those who profit by present conditions and are loath to believe that their life is working harm.

The greatest contribution which any man can make to the social movement is the contribution of a regenerated personality, of a will which sets justice above policy and profit, and of an intellect emancipated from falsehood. Such a man will in some measure incarnate the principles of a higher social order in his attitude to all questions and in all his relations to men, and will be a well-spring of regenerating influences.

The spiritual force of Christianity should be turned against the materialism and mammonism of our industrial and social order.

If a man sacrifices his human dignity and self-respect to increase his income, or stunts his intellectual growth and his human affections to swell his bank account, he is to that extent serving mammon and denying God. Likewise if he uses up and injures the life of his fellow-men to make money for himself, he serves mammon and denies God. But our industrial order does both. It makes property the end, and man the means to produce it.

"Life is more than food and raiment." More, too, than the apparatus which makes food and raiment. What is all the machinery of our industrial organization worth if it does not make human life healthful and happy? But is it doing that? Men are first of all men, folks, members of our human family. To view them first of all as labor force is civilized barbarism. It is the attitude of the exploiter. Yet unconsciously we have all been taught to take that attitude and talk of men as if they were horse-powers or volts. Our commercialism has tainted our sense of fundamental human verities and values. We measure our national prosperity by pig-iron and steel instead of by the welfare of the people.

Our scientific political economy has long been an oracle of the false god. It has taught us to approach economic questions from the point of view of goods and not of man. It tells us how wealth is produced and divided and consumed by man, and not how man's life and development can best be fostered by material wealth.

It is the function of religion to teach the individual to value his soul more than his body, and his moral integrity more than his income. In the same way it is the function of religion to teach society to value human life more than property, and to value property only in so far as it forms the material basis for the higher development of human life. This is not only Christian but prudent.

It is entirely feasible for the Church to mitigate the social hardships of the working classes by lending force to humane customs. Its help would make the Saturday half holiday in summer practicable. It could ease the strain of the

Christmas shopping season. It could secure seats and rest rooms for the girls in the department stores. It could counteract the tendency of tenement owners to crowd the people. It could encourage employers in making a place for their aged employees and discourage the early exploitation of children. A single frank and prayerful discussion of one of these questions in a social meeting of the church or its societies would create more social morality and good custom than many columns in the newspapers. Such an activity would not solve the fundamental questions of capitalism, but it would ease the pressure a little and would save the people from deterioration, while the social movement is moving toward the larger solution.

The working class, which is now engaged in its upward movement, is struggling to secure better conditions of life, an assured status for its class organizations, and ultimately the ownership of the means of production. Its success in the last great aim would mean the closing of the gap which now divides industrial society and the establishment of industry on the principle of solidarity and the method of coöperation. Christianity should enter into a working alliance with this rising class, and by its mediation secure the victory of these principles by a gradual equalization of social opportunity and power.

READING AND DISCUSSION QUESTIONS

1. What mission does Rauschenbusch define for the church in the early twentieth century? Can you infer any criticism of the existing church from his comments?

2. How does Rauschenbusch's Social Gospel mission reflect a clash of values during the turn of the century? What segments of society might have resisted Rauschenbusch's call?

P6-3 | The New Woman Challenges the Social Order

UNDERWOOD & UNDERWOOD, *The New Woman — Wash Day* (1901)

Gender ideals were in flux at the start of the twentieth century. Conventional attitudes that had defined domesticity as the proper sphere of action for respectable women faced pushback from feminists who championed the "New Woman." The New Woman pushed boundaries. She challenged stereotypes by pursuing higher education and professional careers. She discarded the corset and other literal and metaphorical restraints. She was politically engaged. For many women, the New Woman ideal was the culmination of a century of reform activity. For other more conservative women and many males, the New Woman was a threat to society's conventional gender norms. Satire was one way this backlash against the New Woman took form. In the source reproduced here, this stereoview photograph (which gave viewers the illusion of depth in a photograph) lampooned the New Woman and the gender conflict she caused. Here the man is doing the laundry while the woman, dressed in men's clothing, strikes a decidedly masculine pose.

The New Woman — Wash Day.
Copyright 1901 by Underwood & Underwood

Underwood & Underwood/Library of Congress

READING AND DISCUSSION QUESTIONS

1. Examine the elements within this photograph, including the clothes worn by the man and woman, their poses, and the bicycle in the background. What role does each of these details play in the photographer's satire?

2. How is the photographer feminizing the man and masculinizing the woman? What gender norms are being challenged here?

3. Why do you think this photograph was produced and sold? What market do you think the Underwood & Underwood Company, which produced a series of these types of images, was attempting to reach?

P6-4 | Anthropologist Undermines Racial Stereotypes
FRANZ BOAS, *The Mind of Primitive Man* (1911)

Through most of the nineteenth century, "culture" was used to denote high-minded art, literature, and music, but with the rise of university-based social sciences, anthropologists like Franz Boas redefined the term to mean the values, beliefs, and attitudes that shaped people's worldview and influenced their behavior and conduct. Boas chaired the Department of Anthropology at Columbia University after stints working at the Field Museum in Chicago and the American Museum of Natural History in New York, where his controversial approach to anthropology challenged existing ideas of racial determinism.

Until the first decade of our century the opinion that race determines culture had been, in Europe at least, rather a subject of speculation of amateur historians and sociologists than a foundation of public policy. Since that time it has spread among the masses. Slogans like "blood is thicker than water," are expressions of its new emotional appeal. The earlier concept of nationality has been given a new meaning by identifying nationality with racial unity and by assuming that national characteristics are due to racial descent. It is particularly interesting to note that in the anti-Semitic movement in Germany of the time of 1880 it was not the Jew as a member of an alien race who was subject to attack, but the Jew who was not assimilated to German national life. The present policy of Germany is based on an entirely different foundation, for every person is supposed to have a definite, unalterable character according to his racial descent and this determines his political and social status. The conditions are quite analogous to the status assigned to the Negro at an earlier period, when licentiousness, shiftless laziness, lack of initiative were considered as racially determined, unescapable qualities of every Negro. It is a curious spectacle to see that serious scientists, wherever free to express themselves, have on the whole been drifting away from the opinion that race determines mental status, excepting however those biologists who have no appreciation of social factors because they are captivated by the apparent hereditary determinism of morphological forms, while among the uninformed public to which unfortunately a number of powerful European politicians belong, race prejudice has been making and is still making unchecked progress. I believe it would be an error to assume that we are free of this tendency: if nothing else the restrictions imposed upon members of certain "races," abridging their right to own real estate, to tenancy in apartment houses, membership of clubs, to their right to visit hotels and summer resorts, to admission to schools and colleges shows at least that there is no abatement of old prejudices directed against Negroes, Jews, Russians, Armenians or whatever they may be. The excuse that these exclusions are compelled by economic considerations, or by the fear of driving

Franz Boas, *The Mind of Primitive Man* (New York: The Macmillan Company, 1911; revised edition, 1938), 253–254, 268–272.

away from schools or colleges other social groups, is merely an acknowledgment of a widespread attitude. . . .

The Negro problem as it presents itself in the United States is from a biological viewpoint not essentially different from those just discussed. We have found that no proof of an inferiority of the Negro type could be given, except that it seemed barely possible that perhaps the race would not produce quite so many men of highest genius as other races, while there was nothing at all that could be interpreted as suggesting any material difference in the mental capacity of the bulk of the Negro population as compared with the bulk of the White population. There will undoubtedly be endless numbers of men and women who will be able to outrun their White competitors, and who will do better than the defectives whom we permit to drag down and retard the healthy children of our public schools.

Ethnological observation does not countenance the view that the traits observed among our poorest Negro population are in any sense racially determined. A survey of African tribes exhibits to our view cultural achievements of no mean order. To those unfamiliar with the products of native African art and industry, a walk through one of the large museums of Europe would be a revelation. Few of our American museums have made collections that exhibit this subject in any way worthily. The blacksmith, the wood carver, the weaver, the potter these all produce ware original in form, executed with great care, and exhibiting that love of labor, and interest in the results of work, which are apparently so often lacking among the Negroes in our American surroundings. . . . The power of organization as illustrated in the government of native states is of no mean order, and when wielded by men of great personality has led to the foundation of extended empires. All the different kinds of activities that we consider valuable in the citizens of our country may be found in aboriginal Africa. Neither is the wisdom of the philosopher absent. A perusal of any of the collections of African proverbs that have been published will demonstrate the homely practical philosophy of the Negro, which is often proof of sound feeling and judgment.

It would be out of place to enlarge on this subject, because the essential point that anthropology can contribute to the practical discussion of the adaptability of the Negro is a decision of the question how far the undesirable traits that are at present undoubtedly found in our Negro population are due to racial traits, and how far they are due to social surroundings for which we are responsible. To this question anthropology can give the decided answer that the traits of African culture as observed in the aboriginal home of the Negro are those of a healthy primitive people, with a considerable degree of personal initiative, with a talent for organization, with imaginative power, with technical skill and thrift. Neither is a warlike spirit absent in the race, as is proved by the mighty conquerors who overthrew states and founded new empires, and by the courage of the armies that follow the bidding of their leaders. . . .

There is . . . no evidence whatever that would stigmatize the Negro as of weaker build, or as subject to inclinations and powers that are opposed to our social organization. An unbiased estimate of the anthropological evidence so far brought forward does not permit us to countenance the belief in a racial inferiority which would unfit an individual of the Negro race to take his part in modern civilization. We do not know of any demand made on the human body or mind in modern life that anatomical or ethnological evidence would prove to be beyond his powers.

The traits of the American Negro are adequately explained on the basis of his history and social status. The tearing-away from the African soil and the consequent complete loss of the old standards of life, which were replaced by the dependency of slavery and by all it entailed, followed by a period of disorganization and by a severe economic struggle against heavy odds, are sufficient to explain the inferiority of the status of the race, without falling back upon the theory of hereditary inferiority.

In short, there is every reason to believe that the Negro when given facility and opportunity, will be perfectly able to fulfill the duties of citizenship as well as his White neighbor. . . .

Our tendency to evaluate an individual according to the picture that we form of the class to which we assign him, although he may not feel any inner connection with that class, is a survival of primitive forms of thought. The characteristics of the members of the class are highly variable and the type that we construct from the most frequent characteristics supposed to belong to the class is never more than an abstraction hardly ever realized in a single individual, often not even a result of observation, but an often heard tradition that determines our judgment.

Freedom of judgment can be attained only when we learn to estimate an individual according to his own ability and character. Then we shall find, if we were to select the best of mankind, that all races and all nationalities would be represented. Then we shall treasure and cultivate the variety of forms that human thought and activity has taken, and abhor, as leading to complete stagnation, all attempts to impress one pattern of thought upon whole nations or even upon the whole world.

READING AND DISCUSSION QUESTIONS

1. In what way did Boas's understanding of race and culture challenge prevailing ideas that had defined Anglo-Saxon superiority and "Negro" inferiority? What fundamental assumption about race did his anthropological work overturn?

2. Examine the historical context of turn-of-the-century America to understand anthropology's impact on the politics of race and ethnicity. How do the issues raised in this source relate to American debates over immigration and the "Negro problem" from this period?

P6-5 | Modernism and Its Critics

MARCEL DUCHAMP, *Nude Descending a Staircase* (1912), and J. F. GRISWOLD, *The Rude Descending a Staircase (Rush Hour at the Subway)* (1913)

The 1913 Armory Show held at the Sixty-Ninth Street Armory building in New York City introduced Americans to modern art, featuring European postimpressionist and Cubist painters like Paul Cézanne, Henri Matisse, and Marcel Duchamp. These canvases challenged the more academic art Americans were accustomed to seeing by eschewing realism for a different aesthetic, one self-consciously abstract. Cubists, for instance, reduced nature to its elemental forms, as seen in Duchamp's scandalous painting *Nude Descending a Staircase*. Many critics, like J. F. Griswold, the cartoonist who drew the parody *The Rude Descending a Staircase (Rush Hour at the Subway)*, dismissed much of the avant-garde as amateurish, but others caught the significance of the Armory Show as a cultural thunderclap.

Succession Marcel Duchamp/ADAGP, Paris/Artists Rights Society (ARS), New York 2017. The Philadelphia Museum of Art/Art Resource, NY

THE EVENING SUN, THURSDAY, MARCH 20, 1913.

SEEING NEW YORK WITH A CUBIST

The Rude Descending a Staircase
(Rush Hour at the Subway)

Digital Image ©The Museum of Modern Art/Licensed
by SCALA/Art Resource, NY

READING AND DISCUSSION QUESTIONS

1. What does Duchamp's abstract painting suggest about the shift in aesthetic values at the turn of the century? What can you infer from Griswold's cartoon about the popular reception of modernism?

2. Why might Americans have viewed Duchamp's work, and the other canvases at the Armory Show, with alarm?

P6-6 | Solving the Problems Plaguing Native Americans

CARLOS MONTEZUMA, *What Indians Must Do* (1914)

The fate of Native Americans twisted and turned on the changing ideas and attitudes with which whites viewed them. The latter nineteenth century, witness to infamous Indian wars and deliberate efforts to decimate the native population, toggled between policies of assimilation and separation on reservations. Carlos Montezuma, an Apache activist and doctor, emerged in the early twentieth century as a national leader for Indian civil rights, attacking the reservation system and the federal bureaucracy that supported it by drawing on prevailing theories of social philosophy.

Carlos Montezuma, "What Indians Must Do," *The Quarterly Journal of the Society of American Indians* 2, no. 4 (October–December 1914): 294–299.

We must free ourselves. Our peoples' heritage is freedom. Freedom reigned in their whole make-up. They harmonized with nature and lived accordingly. Preaching freedom to our people on reservations does not make them free any more than you can, by preaching, free those prisoners who are in the penitentiary. Reservations are prisons where our people are kept to live and die, where equal possibilities, equal education and equal responsibilities are unknown.

For our people to know what freedom is they must go outside of the reservation and in order for them to harmonize with it and get used to it, they must live outside of the reservations. . . .

Sons of the aboriginal Indians, do you know we have been driven from the heritage of our fathers from generation to generation until we can not take another step! What are we going to do? We must decide for ourselves very quickly. Are we to disappear as the buffaloes or rise above the horizon of the twentieth century and respond, "We are here!" The sound of your own voice at the roll call will be at the end of the final battle to gain your freedom, be your individual self. The Society of American Indians will not cease until Indians have gained that standard that makes one true and free.

We must do away with the Indian Bureau. The reservation system has debarred us as a race from acquiring that knowledge to appreciate our property. The Government after teaching us how to live without work has come to the conclusion "that the Indians are not commercialists" and, therefore, "we (his guardian) will remove them as we think best and use them as long as our administration lasts and make friends." The Indian Department has drifted into commercialism at the expense of our poor benighted people. So they go on and say: "Let us not allot those Indians on that sweet flowing water because there are others who will profit by damming it up and selling it out to the newcomers; that the Indians do not use or develop their lands; five acres of irrigated land is all that one Indian can manage, but in order to be generous, we will give him ten acres and close up the books and call it square; that their vast forest does them no good, before the Indian can open his eyes let us transfer it to the Forestry Reserve Department. Never mind, let the Indian scratch for his wood to cook with and to warm himself in the years to come; that the Indians have no use for rivers, therefore, we will go into damming business and build them on their lands without their consent. Pay? No! Why should we?" They give us "C" class water instead of "A" class. They have got us! Why? Because we do not know the difference. . . .

My Indian friends, it seems that we have no voice in our affairs. It seems that all we can do is to sit there like dummies and see our property fade away and wonder what next. Our woods go to the forestry reserve; our fertile lands to the Irrigation Project; our rich minerals to the miners, and our waters to the interested parties that build dams and reap the profit within our reservations. In all of these it seems that we are counted out. If our Society is going to amount to anything do you not think we ought in some way stand up for our people?

If this taking away what belongs to us continues very much longer, where do you suppose we will land?

As the Society of American Indians, it is our duty to protect and aid in some way, to stop these wholesale smuggling away of our people's property. Can you imagine any other race allowing this without their consent?

The sooner the Government abolishes the Indian Bureau, the better it will be for we Indians in every way. The system that has kept alive the Indian Bureau has been instrumental in dominating over our race for fifty years. In that time the Indian's welfare has grown to the secondary and the Indian Bureau the whole thing, and therefore a necessary political appendage of the Government. It sends out exaggerated and wonderful reports to the public in order to suck the blood of our race, so that it may have perpetual life to sap your life, my life and our children's future prospects. There are many good things to say about the Indian Department. It started out right with our people. It fed them, clothed them and protected them from going outside of the reservations. It was truly a place of refuge. Then they were dominated by agents; now they are called superintendents. On the reservation our people did not act without the consent of the Superintendent; they did not express themselves without the approval of the Superintendent, and they did not dare to think, for that would be to rival, to the Superintendent. Yesterday, today, our people are in the same benighted condition. As Indians they are considered non-entities. They are not anything to themselves and not anything to the world.

It would be wrong for me to come here and tell you that the reservation system is good and helpful to our people, and that the Indian Bureau should be perpetuated when I know in my heart that it has been the greatest hindrance on the road from Indian life to civilization. Look at New York and Chicago, and then at the tepees on reservations. Look at Harvard, Yale, Princeton, and Madison, and then at the day schools on Indian reservations; hear the screeching locomotives and the whirr of industry and see the light of electricity; behold the grand panorama of agriculture of green gardens from the Atlantic to the Pacific coasts, from Canada to the Gulf of Mexico; and then behold the lounging Indians around agency buildings and under shady trees. Paradoxical as the statement may sound, it is nevertheless true, that the greatest obstacle that lies along the path toward the solution of our problem is the existence of the "helpful" Indian Bureau at Washington. It is the power plant that supplies life current to the reservations. It is long range, outside life, and does not grow from within.

The Indian Bureau seems to exist for no other purpose than to preserve the reservations. In other words the source from which the Indian ought to find relief from the evils of the reservation system is the very source without which the evil would not exist. . . .

The time has come that we Indians are ready to battle our own way in the world. Justice from the world can be no worse than the reservation system.

After starvation, rubbing up against the world and perchance surviving our reward will be independence. Once upon a time our ancestors were supremely independent. All they surveyed was theirs. There was none to dispute their claim. It was an ideal independence and worthy of imitation, but time has changed and conditions have changed with it. Somehow and for no other reason but that our people were Indians were they enslaved to separate existence and governed under different rules from the general government of the country. It is an appalling thing to think of such a thing and it does not look right and just. As their children's children we ought to be ashamed of ourselves that we tolerate this national abuse any longer without our resentment, without trying to redeem our people.

To a great extent it is our fault because we have taken no interest, no thought and no consideration to change and to look around to be really free. We Indians must let loose from these things that cause us to be separate from the laws and rules that other races enjoy. It is a delusion to think that we are free when we are reservation Indians and governed by the Indian Bureau.

We must be independent. When with my people for a vacation in Arizona I must live outdoors; I must sleep on the ground; I must cook in the fire on the ground; I must sit on the ground, I must eat nature's food and I must be satisfied with inconveniences that I do not enjoy at my Chicago home. Yet those blood relations of mine are independent, happy, because they were born and brought up in that environment, while as a greenhorn I find myself dependent and helpless in such simple life. In order for we Indians to be independent in the whirl of this other life, we must get into it and get used to it and live up to its requirements and take our chances with the rest of our fellow creatures. Being caged up and not permitted to develop our facilities has made us a dependent race. We are looked upon as hopeless to save and as hopeless to do anything for ourselves. The only Christian way, then, is to leave us alone and let us die in that condition. The conclusion is true that we will die that way if we do not hurry up and get out of it and hustle for our salvation. Did you ever notice how other races hustle and bustle in order to achieve independence? Reservation Indians must do the same as the rest of the wide world.

As a full-blooded Apache Indian I have nothing more to say. Figure out your responsibility and the responsibility of every Indian that hears my voice.

READING AND DISCUSSION QUESTIONS

1. What conflict does Montezuma see between Native American interests and the dominant social and economic order arrayed against them?

2. To what extent does Montezuma draw on Social Darwinist ideas and values regarding survival of the fittest in mounting his attack on the federally supported reservation system?

▪ COMPARATIVE QUESTIONS ▪

1. Using the sources in this chapter, construct an argument demonstrating the role that ideas, beliefs, and creative expression played in effecting a cultural transformation in the period from 1877 to 1917.

2. Compare William Graham Sumner's advocacy of Social Darwinism (Document P6-1) with Walter Rauschenbusch's Social Gospel Movement (Document P6-2). How would each have critiqued the other?

3. How do the values and attitudes toward gender roles demonstrated in the "New Woman — Wash Day" photograph (Document P6-3) compare with those of Theodore Roosevelt (Document 17-1), Elizabeth Shepley Sergeant (Document 17-3), and the Supreme Court's decision in *Muller v. Oregon* (Document 19-4)? To what extent did race and class intersect with gender to shape society's ideals for both sexes?

4. Is the period 1877 to 1917 better defined as the end of Victorianism or the birth of modernism? Which is the more convincing way of interpreting the period? Identify the sources that support your argument.

20

An Emerging World Power

1890–1918

The Protestant minister Josiah Strong (1847–1916) defined America's responsibility to "civilize and Christianize" the world by encouraging missionaries to promote the gospel. This evangelical motive was but one among a number of impulses driving late-nineteenth-century supporters of American expansionism, a latter-day expression of Manifest Destiny. Others emphasized the strategic and economic importance of overseas territories as critical to America's Social Darwinist competition with other world powers. The confluence of motives led policymakers to step offshore into the Caribbean, the Pacific, and Asia as well as Europe during World War I, but not without resistance. Opponents marshaled compelling counterarguments to American imperialism, bolstered by native protests and the evidence of domestic unrest inspired by wartime curtailment of civil liberties. This turn-of-the-century debate about the United States' legitimate and necessary role on the world stage splintered the American public into factions and colored the politics of the period. The disillusionment of World War I tempered overseas enthusiasm, but President Woodrow Wilson's lofty rhetoric about "making the world safe for democracy" established a precedent for future interventions framed as the selfless duty of a privileged nation.

20-1 | Senator Defends America's Imperial Ambitions

ALBERT BEVERIDGE, *"The March of the Flag" Speech* (1898)

In his popular speech before Republicans in the fall 1898 campaign season, Albert Beveridge rallied the party faithful in support of an ambitious international role for the United States. Elected to the Senate from Indiana, Beveridge served two terms as a member of the more progressive wing of the Republican Party, supporting policies he would later renounce, such as expanded government regulation. By the time he delivered his speech, the War of 1898 was over. Spain had already capitulated to the United States, ending what Secretary of State John Hay called the "splendid little war" and bolstering advocates for American expansion.

It is a noble land that God has given us; a land that can feed and clothe the world; a land whose coastlines would inclose half the countries of Europe; a land set like a sentinel between the two imperial oceans of the globe, a greater England with a nobler destiny.

It is a mighty people that He has planted on this soil; a people sprung from the most masterful blood of history; a people perpetually revitalized by the virile, man-producing working-folk of all the earth; a people imperial by virtue of their power, by right of their institutions, by authority of their Heaven-directed purposes—the propagandists and not the misers of liberty.

It is a glorious history our God has bestowed upon His chosen people; a history heroic with faith in our mission and our future; a history of statesmen who flung the boundaries of the Republic out into unexplored lands and savage wilderness; a history of soldiers who carried the flag across blazing deserts and through the ranks of hostile mountains, even to the gates of sunset; a history of a multiplying people who overran a continent in half a century; a history of prophets who saw the consequences of evils inherited from the past and of martyrs who died to save us from them; a history divinely logical, in the process of whose tremendous reasoning we find ourselves to-day.

Therefore, in this campaign, the question is larger than a party question. It is an American question. It is a world question. Shall the American people continue their march toward the commercial supremacy of the world? Shall free institutions broaden their blessed reign as the children of liberty wax in strength, until the empire of our principles is established over the hearts of all mankind?

Have we no mission to perform, no duty to discharge to our fellow-man? Has God endowed us with gifts beyond our deserts and marked us as the people of His peculiar favor, merely to rot in our own selfishness, as men and nations

Albert Beveridge, *The Meaning of the Times and Other Speeches* (Indianapolis: The Bobbs-Merrill Company, 1908), 47–57.

must, who take cowardice for their companion and self for their deity — as China has, as India has, as Egypt has?

Shall we be as the man who had one talent and hid it, or as he who had ten talents and used them until they grew to riches? And shall we reap the reward that waits on our discharge of our high duty; shall we occupy new markets for what our farmers raise, our factories make, our merchants sell — aye, and, please God, new markets for what our ships shall carry?

Hawaii is ours; Porto Rico is to be ours; at the prayer of her people Cuba finally will be ours; in the islands of the East, even to the gates of Asia, coaling stations are to be ours at the very least; the flag of a liberal government is to float over the Philippines, and may it be the banner that Taylor unfurled in Texas and Fremont carried to the coast.

The Opposition tells us that we ought not to govern a people without their consent. I answer, The rule of liberty that all just government derives its authority from the consent of the governed, applies only to those who are capable of self-government. We govern the Indians without their consent, we govern our territories without their consent, we govern our children without their consent. How do they know that our government would be without their consent? Would not the people of the Philippines prefer the just, humane, civilizing government of this Republic to the savage, bloody rule of pillage and extortion from which we have rescued them?

. . . There was not one reason for the land-lust of our statesmen from Jefferson to Grant, other than the prophet and the Saxon within them. But, to-day, we are raising more than we can consume, making more than we can use. Therefore we must find new markets for our produce.

And so, while we did not need the territory taken during the past century at the time it was acquired, we do need what we have taken in 1898, and we need it now. The resources and the commerce of these immensely rich dominions will be increased as much as American energy is greater than Spanish sloth. In Cuba, alone, there are 15,000,000 acres of forest unacquainted with the ax, exhaustless mines of iron, priceless deposits of manganese, millions of dollars' worth of which we must buy, to-day, from the Black Sea districts. There are millions of acres yet unexplored.

The resources of Porto Rico have only been trifled with. The riches of the Philippines have hardly been touched by the finger-tips of modern methods. . . . They sell hemp, sugar, cocoanuts, fruits of the tropics, timber of price like mahogany; they buy flour, clothing, tools, implements, machinery and all that we can raise and make. Their trade will be ours in time.

The commercial supremacy of the Republic means that this Nation is to be the sovereign factor in the peace of the world. For the conflicts of the future are to be conflicts of trade — struggles for markets — commercial wars for existence. . . . So Hawaii furnishes us a naval base in the heart of the Pacific; the Ladrones another, a voyage further on; Manila another, at the gates of Asia — Asia, to the trade of whose hundreds of millions American merchants, manufacturers, farmers, have as good right as those of Germany or France or Russia or England; Asia, whose commerce with the United Kingdom alone amounts to hundreds of millions of dollars every year; Asia, to whom Germany looks to take her surplus products; Asia, whose doors must not be shut against American trade. Within five decades the bulk of Oriental commerce will be ours. . . .

There are so many real things to be done — canals to be dug, railways to be laid, forests to be felled, cities to be builded, fields to be tilled, markets to be won, ships to be launched, peoples to be saved, civilization to be proclaimed and the flag of liberty flung to the eager air of every sea. Is this an hour to waste upon triflers with nature's laws? Is this a season to give our destiny over to word-mongers and prosperity-wreckers? No! It is an hour to remember our duty to our homes. It is a moment to realize the opportunities fate has opened to us. And so it is an hour for us to stand by the Government.

Wonderfully has God guided us. . . . [I]t is ours to set the world its example of right and honor. We can not fly from our world duties; it is ours to execute the purpose of a fate that has driven us to be greater than our small intentions. We can not retreat from any soil where Providence has unfurled our banner; it is ours to save that soil for liberty and civilization.

READING AND DISCUSSION QUESTIONS

1. Analyze Beveridge's language for evidence of his understanding of race and its role in defining "civilization." How does he define the "mission of our race"?

2. To what extent does Beveridge draw on nineteenth-century notions of Manifest Destiny that had supported antebellum territorial expansion? How did he and other pro-expansionists adapt that language to the geopolitical needs of the turn of the century?

3. How does Beveridge answer critics who opposed American imperialism in the latter nineteenth century?

20-2 | Deposed Queen Pleads for Her Island Kingdom

LILIUOKALANI, *Hawaii's Story by Hawaii's Queen* (1898)

In 1898, when the United States entered a war with Spain over Cuba and the Philippines, Congress passed a resolution annexing the Hawaiian Islands, part of a growing colonization interest among many policymakers to extend the power and influence of the United States around the world. Hawaii was key for its strategic position in the central Pacific and for its trade, promoted by those with American business interests who in the early 1890s

Liliuokalani, *Hawaii's Story by Hawaii's Queen* (Boston: Lothrop, Lee & Shepard Co., 1898), 370–374.

engineered the overthrow of Liliuokalani, the island's queen. Liliuokalani's 1898 memoir, published amid failed efforts to lobby American politicians to oppose annexation, presented her island's plea for its restored sovereignty.

I have felt much perplexity over the attitude of the American press, that great vehicle of information for the people, in respect of Hawaiian affairs. Shakespeare has said it is excellent to have a giant's strength, but it is tyrannous to use it like a giant. It is not merely that, with few exceptions, the press has seemed to favor the extinction of Hawaiian sovereignty, but that it has often treated me with coarse allusions and flippancy, and almost uniformly has commented upon me adversely, or has declined to publish letters from myself and friends conveying correct information upon matters which other correspondents had, either wilfully or through being deceived, misrepresented. Perhaps in many cases *libellous* matter was involved. Possibly the press was not conscious of how cruelly it was exerting its strength, and will try, I now trust, to repair the injury.

It has been shown that in Hawaii there is an alien element composed of men of energy and determination, well able to carry through what they undertake, but not scrupulous respecting their methods. They doubtless control all the resources and influence of the present ruling power in Honolulu, and will employ them tirelessly in the future, as they have in the past, to secure their ends. This annexationist party might prove to be a dangerous accession even to American politics, both on account of natural abilities, and because of the training of an autocratic life from earliest youth.

Many of these men are anything but ideal citizens for a democracy. That custom of freely serving each other without stipulation or reward which exists as a very nature among our people has been even exaggerated in our hospitality to our teachers and advisers. Their children, and the associates they have drawn to themselves, are accustomed to it. They have always been treated with distinction. They would hardly know how to submit to the contradictions, disappointments, and discourtesies of a purely emulative society.

It would remain necessary for them to rule in Hawaii, even if the American flag floated over them. And if they found they could be successfully opposed, would they seek no remedy? Where would men, already proved capable of outwitting the conservatism of the United States and defeating its strongest traditions, capable of changing its colonial and foreign policy at a single *coup*, stop in their schemes?

Perhaps I may even venture here upon a final word respecting the American advocates of this annexation of Hawaii. I observe that they have pretty successfully striven to make it a party matter. It is chiefly Republican statesmen and politicians who favor it. But is it really a matter of party interest? Is the American Republic of States to degenerate, and become a colonizer and a land-grabber?

And is this prospect satisfactory to a people who rely upon self-government for their liberties, and whose guaranty of liberty and autonomy to the whole western hemisphere, the grand Monroe doctrine, appealing to the respect and the sense of justice of the masses of every nation on earth, has made any attack upon it practically impossible to the statesmen and rulers of armed empires? There is little question but that the United States could become a successful rival of the European nations in the race for conquest, and could create a vast military and naval power, if such is its ambition. But is such an ambition laudable? Is such a departure from its established principles patriotic or politic?

Here, at least for the present, I rest my pen. During my stay in the capital, I suppose I must have met, by name and by card, at least five thousand callers. From most of these, by word, by grasp of hand, or at least by expression of countenance, I have received a sympathy and encouragement of which I cannot write fully. Let it be understood that I have not failed to notice it, and to be not only flattered by its universality, but further very grateful that I have had the opportunity to know the real American people, quite distinct from those who have assumed this honored name when it suited their selfish ends.

But for the Hawaiian people, for the forty thousand of my own race and blood, descendants of those who welcomed the devoted and pious missionaries of seventy years ago, — for them has this mission of mine accomplished anything?

Oh, honest Americans, as Christians hear me for my down-trodden people! Their form of government is as dear to them as yours is precious to you. Quite as warmly as you love your country, so they love theirs. With all your goodly possessions, covering a territory so immense that there yet remain parts unexplored, possessing islands that, although near at hand, had to be neutral ground in time of war, do not covet the little vineyard of Naboth's, so far from your shores, lest the punishment of Ahab fall upon you, if not in your day, in that of your children, for "be not deceived, God is not mocked." The people to whom your fathers told of the living God, and taught to call "Father," and whom the sons now seek to despoil and destroy, are crying aloud to Him in their time of trouble; and He will keep His promise, and will listen to the voices of His Hawaiian children lamenting for their homes.

It is for them that I would give the last drop of my blood; it is for them that I would spend, nay, am spending, everything belonging to me. Will it be in vain? It is for the American people and their representatives in Congress to answer these questions. As they deal with me and my people, kindly, generously, and justly, so may the Great Ruler of all nations deal with the grand and glorious nation of the United States of America.

READING AND DISCUSSION QUESTIONS

1. What strategy does Liliuokalani use in her memoir to convince Americans to resist annexation? What does she imply will be the consequences for America of its overreach into the Pacific?

2. Whom does she blame for the political crisis in Hawaii? What inferences about American foreign policy can you draw from her assessment of Hawaii's experiences?

20-3 | The New Diplomacy

PUCK, *US President Theodore Roosevelt's New Diplomacy, "Speak Softly and Carry a Big Stick"* (1901)

Theodore Roosevelt had ambitions for the United States. He supported the War of 1898 against Spain, and after he became president he continued the expansionist policies of President McKinley. In this cartoon published in *Puck*, an American magazine of satire and humor, the artist portrays Roosevelt as the world's policeman, perhaps a nod to his time as New York City police commissioner. Here Roosevelt employs two instruments of foreign policy: arbitration and the threat of force.

Universal History Archive/Getty Images

READING AND DISCUSSION QUESTIONS

1. What is the artist suggesting about Roosevelt's foreign policy? What role is he projecting for Roosevelt and the United States?

2. Notice the Capitol building, small in scale, just behind Roosevelt. What might you infer about the artist's perspective regarding the modern presidency? What has happened to the balance of power between the branches of the federal government?

3. Explain why you think the artist supports or opposes Roosevelt's expansionist foreign policy?

"US President Theodore Roosevelt's New Diplomacy, 'Speak Softly and Carry a Big Stick,'" *Puck* 1901, via Getty Images, http://www.gettyimages.com/license/629444493.

20-4 | Defending Those Opposed to War

FRANCES M. WITHERSPOON, *Letter to Newton Baker* (1918)

Frances M. Witherspoon devoted her life to activism. She was a women's suffrage and labor organizer in New York City during the early twentieth century. When World War I broke out in Europe, she helped found the Woman's Peace Party and pioneered direct action campaigns to oppose U.S. entry into the war. Then, when the United States entered the war in 1917, she took up the cause of conscientious objectors, those whose religious beliefs and principles forbade them from participating in war efforts. The Selective Service Act of 1917, however, defined those entitled to objector status as individuals who were members of well-established religious groups whose teachings explicitly forbade war activities. Ultimately, it was up to local draft boards to decide which objectors' claims were justified. Conscientious objectors were frequently imprisoned. Others were segregated within military camps where they suffered harassment and physical abuse. As a co-founder of the New York Bureau of Legal Advice and its Executive Secretary, Witherspoon worked on behalf of conscientious objectors. In this letter to Secretary of War Newton Baker, she raises questions on behalf of conscientious objectors who were court-martialed.

May 3 – 1918

My dear Secretary Baker:

I am making an urgent request for information in regard to court-martial of conscientious objectors in cantonments[1] near New York City. I do this at the suggestion of Mr. Roger Baldwin, Director of the National Civil Liberties Bureau and for the reason that this Bureau which is local in scope, has been closer in touch with the situation in these camps than the national organization.

The New York Press of May first announces the general court-martial of conscientious objectors, the enclosed clipping from the NEW YORK TRIBUNE being a typical report. Those interested in the problem here are anxious to learn if this news is authentic and if a general order for court-martial under Article 96 has been issued by the Department [of War] for all camps.

From Section 3 of the Executive Order of March 20th those interested in the conscientious objectors problem understood

1) That conscientious objectors refusing assignment to non-combatant military service as defined by the President would continue to be segregated under the command of a special officer;

2) That punitive hardships already forbidden by your order of September 15th, were not to be imposed;

3) That such persons would remain as above described until classified by you and until orders from you should be received by the Post Commander as to their disposition;

Witherspoon, Frances, "Letter May 3, 1918 from Frances Witherspoon to Newton Baker," *Conscientious Objection & the Great War: 1914–1920*, accessed September 10, 2019, https://cosandgreatwar.swarthmore.edu/items/show/279.

[1] **Cantonments**: Military camps.

4) That court-martials of absolute conscientious objectors were not to take place until such orders should have been issued direct from the War Department and that when ordered, trials should be conducted under Articles of War 64 and 65.

May I now learn whether those court-martials which have already taken place within the last few days have been held with your consent or through mis-interpretation of the Executive Order? Do they find justification under the last clause of the Order, section 3, which reads "but not to allow their objections to be made the basis of any favor or consideration beyond exemption from actual military service which is not extended to any other soldiers in the service of the United States"?

The whole theory behind the action of the conscientious objector seems to be that his consicence [sic] and principles against war are violated not only by actual military duty in trench and field, but as well by the wearing of the uniform, drilling in training camps and even by the performing of any labor, physical or mental, in any way connected with the military system. It is for this very rea-son that he has refused even those forms of non-combatant service which would seem least connected with the promotion of the war or of the military establish-ment. It is this very unwillingness to cooperate even in ways most remote from actual military operations that their conscientious scruples would appear to have their root. And this being so, it would seem that if court-martials are now being permitted for those whose fault lies merely in a logical adherence to their prin-ciples, then the Executive Order offers them no protection whatsoever. Yet the whole spirit of the order would indicate that this is an entirely false deduction. It seems to provide not only fair and generous treatment for the man who can not conscientiously accept service in fighting units but who can serve his country in non-combatant capacity, but uniform and humane handling as well for those men who can not serve the country in any way connected with the war.

It would at least indicate that the matter is not left to the discretion of the individual commander who might experience extreme difficulty in understanding in the slightest degree the motives back of the conscientious objectors' conduct and it will be an acute disappointment to those who have been relying upon the liberal and humane attitude of the War Department to learn that the paragraph quoted can be taken by commanders as authority for any notion which they may deem desirable.

I enclose the clipping from the NEW YORK WORLD in regard to the case of William Daisenberger, whose offence according to this statement (which, of course, may be wholly inaccurate) seems to have consisted merely in conduct similar to that of all absolute conscientious objectors of whom we have any knowledge. It therefore becomes a test case and information as to whether the War Department approved the court-martial would I suppose answer the general question raised.

Thanking you for your patience with this lengthy inquiry, prompted as I am sure you will understand by very great anxiety.

FRANCES M. WITHERSPOON

READING AND DISCUSSION QUESTIONS

1. What information is Witherspoon seeking from the secretary of war? What is the situation that has given rise to her letter?

2. What does this letter suggest about the roles women played during wartime? To what extent does Witherspoon's letter challenge stereotypes regarding women's activism during this period?

3. How does the plight of the conscientious objectors Witherspoon discusses reveal the limits of civil liberties during wartime?

20-5 | Workers Protest Wartime Attacks

THE LIBERATOR, *Tulsa, November 9th* (1918)

The Industrial Workers of the World (IWW), the radical labor union organized in 1905, opposed America's entry into the world war that started in Europe in 1914, condemning it as a capitalist's war and a laborer's fight. Government propaganda marginalized antiwar activists, and the 1917 Espionage Act criminalized many of their activities. The IWW became an easy target, as members reported in this article (published in April 1918) describing their November 1917 run-in with the Tulsa, Oklahoma, police and the Ku Klux Klan. Among those terrorized by the Klan were blacks, Jews, and immigrants, many of whom were IWW members.

Tulsa, November 9th.

[Editor's Note:—In this story of persecution and outrage at Tulsa, Oklahoma, told in the sworn statement of one of the victims, there is direct and detailed evidence of one of the most menacing by-products of the war. Here in Tulsa, as in Bisbee and Butte and Cincinnati, patriotic fervor was used by employers with the connivance or open cooperation of local officials, as a mask for utterly lawless attacks upon workingmen who attempted to organize for better conditions. This false resort to loyalty on the part of certain war profiteers is emphasized in the recent Report of the President's Mediation Commission. These cowardly masked upper-class mobs, calling themselves "Knights of Liberty" and mumbling hypocritical words about "the women and children of Belgium," will not succeed in terrorizing the labor movement of America, nor will they tend to make it more patriotic.]

On November 9, 1917, seventeen men, taken from the custody of the city police of Tulsa, Oklahoma, were whipped, tarred and feathered, and driven out of the city with a warning never to return.

In a letter dated December 21, a resident of Tulsa, writes:

"I think it is only fair to say that the bottom cause of this trouble locally was that a few men, presumably belonging to the I.W.W. came into the oilfields

---

"Tulsa, November 9th," The Liberator 1 (April 1918): 15–17.

something like a year ago and were meeting with considerable success in getting oil-field workers—especially pipe-line and tank builders—to fight for better wages and shorter hours.

"Not long after the outrage was committed in Butte, Mont., on the crippled I.W.W. leader (Frank Little), the home of J. Edgar Pew in this city was partly destroyed by some kind of explosion and Mr. and Mrs. Pew narrowly escaped being killed. The news agencies at once published it as a dastardly act of the I.W.W.'s. Mr. Pew is the vice-president and active manager of the Carter Oil Co., which by the way, is owned and controlled by Standard Oil and is one of its largest producing subsidiary companies. A few weeks after the Pew home incident, an explosion followed by a fire partially destroyed an oil refinery that is located at Norfolk, Okla. This property was under the Carter Oil Co. management. Two men lost their lives in this accident. The news agencies without exception (so far as I know) exploited this as another I.W.W. outrage."

From this point we take up the story in a sworn statement made by the secretary of the Tulsa local.

"On the night of November 5, 1917, while sitting in the hall at No. 6 W. Brady Street, Tulsa, Okla. (the room leased and occupied by the Industrial Workers of the World, and used as a union meeting room), at about 8:45 P.M., five men entered the hall, to whom I at first paid no attention, as I was busy putting a monthly stamp in a member's union card book. After I had finished with the member, I walked back to where these five men had congregated at the baggage-room at the back of the hall, and spoke to them, asking if there was anything I could do for them.

"One who appeared to be the leader, answered 'No, we're just looking the place over.' Two of them went into the baggage-room flashing an electric flash-light around the room. The other three walked toward the front end of the hall. I stayed at the baggage-room door, and one of the men came out and followed the other three up to the front end of the hall. The one who stayed in the baggage-room asked me if I was 'afraid he would steal something.' I told him we were paying rent for the hall, and I did not think anyone had a right to search this place without a warrant. He replied that he did not give a damn if we were paying rent for four places, they would search them whenever they felt like it. Presently he came out and walked toward the front end of the hall, and I followed a few steps behind him.

"In the meantime the other men, who proved to be officers, appeared to be asking some of our members questions. Shortly after, the patrol-wagon came and all the members in the hall—10 men—were ordered into the wagon. I turned out the light in the back end of the hall, closed the desk, put the key in the door and told the 'officer' to turn out the one light. We stepped out, and I locked the door, and at the request of the 'leader of the officers,' handed him the keys. He told me to get in the wagon, I being the 11th man taken from the hall, and we were taken to the police station.

"November 6th, after staying that night in jail, I put up $100.00 cash bond so that I could attend to the outside business, and the trial was set for 5 o'clock P.M., November 6th. Our lawyer, Chas. Richardson, asked for a continuance and it was granted. Trial on a charge of vagrancy was set for November 7th at 5 P.M. by Police Court Judge Evans. After some argument by both sides the cases were continued until the next night, November 8th, and the case against Gunnard Johnson, one of our men, was called. After four and a half hours' session the case was again adjourned until November 9th at 5 P.M., when we agreed to let the decision in Johnson's case stand for all of us. . . .

"Johnson said he had come into town Saturday, November 3d, to get his money from the Sinclair Oil & Gas Co. and could not get it until Monday, the 5th, and was shipping out Tuesday, the 6th, and that he had $7.08 when arrested. He was reprimanded by the judge for not having a Liberty Bond, and as near as anyone could judge from the closing remarks of Judge Evans, he was found guilty and fined $100 for not having a Liberty Bond.

"Our lawyer made a motion to appeal the case and the bonds were then fixed at $200 each. I was immediately arrested, *as were also five spectators in the open court-room*, for being I.W.W.'s. One arrested was not a member of ours, but a property-owner and citizen. I was searched and $30.87 taken from me, as also was the receipt for the $100 bond, and we then were all placed back in the cells.

"In about forty minutes, as near as we could judge, about 11 P.M., the turnkey came and called 'Get ready to go out you I.W.W. men.' We dressed as rapidly as possible, were taken out of the cells, and the officer gave us back our possessions, Ingersoll watches, pocketknives and money, with the exception of $3 in silver of mine which they kept, giving me back $27.87. I handed the receipt for the $100 bond I had put up to the desk sergeant, and he told me he did not know anything about it, and handed the receipt back to me, which I put in my trousers pocket with the 87 cents. Twenty-seven dollars in bills was in my coat pocket. We were immediately ordered into automobiles waiting in the alley. Then we proceeded one block north to 1st Street, west one-half block to Boulder Street, north across the Frisco tracks and stopped.

"Then the masked mob came up and ordered everybody to throw up their hands. Just here I wish to state I never thought any man could reach so high as those policemen did. We were then bound, some with hands in front, some with hands behind, and others bound with arms hanging down their sides, the rope being wrapped around the body. Then the police were ordered to 'beat it,' which they did, running, and we started for the place of execution.

"When we arrived there, a company of gowned and masked gunmen were there to meet us standing at 'present arms.' We were ordered out of the autos, told to get in line in front of these gunmen and another bunch of men with automatics and pistols, lined up between us. Our hands were still held up, and those who were bound, in front. Then a masked man walked down the line and slashed the ropes that bound us, and we were ordered to strip to the waist, which we did, threw our clothes in front of us, in individual piles—coats, vests, hats, shirts and undershirts. The boys not having had time to distribute their possessions that were given back to them at the police stations, everything was in the coats, everything we owned in the world.

"Then the whipping began. A double piece of new rope, ⅝ or ¾ hemp, being used. A man, 'the chief' of detectives, stopped the whipping of each man when he thought the victim had enough. After each one was whipped another man applied the tar with a large brush, from the head to the seat. Then a brute smeared feathers over and rubbed them in.

"After they had satisfied themselves that our bodies were well abused, our clothing was thrown into a pile, gasoline poured on it and a match applied. By the light of our earthly possessions, we were ordered to leave Tulsa, and leave running and never come back. The night was dark, the road very rough, and as I was one of the last two that was whipped, tarred and feathered, and in the rear when ordered to run, I decided to be shot rather than stumble over the rough road. After going forty or fifty feet I stopped and went into the weeds. I told the man with me to get in the weeds also, as the shots were coming very close over us, and ordered him to lie down flat. We expected to be killed, but after 150 or 200 shots were fired they got in their autos.

"After the last one had left, we went through a barbed-wire fence, across a field, called to the boys, collected them, counted up, and had all the 16 safe, though sore and nasty with tar. After wandering around the hills for some time—ages it seemed to me—we struck the railroad track. One man, Jack Sneed, remembered then that he knew a farmer in that vicinity, and he and J.F. Ryan volunteered to find the house. I built a fire to keep us from freezing.

"We stood around the fire expecting to be shot, as we did not know but what some tool of the commercial club had followed us. After a long time Sneed returned and called to us, and we went with him to a cabin and found an I.W.W. friend in the shack and 5 gallons of coal oil or kerosene, with which we cleaned the filthy stuff off of each other, and our troubles were over, as friends sent clothing and money to us that day, it being about 3 or 3:30 A.M. when we reached the cabin.

"The men abused, whipped and tarred were: Tom McCaffery, John Myers, John Boyle, Charles Walsh, W.H. Walton, L.R. Mitchell, Jos. French, J.R. Hill, Gunnard Johnson, Robt. McDonald, John Fitzsimmons, Jos. Fischer, Gordon Dimikson, J.F. Ryan, E.M. Boyd, Jack Sneed (not an I.W.W.).

"This is a copy of my sworn statement and every word is truth."

In answer to special inquiry the writer added to his statement as follows: "It was very evident that the police force knew what was going to happen when they took us from jail, as there were extra gowns and masks provided *which were put on by the Chief of Police and one detective named Blaine, and the number of blows we received were regulated by the Chief of Police himself, who was easily recognizable by six of us at least.*"

The above account is substantiated at every point by a former employee of The Federal Industrial Relations Commission, who at the request of the National Civil Liberties Bureau made a special investigation of the whole affair. His report names directly nine leaders of the mob, including five members of the police force.

The part played by the press in this orgy of "Patriotism" is illustrated by the following excerpts from an editorial which appeared in the Tulsa Daily World on the afternoon of the 9th:

Get Out the Hemp

"Any man who attempts to stop the supply for one-hundredth part of a second is a traitor and ought to be shot! . . .

"In the meantime, if the I.W.W. or its twin brother, the Oil Workers' Union, gets busy in your neighborhood, kindly take occasion to decrease the supply of hemp. A knowledge of how to tie a knot that will stick might come in handy in a few days. It is no time to dally with the enemies of the country. The unrestricted production of petroleum is as necessary to the winning of the war as the unrestricted production of gunpowder. We are either going to whip Germany or Germany is going to whip us. The first step in the whipping of Germany is to strangle the I.W.W.'s. Kill them, just as you would kill any other kind of a snake. Don't scotch 'em: kill 'em. And kill 'em dead. It is no time to waste money on trials and continuances and things like that. All that is necessary is the evidence and a firing squad. Probably the carpenters' union will contribute the timber for the coffins."

READING AND DISCUSSION QUESTIONS

1. Analyze the testimony of IWW members for evidence of the domestic impact of the war, including its effect on civil liberties. What factors combined to make members of the IWW a particular target?

2. What conclusions can you draw regarding the crimes IWW members were alleged to have committed?

3. How do you interpret the editorial from the *Tulsa Daily World*, which the article quotes? What evidence does it provide for your understanding of the wartime relationship between industry, labor, and government? What veiled threat implied by the editorial is directed to members of the IWW?

20-6 | President's Fourteen Points for Postwar Peace

WOODROW WILSON, *War Aims and Peace Terms* (1918)

President Wilson initially avoided intervening in the world war begun in 1914. However, the resumption of German submarine attacks on American ships reversed Wilson's nonintervention policies, leading him to support the Allies in what he once called a "war to end all wars." American troops joined the fight after Congress declared war against Germany on April 6, 1917. Despite German battlefield gains, Wilson was anticipating peace in January 1918 when he addressed Congress, laying out his famous Fourteen Points, a set of principles upon which he hoped the postwar settlement would be based. His hopes were dashed in the Treaty of Versailles (signed June 28, 1919), which ended the war and established terms very different from the ones he had envisioned.

It will be our wish and purpose that the processes of peace, when they are begun, shall be absolutely open and that they shall involve and permit henceforth no secret understandings of any kind. The day of conquest and aggrandizement is gone by; so is also the day of secret covenants entered into in the interest of particular governments and likely at some unlooked-for moment to upset the peace of the world. It is this happy fact, now clear to the view of every public man whose thoughts do not still linger in an age that is dead and gone, which makes it possible for every nation whose purposes are consistent with justice and the peace of the world to avow [now] or at any other time the objects it has in view.

We entered this war because violations of right had occurred which touched us to the quick and made the life of our own people impossible unless they were corrected and the world secure once for all against their recurrence. What we demand in this war, therefore, is nothing peculiar to ourselves. It is that the world be made fit and safe to live in; and particularly that it be made safe for every peace-loving nation which, like our own, wishes to live its own life, determine its own institutions, be assured of justice and fair dealing by the other peoples of the world as against force and selfish aggression. All the peoples of the world are in effect partners in this interest, and for our own part we see very clearly that unless justice be done to others it will not be done to us. The programme of the world's peace, therefore, is our programme; and that programme, the only possible programme, as we see it, is this:

I. Open covenants of peace, openly arrived at, after which there shall be no private international understandings of any kind but diplomacy shall proceed always frankly and in the public view.

II. Absolute freedom of navigation upon the seas, outside territorial waters, alike in peace and in war, except as the seas may be closed in whole or in part by international action for the enforcement of international covenants.

Woodrow Wilson, Message to Congress, January 8, 1918, Records of the United States Senate; Record Group 46; National Archives.

III.   The removal, so far as possible, of all economic barriers and the establishment of an equality of trade conditions among all the nations consenting to the peace and associating themselves for its maintenance.

IV.   Adequate guarantees given and taken that national armaments will be reduced to the lowest point consistent with domestic safety.

V.   A free, open-minded, and absolutely impartial adjustment of all colonial claims, based upon a strict observance of the principle that in determining all such questions of sovereignty the interests of the populations concerned must have equal weight with the equitable claims of the government whose title is to be determined.

VI.   The evacuation of all Russian territory and such a settlement of all questions affecting Russia as will secure the best and freest cooperation of the other nations of the world in obtaining for her an unhampered and unembarrassed opportunity for the independent determination of her own political development and national policy and assure her of a sincere welcome into the society of free nations under institutions of her own choosing; and, more than a welcome, assistance also of every kind that she may need and may herself desire. The treatment accorded Russia by her sister nations in the months to come will be the acid test of their good will, of their comprehension of her needs as distinguished from their own interests, and of their intelligent and unselfish sympathy.

VII.   Belgium, the whole world will agree, must be evacuated and restored, without any attempt to limit the sovereignty which she enjoys in common with all other free nations. No other single act will serve as this will serve to restore confidence among the nations in the laws which they have themselves set and determined for the government of their relations with one another. Without this healing act the whole structure and validity of international law is forever impaired.

VIII.   All French territory should be freed and the invaded portions restored, and the wrong done to France by Prussia in 1871 in the matter of Alsace-Lorraine, which has unsettled the peace of the world for nearly fifty years, should be righted, in order that peace may once more be made secure in the interest of all.

IX.   A readjustment of the frontiers of Italy should be effected along clearly recognizable lines of nationality.

X.   The peoples of Austria-Hungary, whose place among the nations we wish to see safeguarded and assured, should be accorded the freest opportunity to autonomous development.

XI.   Rumania, Serbia, and Montenegro should be evacuated; occupied territories restored; Serbia accorded free and secure access to the sea; and the relations of the several Balkan states to one another determined by friendly counsel along historically established lines of allegiance and nationality; and international guarantees of the political and economic independence and territorial integrity of the several Balkan states should be entered into.

XII. The Turkish portion of the present Ottoman Empire should be assured a secure sovereignty, but the other nationalities which are now under Turkish rule should be assured an undoubted security of life and an absolutely unmolested opportunity of autonomous development, and the Dardanelles should be permanently opened as a free passage to the ships and commerce of all nations under international guarantees.

XIII. An independent Polish state should be erected which should include the territories inhabited by indisputably Polish populations, which should be assured a free and secure access to the sea, and whose political and economic independence and territorial integrity should be guaranteed by international covenant.

XIV. A general association of nations must be formed under specific covenants for the purpose of affording mutual guarantees of political independence and territorial integrity to great and small states alike.

In regard to these essential rectifications of wrong and assertions of right we feel ourselves to be intimate partners of all the governments and peoples associated together against the Imperialists. We cannot be separated in interest or divided in purpose. We stand together until the end.

For such arrangements and covenants we are willing to fight and to continue to fight until they are achieved; but only because we wish the right to prevail and desire a just and stable peace such as can be secured only by removing the chief provocations to war, which this programme does remove. We have no jealousy of German greatness, and there is nothing in this programme that impairs it. We grudge her no achievement or distinction of learning or of pacific enterprise such as have made her record very bright and very enviable. We do not wish to injure her or to block in any way her legitimate influence or power. We do not wish to fight her either with arms or with hostile arrangements of trade if she is willing to associate herself with us and the other peace-loving nations of the world in covenants of justice and law and fair dealing. We wish her only to accept a place of equality among the peoples of the world,—the new world in which we now live,—instead of a place of mastery.

READING AND DISCUSSION QUESTIONS

1. Analyze Wilson's Fourteen Points to understand the reasons why he believed the war was fought in the first place. What failures did his plan for peace seek to correct?

2. To what extent were Wilson's Fourteen Points a repudiation of the policies of American expansionists like Beveridge?

▪ COMPARATIVE QUESTIONS ▪

1. Compare Albert Beveridge's assumptions about race (Document 20-1) with the anthropological ideas about race articulated by Franz Boas (Document P6-4). How do you imagine Boas would have responded to Beveridge's argument that Anglo-Saxons had a special role to play in world affairs?

2. To what extent did President Wilson's rhetoric about national self-determination (Document 20-6) reflect the policies of the United States during the period from 1890 to 1918? To what extent did the United States' interactions with Hawaii and the Philippines expose gaps between rhetoric and reality?

3. What evidence of Social Darwinist ideas can you identify in the arguments used by those advocating for a more expansive U.S. role in world affairs? Compare the evidence in this chapter with William Graham Sumner's use of Social Darwinism (Document P6-1).

4. What lessons about civil liberties during wartime do you think Americans learned in this period? How relevant are those concerns today?

5. The period from 1890 to 1918 saw the United States assume a more aggressive role in world affairs. To what extent were these years an exception? What were the most significant factors shaping America's interaction with the rest of the world?

21

Unsettled Prosperity: From War to Depression

1919–1932

The years following World War I were hardly the period of "normalcy" President Warren Harding had hoped for. Instead, the twenties both roared and retreated at the same time. For many, the postwar era opened possibilities for self-expression and a turn to life's pleasures, encouraged by a booming consumer culture promising self-fulfillment and high living. For others, the so-called modern world's hedonism beguiled Americans into abandoning traditional values of God and country for false values and empty promises. This core conflict about American values played itself out in the politics of the period. Suffragists finally won ratification of the Nineteenth Amendment in 1920, and African American culture bloomed into a renaissance that proclaimed blacks' self-confident identity. Yet the era's more conservative leanings sought to purge society's demons, whether they took form in liquor bottles, radical labor ideologies, subversive immigrants, or godless attacks on traditional values. The 1929 stock market crash revealed the economic strains that had fueled the 1920s exuberance and ushered in a new era of austerity.

21-1 | Condemned Radical Protests Political Hysteria

BARTOLOMEO VANZETTI, *Last Statement to the Court of Massachusetts* (1927)

The trial and execution of two Italian immigrants, Nicola Sacco and Bartolomeo Vanzetti, illustrate the crippling nativist fear that seized so many Americans in the 1920s. Arrested for allegedly murdering two men during a robbery in Braintree, Massachusetts, Sacco and Vanzetti were convicted in 1920. Appeals were unsuccessful, and the death sentence by electrocution was carried out in 1927. Vanzetti's defiant final statement failed to move the court, but it did provoke a public outcry as well as national and worldwide demonstrations condemning the sentence.

Yes. What I say is that I am innocent, not only of the Braintree crime, but also of the Bridgewater crime.[1] That I am not only innocent of these two crimes, but in all my life I have never stole and I have never killed and I have never spilled blood. That is what I want to say. And it is not all. Not only am I innocent of these two crimes, not only in all my life I have never stole, never killed, never spilled blood, but I have struggled all my life, since I began to reason, to eliminate crime from the earth.

Everybody that knows these two arms knows very well that I did not need to go in between the street and kill a man to take the money. I can live with my two arms and live well. But besides that, I can live even without work with my arm for other people. I have had plenty of chance to live independently and to live what the world conceives to be a higher life than not to gain our bread with the sweat of our brow. . . .

We were tried during a time that has now passed into history. I mean by that, a time when there was a hysteria of resentment and hate against the people of our principles, against the foreigner, against slackers, and it seems to me—rather, I am positive of it, that both you and Mr. Katzmann[2] has done all what it were in your power in order to work out, in order to agitate still more the passion of the juror, the prejudice of the juror, against us. . . .

But the jury were hating us because we were against the war, and the jury don't know that it makes any difference between a man that is against the war because he believes that the war is unjust, because he hate no country, because he is a cosmopolitan, and a man that is against the war because he is in favor of the other country that fights against the country in which he is, and therefore

---

The Sacco-Vanzetti Case: Transcript of the Record of the Trial of Nicola Sacco and Bartolomeo Vanzetti in the Courts of Massachusetts and Subsequent Proceedings, 1920–7, vol. 5: Pages 4360–5621, with General Index (New York: Henry Holt & Company, 1929), 4896–4905.

[1] **Bridgewater crime**: In addition to the Braintree robbery and murder, Vanzetti (though not Sacco) was accused of a robbery in Bridgewater, Massachusetts.

[2] **Mr. Katzmann**: Frederick Katzmann was the district attorney prosecuting the case against Vanzetti.

a spy, and he commits any crime in the country in which he is in behalf of the other country in order to serve the other country. We are not men of that kind. Katzmann know very well that. Katzmann know that we were against the war because we did not believe in the purpose for which they say that the war was done. We believe it that the war is wrong, and we believe this more now after ten years that we understood it day by day,—the consequences and the result of the after war. We believe more now than ever that the war was wrong, and we are against war more now than ever, and I am glad to be on the doomed scaffold if I can say to mankind, "Look out; you are in a catacomb of the flower of mankind. For what? All that they say to you, all that they have promised to you—it was a lie, it was an illusion, it was a cheat, it was a fraud, it was a crime. They promised you liberty. Where is liberty? They promised you prosperity. Where is prosperity? They have promised you elevation. Where is the elevation?" . . .

Where is the moral good that the War has given to the world? Where is the spiritual progress that we have achieved from the War? Where are the security of life, the security of the things that we possess for our necessity? Where are the respect for human life? Where are the respect and the admiration for the good characteristics and the good of the human nature? Never as now before the war there have been so many crimes, so many corruptions, so many degeneration as there is now. . . .

Well, I have already say that I not only am not guilty of these two crimes, but I never commit a crime in my life,—I have never steal and I have never kill and I have never spilt blood, and I have fought against the crime, and I have fought and I have sacrificed myself even to eliminate the crimes that the law and the church legitimate and sanctify.

This is what I say: I would not wish to a dog or to a snake, to the most low and misfortunate creature of the earth—I would not wish to any of them what I have had to suffer for things that I am not guilty of. But my conviction is that I have suffered for things that I am guilty of. I am suffering because I am a radical and indeed I am a radical; I have suffered because I was an Italian, and indeed I am an Italian; I have suffered more for my family and for my beloved than for myself; but I am so convinced to be right that if you could execute me two times, and if I could be reborn two other times, I would live again to do what I have done already.

I have finished. Thank you.

READING AND DISCUSSION QUESTIONS

1. Why does Vanzetti believe that he and Sacco were tried and convicted of the murders?

2. What does the Sacco and Vanzetti trial reveal about the anti-immigrant and anti-radical politics of the 1920s? How does this trial help you to understand the passage of the 1924 National Origins Act limiting immigration?

21-2 | Fighting for (All) Women's Right to Vote

CARRIE CHAPMAN CATT, *Passing the Federal Suffrage Amendment* (1918) and NEW-YORK TRIBUNE, *"Just Like the Men!"* (March 1, 1913)

By the time Carrie Chapman Catt wrote this introduction to *The Woman Citizen* in 1918, seventy years after the 1848 Women's Rights Convention at Seneca Falls, New York had first called for equal suffrage, women were on the cusp of victory. Catt was twice elected president of the National American Woman Suffrage Association (NAWSA), and her superior skills at organizing were instrumental in national and international efforts to advance women's rights. But the movement itself faced divisions, as is hinted at by this cartoon published in 1913. Did women's suffrage mean all women, regardless of race? African American women who formed the National Association of Colored Women hoped to take part in NAWSA's 1913 parade in Washington, D.C. NAWSA's leaders balked. They did not want to jeopardize support from southern congressmen by "muddying" women's suffrage with voting rights for black women. Women's suffrage advocates were ultimately successful. The Nineteenth Amendment was ratified in 1920, but African American women, like many African American men, faced on-going obstacles in exercising their right to vote, a reality only addressed with the passage of civil rights legislation in the 1960s.

Prejudice and tradition are breaking down everywhere before the onslaughts of reason. Women have proved that their service to the State is efficient and essential. Arguments against their complete enfranchisement now sound churlish. And men are in a mood of gratitude and appreciation, and not disposed to be churlish.

Ideas of freedom, locked and padlocked in the back of men's minds, have been breaking jail. Men had not previously shut the door on women deliberately. They had been serenely sure they didn't need them in public life until of late. Now they are getting strangely humble. Doubtless statesmen in the United States are thinking in terms of political freedom as they have not since the Civil War.

Thus the political significance of an issue which now affects many millions of women is not lost upon political leaders.

Leaders of all political parties, major and minor, have begun to demand it, and the national committees of the major parties have endorsed the Federal Amendment. Almost 8,000,000 voters, men and women, demand it in the twelve equal suffrage states and already the legislatures of many of these states, notably New York, the youngest of the group, have virtually ratified the Amendment in advance by sending resolutions to the Senate, urging its passage. Two million

Carrie Chapman Catt, "Passing the Federal Suffrage Amendment," Introduction to *The Woman Citizen,* by Mary Sumner Boyd (New York: Frederick A. Stokes Company, 1918), 1–9.

organized suffragists, uncounted millions of their unorganized helpers, women who are to-day trying to give themselves in two directions by laboring for suffrage and for the war, clamor to be relieved from their double task and to be allowed to give all their time to war work. . . .

Votes for women is a movement concerned far less with numbers than with inner meanings. It means informing the whole field of public life with the woman spirit, if it means anything at all. It is this that war has made evident in Europe, and will make evident in America. Woman suffrage is preeminently a war measure.

It is this which has recently aroused women of the South and Middle West to renewed demand for the vote in those states where the alien man has been permitted to vote when he was too little in sympathy with the ideals of this government to fight for them.

Not only a burning patriotism has aroused the women of these states as never before to work for their right to voice their own principles of government, but a real desire to protect the interests of their sons and husbands at the front from possible domination by a hostile spirit at home has inflamed them into a new crusade.

It is the spirit of the mother, the wife, the loyal American which has been injected into the states where this question is acute. And having once been awakened, men and women everywhere see that the woman's point of view cannot be pushed out of the councils which are to make for a better State.

The housewife's own knowledge must enter into food conservation if it is to be an effective conservation. The nurse's own experience must obtain to make the Red Cross do its effective best. The understanding women have of woman must be taken into account to keep the camp zone clean, for this is a problem that touches women and men both. The mother's voice is above all the one which will be wanted for deliberations about an increased birth rate to make up for war's ravages unless the world is to be thrust back into that disrespect for the child's right to be well born out of which it has been slowly emerging.

It is these considerations and not the granting of rewards to ammunition-making women, which has made statesmen declare that the ballot for women is a measure needed by a world at war as a safeguard of civilization and an assurance that the world is safe for democracy.

Library of Congress

READING AND DISCUSSION QUESTIONS

1. By the time Carrie Chapman Catt wrote this introduction, she had become convinced that ratification was certain. What do you think encouraged her in this view? How do you differentiate between long- and short-term causes of ratification?

2. What inference can you draw regarding Catt's understanding of women's role in American society? What role does she envision women playing in shaping the modern world?

3. What does this cartoon suggest about the movement for women's suffrage? How was race a complicating factor in achieving the movement's goals?

21-3 | Progressive Party's Call for Greater Democracy

Platform of the Conference for Progressive Political Action (1924)

Progressivism crested in the prewar years but crashed due to the political divisions regarding America's entry into World War I. In 1924, Wisconsin senator Robert M. La Follette organized a revived Progressive Party, embracing usual progressive ideas together with earlier proposals pushed by late-nineteenth-century Populists. La Follette ran unsuccessfully against Republican Calvin Coolidge for president in 1924, losing every state except his native Wisconsin but winning 17 percent of the popular vote nationwide, a remarkable showing for a candidate endorsed by the Socialist Party. The 1924 Progressive Party platform lays out its ambitious agenda for democratic mobilization.

For 148 years the American people have been seeking to establish a government for the service of all and to prevent the establishment of a government for the mastery of the few. Free men of every generation must combat renewed efforts of organized force and greed to destroy liberty. Every generation must wage a new war for freedom against new forces that seek through new devices to enslave mankind.

Under our representative democracy the people protect their liberties through their public agents.

The test of public officials and public polities alike must be: Will they serve or will they exploit the common need?

The reactionary continues to put his faith in mastery for the solution of all problems. He seeks to have what he calls the strong men and best minds rule and impose their decisions upon the masses of their weaker brethren.

The progressive, on the contrary, contends for less autocracy and more democracy in government, for less power of privilege and greater obligations of service.

Under the principle of ruthless individualism and competition, that government is deemed best which offers to the few the greatest chance of individual gain.

Under the progressive principle of co-operation, that government is deemed best which offers to the many the highest level of average happiness and well being.

It is our faith that we all go up or down together — that class gains are temporary delusions and that eternal laws of compensation make every man his brother's keeper.

"Platform of the Conference for Progressive Political Action," *The Socialist World* 5, no. 7 (July 1924): 2–3.

Program of Public Service

In that faith we present our program of public service:
1. The use of the power of the federal government to crush private monopoly, not to foster it.
2. Unqualified enforcement of the constitutional guarantees of freedom of speech, press and assemblage.
3. Public ownership of the nation's water power and creation of a public super-power system. Strict public control and permanent conservation of all natural resources, including coal, iron and other ores, oil and timber lands in the interest of the people. Promotion of public works in times of business depression.
4. Retention of surtax on swollen incomes, restoration of the tax on excess prof-its, taxation of stock dividends, profits undistributed to evade taxes, rapidly progressive taxes on large estates and inheritances, and repeal of excessive tariff duties, especially on trust-controlled necessities of life and of nuisance taxes on consumption, to relieve the people of the present unjust burden of taxation and compel those who profited by the war to pay their share of the war's costs, and to provide the funds for adjusted compensation solemnly pledged to the veterans of the World War.
5. Reconstruction of the federal reserve and federal farm loan systems to provide for direct public control of the nation's money and credit to make it available on fair terms to all, and national and state legislation to permit and promote co-operative banking.
6. Adequate laws to guarantee to farmers and industrial workers the right to organize and bargain collectively through representatives of their own choosing for the maintenance or improvement of their standard of life.
7. Creation of a government marketing corporation to provide a direct route between farm producer and city consumer and to assure farmers fair prices for their products, and protect consumers from the profiteers in foodstuffs and other necessaries of life. Legislation to control the meat-packing industry.
8. Protection and aid of cooperative enterprises by national and state legislation.
9. Common international action to effect the economic recovery of the world from the effects of the World War.
10. Repeal of the Cummins-Esch law. Public ownership of railroads, with dem-ocratic operation, and with definite safeguards against bureaucratic control.
11. Abolition of the tyranny and usurpation of the courts, including the practice of nullifying legislation in conflict with the political, social or economic theories of the judges. Abolition of injunctions in labor disputes and of the power to punish for contempt without trial by jury. Election of all federal judges without party designation for limited terms.

For Child Labor Amendment

12. Prompt ratification of the child labor amendment and subsequent enact-ment of a federal law to protect children in industry. Removal of legal discriminations against women by measures not prejudicial to legislation nec-essary for the protection of women and for the advancement of social welfare.

13. A deep waterway from the great lakes to the sea.
14. We denounce the mercenary system of degraded foreign policy under recent administrations in the interests of financial imperialists, oil monopolists and international bankers, which has at times degraded our state department from its high service as a strong and kindly intermediary of defenseless governments to a trading outpost for those interests and concession seekers engaged in the exploitation of weaker nations, as contrary to the will of the American people, destructive of domestic development and provocative of war. We favor an active foreign policy to bring about a revision of the Versailles treaty in accordance with the terms of the armistice, and to promote firm treaty agreements with all nations to outlaw wars, abolish conscription, drastically reduce land, air and naval armaments and guarantee public referendum on peace and war.

In supporting this program we are applying to the needs of today the fundamental principles of American democracy, opposing equally the dictatorship of plutocracy and the dictatorship of the proletariat.

We appeal to all Americans without regard to partisan affiliation and we raise the standards of our faith so that all of like purpose may rally and march in this campaign under the banners of progressive union.

The nation may grow rich in the vision of greed. The nation will grow great in the vision of service.

READING AND DISCUSSION QUESTIONS

1. What were the problems Progressives saw in the existing social, political, and economic conditions in America? What were their solutions to these problems?

2. What examples of "autocracy" do you think Progressives in 1924 were referencing in their platform?

3. How might historians account for the electoral loss Progressives faced in the 1924 election? Were the party's political ideas out of sync with the political culture of the twenties?

21-4 | Pushing for Prohibition

"Boys, Decide Between Us and Booze" (c. 1910s) and *"Women Picketing for Prohibition, Madison"* (c. 1910s)

Early twentieth century efforts to ban alcohol were part of a long struggle that began in the early nineteenth century. Women were often leaders of these efforts and pioneered mobilizing tactics like petition drives, parades, and direct action against saloons and bars. The Women's Christian Temperance Union (WCTU) became the largest national reform organization with state-level chapters across the country. Groups like the WCTU pressed for state and local legislation to curb alcohol consumption and, by the time the Eighteenth Amendment was ratified in 1919, many states had already passed such legislation. These photographs, one depicting women from Madison, Minnesota and a second featuring female students from Martin College in Tennessee, highlight the state-level activism that led to ratification.

Looking Back at Tennessee Collection/Tennessee Virtual Archive

Minnesota Historical Society/Getty Images

READING AND DISCUSSION QUESTIONS

1. Compare these two photographs. What similarities do you see? Why, for example, are the women wearing white?

2. Analyze the signs in both photographs. What are the messages being sent? What argument for prohibition are they making? To whom are they appealing and how?

21-5 | Harlem Renaissance Poet Sings the Blues

LANGSTON HUGHES, *"The Weary Blues"* (1926)

The Great Migration of African Americans out of the South to northern cities, including New York's Harlem neighborhood, constitutes one of the major demographic transformations of the twentieth century. The development of a black middle class supported the self-conscious cultural flowering known as the Harlem Renaissance, a 1920s outpouring of black artistic expression visible in paintings and sculpture, novels, jazz and blues music, and poetry. This work often depicted self-confident black Americans asserting their individuality in the face of haunting racial oppression. In one of his 1920s essays Langston Hughes wrote, "I am a Negro—and beautiful!" Here, in "The Weary Blues," the title poem in his 1926 collection, Hughes pays homage to a jazz aesthetic that defined the Harlem Renaissance.

The Weary Blues

Droning a drowsy syncopated tune,
Rocking back and forth to a mellow croon,
    I heard a Negro play.
Down on Lenox Avenue the other night
By the pale dull pallor of an old gas light
    He did a lazy sway. . . .
    He did a lazy sway. . . .
To the tune o' those Weary Blues.
With his ebony hands on each ivory key
He made that poor piano moan with melody.
    O Blues!
Swaying to and fro on his rickety stool
He played that sad raggy tune like a musical fool.
    Sweet Blues!
Coming from a black man's soul.
    O Blues!

In a deep song voice with a melancholy tone
I heard that Negro sing, that old piano moan—
    "Ain't got nobody in all this world,
        Ain't got nobody but ma self.
        I's gwine to quit ma frownin'
        And put ma troubles on the shelf."
Thump, thump, thump, went his foot on the floor.
He played a few chords then he sang some more—
    "I got the Weary Blues
        And I can't be satisfied.
        Got the Weary Blues
        And can't be satisfied—
        I ain't happy no mo'
        And I wish that I had died."
And far into the night he crooned that tune.
The stars went out and so did the moon.
The singer stopped playing and went to bed
While the Weary Blues echoed through his head.
He slept like a rock or a man that's dead.

READING AND DISCUSSION QUESTIONS

1. What does Hughes observe on Lenox Avenue, the famous street in New York City's Harlem neighborhood?

2. What does Hughes communicate about black culture? What role did the blues play in defining African American culture in the early twentieth century?

3. How did Hughes use language in this poem to evoke the music he heard?

21-6 | Advertising the American Dream

Westinghouse Advertisement (1924) and *Chevrolet Advertisement* (1927)

After an initial postwar recession, many sectors of the American economy rebounded, inducing the middle and upper class to indulge in a consumer culture manufactured by sophisticated marketers and advertisers. Americans bought products to adorn themselves and their homes in the latest and most modern fashions. Not everyone had the means to participate, and even those who purchased their way to happiness often did so on borrowed money, an overextension that snapped when the stock market crashed. These advertisements show the marketing strategies used to sell goods and an ideal of the good life.

READING AND DISCUSSION QUESTIONS

1. Examine these advertisements from the 1920s for evidence of the consumer culture that had emerged in that decade. What appeal to consumers do these advertisements make?

2. From these advertisements, what inference can you draw about the consumers these marketers targeted with their advertising campaign? Which consumers were excluded from the appeal in these ads and why? What do these advertisements reveal about 1920s society?

▪ COMPARATIVE QUESTIONS ▪

1. Compare the views of Langston Hughes on African American culture (Document 21-5) with the perspectives of Booker T. Washington (Document 17-5) and W. E. B. Du Bois (Document 19-6). To what extent did they agree on the means for surpassing the social, economic, and political limitations imposed by a majority white culture?

2. What do the sources in this chapter about women's suffrage (Document 21-2) and prohibition (Document 21-4) tell us about the role of women in reform? Do you see continuities over time in the causes they fought for? Compare these sources with Minnie U. Rutherford (Document 17-6), Jane Addams (Document 18-2), and "The New Woman—Wash Day" (Document P6-3).

3. What argument about the immigrant experience in America can you make using the evidence from the Sacco and Vanzetti trial (Document 21-1) together with Antanas Kaztauskis's experience (Document 16-3), the Border Wall cartoon (Document 16-5), and Marie Ganz's memory of the tenements (Document 18-3)?

4. How do Langston Hughes (Document 21-5) and Carrie Chapman Catt (Document 21-2) use the popular impressions of their respective groups to advocate for their betterment or recognition? What other parallels do you find between the Harlem Renaissance and the women's rights movement?

22

Managing the Great Depression, Forging the New Deal

1929–1938

The stock market crash of 1929 and the resulting depression burst the inflated economic bubble of the 1920s and plunged many Americans into an uncertain future. The thousands of letters that Eleanor Roosevelt received from distressed Americans recounting their tragic circumstances hint at the despair the economic crisis caused. When Franklin Delano Roosevelt entered the White House in 1933, he replaced Herbert Hoover's fiscally conservative approach, launching the New Deal, a program of reforms demonstrating the active engagement of the federal government. Some critics complained that FDR did not go far enough, while others described him as dictatorial in his control of the economy. To the broad coalition of American voters, however, FDR inspired hope that "happy days" were fast approaching. From its initial efforts to shore up financial institutions, Roosevelt's New Deal broadened in response to labor and working-class concerns to embrace public programs providing basic necessities and creating "safety net" guarantees that came to define a liberal consensus regarding government's role and responsibility in the twentieth century.

22-1 | President Inspires Depressed Nation with Promise of Action

FRANKLIN D. ROOSEVELT, *Inaugural Address* (1933)

During the 1932 election, Roosevelt's campaign had exuded a desperately needed optimism in the face of the worst economic collapse in American history. His inaugural address, where he allayed the fear Americans felt, called for immediate action, a counterpoint to the more conservative approach of his predecessor, who had presided over the first years of the Great Depression. Roosevelt's call for "action, and action now" anticipated the frenzy of his first hundred days, when he launched the programs collectively described as the New Deal.

I am certain that my fellow Americans expect that on my induction into the Presidency I will address them with a candor and a decision which the present situation of our Nation impels. This is preeminently the time to speak the truth, the whole truth, frankly and boldly. Nor need we shrink from honestly facing conditions in our country today. This great Nation will endure as it has endured, will revive and will prosper. So, first of all, let me assert my firm belief that the only thing we have to fear is fear itself—nameless, unreasoning, unjustified terror which paralyzes needed efforts to convert retreat into advance. In every dark hour of our national life a leadership of frankness and vigor has met with that understanding and support of the people themselves which is essential to victory. I am convinced that you will again give that support to leadership in these critical days. . . .

Our greatest primary task is to put people to work. This is no unsolvable problem if we face it wisely and courageously. It can be accomplished in part by direct recruiting by the Government itself, treating the task as we would treat the emergency of a war, but at the same time, through this employment, accomplishing greatly needed projects to stimulate and reorganize the use of our natural resources.

Hand in hand with this we must frankly recognize the overbalance of population in our industrial centers and, by engaging on a national scale in a redistribution, endeavor to provide a better use of the land for those best fitted for the land. The task can be helped by definite efforts to raise the values of agricultural products and with this the power to purchase the output of our cities. It can be helped by preventing realistically the tragedy of the growing loss through foreclosure of our small homes and our farms. It can be helped by insistence that the Federal, State, and local governments act forthwith on the demand that their cost be drastically reduced. It can be helped by

Franklin D. Roosevelt, Inaugural Address, March 4, 1933. Online by Gerhard Peters and John T. Woolley, *The American Presidency Project*, www.presidency.ucsb.edu/ws/?pid=1447.

the unifying of relief activities which today are often scattered, uneconomical, and unequal. It can be helped by national planning for and supervision of all forms of transportation and of communications and other utilities which have a definitely public character. There are many ways in which it can be helped, but it can never be helped merely by talking about it. We must act and act quickly.

Finally, in our progress toward a resumption of work we require two safeguards against a return of the evils of the old order: there must be a strict supervision of all banking and credits and investments, so that there will be an end to speculation with other people's money; and there must be provision for an adequate but sound currency.

These are the lines of attack. I shall presently urge upon a new Congress, in special session, detailed measures for their fulfillment, and I shall seek the immediate assistance of the several States.

Through this program of action we address ourselves to putting our own national house in order and making income balance outgo. Our international trade relations, though vastly important, are in point of time and necessity secondary to the establishment of a sound national economy. I favor as a practical policy the putting of first things first. I shall spare no effort to restore world trade by international economic readjustment, but the emergency at home cannot wait on that accomplishment.

The basic thought that guides these specific means of national recovery is not narrowly nationalistic. It is the insistence, as a first consideration, upon the interdependence of the various elements in, and parts of, the United States—a recognition of the old and permanently important manifestation of the American spirit of the pioneer. It is the way to recovery. It is the immediate way. It is the strongest assurance that the recovery will endure. . . .

It is to be hoped that the normal balance of Executive and legislative authority may be wholly adequate to meet the unprecedented task before us. But it may be that an unprecedented demand and need for undelayed action may call for temporary departure from that normal balance of public procedure.

I am prepared under my constitutional duty to recommend the measures that a stricken Nation in the midst of a stricken world may require. These measures, or such other measures as the Congress may build out of its experience and wisdom, I shall seek, within my constitutional authority, to bring to speedy adoption.

But in the event that the Congress shall fail to take one of these two courses, and in the event that the national emergency is still critical, I shall not evade the clear course of duty that will then confront me. I shall ask the Congress for the one remaining instrument to meet the crisis—broad Executive power to wage a war against the emergency, as great as the power that would be given to me if we were in fact invaded by a foreign foe.

For the trust reposed in me I will return the courage and the devotion that befit the time. I can do no less. . . .

We do not distrust the future of essential democracy. The people of the United States have not failed. In their need they have registered a mandate that they want direct, vigorous action. They have asked for discipline and direction under leadership. They have made me the present instrument of their wishes. In the spirit of the gift I take it.

In this dedication of a Nation we humbly ask the blessing of God. May He protect each and every one of us. May He guide me in the days to come.

READING AND DISCUSSION QUESTIONS

1. How would you describe the tone of Roosevelt's inaugural address? What do you think he hoped to accomplish with the speech, given at the height of the Great Depression?

2. What might Roosevelt's audience have anticipated about his approach to solving the economic crisis based on his inaugural address? Which lines might have cheered those hit hard by the depression? Which lines might have worried big business?

22-2 | Outflanking Roosevelt with Plan to Share the Nation's Wealth

HUEY LONG, *Every Man a King* (1934)

Two years into the New Deal, recovery still seemed distant for many Americans. Their continued despair buoyed the political ambitions of Democratic senator Huey Long from Louisiana. A brilliant orator and political operator, Long took advantage of the new popularity of radio to blast the New Deal's failures and cultivate a national audience for his radical "Share Our Wealth" program. Long's presidential ambitions, which could have compromised Roosevelt's support, were cut short when an assassin's bullet silenced him in 1935.

We have in America today more wealth, more goods, more food, more clothing, more houses than we have ever had. We have everything in abundance here.

We have the farm problem, my friends, because we have too much cotton, because we have too much wheat, and have too much corn, and too much potatoes.

We have a home loan problem, because we have too many houses, and yet nobody can buy them and live in them.

We have trouble, my friends, in the country, because we have too much money owing, the greatest indebtedness that has ever been given to civilization, where

---

Huey Long, *Share Our Wealth, Every Man a King* (Washington, DC, n.d.), 7–17.

it has been shown that we are incapable of distributing the actual things that are here, because the people have not money enough to supply themselves with them, and because the greed of a few men is such that they think it is necessary that they own everything, and their pleasure consists in the starvation of the masses, and in their possessing things they cannot use, and their children cannot use, but who bask in the splendor of sunlight and wealth, casting darkness and despair and impressing it on everyone else. . . .

We have in America today, ladies and gentlemen, $272,000,000,000 of debt. Two hundred and seventy-two thousand millions of dollars of debts are owed by the various people of this country today. Why, my friends, that cannot be paid. It is not possible for that kind of debt to be paid.

The entire currency of the United States is only $6,000,000,000. That is all of the money that we have got in America today. All the actual money you have got in all of your banks, all that you have got in the Government Treasury, is $6,000,000,000; and if you took all that money and paid it out today you would still owe $266,000,000,000; and if you took all that money and paid again you would still owe $260,000,000,000; and if you took it, my friends, 20 times and paid it you would still owe $150,000,000,000.

You would have to have 45 times the entire money supply of the United States today to pay the debts of the people of America and then they would just have to start out from scratch, without a dime to go on with. . . .

So, we have in America today, my friends, a condition by which about 10 men dominate the means of activity in at least 85 percent of the activities that you own. They either own directly everything or they have got some kind of mortgage on it, with a very small percentage to be excepted. They own the banks, they own the steel mills, they own the railroads, they own the bonds, they own the mortgages, they own the stores, and they have chained the country from one end to the other until there is not any kind of business that a small, independent man could go into today and make a living, and there is not any kind of business that an independent man can go into and make any money to buy an automobile with; and they have finally and gradually and steadily eliminated everybody from the fields in which there is a living to be made, and still they have got little enough sense to think they ought to be able to get more business out of it anyway.

If you reduce a man to the point where he is starving to death and bleeding and dying, how do you expect that man to get hold of any money to spend with you? It is not possible. . . .

Now, we have organized a society, and we call it "Share Our Wealth Society," a society with the motto "Every Man a King."

Every man a king, so there would be no such thing as a man or woman who did not have the necessities of life, who would not be dependent upon the whims and caprices and ipsi dixit[1] of the financial barons for a living. What do

---

[1] **Ipsi dixit**: That is, *ipse dixit* (Latin, "he himself says it"), the logical fallacy of making an assertion without proof.

we propose by this society? We propose to limit the wealth of big men in the country. There is an average of $15,000 in wealth to every family in America. That is right here today.

We do not propose to divide it up equally. We do not propose a division of wealth, but we propose to limit poverty that we will allow to be inflicted upon any man's family. We will not say we are going to try to guarantee any equality, or $15,000 to a family. No; but we do say that one third of the average is low enough for any one family to hold, that there should be a guarantee of a family wealth of around $5,000; enough for a home, an automobile, a radio, and the ordinary conveniences, and the opportunity to educate their children; a fair share of the income of this land thereafter to that family so there will be no such thing as merely the select to have those things, and so there will be no such thing as a family living in poverty and distress.

We have to limit fortunes. Our present plan is that we will allow no one man to own more tha[n] $50,000,000. We think that with that limit we will be able to carry out the balance of the program. It may be necessary that we limit it to less than $50,000,000. It may be necessary, in working out of the plans that no man's fortune would be more than $10,000,000 or $15,000,000. But be that as it may, it will still be more than any one man, or any one man and his children and their children, will be able to spend in their lifetimes; and it is not necessary or reasonable to have wealth piled up beyond that point where we cannot prevent poverty among the masses.

Another thing we propose is old-age pension of $30 a month for everyone that is 60 years old. Now, we do not give this pension to a man making $1,000 a year, and we do not give it to him if he has $10,000 in property, but outside of that we do.

We will limit hours of work. There is not any necessity of having over-production. I think all you have got to do, ladies and gentlemen, is just limit the hours of work to such an extent as people will work only so long as it is necessary to produce enough for all of the people to have what they need. Why, ladies and gentlemen, let us say that all of these labor-saving devices reduce hours down to where you do not have to work but 4 hours a day; that is enough for these people, and then praise be the name of the Lord, if it gets that good. Let it be good and not a curse, and then we will have 5 hours a day and 5 days a week, or even less than that, and we might give a man a whole month off during a year, or give him 2 months; and we might do what other countries have seen fit to do, and what I did in Louisiana, by having schools by which adults could go back and learn the things that have been discovered since they went to school.

We will not have any trouble taking care of the agricultural situation. All you have to do is balance your production with your consumption. You simply have to abandon a particular crop that you have too much of, and all you have to do is store the surplus for the next year, and the Government will take it over. When you have good crops in the area in which the crops that have been planted are sufficient for another year, put in your public works in the particular year when you do not need to raise any more, and by that means you get everybody employed. When the Government has enough of any particular crop to take care of all of the people, that will be all that is necessary; and in order to do all of this, our taxation is going to be to take the billion-dollar fortunes and strip them down to frying size, not to exceed $50,000,000, and if it is necessary to come to $10,000,000, we will come to $10,000,000. We have worked the proposition out to guarantee a limit upon property (and no man will own less than one-third the average), and guarantee a reduction of fortunes and a reduction of hours to spread wealth throughout this country. We would care for the old people above 60 and take them away from this thriving industry and give them a chance to enjoy the necessities and live in ease, and thereby lift from the market the labor which would probably create a surplus of commodities.

Those are the things we propose to do. "Every Man a King." Every man to eat when there is something to eat; all to wear something when there is something to wear. That makes us all a sovereign.

You cannot solve these things through these various and sundry alphabetical codes. You can have the N. R. A. and P. W. A. and C. W. A. and the U. U. G. and G. I. N. and any other kind of dad-gummed lettered code. You can wait until doomsday and see 25 more alphabets, but that is not going to solve this proposition. Why hide? Why quibble? You know what the trouble is. The man that says he does not know what the trouble is is just hiding his face to keep from seeing the sunlight. . . .

Now, my friends, we have got to hit the root with the ax. Centralized power in the hands of a few, with centralized credit in the hands of a few, is the trouble.

Get together in your community tonight or tomorrow and organize one of our Share Our Wealth Societies. If you do not understand it, write me and let me send you the platform; let me give you the proof of it.

This is Huey P. Long talking, United States Senator, Washington, D.C. Write me and let me send you the data on this proposition. Enroll with us. Let us make known to the people what we are going to do. I will send you a button, if I have got enough of them left. We have got a little button that some of our friends designed, with our message around the rim of the button, and in the center "Every Man a King." Many thousands of them are meeting through the United States, and every day we are getting hundreds and hundreds of letters. Share Our Wealth Societies are now being organized, and people have it within their power to relieve themselves from this terrible situation. . . .

I thank you, my friends, for your kind attention, and I hope you will enroll with us, take care of your own work in the work of this Government, and share or help in our Share Our Wealth Societies.

I thank you.

READING AND DISCUSSION QUESTIONS

1. Analyze Long's proposal for evidence of his political solution to the economic crisis of the Great Depression. How does he define the crisis and the solution?

2. What similarities to populism and progressivism can you identify in Long's "Share Our Wealth" program? What audience was he addressing, and what strategies did he use in his appeal?

22-3 | FDR's New Deal Programs in Action

Michigan Artist Alfred Castagne Sketching WPA Construction Workers (1939)

Roosevelt's New Deal embraced several aims as it evolved, but a central focus was finding jobs for the unemployed. The 1933 Public Works Administration (PWA) funded municipal projects including the building of roads, dams, bridges, and schools, funneling federal money to states and localities to hire workers. Two years later, Roosevelt created the Works Progress Administration (WPA), which funded similar projects and programs, such as the Federal Art Project and the Federal Writers' Project, which employed artists, novelists, and actors. This image, by an unknown photographer, depicts both programs at work.

National Archives, Records of the Work Projects Administration (69-AG-410)

READING AND DISCUSSION QUESTIONS

1. Analyze this photograph for evidence of Roosevelt's goals for his New Deal programs. What do you think Roosevelt was trying to accomplish beyond just providing jobs? Why, for instance, do you think the WPA funded artists like the one shown sketching in this scene?

2. By examining this photograph and evaluating the WPA, what conclusions might you draw about the evolving relationship between the American people and the federal government? To what extent do you think Americans began changing their understanding of government's role and responsibility in supporting those in need?

22-4 | Two Views of the National Recovery Administration

CLIFFORD K. BERRYMAN, *"The Spirit of the New Deal"* (1933) and *"It's So Hard to Find a Place for You"* (1935)

In 1933, Congress passed the National Industrial Recovery Act, creating a new federal agency, the National Recovery Administration (NRA). Designed to counter the economic fallout of the Great Depression, the NRA worked with labor and industry to establish "fair practices" codes within industries, regulating minimum wages, maximum working hours, and prices. Businesses adopting these codes displayed the Blue Eagle "We Do Our Part" sign. Many businesses, however, quickly resisted the regulations as an example of government overreach. For African Americans, the NRA did not go far enough. Many of the agricultural and domestic service industries (where southern African Americans were typically employed) were exempt from NRA minimum wage regulations, enabling employers to discriminate against black workers.

MPI/Getty Images

Chicago History Museum/Getty Images

READING AND DISCUSSION QUESTIONS

1. Compare the point of view of these cartoons. What is the artist of each image suggesting about the merits of the NRA?

2. What do these images suggest about race as a factor in shaping the design, implementation, and success of the NRA in particular and the New Deal in general?

22-5 | Reporting the Plight of Depression Families

MARTHA GELLHORN, *Field Report to Harry Hopkins* (1934)

Journalist and novelist Martha Gellhorn's heartrending field report describing impoverished Gastonia, North Carolina, families vividly captures the desperate hope of depression-era families. Hired by Harry Hopkins, Franklin Roosevelt's point man for federal relief efforts, Gellhorn detailed the enormous challenge facing the administration. Compounding the epic humanitarian crisis she encountered was the political opposition, which she singled out as one among many obstacles hampering relief efforts.

From Martha Gellhorn to Harry Hopkins, Report, Gaston County, North Carolina, November 11, 1934, Franklin D. Roosevelt Library, Harry Hopkins Papers, Box 66. Online transcript available at http://newdeal.feri.org/hopkins/hop08.htm.

All during this trip [to North Carolina] I have been thinking to myself about that curious phrase "red menace," and wondering where said menace hid itself. Every house I visited — mill worker or unemployed — had a picture of the President. These ranged from newspaper clippings (in destitute homes) to large colored prints, framed in gilt cardboard. The portrait holds the place of honour over the mantel. . . . He is at once God and their intimate friend; he knows them all by name, knows their little town and mill, their little lives and problems. And, though everything else fails, he is there, and will not let them down.

I have been seeing people who, according to almost any standard, have practically nothing in life and practically nothing to look forward to or hope for. But there is hope; confidence, something intangible and real: "the president isn't going to forget us."

Let me cite cases: I went to see a woman with five children who was living on relief ($3.40 a week). Her picture of the President was a small one, and she told me her oldest daughter had been married some months ago and had cried for the big, coloured picture as a wedding present. The children have no shoes and that woman is terrified of the coming cold as if it were a definite physical entity. There is practically no furniture left in the home, and you can imagine what and how they eat. But she said, suddenly brightening, "I'd give my heart to see the President. I know he means to do everything he can for us; but they make it hard for him; they won't let him." I note this case as something special; because here the faith was coupled with a feeling (entirely sympathetic) that the President was not entirely omnipotent.

I have been seeing mill workers; and in every mill when possible, the local Union president. There has been widespread discrimination in the south; and many mills haven't re-opened since the strike. Those open often run on such curtailment that workers are getting from 2 to 3 days work a week. The price of food has risen (especially the kind of food they eat: fat-back bacon, flour, meal, sorghum) as high as 100%. It is getting cold; and they have no clothes. The Union presidents are almost all out of work, since the strike. In many mill villages, evictions have been served; more threatened. These men are in a terrible fix. (Lord, how barren the language seems: these men are faced by hunger and cold, by the prospect of becoming dependent beggars — in their own eyes: by the threat of homelessness, and their families dispersed. What more can a man face, I don't know.) You would expect to find them maddened with fear; with hostility. I expected and waited for "lawless" talk; threats; or at least, blank despair. And I didn't find it. I found a kind of contained and quiet misery; fear for their families and fear that their children wouldn't be able to go to school. ("All we want is work and the chance to care for our families like a man should.") But what is keeping them sane, keeping them going on and hoping, is their belief in the President. . . .

These are the things they say to me: "We trust in the Supreme Being and Franklin Roosevelt." — "You heard him talk over the radio, ain't you? He's the only president who ever said anything about the forgotten man. We know he's going to stand by us." — "He's a man of his word and he promised us;

we aren't worrying as long as we got him." — "The president won't let these awful conditions go on." — "The president wanted the Code. The president knows why we struck." — "The president said no man was going to go hungry and cold; he'll get us our jobs." . . .

I am going on and on about this because I think it has vast importance. These people will be slow to give up hope; terribly slow to doubt the president. But if they don't get their jobs; then what? If the winter comes on and they find themselves on our below-subsistence relief; then what? I think they might strike again; hopelessly and apathetically. In very few places, there might be some violence speedily crushed. But if they lose this hope, there isn't much left for them as a group. And I feel [if] this class (whatever marvelous stock they are, too) loses its courage or morale or whatever you want to call it, there will be an even worse social problem than there now is. And I think that with time, adding disillusionment and suffering, they might actually go against their own grain and turn into desperate people. As it is, between them and fear, stands the President. But only the President. . . .

What has been constantly before me is the health problem. To write about it is difficult only in that one doesn't know where to begin. Our relief people are definitely on below subsistence living scales. (This is the unanimous verdict of anyone connected with relief; and a brief study of budgets clinches the matter.)

The result is that dietary diseases abound. I know that in this area there has always been pelagra;[2] but that doesn't make matters better. In any case it is increasing; and I have seen it ranging from scaly elbows in children to insanity in a grown man. Here is what doctors say: "It's no use telling mothers what to feed their children; they haven't the food to give." . . . "Conditions are really horrible here; it seems as if the people were degenerating before your eyes: the children are worse mentally and physically than their parents." . . . "All the mill workers I see are definite cases of undernourishment; that's the best breeding ground I know for disease." . . . "There's not much use prescribing medicine; they haven't the money to buy it." . . . "You can't do anything with these people until they're educated to take care of themselves; they don't know what to eat; they haven't the beginning of an idea how to protect themselves against sickness." . . .

The medical set-up, from every point of view, in this area is tragic. In Gaston County there is not one county clinic or hospital; and only one health officer (appointed or elected?). This gentleman has held his job for more than a dozen years; and must have had droll medical training sometime during the last century. He believes oddly that three shots of neo-salvarsan will cure syphilis; and thinks that injecting this into the arm muscle is as good as anything. Result: he cripples and paralyzes his patients who won't go back. He likewise refuses to sign sterilization warrants on imbeciles: grounds "It's a man's prerogative to

---

[2] **Pelagra**: A serious vitamin deficiency caused by poor nutrition.

have children." Another doctor in this area owns a drug store. He was selling bottled tonic (home-made I think) to his mill worker patients as a cure for syphilis. This was discovered by a 21 year old case worker, who wondered why her clients' money was disappearing so fast. When asked why he did this he said that syphilis was partly a "run-down" condition, and that "you ought to build the patients up." Every doctor says that syphilis is spreading unchecked and uncured. One doctor even said that it had assumed the proportions of an epidemic and wouldn't be stopped unless the government stepped in; and treated it like small-pox. . . .

Which brings us to birth control. Every social worker I saw, and every doctor, and the majority of mill owners, talked about birth control as the basic need of this class. I have seen three generations of unemployed (14 in all) living in one room; and both mother and daughter were pregnant. Our relief people have a child a year; large families are the despair of the social worker and the doctor. The doctors say that the more children in a family the lower the health rating. These people regard children as something the Lord has seen fit to send them, and you can't question the Lord even if you don't agree with him. There is absolutely no hope for these children; I feel that our relief rolls will double themselves given time. The children are growing up in terrible surroundings; dirt, disease, overcrowding, undernourishment. Often their parents were farm people, who at least had air and enough food. This cannot be said for the children. I know we could do birth control in this area; it would be a slow and trying job beginning with education. (You have to fight superstition, stupidity and lack of hygiene.) But birth control would be worked into prenatal clinics; and the grape vine telegraph is the best propaganda I know. I think if it isn't done that we may as well fold up; these people cannot be bettered under present circumstances. Their health is going to pieces; the present generation of unemployed will be useless human material in no time; their housing is frightful (talk about European slums); they are ignorant and often below-par intelligence. What can we do: feed them—feed them pinto beans and corn bread and sorghum and watch the pelagra spread. And in twenty years, what will there be; how can a decent civilization be based on a decayed substrata, which is incapable physically and mentally to cope with life?

As for their homes: I have seen a village where the latrines drain nicely down a gully to a well from which they get their drinking water. Nobody thinks anything about this; but half the population is both syphilitic and moronic; and why they aren't all dead of typhoid I don't know. (It would probably be a blessing if they were.) . . . .

[T]here is [also] a problem of education. (Do you know that the highest paid teacher in a school in North Carolina gets $720 a year? This is not criticism of the teachers; it is a downright woe.) But the schooling is such awful nonsense. Teach the kids to recite the Gettysburg address by heart: somehow one is not impressed. And they don't know what to eat or how to cook it; they don't even know that their bodies can be maintained in health by protective measures; they don't know that one needn't have ten children when one can't feed one; they don't know that syphilis is destroying and contagious. And with all this, they are grand people. If there is any meaning in the phrase "American stock" it has some meaning here. They are sound and good humored; kind and loyal. I don't believe they are lazy; I believe they are mostly ill and ignorant. They have a strong family feeling; and one sees this in pitiful ways — for instance: if there is any means of keeping the children properly or prettily clothed, it is done; but the mother will be a prematurely aged, ugly woman who has nothing to put on her back. And the father's first comment will be: could we get shoes for the children so they can go to school (though the father himself may be walking on the ground). . . .

I hope you won't misunderstand this report. It's easy to see what the government is up against. What with a bunch of loathsome ignoramuses talking about "lavish expenditure" and etc. And all right-minded citizens virtuously protesting against anything which makes sense or sounds new. I'm writing this extra report because you did send us out to look; and you ought to get as much as we see. It isn't all there is to see, by any means; and naturally I have been looking at the worst and darkest side. But it is a terribly frightening picture. Is there no way we can get it before the public, no way to make them realize that you cannot build a future on bad basic material? We are so proud of being a new people in a free land. And we have a serf class; a serf class which seems to me to be in as bad a state of degeneration maybe, in this area, worse than the low class European who has learned self-protection through centuries of hardship. It makes me raging mad to hear talk of "red revolution," the talk of cowards who would deserve what they got, having blindly and selfishly fomented revolution themselves. Besides I don't believe it; it takes time for all things including successful rebellion; time and a tradition for revolutions which does not exist in this country. But it's far more terrible to think that the basis of our race is slowly rotting, almost before we have had time to become a race.

READING AND DISCUSSION QUESTIONS

1. What does Gellhorn's discussion of the "red menace" suggest about the opposition Roosevelt faced in administering relief programs as part of the New Deal? What evidence of the "red menace" did she find in her field observations among North Carolina's poor?

2. How would you describe the tone of Gellhorn's reporting? How optimistic is she that these families will survive the Great Depression? What does she describe as the short- and long-term consequences of the depression?

3. Imagine you are Harry Hopkins reading Gellhorn's report. What advice would you give to Roosevelt concerning relief efforts for the nation's poor? How would you advise Roosevelt to navigate the obstacles to relief?

▪ COMPARATIVE QUESTIONS ▪

1. Compare Roosevelt's first inaugural address (Document 22-1) with the economic and social philosophy of William Graham Sumner (Document P6-1). What evidence do these documents provide on how the role of government changed over time?

2. What similarities can you identify between Martha Gellhorn's reporting (Document 22-5) and Upton Sinclair's *The Jungle* (Document 18-6)? To what extent is Gellhorn an heir to a Progressive Era tradition of muckraking journalism?

3. Assess the New Deal by identifying the arguments for and against Roosevelt's programs. To what extent are those arguments of the 1930s relevant today?

4. How might you interpret the New Deal within the broader narrative of American history? Would you emphasize continuities in the New Deal by linking Roosevelt's ideas to the earlier Populist and progressive reform movements? Or would you see the New Deal as a break with the past and the beginning of something new? Explain.

The World at War

1937–1945

Physicist Luis Alvarez was in one of the B-29 bomber planes accompanying the *Enola Gay*, the U.S. plane that dropped an atomic bomb on the Japanese city of Hiroshima on August 6, 1945. Moments after the blast, Alvarez wrote a letter to his young son, describing the mushroom cloud as "awe-inspiring" and the light flash "many times brighter than the sun." His front-row seat to history marked a beginning and an end. The bombs dropped on Hiroshima and, three days later, Nagasaki led to the end of World War II, the second fantastically destructive war of the twentieth century. Those bombs also inaugurated a new era in America's global dominance. The war had significant and immediate effects on the United States, even before the 1941 attack on Pearl Harbor. This global conflict transformed the lives of those American soldiers called to fight and those they left behind. The social and political consequences of war on the home front took many forms, from the mobilization of the wartime economy to constraints on economics and civil liberties. Many Americans who fought in World War II hoped to preserve liberty and freedom, while at the same time the war effort highlighted the persistent shortcomings plaguing race relations in the United States. Alvarez witnessed the end of the war but could only imagine the battles yet to come.

23-1 | President Roosevelt Defines the Four Freedoms at Risk

FRANKLIN D. ROOSEVELT, *Annual Message to Congress on the State of the Union* (1941)

Following the disaster of World War I, Americans had little taste for another European war when conflict erupted on the Continent once again in 1939. In his January 1941 State of the Union address, eleven months before the attack on Pearl Harbor, President Roosevelt pressed the case against isolationism and for the protection of American security. Here, Roosevelt articulates a vision for the world defined by guarantees of four essential freedoms.

Every realist knows that the democratic way of life is at this moment being directly assailed in every part of the world — assailed either by arms, or by secret spreading of poisonous propaganda by those who seek to destroy unity and promote discord in nations that are still at peace.

During sixteen long months this assault has blotted out the whole pattern of democratic life in an appalling number of independent nations, great and small. The assailants are still on the march, threatening other nations, great and small.

Therefore, as your President, performing my constitutional duty to "give to the Congress information of the state of the Union," I find it, unhappily, necessary to report that the future and the safety of our country and of our democracy are overwhelmingly involved in events far beyond our borders.

Armed defense of democratic existence is now being gallantly waged in four continents. If that defense fails, all the population and all the resources of Europe, Asia, Africa and Australasia will be dominated by the conquerors. . . .

In times like these it is immature — and incidentally, untrue — for anybody to brag that an unprepared America, single-handed, and with one hand tied behind its back, can hold off the whole world.

No realistic American can expect from a dictator's peace international generosity, or return of true independence, or world disarmament, or freedom of expression, or freedom of religion — or even good business.

Such a peace would bring no security for us or for our neighbors. "Those, who would give up essential liberty to purchase a little temporary safety, deserve neither liberty nor safety."

As a nation, we may take pride in the fact that we are softhearted; but we cannot afford to be soft-headed.

We must always be wary of those who with sounding brass and a tinkling cymbal preach the "ism" of appeasement.

We must especially beware of that small group of selfish men who would clip the wings of the American eagle in order to feather their own nests. . . .

Franklin D. Roosevelt, "Annual Message to Congress on the State of the Union," January 6, 1941. Online by Gerhard Peters and John T. Woolley, *The American Presidency Project,* www .presidency.ucsb.edu/ws/?pid=16092.

The need of the moment is that our actions and our policy should be devoted primarily — almost exclusively — to meeting this foreign peril. For all our domestic problems are now a part of the great emergency.

Just as our national policy in internal affairs has been based upon a decent respect for the rights and the dignity of all our fellow men within our gates, so our national policy in foreign affairs has been based on a decent respect for the rights and dignity of all nations, large and small. And the justice of morality must and will win in the end.

Our national policy is this:

First, by an impressive expression of the public will and without regard to partisanship, we are committed to all-inclusive national defense.

Second, by an impressive expression of the public will and without regard to partisanship, we are committed to full support of all those resolute peoples, everywhere, who are resisting aggression and are thereby keeping war away from our Hemisphere. By this support, we express our determination that the democratic cause shall prevail; and we strengthen the defense and the security of our own nation.

Third, by an impressive expression of the public will and without regard to partisanship, we are committed to the proposition that principles of morality and considerations for our own security will never permit us to acquiesce in a peace dictated by aggressors and sponsored by appeasers. We know that enduring peace cannot be bought at the cost of other people's freedom.

I . . . ask this Congress for authority and for funds sufficient to manufacture additional munitions and war supplies of many kinds, to be turned over to those nations which are now in actual war with aggressor nations.

Our most useful and immediate role is to act as an arsenal for them as well as for ourselves. They do not need man power, but they do need billions of dollars worth of the weapons of defense.

The time is near when they will not be able to pay for them all in ready cash. We cannot, and we will not, tell them that they must surrender, merely because of present inability to pay for the weapons which we know they must have. . . .

Let us say to the democracies: "We Americans are vitally concerned in your defense of freedom. We are putting forth our energies, our resources and our organizing powers to give you the strength to regain and maintain a free world. We shall send you, in ever-increasing numbers, ships, planes, tanks, guns. This is our purpose and our pledge." . . .

The happiness of future generations of Americans may well depend upon how effective and how immediate we can make our aid felt. No one can tell the exact character of the emergency situations that we may be called upon to meet. The Nation's hands must not be tied when the Nation's life is in danger.

We must all prepare to make the sacrifices that the emergency — almost as serious as war itself — demands. Whatever stands in the way of speed and efficiency in defense preparations must give way to the national need.

A free nation has the right to expect full cooperation from all groups. A free nation has the right to look to the leaders of business, of labor, and of agriculture to take the lead in stimulating effort, not among other groups but within their own groups. . . .

As men do not live by bread alone, they do not fight by armaments alone. Those who man our defenses, and those behind them who build our defenses, must have the stamina and the courage which come from unshakable belief in the manner of life which they are defending. The mighty action that we are calling for cannot be based on a disregard of all things worth fighting for.

The Nation takes great satisfaction and much strength from the things which have been done to make its people conscious of their individual stake in the preservation of democratic life in America. Those things have toughened the fibre of our people, have renewed their faith and strengthened their devotion to the institutions we make ready to protect.

Certainly this is no time for any of us to stop thinking about the social and economic problems which are the root cause of the social revolution which is today a supreme factor in the world.

For there is nothing mysterious about the foundations of a healthy and strong democracy. The basic things expected by our people of their political and economic systems are simple. They are:

Equality of opportunity for youth and for others.

Jobs for those who can work.

Security for those who need it.

The ending of special privilege for the few.

The preservation of civil liberties for all.

The enjoyment of the fruits of scientific progress in a wider and constantly rising standard of living.

These are the simple, basic things that must never be lost sight of in the turmoil and unbelievable complexity of our modern world. The inner and abiding strength of our economic and political systems is dependent upon the degree to which they fulfill these expectations.

Many subjects connected with our social economy call for immediate improvement.

As examples:

We should bring more citizens under the coverage of old-age pensions and unemployment insurance.

We should widen the opportunities for adequate medical care.

We should plan a better system by which persons deserving or needing gainful employment may obtain it.

I have called for personal sacrifice. I am assured of the willingness of almost all Americans to respond to that call.

A part of the sacrifice means the payment of more money in taxes. In my Budget Message I shall recommend that a greater portion of this great defense program be paid for from taxation than we are paying today. No person should try, or be allowed, to get rich out of this program; and the principle of tax payments in accordance with ability to pay should be constantly before our eyes to guide our legislation.

In the future days, which we seek to make secure, we look forward to a world founded upon four essential human freedoms.

The first is freedom of speech and expression—everywhere in the world.

The second is freedom of every person to worship God in his own way—everywhere in the world.

The third is freedom from want—which, translated into world terms, means economic understandings which will secure to every nation a healthy peacetime life for its inhabitants—everywhere in the world.

The fourth is freedom from fear—which, translated into world terms, means a world-wide reduction of armaments to such a point and in such a thorough fashion that no nation will be in a position to commit an act of physical aggression against any neighbor—anywhere in the world.

That is no vision of a distant millennium. It is a definite basis for a kind of world attainable in our own time and generation. That kind of world is the very antithesis of the so-called new order of tyranny which the dictators seek to create with the crash of a bomb. . . .

This nation has placed its destiny in the hands and heads and hearts of its millions of free men and women; and its faith in freedom under the guidance of God. Freedom means the supremacy of human rights everywhere. Our support goes to those who struggle to gain those rights or keep them. Our strength is our unity of purpose. To that high concept there can be no end save victory.

READING AND DISCUSSION QUESTIONS

1. Examine the argument Roosevelt made to Congress regarding the threats America faced from the war in Europe. How was America's security tied to events overseas?

2. How did Roosevelt define America's interest in the war in Europe? What were the freedoms at stake that he challenged Congress and the American people to defend?

23-2 | Soldiers Describe D-Day Experience

Interviews with the Library of Congress Veterans History Project (2001, 2003)

The June 1944 Normandy invasion began the liberation of Europe from German control. Planned by General Dwight D. Eisenhower, the amphibious assault of German-occupied France, known as Operation Overlord, resulted in the landing of 160,000 soldiers along France's coastline. Nine thousand of them died there. Their comrades, including Sergeant Claud C. Woodring and Private First Class Jay S. Adams, pushed forward, with the goal of capturing Germany and ending the war. These excerpts of interviews done as part of the Library of Congress's Veterans History Project vividly evoke the soldier's experience of war.

Interview with Claud Woodring, January 2, 2003, from Veterans History Project, American Folklife Center, Library of Congress. http://lcweb2.loc.gov/diglib/vhp-stories/loc.natlib .afc2001001.05288/. Courtesy of Claud Woodring.

Interview with Jay S. Adams, July 5, 2001, from Veterans History Project, Americans Folklife Center, Library of Congress. https://memory.loc.gov/diglib/vhp-stories/loc.natlib .afc2001001.00151/transcript?ID=sr0001

Interview with Jay S. Adams, July 5, 2001

The order came on the sixth for us . . . to go across the channel. . . . I went across on an LCT [landing craft tank], with my crane and my dozer on there. I was a dozer operator . . . and when we got out in the channel it got pretty rough, and I had to chain my dozer down because it was sliding down the deck. I was afraid it'd punch a hole in the side and we'd sink before we got there. [M]any of the men on the boats were . . . seasick because that channel was very rough. It was a storm, really, when we was going over, and as we approached the coastline in the morning, Navy was shelling the coast, and it was just like a fog on the coast. . . . [O]n the left, our Rangers are trying to get up the cliff there with pillboxes to step on the cliff, and we was coming right into the pillboxes, and we was supposed to have been on the second wave, and I don't know what time we got in there and dropped the ramp, and the jeep that came off, the guy got wounded, and then the fire was so heavy that the ship's Captain backed us off and we went back out into the channel. . . . [T]he guy driving the jeep, they sent him back to the States, and he had a sister that lived in Ashtabula. He wrote his sister and told his sister about me, and she got a hold of my parents and told them where I was at. They hadn't heard from me for so long and they didn't know that — then they knew that I was in the invasion in the French coast. . . .

[W]e backed off, and then we started in again, and we got stuck on a sand bar and was kind of like that, and an 88 come in under and explode it, and they pushed our boat aside just like that, and just as we done that, three 88 shells come right in where we was at and that pushed us back out, and then we tried to get in again, and the Captain of the ship, he dropped a ramp and I looked down there, and there was a .50 caliber sticking out of the water from a half track, and I told my officer, "We can't get the dozer in until we ground it out." So he said, "I'll take care of it." So he went up to see the Captain and he says, "You gotta get him in there." To this day, I'm convinced that he pulled a gun on that ship's Captain to get him in there because what they were doing, a lot of Navy guys were dropping them off in the water, and some of the quick movers going down and drowning out, and the men were drowning out. Getting drowned with the heavy packs on because it was too far out and some of the operators had flak vests on. I had a flak vest on, and I told the officer I'd take that off right here and I'd swim ashore [but] — we'll lose our equipment. He said, "We'll get her in." And so, when we finally did get in there . . . [it was] kind of gruesome to see all the dead soldiers laying on that beach. You had to zig zag around . . . to keep from running over them. One of my other buddies, that drove a dozer, he came in. I guess he got in a little ahead of me, and he heard a shell coming in, and they jumped off, and the shell came underneath his dozer and blowed the bottom out, and he . . . had a trailer behind him with TNT in there. The only thing was left was a short piece of the tongue left. Dove, Lynton Dove, had another dozer in our Company C, and he made a pass up through there. Some way or another he got through the mine field, and filled in an antitank dish, and got up over the hill so that the traffic could get going, and he received a DSC [Distinguished Service Cross] for that. . . .

And then we kind of, took us a few days to try to get organized again and get back together, and then our job was working on the beach for quite a while. We made roads in that area, and we built loading docks for the ducks that come in. . . . [W]hile we was down there, I helped clean the mine field with my dozer, and one day as I was walking down there, to get on my dozer, something grabbed—just seemed like somebody grabbed me by the shoulder and stopped me. And when I stopped and I moved my foot aside, there's a mine about an inch and a half from being stepped on, and now God was watching over us. I tell you, it's—you can't imagine it until you have something like that happen. It's just like somebody reached up, and took a hold of you, and made you stop. Just like I'm looking out at that tree, not thinking nothing about it. Walking through there, you know. Just that quick I stopped. You know, it was, and for many instances, like just a few seconds that I shifted gears or something, and a sniper shot at me one time, and I shifted a little quicker one time and a bullet went behind me, and lot of different instances went on like that. Just, moving just a little bit one way or another. A lot of our—we lost I forget how many men, but quite a few of us got through it. It's a wonder any of us made it. Within a 24-hour period there was around 5,000 men killed right there on the beach, and that's not counting the wounded. I don't know how many wounded. To this day there's probably a lot of them in the hospitals that have never come out from there. . . .

[A]fter we got done there, after they got the port open, then we moved on up . . . all the way through France, and up into Belgium, and up into Holland . . . it was getting colder weather . . . and everybody sleeping in the pup tents and everything, and there's a guy came from this village. He said, "I'd like a couple guys to come and sleep in my house where it's warm tonight." . . . They were still thankful that they'd been liberated and they was free, 'cause I don't know exactly how many years they were under German . . . control, and they couldn't do enough for the GI's going through there, and that happened through all of the towns that we went through.

Interview with Claud Woodring, January 2, 2003

I was inducted May 6th of '43. I went to Camp Perry, Ohio. Shipped from there to Camp Shelby, Mississippi, for my basic training. Basic training was to be 13 weeks. At 11 weeks, I was shipped out of Camp Shelby, Mississippi, to Fort George G. Meade, Baltimore, Maryland. I went to a staging area somewhere [in] upstate New York. I shipped out of New York on November 2, 1943. . . . We landed in Glasgow, Scotland, on November the 9th of '43. From there I went to Dorchester, Dorset, England, assigned to the First Infantry Division Company of the 18th Regiment. . . .

All of my combat training was in England. . . . I was not a good soldier when I first went into the Army. When I went to Camp Shelby, Mississippi, the first day I was taking pictures with a two-dollar Brownie camera. The company commander objected to that. We had a few words and he stomped on my camera. From then on I did not like the Army's attitude. . . . After 11 weeks, my name was posted on a shipping order. I shipped out. I did not get a three-day pass after I was inducted. I did not get a seven-day furlough after basic training. When I left home, I kissed mom goodbye, and I didn't see my mother again until after I got back after I was wounded. All of these things led up to—I developed an attitude and when I was assigned to the First Infantry Division in England I had a sergeant, Sergeant St. John, he took me aside and beat the hell out of me and convinced me I should become a soldier or I wasn't going to survive the war. He taught me to be a soldier in England. While training in England, I . . . had sniper training and demolition training. I did a lot of demolition training in anticipation of the landing. . . .

I was charged with the job of blowing up the barbed wire on the beach. That's what I trained for, specifically, along with being a foot soldier. . . . We went down to Portsmouth and we were put on LCVP, landing craft vehicle and personnel, and . . . we was on that ship all night . . . June the 5th, [the night] prior to the invasion, and when we went across the channel it was dark, of course, at night, but it was almost wall-to-wall LCVP's landing craft. Our landing craft hit a submerged mine two, three hundred yards from shore and sunk. In the process of the ship hitting the mine, one of my buddies went overboard and I let my rifle down to help ease him up. He weighed 200 pounds, I weighed 125 pounds. He won. He was in the water with two guns, so when we abandoned the ship, so to speak, I had two bangalore torpedos and inflated our life belts . . . and we swam ashore. At this point in time it was just breaking daylight. . . .

[The trip across the channel had been] terribly rough. . . . The weather was horrible, windy rough, high waves. Ships banging against each other almost. It was so bad. . . . When I got off of the ship, I swam ashore. . . . Fully clothed with all the gear on we had and no rifle and at that point I didn't need a rifle. The day and evening before the invasion the air corps had dropped thousands of little bombs on the beach to make ready-made foxholes, which were a Godsend, so I approached the barbed wire, which is strung out in coils several layers thick. You couldn't cut one strand of barbed wire. If you did, it would fly and grab you and tear you all apart and it was impossible to cut through it. It would take too much time. We had the bangalore torpedoes which screwed together with a hand grenade detonator in it and slid them under the barbed wire, pulled the pin, ducked in a foxhole and blew a hole in the barbed wire that was probably, oh, 50, 60 yards wide and all the time there's people pushing right behind you. There are thousands coming on. Probably the only reason I survived the assault on the beach was the Germans could fire into a massive crowd behind me and they weren't worried about the first person up ahead. . . .

As I remember, we were on top of the beach—on top of the sand dunes at the beach probably by two o'clock in the afternoon, maybe a little earlier than that, but at that point the beach was completely full of people and equipment and litter and the tide was coming in. . . . After we left the beaches, we got right into the hedgerow country and that was horrendous fighting, probably as diffi-cult as the beach because of the cover they had. This hedgerow country had been there—they're little two or three acre field with hedgerows for fences. . . . Every day we ran into the enemy, whether it be Panzer or rear action—rear guard. After we got through the hedgerow country out into open country, the Germans had to travel at night because we had air supremacy. . . . As soon as it got dark, you would hear the German equipment heading towards Germany. They had a short night and can't travel very fast in the dark, consequently every day about two o'clock in the afternoon or three or noon, whatever, we would have advanced as far during the daytime as they did at night and then there would be another little war fought every day. Every day we caught the enemy and had a scrimmage. . . . The Germans that we captured, though, were conscription army, Czechs, Poles, whoever. They didn't want to fight and they [were] way—underequipped. They were still using World War I horse-drawn artillery. These people surrendered by the hundreds. One soldier could take 50 prisoners back and not have a problem. . . . The frequency and the fierceness of the fighting would decrease at that point pretty much every day because the German—hardline German soldiers were heading for Germany and they had occupation troops that were just holding us up. They were just there to irritate us. . . . The local French people were great. If there was a sniper in a tower, they told you where he was. They were informants. They were glad to see us. They helped us in any way they could.

READING AND DISCUSSION QUESTIONS

1. What perspective of war and the D-Day invasion in particular emerges from these interview transcripts? How might an account of D-Day differ if you read, for example, a report from General Dwight Eisenhower, who planned the Normandy invasion?

2. From these interviews, what can you infer about the meaning and significance of D-Day from these soldiers' perspectives? What about the invasion stands out in their memories?

23-3 | Japanese Americans in the Crosshairs of War

GORDON HIRABAYASHI, *Why I Refused to Register for Evacuation* (1942)

After Japan's 1941 attack on Pearl Harbor, President Roosevelt imposed restraints on Japanese immigrants (known as Issei) and their American-born descendants (Nisei), including curfews and eventually evacuation to internment camps. Gordon Hirabayashi, an American citizen of Japanese descent, refused to register for the forced evacuation and was convicted and sentenced to jail. His appeal to the Supreme Court ended in defeat. When the evacuation order was announced, Hirabayashi penned this note describing his reasons for resisting.

Gordon K. Hirabayashi, "Why I Refused to Register for Evacuation," May 13, 1942, Ring Family Papers, Box 1, Folder 17, University of Washington, Special Collections, Seattle, Washington. http://digitalcollections.lib.washington.edu/cdm/singleitem/collection/pioneerlife /id/21356/rec/106.

Over and above any man-made creed or law is the natural law of life—the right of human individuals to live and to creatively express themselves. No man was born with the right to limit that law. Nor, do I believe, can anyone justifiably work himself to such a position.

Down through the ages, we have had various individuals doing their bit to establish more securely these fundamental rights. They have tried to help society see the necessity of understanding those fundamental laws; some have succeeded to the extent of having these natural laws recorded. Many have suffered unnatural deaths as a result of their convictions. Yet, today, because of the efforts of some of these individuals, we have recorded in the laws of our nation certain rights for all men and certain additional rights for citizens. These fundamental moral rights and civil liberties are included in the Bill of Rights, U.S. Constitution and other legal records. They guarantee that these fundamental rights shall not be denied without due process of law.

The principles or the ideals are the things which give value to a person's life. They are the qualities which give impetus and purpose toward meaningful experiences. The violation of human personality is the violation of the most sacred thing which man owns.

This order for the mass evacuation of all persons of Japanese descent denies them the right to live. It forces thousands of energetic, law-abiding individuals to exist in a miserable psychological and a horrible physical atmosphere. This order limits to almost the full extent the creative expressions of those subjected. It kills the desire for a higher life. Hope for the future is exterminated. Human personalities are poisoned. The very qualities which are essential to a peaceful, creative community are being thrown out and abused. Over 60 percent are American citizens, yet they are denied on a wholesale scale without due process of law the civil liberties which are theirs.

If I were to register and cooperate under those circumstances, I would be giving helpless consent to the denial of practically all of the things which give me incentive to live. I must maintain my Christian principles. I consider it my duty to maintain the democratic standards for which this nation lives. Therefore, I must refuse this order for evacuation.

Let me add, however, that in refusing to register, I am well aware of the excellent qualities of the army and government personnel connected with the prosecution of this exclusion order. They are men of the finest type, and I sincerely appreciate their sympathetic and honest efforts. Nor do I intend to cast any shadow upon the Japanese and the other Nisei who have registered for evacuation. They have faced tragedy admirably. I am objecting to the principle of this order, which denies the rights of human beings, including citizens.

GORDON K. HIRABAYASHI
May 13, 1942

READING AND DISCUSSION QUESTIONS

1. Analyze Hirabayashi's statement to determine the argument he makes against the U.S. policy regarding Japanese internment camps. Upon what sources of authority does he base his refusal?

2. What does his form of civil disobedience reveal to you about the wartime pressures and constraints on civil liberties?

23-4 | Fighting for Democracy and Civil Rights at Home and Abroad

LULAC NEWS, *Editorial* (1945)

When the League of United Latin American Citizens (LULAC) was organized in 1929, those of Latin American descent faced racial and ethnic discrimination, exacerbated by the economic tensions of the Great Depression. Franklin Roosevelt supported a policy of repatriating many to Mexico in an effort to ease the economic crisis, but when wartime labor demands spiked, Mexican contract laborers were brought in to work the farms. Latin Americans also fought in the war yet faced discrimination similar to that experienced by African American veterans upon their return home. This 1945 editorial from the *LULAC News* raises questions about the meaning of race and the hypocrisy of America's freedom rhetoric in a culture of discrimination.

"We do not serve Mexicans here." "You will have to get out as no Mexicans are allowed." "Your uniform and service ribbons mean nothing here. We still do not allow Mexicans."

These, and many other stronger-worded ones, are the embarrassing and humiliating retorts given our returning veterans of Latin American descent and their families. They may all be worded differently, and whereas some are toned with hate and loathness while others are toned with sympathy and remorse, still the implication remains that these so-called "Mexicans" are considered unworthy of equality, regardless of birthright or service. This situation is ironic indeed, in view of the fact that these same "Mexicans" have just finished helping this country to defeat countries to the east and west who would impose upon the world a superior people, a superior culture.

Why this hate, this prejudice, this tendency to discriminate against a people whose only fault seems to be that they are heirs of a culture older

"Editorial". From LULAC News Volume 12 (October 1945), pp. 5–6 is reprinted with permission from the publisher of "Testimonio: A Documentary History of the Mexican American Struggle for Civil Rights", edited by F. Arturo Gonzalez (©2000 Arte Publico Press — University of Houston)

than any known "American Culture," to find themselves a part of a land and people they have helped to build and to defend, to find themselves a part of a minority group whose acquired passive nature keeps them from boldly demanding those rights and privileges which are rightfully theirs? Can it be the result of difference in race, nationality, language, loyalty, intelligence or ability?

There is no difference in race. Latin Americans, or so-called "Mexicans," are Caucasian or white. There are only three races: the Caucasian, the Negroid, and the Mongoloid. Racial characteristics place the Latin American among the white. Who dares contradict nature? There is no difference in nationality. These "Mexicans" were born and bred in this country and are just as American as Jones or Smith. In fact, the ancestors of these "Mexicans" were here before those of Jones or Smith decided to take up abode. Differences in language? No. These "Mexicans" speak English. Accented, perhaps, in some cases, but English all over the United States seems to be accented. That these "Mexicans" can speak Spanish is not a detriment; it is an asset. After all, there are not too many people in this country who can boast a knowledge of the most widely spoken languages of the world. Difference in loyalty? How can that be when all revere the same stars and stripes, when they don the same service uniforms for the same principles? Difference in intelligence and ability? Impossible. For every profession and category of work, from menial labor to the most scientific and technical matter, there is a qualified group of "Mexicans." All they need is the opportunity minus the discrimination and jealousy.

We could go on and on naming erroneously imagined differences to be used as a basis for this hate and find each one false. This condition is not a case of difference; it is a case of ignorance. Yes, ignorance. Odd indeed to find this banal state of mind in a country of such enlightenment and progress. But then, ignorance is like a disease that is contagious, but contagious only for those who wish to suffer from it. Ignorance, bigotry, prejudice, and intolerance all down through the centuries have tried to crush intelligence with cruelty, reason with brutality, and spirituality with madness. This quartet of banalities constitutes the curse of the world. Ignorance is the parent of the other three.

Yes, ignorance broods hate and all its resultant actions of jealousy, misunderstandings, erroneous opinions, and premeditated feelings of discord and confusion. In this particular case of unjustified failure to foment a fraternal feeling between two groups of Americans, it is an ignorance of facts that poisons the atmosphere. An ignorance of the cultural contributions of Americans of Latin American descent to the still young American Culture; an ignorance of the blood, sweat, and efforts given to this country for its betterment; an ignorance of the sufferings withstood and the lives given to preserve this country free and independent through its various periods of strife and conflict; and finally, an ignorance of a sense of appreciation for a long, profitable, and loyal association with a group of Americans whose voice cries out in desperate supplication:

"We have proved ourselves true and loyal Americans by every trial and test that has confronted us; now give us social, political, and economic equality and the opportunity to practice and enjoy that equality. We ask for it not as a favor, but as a delegated right guaranteed by our Constitution, and as a reward for faithful service."

READING AND DISCUSSION QUESTIONS

1. What conclusions can you draw from the editorial regarding the construction of race in midcentury American culture? What argument about "whiteness" did LULAC make, and why did the organization object to the term "Mexicans" as Americans used it?

2. What impact do you think the concerns raised by LULAC had on the postwar civil rights movement? How does LULAC define the source of the discrimination its members faced?

23-5 | African American Women and the War Effort

U.S. Army Nurses Arrive in European Theater of War (1944)

Women played an important role in the wartime effort. Many "Rosie the Riveters" joined sectors of the industrial economy once dominated by men. Others took jobs in the federal bureaucracy as secretaries for government agencies. Almost 350,000 women joined one of the military branches in auxiliary or reserve corps. These WAACS (Women's Army Auxiliary Corps) and WAVES (the Navy's female reserve unit) tackled many roles, including laboratory technicians in government hospitals, test pilots for newly manufactured planes, radio operators, analysts, and mechanics. The federal government undertook a major advertising campaign to enlist women's support for the war, and by war's end, a third of U.S. women were working outside the home. Despite these expanded opportunities, women earned much less than the men who held the same jobs before the war. In addition to earning less than their male counterparts, African American women faced persistent discrimination. Many African Americans embraced the Double V campaign, fighting both for victory over Nazism and fascism overseas and victory over racial discrimination at home. African Americans pointed to their wartime contributions, including those of the U.S. Army nurses shown in this photograph, in making their case for equal citizenship. Here, a group of African American nurses arrive in Scotland by ship in August 1944 to serve in the European Theater of Operations.

National Archives

READING AND DISCUSSION QUESTIONS

1. What does this photograph suggest about the role of women during wartime? What opportunities did World War II open to African American women?

2. What do you think their military service meant to these African American women? What might you infer about the impact of their wartime service on the subsequent civil rights movement?

23-6 | President Explains Use of Atomic Bomb to End War

HARRY TRUMAN, *Statement by the President Announcing the Use of the A-Bomb at Hiroshima* (1945)

Harry Truman entered the presidency in April 1945 following the death of FDR. It fell to him to oversee the end of the war in the Pacific against the Japanese. When the government of Japan ignored the Allied demand for surrender made at the Potsdam Conference in July, Truman decided to use the atomic bomb secretly developed by American scientists. Ultimately two bombs were dropped, the first on Hiroshima on August 6, the second three days later on Nagasaki. In this August 6 statement, Truman announced the bombing of Hiroshima to the American people.

Harry S. Truman, "Statement by the President Announcing the Use of the A-Bomb at Hiroshima," August 6, 1945. Online by Gerhard Peters and John T. Woolley, *The American Presidency Project*, www.presidency.ucsb.edu/ws/?pid=12169.

Sixteen hours ago an American airplane dropped one bomb on Hiroshima, an important Japanese Army base. That bomb had more power than 20,000 tons of T.N.T. It had more than two thousand times the blast power of the British "Grand Slam" which is the largest bomb ever yet used in the history of warfare.

The Japanese began the war from the air at Pearl Harbor. They have been repaid many fold. And the end is not yet. With this bomb we have now added a new and revolutionary increase in destruction to supplement the growing power of our armed forces. In their present form these bombs are now in production and even more powerful forms are in development.

It is an atomic bomb. It is a harnessing of the basic power of the universe. The force from which the sun draws its power has been loosed against those who brought war to the Far East.

Before 1939, it was the accepted belief of scientists that it was theoretically possible to release atomic energy. But no one knew any practical method of doing it. By 1942, however, we knew that the Germans were working feverishly to find a way to add atomic energy to the other engines of war with which they hoped to enslave the world. But they failed. We may be grateful to Providence that the Germans got the V-1's and V-2's late and in limited quantities and even more grateful that they did not get the atomic bomb at all.

The battle of the laboratories held fateful risks for us as well as the battles of the air, land and sea, and we have now won the battle of the laboratories as we have won the other battles.

Beginning in 1940, before Pearl Harbor, scientific knowledge useful in war was pooled between the United States and Great Britain, and many priceless helps to our victories have come from that arrangement. Under that general policy the research on the atomic bomb was begun. With American and British scientists working together we entered the race of discovery against the Germans.

The United States had available the large number of scientists of distinction in the many needed areas of knowledge. It had the tremendous industrial and financial resources necessary for the project and they could be devoted to it without undue impairment of other vital war work. In the United States the laboratory work and the production plants, on which a substantial start had already been made, would be out of reach of enemy bombing, while at that time Britain was exposed to constant air attack and was still threatened with the possibility of invasion. For these reasons Prime Minister Churchill and President Roosevelt agreed that it was wise to carry on the project here. We now have two great plants and many lesser works devoted to the production of atomic power. Employment during peak construction numbered 125,000 and over 65,000 individuals are even now engaged in operating the plants. Many have worked there for two and a half years. Few know what they have been producing. They see great quantities of material going in and they see nothing coming out of these plants, for the physical size of the explosive charge is exceedingly small. We have spent two billion dollars on the greatest scientific gamble in history—and won.

But the greatest marvel is not the size of the enterprise, its secrecy, nor its cost, but the achievement of scientific brains in putting together infinitely complex pieces of knowledge held by many men in different fields of science into a workable plan. And hardly less marvelous has been the capacity of industry to design, and of labor to operate, the machines and methods to do things never done before so that the brain child of many minds came forth in physical shape and performed as it was supposed to do. Both science and industry worked under the direction of the United States Army, which achieved a unique success in managing so diverse a problem in the advancement of knowledge in an amazingly short time. It is doubtful if such another combination could be got together in the world. What has been done is the greatest achievement of organized science in history. It was done under high pressure and without failure.

We are now prepared to obliterate more rapidly and completely every productive enterprise the Japanese have above ground in any city. We shall destroy their docks, their factories, and their communications. Let there be no mistake; we shall completely destroy Japan's power to make war.

It was to spare the Japanese people from utter destruction that the ultimatum of July 26 was issued at Potsdam. Their leaders promptly rejected that ultimatum. If they do not now accept our terms they may expect a rain of ruin from the air, the like of which has never been seen on this earth. Behind this air attack will follow sea and land forces in such numbers and power as they have not yet seen and with the fighting skill of which they are already well aware.

The Secretary of War, who has kept in personal touch with all phases of the project, will immediately make public a statement giving further details.

His statement will give facts concerning the sites at Oak Ridge near Knoxville, Tennessee, and at Richland near Pasco, Washington, and an installation near Santa Fe, New Mexico. Although the workers at the sites have been making materials to be used in producing the greatest destructive force in history they have not themselves been in danger beyond that of many other occupations, for the utmost care has been taken of their safety.

The fact that we can release atomic energy ushers in a new era in man's understanding of nature's forces. Atomic energy may in the future supplement the power that now comes from coal, oil, and falling water, but at present it cannot be produced on a basis to compete with them commercially. Before that comes there must be a long period of intensive research.

It has never been the habit of the scientists of this country or the policy of this Government to withhold from the world scientific knowledge. Normally, therefore, everything about the work with atomic energy would be made public.

But under present circumstances it is not intended to divulge the technical processes of production or all the military applications, pending further examination of possible methods of protecting us and the rest of the world from the danger of sudden destruction.

I shall recommend that the Congress of the United States consider promptly the establishment of an appropriate commission to control the production and use of atomic power within the United States. I shall give further consideration and make further recommendations to the Congress as to how atomic power can become a powerful and forceful influence towards the maintenance of world peace.

READING AND DISCUSSION QUESTIONS

1. Beyond simply announcing the dropping of the atomic bomb, what does Truman hope to accomplish with his statement to the American people? Do you think Americans were his only audience?

2. How do you assess the tone of Truman's statement? How, for instance, does he describe the work of the scientists who created the bomb?

3. Imagine yourself an advisor to Truman on August 5. What advice would you have given him concerning the use of the atomic bomb? What do you think were the common arguments for and against its use?

■ COMPARATIVE QUESTIONS ■

1. Compare Franklin D. Roosevelt's "Four Freedoms" speech (Document 23-1) with Woodrow Wilson's Fourteen Points (Document 20-6) to understand how the definition of America's values changed and remained consistent over time. What similarities do you see in the way the two presidents spoke about war's potential to change the world?

2. Did the experience of World War II change the way people of different races and ethnicities were treated in the United States? Consider the United States' treatment of immigrants (see Bartolomeo Vanzetti's last statement [Document 21-1] and the anti-immigrant political cartoon [Document 16-5]) and African Americans (see "New York Negroes Stage Silent Parade of Protest" [Document 18-4]) in the late nineteenth and early twentieth centuries and compare that to the evidence in Gordon Hirabayashi's statement (Document 23-3) and the *LULAC News* editorial (Document 23-4). What can you conclude about America's history of race and ethnic relations through the mid-twentieth century?

3. What editorial reaction can you imagine *LULAC News* (Document 23-4) having in response to Franklin D. Roosevelt's "Four Freedoms" speech (Document 23-1)? How might readers of *LULAC News* have reacted to Roosevelt's description of American ideals?

4. How would you assess the cost of war on American society? To what extent do you see evidence of war helping or hindering the resolution of persistent social, political, and economic problems?

DOCUMENT SET

Global Ambitions and Domestic Turmoil

1890–1945

CHAPTER 20
An Emerging World Power, 1890–1918

CHAPTER 21
Unsettled Prosperity: From War to Depression, 1919–1932

CHAPTER 22
Managing the Great Depression, Forging the New Deal, 1929–1938

CHAPTER 23
The World at War, 1937–1945

While the United States entered the 1890s without significant international engagements, fifty-five years later, it had emerged as the leading power in the world. Critics of America's imperial ambitions might well have wondered what their country had become. This global expansion was driven by economic and geopolitical considerations, but many Americans maintained a centuries-old belief that they had a "rendezvous with destiny," and that their ventures overseas were selfless acts in support of democracy's onward progress. The reality at home, however, raised questions for many groups: women advocating for suffrage, immigrants, ethnic minorities, and Native Americans defending their rights, and African Americans facing persistent racism. As the various groups defined their identity within American society, they faced the juxtaposition of their experience with the American ideal. The theme of identity was critical to these groups as they sought to imagine their place as part of America, and as gender, class, ethnic, religious, regional, and racial factors affected the way they saw themselves and the way that others viewed them. For some, merging their identity into an American melting pot seemed best, while others saw strength in maintaining America's diversity. The tension between these perspectives fueled discussions of American identity throughout the twentieth century.

P7-1 | Lower East Side Residents Condemn Immigration Commissioner

Citizens Committee of Orchard, Rivington, and East Houston Streets, New York City to William Howard Taft (1912)

More than 600,000 immigrants passed through Ellis Island in 1912, the year residents of the Lower East Side wrote this letter to President Taft criticizing the disparaging remarks of the New York commissioner of immigration. Unlike earlier waves of immigration, increasing numbers hailed from Southern and Eastern Europe, including Jews and other groups that many Americans feared as radical and unassimilable. This anxiety led to a study published in 1911 by the Dillingham Commission recommending immigration restriction, which would later be enacted in the early 1920s. Here, a citizens' committee of the Lower East Side responds by affirming their identity as Americans.

Hon. WILLIAM H. TAFT,
President of the United States of America,
Washington, D.C.

Sir: —
The undersigned are residents of Orchard, Rivington, and East Houston Streets, in the Borough of Manhattan, City of New York. As such they respectfully call your attention to the following statement contained in the annual report for the year ending June 30, 1911, of William Williams, Esq., Commissioner of Immigration for the Port of New York:

"The new immigration, unlike that of the earlier years, proceeds in part from the poorer elements of the countries of Southern and Eastern Europe and from backward races with customs and institutions widely different from ours and without the capacity of assimilating with our people as did the early immigrants. Many of those coming from these sources have very low standards of living, possess filthy habits, and are of an ignorance which passes belief. Types of the classes referred to, representing various alien races and nationalities may be

Citizens Committee of Orchard, Rivington, and East Houston Streets, New York City to William Howard Taft, April 9, 1912, Records of the Immigration and Naturalization Service, Record Group 85, National Archives, ARC 3854680.

observed in some of the tenement districts of Elizabeth, Orchard and Rivington, and East Houston Streets, New York City. * * * They often herd together, forming in effect foreign colonies in which the English language is almost unknown." . . .

Although this report of Mr. Williams is supposed to relate solely to Ellis Island affairs, fully two pages are devoted to matters having no bearing whatsoever upon the affairs at Ellis Island, but are evidently interpolated for restrictionistic purposes.

While the individual views of the Commissioner are no concern of ours, we are vitally interested in that portion of his report which undertakes to reflect upon us, as indicated in the foregoing excerpt. We deny emphatically that there is any truth in the strictures imposed by this public official upon the inhabitants of Orchard, Rivington and East Houston Streets. A large proportion of them are citizens of the United States, loyal to their country and to its institutions, seeking by their industry to add to the well-being of the community in which they reside. Those who are not citizens, intend to become such at the earliest opportunity. Although most of the residents of these streets are of foreign birth, they have come to this country for the purpose of establishing permanent homes, of rearing and educating their children as good Americans, and of enjoying the blessings of freedom, at the same time assuming and performing the obligations which residence and citizenship entail.

A survey of the district whose good name is involved in the strictures contained in Mr. Williams's report, indicating the nationalities and the moral, social and industrial activities of the population included in such district, is hereto appended. It is believed that the statistics thus presented for your consideration will demonstrate, not only that the statements made by Mr. Williams are false, but that they are libelous, and that no public official should be permitted with impunity thus to malign a large and populous section of this great city.

Remarks of this character, emanating from one occupying the official position that Mr. Williams fills, are calculated to do great injury to those who are included within them. They are particularly objectionable because they are apt to arouse unwarranted prejudices against immigrants, and especially among immigration inspectors, who are his subordinates and who, as has been pointed out by the Congressional Immigration Commission, are at present disposed "in a greater or less degree to reflect in their decisions the attitude of the commissioner," thus "tending to impair the judicial character of the board."

Under the circumstances we are impelled, not only for self-protection but because we believe it to be our duty as citizens, to protest against these wanton and unjustifiable reflections upon us; against this attempt on the part of a public official to discriminate among those who have passed through the gate at Ellis Island, and who have become absorbed in the general population of this country.

Moreover, we consider the remarks to which we have taken umbrage as a gratuitous insult, because in making them Mr. Williams did not deal with any matters which came within his jurisdiction, which is confined to Ellis Island, but has seen fit, either maliciously or without knowledge of the conditions which he seeks to describe, to animadvert upon us and those whom we represent, all of whom are striving to the utmost of their power to maintain the respect and good will of their fellow citizens.

We therefore respectfully pray, that such action may be taken in the premises as will vindicate our reputation and that of our families and neighbors, and will result in the retraction of the libelous charge of which we complain.

Dated, New York, April 9, 1912.

Respectfully submitted,

CITIZENS COMMITTEE

of

ORCHARD, RIVINGTON AND EAST HOUSTON STREETS,
NEW YORK CITY.

READING AND DISCUSSION QUESTIONS

1. Examine the role of ethnic identity in shaping both the commissioner of immigration's characterization of Lower East Side residents and their response. To what extent did their ethnicity define them in their own minds?

2. What stereotypes about ethnic groups are these residents challenging in their letter of protest? How do they defend themselves against the commissioner's representations?

3. What can you conclude from this document about how changing patterns of migration to the United States during this period influenced the growth of racial and ethnic identities?

P7-2 | Native American Citizenship

CHIEFS OF THE ONONDAGA NATION, *Letter to President Calvin Coolidge* (1924) and *President Coolidge Becoming a Member of the Sioux Indians* (1927)

For the residents of the Lower East Side, citizenship was part of the American identity they sought. The same was not true for many Native Americans, especially the Onondaga, whose tribal lands lay in upstate New York. When the United States Congress passed legislation sponsored by New York Representative Homer Snyder in 1924 conferring citizenship on all Native Americans born in the United States, the Onondaga protested. Native Americans had a complicated legal relationship to the United States. Some had become U.S. citizens through their military service, marriage, or through their acceptance of land allotments. But in 1924 there were many Native peoples who were not citizens. The Indian Citizenship Act of 1924 changed that. But what did U.S. citizenship mean to Native Americans whose ancestors inhabited this continent centuries before the arrival of Europeans? These two sources provide different perspectives on Native American responses to the Act. In their letter to President Calvin Coolidge, who signed the 1924 act into law, the Onondaga Chiefs condemned the grant of citizenship as a "destructive and an injurious weapon" against them. In comparison, the photograph of

Chiefs of the Onondaga Nation to Calvin A. Coolidge, December 30, 1924 at https://www .onondaganation.org/news/2018/the-citizenship-act-of-1924/

Coolidge with Sioux Indians in Deadwood, South Dakota depicts the aftermath of a 1927 ceremony where he was adopted into the tribe and named Leading Eagle. Standing with him are Princess Rose Bud Yellow Robe, Chief Yellow Robe, and Chief Standing Bear.

Therefore, Our Brother, be it resolved that inasmuch as the Snyder Bill is a destructive and an injurious weapon in nature and aspect to the Indians at large, individually and collectively: We Indians as a party to the Treaty between the United States and the Six Nations in [1794], do hereby protest the Snyder Bill, inasmuch as it abrogates sections 1, 2, & 4 of the Treaty. . . .

Therefore, be it resolved, that we, the Indians of the Onondaga Tribe of the Six Nations, duly depose and sternly protest the principal and object of the aforesaid Snyder Bill, . . .

We, the Indians have not as yet tired of the free use and enjoyment of our rights as Indians living on reservations. For the reason of safeguarding the Indians as a whole against unscrupulous advances of any element to the detriment of our welfare, present and future, we again and further protest the principal and aim of the Snyder Bill, . . .

Wherefore, we the undersigned counselling (sic) Chiefs of the Onondaga Nation, recommend the abandonment and repeal of the Snyder Bill.

Bettmann/Getty Images

READING AND DISCUSSION QUESTIONS

1. What arguments against the Indian Citizenship Act of 1924 do the Onondaga chiefs make?

2. What do you think U.S. citizenship meant to the Onondaga? What might account for the different reactions to the conferral of citizenship between the Onondaga and the Sioux?

3. What do these sources say about the relationship between the federal government and native peoples?

P7-3 | Suffragists Bring Battle to the President

Woman Suffrage in Washington, District of Columbia (c. 1917–1918)

Gender identity was at the heart of the women's rights movement. Reformers frequently based their arguments for the vote on the notion that women's gender peculiarly fitted them to contribute to public discussions. In the years leading to the ratification of the Nineteenth Amendment, the National American Woman Suffrage Association led organizing drives, protests, and parades, rallying women as "sisters in the cause" to push for voting rights, even, as shown here, staging vigils at the White House.

Library of Congress, Prints & Photographs Division, Reproduction number LC-DIG-hec-11589 (digital file from original negative)

READING AND DISCUSSION QUESTIONS

1. What point of view concerning women's rights does this photograph reveal? Analyze the message these women are expressing. What argument are they making?

2. Who was the audience for this photograph? To what extent do you think images like this one were created to aid in the formation of gender identity among women in support of voting rights?

P7-4 | Conservative Minister Defines Antimodern Identity

W. B. RILEY, *The Faith of the Fundamentalists* (1927)

In the latter nineteenth century, many Christian ministers found ways to reconcile belief with Darwin's theories regarding natural selection, but in the early twentieth century divisions emerged between those who favored a more liberal reading of scripture (which made room for Darwin) and literalists who accepted the Bible as the inerrant word of God. Conservatives mobilized, embracing metaphors of battle, waging war against "modernism" and its liberal and atheistic associations. By 1920, these religious conservatives embraced the term *fundamentalists* to describe their devotion to core Christian beliefs. Riley's 1927 essay sketched out the fundamentalist identity in an increasingly liberal culture.

Fundamentalism undertakes to reaffirm the greater Christian doctrines. Mark this phrase, "the greater Christian doctrines." It does not attempt to set forth every Christian doctrine. It has never known the elaboration that characterizes the great denominational confessions. But it did lay them side by side, and, out of their extensive statements, elect nine points upon which to rest its claims to Christian attention. They were and are as follows:

1. We believe in the Scriptures of the Old and New Testaments as verbally inspired by God, and inerrant in the original writings, and that they are of supreme and final authority in faith and life.

2. We believe in one God, eternally existing in three persons, Father, Son, and Holy Spirit.

3. We believe that Jesus Christ was begotten by the Holy Spirit, and born of the Virgin Mary, and is true God and true man.

4. We believe that man was created in the image of God, that he sinned and thereby incurred not only physical death, but also that spiritual death which is separation from God; and that all human beings are born with a sinful nature, and, in the case of those who reach moral responsibility, become sinners in thought, word, and deed.

5. We believe that the Lord Jesus Christ died for our sins according to the Scriptures as a representative and substitutionary sacrifice; and that all that believe in Him are justified on the ground of His shed blood.

6. We believe in the resurrection of the crucified body of our Lord, in His ascension into Heaven, and in His present life there for us, as High Priest and Advocate.

W. B. Riley, *The Faith of the Fundamentalists* (1927) from W. B. Riley, "The Faith of the Fundamentalists," Church History 24 (June 1927): 434–440. Reprinted with permission from Current History magazine (June 1927). © 2020 Current History, Inc.

7. We believe in "that blessed hope," the personal, premillennial, and imminent return of our Lord and Saviour, Jesus Christ.
8. We believe that all who receive by faith the Lord Jesus Christ are born again of the Holy Spirit and thereby become children of God.
9. We believe in the bodily resurrection of the just and the unjust, the everlasting felicity of the saved and the everlasting conscious suffering of the lost. . . .

Modernism when it comes to deal with the Fundamentals movement is suddenly possessed with a strange imagination. If you want to know what the movement is *not* and who its leaders are *not*, read their descriptions of both. Certainly as to what we believe, the above declaration leaves no doubt, and only the man ignorant of the Bible or utterly indifferent to its teachings, could ever call into question that these nine points constitute the greater essentials in the New Testament doctrinal system.

Fundamentalism insists upon the plain intent of Scripture-speech. The members of this movement have no sympathy whatever for that weasel method of sucking the meaning out of words and then presenting the empty shells in an attempt to palm them off as giving the Christian faith a new and another interpretation. The absurdities to which such a spiritualizing method may lead are fully revealed in the writings of Mary Baker Eddy[1] and modernists in general. When one is permitted to discard established and scientific definitions and to create, at will, his own glossary, language fails to be longer a vehicle of thought, and inspiration itself may mean anything or nothing, according to the preference of its employer. . . .

Fundamentalism is forever the antithesis of modernist critical theology. It is made up of another and an opposing school. Modernism submits all Scripture to the judgment of man. According to its method he may reject any portion of the Book as uninspired, unprofitable, and even undesirable, and accept another portion as from God because its sentences suit him, or its teachings inspire him. Fundamentalism, on the contrary, makes the Bible "the supreme and final authority in faith and life." Its teachings determine every question upon which they have spoken with some degree of fullness, and its mandates are only disregarded by the unbelieving, the materialistic, and the immoral. Fundamentalists hold that the world is illumined and the Church is instructed and even science itself is confirmed, when true, and condemned when false, by the clear teachings of the open Book. . . .

The future of Fundamentalism is not with claims, but with conquests. Glorious as is our past, history provides only an adequate base upon which to build. Fundamentalists will never need to apologize for the part they have played in education; they have produced it; or for their relationship to colleges and universities and theological seminaries, and all forms of social service; they have created them! . . .

But even that is not enough! Now that modernism has come in to filch from us these creations of our creed, we must either wrest them from bandit hands or begin and build again. In the last few years, in fact, since the modernist-highwaymen rose up to trouble the Church and snatch its dearest treasures,[2] it has shown

---

[1] **Mary Baker Eddy**: Founder of the Church of Christ, Scientist, a Christian denomination advocating the spiritual healing of diseases.

[2] **Dearest treasures**: Riley is claiming modernists have taken over schools, colleges, seminaries, hospitals, and publishing ventures originally created and funded by Fundamentalists.

itself as virile as the promise of Christ, "The gates of hell shall not prevail against it," ever indicated. Today there are one hundred schools and colleges connected with our Fundamentalist Association, some of which have escaped the covetous clutches of modernism, but most of which have been brought into being as a protest against modernism itself. Their growth has been so phenomenal as to prove that the old tree is fruitful still, and that the finest fruit is to be found upon its newest branches, orthodox churches, Fundamentalist colleges, sound Bible training schools, evangelical publication societies, multiplied Bible conferences and stanch defenders of the faith in ever increasing numbers in each denomination. . . .

Who are my brethren? Baptists? Not necessarily, and, in thousands of instances, no! My brethren are those who believe in a personal God, in an inspired Book, and in a redeeming Christ.

READING AND DISCUSSION QUESTIONS

1. Analyze Riley's essay to see how he creates a fundamentalist identity in opposition to modernism. What definition of each emerges from his discussion?

2. To what extent does Riley see fellow fundamentalists as an oppressed group? Were fundamentalists on the defensive in the early twentieth century, and if so, did their "outsider" status help them to create and maintain a distinct religious and cultural identity?

P7-5 | African American Soldier Stands Up to Racial Discrimination
Private Charles F. Wilson to Franklin D. Roosevelt (1944)

Roosevelt's presidency was significant for the political shift it produced by luring African Americans away from their traditional Republican Party loyalties. His Executive Order 8802, issued in 1941, prohibited racially discriminatory practices in the federal government and its wartime union and private-sector contractors. The military, however, remained segregated by race. For many soldiers, their identity in the armed forces was defined almost exclusively by their race. In this letter, Private Wilson, an African American airman based in Arizona, points out the paradox to President Roosevelt, reminding him of the work remaining to be done.

> 33rd AAF Base Unit (CCTS(H))
> Section C
> DAVIS-MONTHAN FIELD
> Tucson, Arizona
> 9 May 1944.

Phillip McGuire, ed., *Taps for a Jim Crow Army: Letters from Black Soldiers in World War II* (Lexington: University Press of Kentucky, 1993), 134–139.

President Franklin Delano Roosevelt
White House
Washington, D.C.

Dear President Roosevelt:

It was with extreme pride that I, a soldier in the Armed Forces of our country, read the following affirmation of our war aims, pronounced by you at a recent press conference:

"The United Nations are fighting to make a world in which tyranny, and aggression cannot exist; a world based upon freedom, equality, and justice; a world in which all persons, regardless of race, color, and creed, may live in peace, honor, and dignity."

Your use of the word "world" means that we are fighting for "freedom, equality, and justice" for "all persons, regardless of race, color, and creed" in our own part of the world, the United States of America, as well as all other countries where such a fight is needed to be carried through. Your use of the words "all persons, regardless of race, color, and creed" means that we are fighting for "freedom, equality, and justice" for our Negro American, no less than for our white Americans, or our Jewish, Protestant and Catholic Americans, or for the subjugated peoples in Europe and China and all other lands.

And the part that our country is playing in the United Nations world struggle against "tyranny and aggression" and for "a world based upon freedom, equality, and justice," although lacking in many respects, is certainly not one to be ashamed of. . . .

But the picture in our country is marred by one of the strangest paradoxes in our whole fight against world fascism. The United States Armed Forces, to fight for World Democracy, is within itself undemocratic. The undemocratic policy of jim crow and segregation is practiced by our Armed Forces against its Negro members. Totally inadequate opportunities are given to the Negro members of our Armed Forces, nearly one tenth of the whole, to participate with "equality" . . . "regardless of race and color" in the fight for our war aims. In fact it appears that the army intends to follow the very policy that the FEPC is battling against in civilian life, the pattern of assigning Negroes to the lowest types of work.

Let me give you an example of the lack of democracy in our Field, where I am now stationed. Negro soldiers are completely segregated from the white soldiers on the base. And to make doubly sure that no mistake is made about this, the barracks and other housing facilities (supply room, mess hall, etc.) of the Negro Section C are covered with black tar paper, while all other barracks and housing facilities on the base are painted white.

It is the stated policy of the Second Air Force that "every potential fighting man must be used as a fighting man. If you have such a man in a base job, you have no choice. His job must be eliminated or be filled by a limited service man, WAC, or civilian." And yet . . . fully 50% of the Negro soldiers are working in base jobs, such as, for example, at the Resident Officers' Mess, Bachelor Officers' Quarters, and Officers' Club, as mess personnel, BOQ orderlies, and bar tenders. . . .

Thus we see that the maintenance of the ideology of "white supremacy" resulting in the undemocratic practices of jim crow and segregation of the Negro members of the Armed Forces brings about the condition on Davis-Monthan Field whereby 80% of the whole Section is removed from the fighting activities on the base. . . .

How can we convince nearly one tenth of the Armed Forces, the Negro members, that your pronouncement of the war aims of the United Nations means what it says, when their experience with one of the United Nations, the United States of America, is just the opposite?

Are the Chinese people to believe that we are fighting to bring them "freedom, equality, and justice," when they can see that in our Armed Forces we are not even practicing ourselves what we are preaching?

However, we leave ourselves wide open for sowers of disunity. Nothing would suit Hitler, Tojo, and our native fascists better, than disunity. The lead editorial in the Afro-American of April the 1st entitled "Soldiers or Sissies" is a tragic example of this. The editorial after relating two cases of *tyranny* against two Negro soldiers: one in Alabama where the "civil police lynched a hand-cuffed, defenseless soldier when they were moving from one prison to another," and another case in Louisiana, where a "Bus driver shot and killed a New York [soldier] who refused to move to a rear seat," goes on to say: "This is terrorism, and the army has no answer for it. Have the soldiers themselves an answer? There are thousands of them and only a few police or bus drivers." If the advice of that editorial were followed it could only lead to disunity and civil strife. We know that isn't the answer. Disunity and civil strife would only weaken our fight against the German and Japanese fascists, or more than that result in our defeat. A victory for the German and Japanese fascists would mean a victory for our native fascists, who are at the bottom [of] this whole program of "white supremacy," race hatred, jim-crowism, and segregation. . . . Such an editorial is totally irresponsible. But decrying such an editorial will get us nowhere. The only answer is to remove the conditions which give rise to such an editorial. That means fighting for the war aims of the United Nations in our own country as well as throughout the rest of the world. That means that we must fight against the fascist shouters of "white supremacy," against the labor baiters, against segregation and jim-crowism, wherever these evils show their fangs, whether in the Armed Forces, or in the civilian population. . . .

President Roosevelt, in the interest of the war effort you issued Executive Order 8802, which established the Fair Employment Practices Committee. Although there is still much to be done, nevertheless this committee, against heavy opposition, has played, and is playing a gallant role in fighting for democracy for the men and women behind the lines, in the industries that produce the guns, and tanks, and bombers for victory over world fascism.

With your issuance of Executive Order 8802, and the setting up of the Fair Employment Practices Committee, you established the foundation for fighting for democracy in the industrial forces of our country, in the interest of victory for the United Nations. In the interest of victory for the United Nations, another Executive Order is now needed. An Executive Order which will lay the base for fighting for democracy in the Armed Forces of our country. An Executive Order which would bring about the result here at Davis-Monthan Field whereby the Negro soldiers would be integrated into all of the Sections on the base, as fighting men, instead of in the segregated Section C as housekeepers.

Then and only then can your pronouncement of the war aims of the United Nations mean to *all* that we "are fighting to make a world in which tyranny, and aggression cannot exist; a world based upon freedom, equality, and justice; a world in which all persons, regardless of race, color, and creed, may live in peace, honor, and dignity."

Respectfully yours,
Charles F. Wilson, 36794590
Private, Air Corps.

READING AND DISCUSSION QUESTIONS

1. To what extent did African American experiences during World War II, as described here, focus attention on public discussions regarding American national identity?

2. How does Private Wilson frame the paradox of race and democracy as he experienced it? From his perspective, how did America's involvement in international crises like World War II affect debates over national identity?

3. How important was World War II in the formation of Wilson's identity as both an American and an African American? Were these identities for him overlapping, distinct, or contradictory?

P7-6 | Labor Organizer Describes Latino Plight in America

LUISA MORENO, *Caravans of Sorrow* (1940)

The crisis of the Great Depression impacted the Latino population of the American Southwest, magnifying their economic vulnerabilities and exacerbating ethnic discrimination. In response, labor and civil rights activists rallied, creating an infrastructure of advocacy to affirm Latino rights and identity. Guatemalan immigrant Luisa Moreno emerged as a leader of these efforts, organizing the Spanish-Speaking Peoples' Congress in 1939. In her statement before the American Committee for the Protection of the Foreign Born in 1940, which came to be known as the "Caravans of Sorrow" speech, she raised awareness of the discrimination facing Spanish-speaking people and demanded equal justice for them.

"Caravans of Sorrow" (1940) Address delivered at the panel of Deportation and Right of Asylum of the 4th Conference of the American Committee for Protection of the Foreign Born, Washington D.C. March 3, 1940. Box 1, Folder 1, Carey McWilliams Collection, University Research Library, Department of Special Collections UCLA. Published by permission of Nancy McWilliams, PhD.

Today the Latin Americans of the United States are seriously alarmed by the "antialien" drive fostered by certain un-American elements; for them, the Palmer days[3] . . . have never ended. In recent years while deportations in general have decreased, the number of persons deported to Mexico has constantly increased. During the period of 1933 to 1937, of a total of 55,087 deported, 25,135 were deportations of Mexicans. This is 45.5 percent of the total and does not include an almost equal number of so-called voluntary departures.

Commenting on these figures, the American Committee for Protection of Foreign Born wrote to the Spanish-Speaking Peoples' Congress in 1939: "One conclusion can be drawn, and that is, where there is such a highly organized set-up as to effect deportations of so many thousands, this set-up must be surrounded with a complete system of intimidation and discrimination of that section of the population victimized by the deportation drive."

Confirming the fact of a system of extensive discrimination are university studies by . . . many other professors and social workers of the Southwest. Let me state the simple truth. The majority of the Spanish-speaking peoples of the United States are victims of a setup for discrimination, be they descendants of the first white settlers in America or noncitizens. . . .

Only some 5 or 6 percent of Latin American immigrants have become naturalized [because of] the lack of documentary proof of entry, because entry was not recorded or because the immigrants were brought over en masse by large interests handling transportation from Mexico in their own peculiar way.

Arriving at logical conclusions, the Latin American noncitizens, rooted in this country, are increasingly seeing the importance and need for naturalization. But how will the thousands of migrants establish residence? What possibility have these people had, segregated in "Little Mexicos," to learn English and meet educational requirements? How can they, receiving hunger wages while enriching the stockholders of the Great Western Sugar Company, the Bank of America, and other large interests, pay high naturalization fees? A Mexican family living on relief in Colorado would have to stop eating for two and a half months to pay for the citizenship papers of one member of the family. Is this humanly possible?

But why have "aliens" on relief while the taxpayers "bleed"? Let me ask those who would raise such a question: what would the Imperial Valley, the Rio Grande Valley, and other rich irrigated valleys in the Southwest be without the arduous, self-sacrificing labor of these noncitizen Americans? . . . Has anyone counted the miles of railroads built by these same noncitizens? One can hardly imagine how many bales of cotton have passed through the nimble fingers of Mexican men, women, and children. And what conditions have they had to endure to pick that cotton? . . .

These people are not aliens. They have contributed their endurance, sacrifices, youth, and labor to the Southwest. Indirectly, they have paid more taxes

---

[3] **Palmer days**: Reference to the series of raids resulting in the deportation of foreign-born radicals conducted by Attorney General A. Mitchell Palmer from November 1919 to January 1920.

than all the stockholders of California's industrialized agriculture, the sugar beet companies and the large cotton interests that operate or have operated with the labor of Mexican workers.

Surely the sugar beet growers have not been asked if they want to dispense with the skilled labor cultivating and harvesting their crops season after season. It is only the large interests, their stooges, and some badly misinformed people who claim that Mexicans are no longer wanted.

And let us assume that 1.4 million men, women, and children were no longer wanted, what could be done that would be different from the anti-Semitic persecutions in Europe? A people who have lived twenty and thirty years in this country, tied up by family relations with the early settlers, with American-born children, cannot be uprooted without the complete destruction of the faintest semblance of democracy and human liberties for the whole population.

What then may the answer to this specific noncitizen problem be? The Spanish-Speaking Peoples' Congress of the United States proposes legislation that would encourage naturalization of Latin American, West Indian, and Canadian residents of the United States and that would nurture greater friendships among the peoples of the Western Hemisphere.

The question of hemispheric unity will remain an empty phrase while this problem at home remains ignored and is aggravated by the fierce "antialien" drive.

Legislation to facilitate citizenship to all natural-born citizens from the countries of the Western Hemisphere, waiving excessive fees and educational and other requirements of a technical nature, is urgently needed. . . .

You have seen the forgotten character in the present American scene — a scene of the Americas. Let me say that, in the face of greater hardships, the "Caravans of Sorrow" are becoming the "Caravans of Hope." They are organizing in trade unions with other workers in agriculture and industry. The unity of Spanish-speaking citizens and noncitizens is being furthered through the Spanish-Speaking Peoples' Congress of the United States, an organization embracing trade unions and fraternal, civic, and cultural organizations, mainly in California. The purpose of this movement is to seek an improvement of social, economic, and cultural conditions, and for the integration of Spanish-speaking citizens and noncitizens into the American nation. The United Cannery, Agricultural, Packing, and Allied Workers of America, with thousands of Spanish-speaking workers in its membership, and Liga Obrera of New Mexico, were the initiators of the Congress.

This Congress stands with all progressive forces against the badly labeled "antialien" legislation and asks the support of this Conference for democratic legislation to facilitate and encourage naturalization. We hope that this Conference will serve to express the sentiment of the people of this country in condemnation of undemocratic discrimination practiced against any person of foreign birth and that it will rally the American people, native and foreign born, for the defeat of un-American proposals. The Spanish-speaking peoples in the United States extend their fullest support and cooperation to your efforts.

READING AND DISCUSSION QUESTIONS

1. What role did the Great Depression play in shaping public debates regarding American national identity as they related to minority groups like Latinos? How did the economic crisis focus these debates?

2. Examine how ethnicity, class, and gender intersected in the civil rights advocacy Moreno pushed for Latinos in America. How did the work of activists like Moreno help to shape or change ideas about American national identity?

▪ COMPARATIVE QUESTIONS ▪

1. How did Luisa Moreno's civil rights activism on behalf of Latinos (Document P7-6) compare with similar efforts promoting the interests of minority groups in America? What similarities or differences can you see?

2. Compare the suffrage photograph (Document P7-3) with Carrie Chapman Catt's 1918 statement (Document 21-2) and Josephine Conger-Kaneko's speech (Document 19-3). How do the documents illuminate the role that gender played in shaping women's response to their political and social marginalization?

3. What do the documents in this set reveal about the ways that American identity has been debated by various groups in the decades between the Civil War and World War II? How have these debates related to economic, social, and cultural transformations that have occurred in society?

4. How does the historian assess the significance of factors such as race, class, gender, and religion in shaping individual and group identities?

5. To what extent are issues of identity central to the American experience? How much are the debates raised in these sources continuing concerns for Americans?

24

PART 8

The Cold War Dawns

1945–1963

Despite the alliance between the United States and the Soviet Union during World War II, a "cold war" of words and ideas rapidly emerged in the immediate wake of that global conflict. Beginning with the Truman administration, American policymakers increasingly viewed the Soviet Union as a hostile force committed to the worldwide expansion of its anti-capitalist and atheistic, communist ideology. How best to counter Soviet aggression became the leading policy debate in the first decades of the Cold War. The urgency of addressing the Soviet menace led to the creation of the national security state, the infrastructure within the federal government created to gather information about Soviet intentions worldwide and to orchestrate the American response. Fears of communist infiltration of the federal government by spies and "fellow travelers," those sympathetic to the communist cause, resulted in a new Red Scare led by Senator Joseph McCarthy, whose investigations into alleged communist activity brought him both enormous popularity and eventual scorn and disgrace. Though the McCarthy persecutions petered out in the mid-1950s, Cold War anxieties persisted, shaping a culture shadowed by the fear of a nuclear cloud mushrooming over the skies of America. The first two documents included in this chapter show how policy makers and critics debated Cold War strategy. The remaining sources explore the effect of the Cold War on American society and culture.

24-1 | Containing the Communist Threat

GEORGE KENNAN, *"Long Telegram" to James Byrnes* (1946)

American diplomat George Kennan was stationed in Moscow in the mid-1940s when he sent a "long telegram" to his superior in Washington, James Byrnes, President Truman's secretary of state. Subsequently published as "The Sources of Soviet Conduct" in the influential policy magazine *Foreign Affairs* under the signature X, the telegram outlined Kennan's views on the Soviet Union. To counter Soviet aggression, he called for a policy of containing the communist threat, a policy soon formulated as the Truman Doctrine, the central foreign policy strategy of the Truman administration.

We have here a political force committed fanatically to the belief that with US there can be no permanent modus vivendi,[1] that it is desirable and necessary that the internal harmony of our society be disrupted, our traditional way of life be destroyed, the international authority of our state be broken, if Soviet power is to be secure. This political force has complete power of disposition over energies of one of world's greatest peoples and resources of world's richest national territory, and is borne along by deep and powerful currents of Russian nationalism. In addition, it has an elaborate and far flung apparatus for exertion of its influence in other countries, an apparatus of amazing flexibility and versatility, managed by people whose experience and skill in underground methods are presumably without parallel in history. Finally, it is seemingly inaccessible to considerations of reality in its basic reactions. For it, the vast fund of objective fact about human society is not, as with us, the measure against which outlook is constantly being tested and re-formed, but a grab bag from which individual items are selected arbitrarily and tendentiously to bolster an outlook already preconceived. This is admittedly not a pleasant picture. Problem of how to cope with this force is undoubtedly greatest task our diplomacy has ever faced and probably greatest it will ever have to face. It should be point of departure from which our political general staff work at present juncture should proceed. It should be approached with same thoroughness and care as solution of major strategic problem in war, and if necessary, with no smaller outlay in planning effort. I cannot attempt to suggest all answers here. But I would like to record my conviction that problem is within our power to solve—and that without recourse to any general military conflict. And in support of this conviction there are certain observations of a more encouraging nature I should like to make:

Telegram from George Kennan, *Charge d'Affaires* at United States Embassy in Moscow to the Secretary of State: The Long Telegram, February 22, 1946, Record Group 59: General Records of the Department of State, 1763–2002, ARC Identifier 2642322, National Archives.

[1]**Modus vivendi:** Latin, meaning a way of living together despite differences.

(One) Soviet power, unlike that of Hitlerite Germany, is neither schematic nor adventuristic. It does not work by fixed plans. It does not take unnecessary risks. Impervious to logic of reason, and it is highly sensitive to logic of force. For this reason it can easily withdraw—and usually does—when strong resistance is encountered at any point. . . . Thus, if the adversary has sufficient force and makes clear his readiness to use it, he rarely has to do so. If situations are properly handled there need be no prestige engaging showdowns.

(Two) Gauged against western world as a whole, Soviets are still by far the weaker force. Thus, their success will really depend on degree of cohesion, firmness and vigor which western world can muster. And this is factor which it is within our power to influence.

(Three) Success of Soviet system, as form of internal power, is not yet finally proven. . . . In Russia, party has now become a great and—for the moment—highly successful apparatus of dictatorial administration, but it has ceased to be a source of emotional inspiration. Thus, internal soundness and permanence of movement need not yet be regarded as assured.

(Four) All Soviet propaganda beyond Soviet security sphere is basically negative and destructive. It should therefore be relatively easy to combat it by any intelligent and really constructive program.

For these reasons I think we may approach calmly and with good heart problem of how to deal with Russia. As to how this approach should be made, I only wish to advance, by way of conclusion, following comments:

(One) Our first step must be to apprehend, and recognize for what it is, the nature of the movement with which we are dealing. We must study it with same courage, detachment, objectivity, and same determination not to be emotionally provoked or unseated by it, with which doctor studies unruly and unreasonable individual.

(Two) We must see that our public is educated to realities of Russian situation. . . . I am convinced that there would be far less hysterical anti-Sovietism in our country today if realities of this situation were better understood by our people. There is nothing as dangerous or as terrifying as the unknown. It may also be argued that to reveal more information on our difficulties with Russia would reflect unfavorably on Russian American relations. I feel that if there is any real risk here involved, it is one which we should have courage to face, and sooner the better. But I cannot see what we would be risking. Our stake in this country, even coming on heels of tremendous demonstrations of our friendship for Russian people, is remarkably small. We have here no investments to guard, no actual trade to lose, virtually no citizens to protect, few cultural contacts to preserve. Our only stake lies in what we hope rather than what we have; and I am convinced we have better chance of realizing those hopes if our public is enlightened. . . .

World communism is like malignant parasite which feeds only on diseased tissue. This is point at which domestic and foreign policies meet. Every courageous and incisive measure to solve internal problems of our own society . . . is a diplomatic victory over Moscow worth a thousand diplomatic notes and joint communiques. If we cannot abandon fatalism and indifference in face of deficiencies of our own society, Moscow will profit—Moscow cannot help profiting by them in its foreign policies.

READING AND DISCUSSION QUESTIONS

1. What conclusions can you draw about Kennan's assessment of the Soviet threat to American interests around the world? What can you infer about his opinion of this larger threat, based on his description of the factors motivating Soviet aggression?

2. What advice does Kennan offer his superiors in the State Department about thwarting the Soviet threat? Why does he think his policy would be an effective counter to Soviet intentions?

3. How does Kennan's telegram help you to understand the broader context of the Cold War in the 1940s? To what extent might his telegram be seen as the start of the Cold War?

24-2 | Challenging Truman's Containment Policy

WALTER LIPPMANN, *Cold War: A Study in U.S. Foreign Policy* (1947)

Few journalists have led as influential a life as Walter Lippmann. His work was highly regarded and brought him into the personal orbit of every president from Woodrow Wilson to Lyndon Johnson. As a foreign policy intellectual, Lippmann offered a powerful counter to Truman's containment strategy by questioning the assumptions of Mr. X (George Kennan) about Soviet ambitions.

[M]y criticism of the policy of containment, or the so-called Truman Doctrine, does not spring from any hope or belief that the Soviet pressure to expand can be "charmed or talked out of existence." I agree entirely with Mr. X that we must make up our minds that the Soviet power is not amenable to our arguments, but only "to contrary force" that "is felt to be too strong, and thus more rational in the logic and rhetoric of power."

My objection, then, to the policy of containment is not that it seeks to confront the Soviet power with American power, but that the policy is misconceived, and must result in a misuse of American power. For as I have sought to show, it commits this country to a struggle which has for its objective nothing more substantial than the hope that in ten or fifteen years the Soviet power will, as the result of long frustration, "break up" or "mellow." In this prolonged struggle the role of the United States is, according to Mr. X, to react "at a series of constantly shifting geographical and political points" to the encroachments of the Soviet power.

The policy, therefore, concedes to the Kremlin the strategical initiative as to when, where and under what local circumstances the issue is to be joined. It compels the United States to meet the Soviet pressure at these shifting geographical and political points by using satellite states, puppet governments and agents which have been subsidized and supported, though their effectiveness is meager and their reliability uncertain. By forcing us to expend our energies and our substance upon these dubious and unnatural allies on the perimeter of the Soviet Union, the effect of the policy is to neglect our natural allies in the Atlantic community, and to alienate them.

They are alienated also by the fact that they do not wish to become, like the nations of the perimeter, the clients of the United States in whose affairs we intervene, asking as the price of our support that they take the directives of their own policy from Washington. They are alienated above all by the prospect of war, which could break out by design or accident, by miscalculation or provocation, if at any of these constantly shifting geographical and political points the Russians or Americans became so deeply engaged that no retreat or compromise was possible. In this war their lands would be the battlefield. Their peoples would be divided by civil conflict. Their cities and their fields would be the bases and the bridgeheads in a total war which, because it would merge into a general civil war, would be as indecisive as it was savage.

We may now ask why the official diagnosis of Soviet conduct, as disclosed by Mr. X's article, has led to such an unworkable policy for dealing with Russia. It is, I believe because Mr. X has neglected even to mention the fact that the Soviet Union is the successor of the Russian Empire and that Stalin is not only the heir of Marx and of Lenin but of Peter the Great, and the Czars of all the Russians.

For reasons which I do not understand, Mr. X decided not to consider the men in the Kremlin as the rulers of the Russian State and Empire, and has limited his analysis to the interaction of "two forces": "the ideology inherited by the present Soviet leaders from the movement in which they had their political origin" and the "circumstances of the power which they have now exercised for nearly three decades in Russia."

Thus he dwells on the indubitable fact that they believe in the Marxian ideology and that "they have continued to be predominantly absorbed with the struggle to secure and make absolute the power which they seized in November 1917." But with these two observations alone he cannot, and does not, explain the conduct of the Soviet government in this postwar era—that is to say its aims and claims to territory and to the sphere of influence which it dominates. The Soviet government has been run by Marxian revolutionists for thirty years; what has to be explained by a planner of American foreign policy is why in 1945 the Soviet government expanded its frontiers and its orbit, and what was the plan and pattern of its expansion. That can be done only by remembering that the Soviet government is a Russian government and that this Russian government has emerged victorious over Germany and Japan.

Having omitted from his analysis the fact that we are dealing with a victorious Russia—having become exclusively preoccupied with the Marxian ideology, and with the communist revolution—it is no wonder that the outcome of Mr. X's analysis is nothing more definite, concrete and practical than that the Soviets will encroach and expand "at a series of constantly shifting geographical and political points." Mr. X's picture of the Soviet conduct has no pattern. It is amorphous. That is why his conclusions about how we should deal with the Soviets have no pattern, and are also amorphous. . . .

I am contending that the American diplomatic effort should be concentrated on the problem created by the armistice—which is on how the continent of Europe can be evacuated by the three non-European armies which are now inside Europe. This is the problem which will have to be solved if the independence of the European nations is to be restored. Without that there is no possibility of a tolerable peace. But if these armies withdraw, there will be a very different balance of power in the world than there is today, and one which cannot easily be upset. For the nations of Europe, separately and in groups, perhaps even in unity, will then, and then only, cease to be the stakes and the pawns of the Russian-American conflict. . . .

It would be a strategic change in the balance of power. For once the Red Army had been withdrawn behind the frontiers of the Soviet Union, it could not re-enter Europe without commit[t]ing an obvious act of military aggression, which would precipitate a general war. The pressure of the Soviets upon Europe by propaganda and infiltration would continue, but that pressure would no longer be backed up by overwhelming military power throughout eastern Europe and by the threat of military intervention in western Europe. . . .

If the Kremlin really means to dominate Europe, it will not withdraw its armies which are halfway across Europe. Standing on the Elbe line in the middle of Europe and Austria, and on the vulnerable frontier of Italy, the Kremlin is in a far better position to advance farther west than it can be if it withdraws and stands on its own frontiers. The withdrawal of the army is, therefore, the acid test of Soviet conduct and purpose, incomparably clearer, more definite, more practical than whether or not they observe the Yalta Declaration in countries liberated from the Nazis but still occupied by the Red Army. . . .

Instead of seeking "to contain" the Soviet Union all over the Eurasian continent, we shall have the initiative and a definite and concrete objective; at the best we shall know the terms on which the main conflict can be settled; at the worst the Soviet Union will have shown its hand on an issue—the liberation of Europe from non-European armies—where there will be no doubt whatever that our cause is just, and that we are the champions of freedom, and that the great masses of the people of Europe will be with us because we stand for the very thing which only traitors can oppose.

We shall have written off the liabilities of the Truman Doctrine which must in practice mean inexorably an unending intervention in all the countries that are supposed to "contain" the Soviet Union. We shall be acting once more in the great American tradition which is to foster the independence of other countries, not to use other countries as the satellites of our own power, however beneficent, and as the instruments of our own policy, however well meant. Our aim will not be to organize an ideological crusade. It will not be to make Jeffersonian democrats out of the peasants of eastern Europe, the tribal chieftains, the feudal lords, the pashas, and the warlords of the Middle East and Asia, but to settle the war and to restore the independence of the nations of Europe by removing the alien armies—all of them, our own included.

We shall have a diplomatic policy that it would be exceedingly difficult for the cleverest propagandist to misrepresent. For everyone can understand such a policy. Practically everyone will wish us to succeed in it. For alien armies are hateful, however well behaved, just because they represent an alien power and are, therefore, a perpetual reminder that the people on whom they are quartered are not masters of their own destiny.

Alien armies are, however, never well behaved: invariably they become corrupted. Thus we may count confidently upon a mounting popular support if we make it our mission to emancipate the ancient and proud continent of Europe from the military control of non-European powers. We shall be drawing upon the elemental and unifying passion of patriotism in Europe which, when it is aroused, is a much stronger passion than factionalism or any ideology.

READING AND DISCUSSION QUESTIONS

1. How does Lippmann's perspective on the Soviet Union compare to Mr. X's assessment? What factors does Lippmann say Mr. X missed in his diagnosis of Soviet ambition?

2. Lippmann says "containment" was based on Mr. X's faulty assumptions; beyond that, what doesn't he like about the containment strategy? What alternative focus of American foreign policy does he advocate in its place?

24-3 | Environmental Consequences of the Cold War
Hanford Site Nuclear Reactors (1960)

During World War II, the federal government's Manhattan Project developed the atomic bombs that leveled the Japanese cities of Hiroshima and Nagasaki. The plutonium for those bombs was extracted from uranium fuel rods produced at Hanford, the top-secret nuclear reactor site located along the Columbia River in southeastern Washington State. This aerial photograph from 1960 shows the reactor site during the height of the Cold War. By this time, the United States had stockpiled more than 18,000 nuclear weapons, almost twelve times more than the Soviet Union. The federal government purchased more than 400,000 acres of land to create the Hanford site. Federal officials believed its remote location on the Columbia River, distant from any population centers, provided security and safety in the case of nuclear accidents. The water from the Columbia River cooled the fuel rods, but the reactors produced radioactive waste, some of which leaked from underground storage tanks. Since the last reactor shut down in the 1980s, the U.S. Department of Energy has assumed responsibility for the site's environmental mitigation efforts.

U.S. Department of Energy

READING AND DISCUSSION QUESTIONS

1. Describe the Hanford site in relationship to the surrounding landscape. What do you notice? What do the tread marks in the foreground suggest?

2. What does the scope of the Hanford site tell us about the economic resources the federal government committed to Cold War projects?

3. How might a historian use the evidence from this photograph to write an environmental history of the Cold War?

24-4 | Expert Offers Diagram of Homosexual Personality

CAPT. GEORGE RAINES, *Testimony Before the U.S. Senate Committee Investigating the Employment of Homosexuals and Other Sex Perverts in Government* (1950)

In this source and the next, we probe the work of the federal government in exposing what many members of Congress at the time considered to be threats to American security. This source was an exhibit submitted by Captain George Raines, a professor of psychiatry at Georgetown University, who was called in 1950 as an expert witness by the U.S.

Senate committee investigating homosexuality within the federal work force. There was much negative social stigma attached to homosexual identity in the twentieth century; in fact, the leading professional organization for psychiatrists defined homosexuality as a "sociopathic personality disturbance." Many men and women during the Cold War hid their homosexual identity for fear that their exposure would result in social ostracism and the loss of employment. Senators were looking for an easy way to identify homosexuals so that they could be removed from sensitive positions within the federal workforce. The diagram Raines shared with senators shows what leaders within the medical community understood about homosexuality in the 1950s. While their views largely contributed to persisting discrimination against homosexuals, Raines's testimony attempted to demonstrate the complexity of human sexuality.

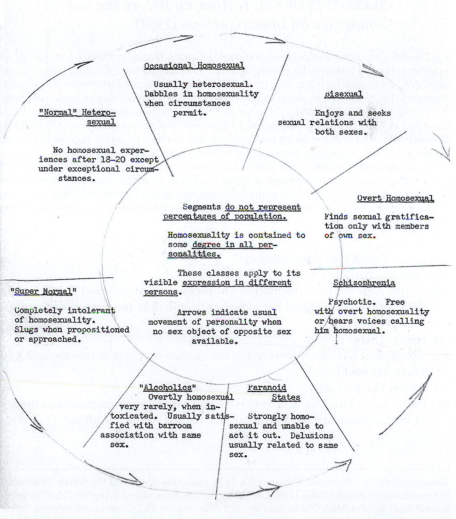

Occasional Homosexual

Usually heterosexual.
Dabbles in homosexuality
when circumstances
permit.

"Normal" Hetero-
sexual

Bisexual

Enjoys and seeks
sexual relations with
both sexes.

No homosexual exper-
iences after 18–20 except
under exceptional circum-
stances.

Overt Homosexual

Finds sexual gratifica-
tion only with members
of own sex.

Segments do not represent
percentages of population.

Homosexuality is contained to
some degree in all per-
sonalities.

These classes apply to its
visible expression in different
persons.

Schizophrenia

Psychotic. Free
with overt homosexuality
or hears voices calling
him homosexual.

"Super Normal"

Completely intolerant
of homosexuality.
Slugs when propositioned
or approached.

Arrows indicate usual
movement of personality when
no sex object of opposite sex
available.

"Alcoholics"
Overtly homosexual
very rarely, when in-
toxicated. Usually satis-
fied with barroom
association with same
sex.

Paranoid
States

Strongly homo-
sexual and unable to
act it out. Delusions
usually related to same
sex.

READING AND DISCUSSION QUESTIONS

1. What does this diagram suggest about the medical profession's understanding of homosexuality in the 1950s? How do you interpret Raines's statement that homosexuality "is contained to some *degree in all personalities*"?

2. Why do you think the U.S. Congress was so concerned about the presence of homosexual men and women within the federal workforce? Given the context of the Cold War and the assumptions medical professionals made about homosexuality, what fueled their anxiety?

24-5 | Investigating the Communist Threat

CHARLOTTE ORAM, *Testimony Before the Senate Committee on Investigations* (1954)

The Senate Committee investigating homosexuals in the federal workforce was part of an extended effort by Congress to identify security threats during the Cold War. Many in Congress saw homosexual men and women as such a threat; some assumed they were peculiarly susceptible to communist influence. That was the particular focus of Senator Joseph McCarthy (R-Wisconsin), who, as chairman of the Senate Subcommittee on Investigations, launched a campaign in 1953 to identify communist infiltration in the federal government. Thousands of Americans were affected by his allegations, many of them based on false or inaccurate evidence. McCarthy's excesses eventually led to his censure by the Senate. In 1954, Charlotte Oram, a suspected member of the Communist Party, faced questions from the committee's chief counsel, Roy Cohn, about whether Annie Lee Moss, an African American woman who worked as a communications clerk in the Pentagon, was also a Communist. Moss was a target because McCarthy had charged, erroneously, that she had access to the codes deciphering diplomatic messages.

MR. COHN: Could I get your full name?

MRS. ORAM: Charlotte Oram.

MR. COHN: And for the information of others present, counsel is Mr. Joseph Forer of the Washington Bar, who has been before the committee on prior occasions.

MR. FORER: That is correct.

MR. COHN: You have been before the committee on prior occasions and you know the rules?

MR. FORER: Yes, sir; I do.

MR. COHN: Now, Mrs. Oram, in 1944 were you a member of the northeast branch of the Communist party with a woman named Annie Lee Moss?

Testimony of Charlotte Oram, February 23, 1954, Executive Session of the Senate Permanent Subcommittee on Investigations of the Committee on Government, vol. 5, Eighty-Third Congress, Second Session, 1954, Made Public January 2002 (Washington, DC: Government Printing Office, 2003), 63–73.

MRS. ORAM: I decline to answer that question on the basis of my privilege under the Fifth Amendment not to be a witness against myself.

MR. COHN: Did you hold membership card 53582 in the Communist party during those years?

MRS. ORAM: My answer to that question is on the same basis.

MR. COHN: Do you know Annie Lee Moss?

MRS. ORAM: I am sorry.

MR. COHN: Do you know Annie Lee Moss?

MRS. ORAM: That name doesn't mean anything to me.

MR. COHN: Can you name for us the members of the Communist cell to which you belonged?

MRS. ORAM: I decline to answer that question on the basis I stated previously.

MR. COHN: Are you a Communist as of today?

MRS. ORAM: I decline to answer that question on the same basis.

SENATOR JACKSON: I had a question. What is your occupation?

MRS. ORAM: I am a housewife.

SENATOR JACKSON: What is your occupation?

MRS. ORAM: I am a housewife.

SENATOR JACKSON: What does your husband do?

MRS. ORAM: He works in a drugstore.

SENATOR JACKSON: He works here in Washington, D.C.?

MRS. ORAM: Well, in Arlington County.

SENATOR JACKSON: Did you know a Mrs. Markward?[2]

MRS. ORAM: I decline to answer that question on the basis that I have stated previously.

SENATOR JACKSON: That is all.

SENATOR MCCLELLAN: May I ask you a question? Are you now employed in the government in any way?

MRS. ORAM: No, I am not.

SENATOR MCCLELLAN: Have you ever been?

MRS. ORAM: No, I never have been.

SENATOR MCCLELLAN: You are declining to answer whether you are a Communist or have ever been a Communist? Is that correct?

MRS. ORAM: I am declining to answer that question.

SENATOR MCCLELLAN: You are unwilling to cooperate with your government and its agencies to the extent of giving it any information that you may have that the government or its agencies may need in order to properly function and discharge its responsibilities in preserving our country, are you?

[The witness consulted with her counsel.]

MRS. ORAM: I decline to answer the questions for the reasons I gave.

SENATOR MCCLELLAN: Are you an American citizen?

---

[2]**Mrs. Markward:** Mary Stalcup Markward, a member of the Communist Party, had cast suspicion on Annie Lee Moss when she claimed that Moss's name appeared on the party's membership roster.

MRS. ORAM: Yes.

SENATOR McCLELLAN: Do you owe any obligations to your country as a citizen?

MRS. ORAM: Certainly.

SENATOR McCLELLAN: Do you regard an obligation to your country that protects you—

MRS. ORAM: I don't believe I understand that.

SENATOR McCLELLAN: Yes, you know what I mean. Do you regard an obligation to the country in which you have citizenship to try to serve it?

MRS. ORAM: Yes, of course.

SENATOR McCLELLAN: You do?

MRS. ORAM: Certainly.

SENATOR McCLELLAN: Do you think that you are serving your country as a good citizen and as a patriotic citizen when you refuse to give information that your government needs?

[The witness consulted with her counsel.]

MRS. ORAM: I believe it is my duty and every citizen's duty to protect and uphold the Constitution and I believe that in relying upon my constitutional rights I am certainly carrying that out.

SENATOR McCLELLAN: Is there any part of the Constitution that you hold allegiance to except the Fifth Amendment?

MRS. ORAM: I hold allegiance to every part, including the First Amendment.

SENATOR McCLELLAN: One of the parts of the Constitution is to preserve the United States, is it not?

MRS. ORAM: That is right.

SENATOR McCLELLAN: Are you going to contribute anything towards preserving your country?

MRS. ORAM: I believe I am doing that.

SENATOR McCLELLAN: If you are willing to do that, will you tell us and give us the information that has been asked as a good citizen of this country?

MRS. ORAM: I give you what information I feel I can and should give you.

SENATOR McCLELLAN: What information you feel you can and should give?

MRS. ORAM: Under the rights of the Constitution.

SENATOR McCLELLAN: Is there any information that you can, or that you are willing to give us, under the Constitution?

MRS. ORAM: That is rather a broad question.

SENATOR McCLELLAN: It is a broad question, but is there any, and I make it broad for your benefit? If you can indicate any information that you are willing to give us, to help to this fight against communism and to preserve our country. Is there any, and I make it broad to cover everything? Is there any that you are willing to give us?

MRS. ORAM: Well, of course.

SENATOR McCLELLAN: All right. Tell us. What is it? Mention one thing.

MRS. ORAM: Well, I don't know. I would have to have a specific question. I can't answer anything out of the blue.

SENATOR MCCLELLAN: Are you willing to help your government fight this conspiracy of communism?

MRS. ORAM: I refuse to answer that question on the basis that I have already stated.

SENATOR MCCLELLAN: You think that would incriminate you to say that you are willing to help fight a conspiracy against the United States of America?

MRS. ORAM: I think that I have to stick to my declination to answer.

SENATOR MCCLELLAN: Do you think that would incriminate you? I am not asking you; I want you to state it under oath.

MRS. ORAM: It might.

SENATOR MCCLELLAN: Do you think that it would incriminate you to help your government fight a conspiracy that is trying to destroy it?
[The witness consulted with her counsel.]

MRS. ORAM: I am afraid I don't understand that question, sir.

SENATOR MCCLELLAN: You do understand the question and it is just as simple as it can be. Do you think that you would be incriminated if you gave information that would help your government fight a conspiracy, the conspiracy of communism that is undertaking to destroy it? You certainly understand that.

MRS. ORAM: I am afraid I don't.

SENATOR MCCLELLAN: That is all, Mr. Chairman.

READING AND DISCUSSION QUESTIONS

1. From the transcript, what conclusions can you draw about the threat McClellan believed communism posed to America's national security?

2. How would you describe the strategies and tactics the committee used in attempting to understand the extent and impact of the Communist Party's influence in government?

3. Explain and evaluate how Oram's testimony reflects the broader Cold War fears concerning communism. Given this testimony, what argument about Cold War political culture in the 1950s might a historian make?

24-6 | Finding Security in an Age of Anxiety
"Get the Feel of a Fallout Shelter" (c. 1950s)

Cold War anxiety was fueled by the threat of a nuclear war between the United States and the Soviet Union, each of which had a massive arsenal of nuclear weapons pointed at the other. The government's Office of Civil Defense (OCD) and similar state-level offices both stoked this anxiety and helped to alleviate it by promoting readiness and preparedness campaigns to protect Americans. Do-it-yourself fallout shelters became a popular civil defense measure. In this photograph a couple shows off the "Family Room of Tomorrow," a $2,500 model shelter sponsored jointly by the OCD and the American Institute of Decorators.

Bettmann/Getty Images

READING AND DISCUSSION QUESTIONS

1. Do you think promotional materials such as this "model shelter" heightened or allayed anxiety about nuclear war with the Soviet Union? Why do you think promoters called this model the "family room of tomorrow"?

2. What can you conclude about gender expectations during the Cold War? How are the roles of men and women depicted here?

3. What midcentury middle-class norms were duplicated in the underground shelter? What "essentials" were stocked for a potential nuclear fallout?

▪ COMPARATIVE QUESTIONS ▪

1. Consider Charlotte Oram's testimony (Document 24-5) and Bartolomeo Vanzetti's last statement (Document 21-1) to compare the ways that the Red Scare manifested itself in the 1920s and 1950s. How do you account for the timing of these outbreaks, and what similarities and differences can you identify between them?

2. Synthesize the multiple perspectives from the sources in this chapter to create a persuasive argument regarding the origins of the Cold War. How did foreign policy analysts interpret the Soviet threat, and how might those interpretations have affected U.S. foreign policy?

3. What do the sources in this chapter suggest about the effect of the Cold War on American society? Consider the role of the federal government in identifying what policymakers at the time determined to be threats to American security. To what extent did the federal investigations into homosexuality and communism restrict American civil liberties?

4. What conclusion can you make about the role ideology has played in shaping America's foreign policy? What comparisons can you draw with the imperialism of the late-nineteenth- and early-twentieth-century era and World War II?

25

Triumph of the Middle Class
1945–1963

Following a decade and a half of economic depression and war, consumer spending burst from the constraints imposed by an era of sacrifice to power a postwar boom. The economics of the Cold War era resulted in an expanding economy and a rising standard of living that swelled the middle class. Returning veterans benefited directly from the federal government's generous subsidies. Men who filled the growing ranks of white-collar employment were able to provide the material comforts mass media and advertising defined as indispensable to suburban living. The full-color spreads in leading magazines helped propagate an idealized image of America as a middle-class nation. The glossy images of contented housewives and happy children, however, represented only one face of Cold War America. Not all housewives were content, not all children were happy, and not all Americans could afford a middle-class lifestyle. A small but swelling chorus of social criticism pierced the veil of apparent middle-class satisfaction. These counterpoints portrayed Cold War America not as the middle-class utopia many imagined, but as a fool's paradise, presenting a social critique that would gain traction among the generation coming of age in the sixties.

25-1 | Congress Passes GI Bill of Rights
Servicemen's Readjustment Act (1944)

Even before the end of World War II, Congress passed the Servicemen's Readjustment Act, popularly known as the GI Bill of Rights, to provide federal benefits to veterans of the armed services. With the post–World War I recession in mind, policymakers attempted to soften the economic consequences of demobilization following World War II by providing jobs, education, and housing benefits. It worked. More than two million veterans used the benefits to pursue college degrees, and the legislation enabled millions of veterans' families to become home owners, pulling them into a broadening middle class.

**An Act to Provide Federal Government Aid for the Readjustment
in Civilian Life of Returning World War II Veterans**
*Be it enacted by the Senate and House of Representatives of the United States
of America in Congress assembled, That this Act may be cited as the
Servicemen's Readjustment Act of 1944.*

Title I

Chapter I—Hospitalization, Claims, and Procedures

Sec. 100. The Veterans Administration is hereby declared to be an essential war agency and entitled, second only to the War and Navy Departments, to priorities in personnel, equipment, supplies, and material under any laws, Executive orders, and regulations pertaining to priorities, and in appointments of personnel from civil-service registers the Administrator of Veterans Affairs is hereby granted the same authority and discretion as the War and Navy Departments and the United States Public Health Service. . . .

Title II

Chapter IV—Education of Veterans

1. Any person who served in the active military or naval service on or after September 16, 1940, and prior to the termination of the present war, and who shall have been discharged or released there-from under conditions other than dishonorable, and whose education or training was impeded, delayed, interrupted, or interfered with by reason of his entrance into the service, or who desires a refresher or retraining course, and who either shall have served ninety days or more, exclusive of any period he was assigned for a course of education or training under the Army specialized training program or the Navy college training program, which course was a continuation of his civilian

An Act to Provide Federal Government Aid for the Readjustment in Civilian Life of Returning World War II Veterans, June 22, 1944; Enrolled Acts and Resolutions of Congress, 1789–1996; General Records of the United States Government; Record Group 11; National Archives.

course and was pursued to completion, or as a cadet or midshipman at one of the service academies, or shall have been discharged or released from active service by reason of an actual service-incurred injury or disability, shall be eligible for and entitled to receive education or training under this part. . . .

5. The Administrator shall pay to the educational or training institution, for each person enrolled in full time or part time course of education or training, the customary cost of tuition, and such laboratory, library, health, infirmary, and other similar fees as are customarily charged, and may pay for books, supplies, equipment, and other necessary expenses, exclusive of board, lodging, other living expenses, and travel, as are generally required for the successful pursuit and completion of the course by other students in the institution: Provided, That in no event shall such payments, with respect to any person, exceed $500 for an ordinary school year. . . .

6. While enrolled in and pursuing a course under this part, such person, upon application to the Administrator, shall be paid a subsistence allowance of $50 per month, if without a dependent or dependents, or $75 per month, if he has a dependent or dependents, including regular holidays and leave not exceeding thirty days in a calendar year. . . .

Title III

Loans for the Purchase or Construction of Homes, Farms, and Business Property

Chapter V—General Provisions for Loans

SEC. 501. (a) Any application made by a veteran under this title for the guaranty of a loan to be used in purchasing residential property or in constructing a dwelling on unimproved property owned by him to be occupied as his home may be approved [by] the Administrator of Veterans Affairs if he finds

(1) that the proceeds of such loans will be used for payment for such property to be purchased or constructed by the veteran;

(2) that the contemplated terms of payment required in any mortgage to be given in part payment of the purchase price or the construction cost bear a proper relation to the veteran's present and anticipated income and expenses; and that the nature and condition of the property is such as to be suitable for dwelling purposes; and

(3) that the purchase price paid or to be paid by the veteran for such property or the construction cost, including the value of the unimproved lot, does not exceed the reasonable normal value thereof as determined by proper appraisal.

Purchase of Farms and Farm Equipment

SEC. 502. Any application made under this title for the guaranty of a loan to be used in purchasing any land, buildings, livestock, equipment, machinery, or implements, or in repairing, altering, or improving any buildings or equipment, to be used in farming operations conducted by the applicant, may be approved by the Administrator of Veterans Affairs if he finds

(1) that the proceeds of such loan will be used in payment for or personal property purchased or to be purchased by the veteran, or for repairing, altering, or improving any buildings or equipment to be used in bona fide farming operations conducted by him;

(2) that such property will be useful in and reasonably necessary for efficiently conducting such operations;

(3) that the ability and experience of the veteran, and the nature of the proposed farming operations to be conducted by him, are such that there is a reasonable likelihood that such operations will be successful; and

(4) that the purchase price paid or to be paid by the veteran for such property does not exceed the reasonable normal value thereof as determined by proper appraisal.

Purchase of Business Property

SEC. 503. Any application made under this title for the guaranty of a loan to be used in purchasing any business, land, buildings, supplies, equipment, machinery, or tools, to be used by the applicant in pursuing a gainful occupation (other than farming) may be approved by the Administrator of Veterans Affairs if he finds

(1) that the proceeds of such loan will be used for payment for real or personal property purchased or to be purchased by the veteran and used by him in the bona fide pursuit of such gainful occupation;

(2) that such property will be useful in and reasonably necessary for the efficient and successful pursuit of such occupation;

(3) that the ability and experience of the veteran, and the conditions under which he proposes to pursue such occupation, are such that there is a reasonable likelihood that he will be successful in the pursuit of such occupation; and

(4) that the purchase price paid or to be paid by the veteran for such property does not exceed the reasonable normal value thereof as determined by proper appraisal. . . .

Title IV

Chapter VI—Employment of Veterans

SEC. 600. (a) In the enactment of the provisions of this title Congress declares as its intent and purpose that there shall be an effective job counseling and employment placement service for veterans . . . so as to provide for them the maximum of job opportunity in the field of gainful employment. [A] Veterans Placement Service Board . . . shall determine all matters of policy relating to the administration of the Veterans Employment Service of the United States Employment Service. . . .

Sec. 601. The United States Employment Service shall assign to each of the States a Veterans employment representative, who shall . . .

(a) be functionally responsible for the supervision of the registration of veterans in local employment offices for suitable types of employment and for placement of veterans in employment;

(b) assist in securing and maintaining current information as to the various types of available employment in public works and private industry or business;

(c) promote the interest of employers in employing veterans;

(d) maintain regular contact with employers and Veterans organizations with a view of keeping employers advised of veterans available for employment and veterans advised of opportunities for employment; and

(e) assist in every possible way in improving working conditions and the advancement of employment of veterans.

Title V

Chapter VII—Readjustment Allowances for Former Members of the Armed Forces Who Are Unemployed

Sec. 700. (a) Any person who shall have served in the active military or naval service of the United States at any time after September 16, 1940, and prior to the termination of the present war, and who shall have been discharged or released from active service under conditions other than dishonorable, after active service of ninety days or more, or by reason of an injury or disability incurred in service in line of duty, shall be entitled . . . to receive a readjustment allowance as provided herein for each week of unemployment, not to exceed a total of fifty-two weeks.

READING AND DISCUSSION QUESTIONS

1. Analyze the GI Bill for evidence of policymakers' concerns regarding returning veterans. What categories of help did they assume veterans would most likely need, and how was this legislation designed to meet those needs?

2. How might a historian seeking to understand the emergence of the post–World War II middle class use the evidence from this source? What short- and long-term consequences do you think the bill's sponsors anticipated?

25-2 | Teen Culture in the Fifties

1950s Rock 'n' Roll Dancers (c. 1950)

Many of the parents of 1950s teenagers saw the new rock 'n' roll music blasting from the radio, jukeboxes, and their children's turntables as deeply transgressive. Parents blushed at the sexually suggestive dancing of rock stars such as Elvis Presley and lyrics that strained the boundaries of middle-class propriety. Access to cars and middle-class affluence provided the means for teens to create and sustain a culture separate from their parents and beyond their prying eyes. Some parents believed they had a full-scale rebellion on their hands. They may have exaggerated the dangers teen culture posed, but photographs such as this one did nothing to calm their nerves.

Michael Ochs Archives/Getty Images

READING AND DISCUSSION QUESTIONS

1. What can you tell from this photograph about social relationships among teens in the 1950s?

2. Imagine the reaction of parents to such a scene. What might have worried them?

3. To what extent was postwar social and economic development shaped by the emergence of a teen culture?

25-3 | Evangelical Calls America to Christ

BILLY GRAHAM, *Our Right to Require Belief* (1962)

In 1956, "In God We Trust" became the official national motto, reflecting both a Cold War culture in which Americans contrasted the United States with the atheistic Soviet Union and the widespread appeal of traditional moral values embodied in the Judeo-Christian tradition. Evangelist Billy Graham emerged within this context, becoming the most significant evangelical preacher of the postwar era. His message of salvation through Christ spoke to middle-class Americans in search of some meaning in their lives.

There is a movement gathering momentum in America to take the traditional concept of God out of our national life. If this movement succeeds, IN GOD WE TRUST will be taken from our coins, the Bible will be removed from our courtrooms, future Presidents will be sworn into office with their hand on a copy of the Constitution instead of the Bible, and chaplains will be removed from the Armed Forces.

The issue of prayers in public schools is now before the Supreme Court and, if the Court decrees negatively, another victory will be gained by those forces which conspire to remove faith in God from the public conscience.

With each passing Christmas season the observing of Christmas in the school becomes a sharper issue. Many public schools, from California to New Jersey, have already ruled out the singing of carols in the classroom.

Those who are trying to remove God from our culture are rewriting history and distorting the truth. But those who advocate drastic changes in our traditional faith are only a tiny minority. Most Americans not only believe in God themselves but want their leaders to have faith in God. The Associated Press recently reported the findings of Dr. Paul Bussard, editor of the *Catholic Digest*, who learned that 99 percent of the American people believe in God; that 77 percent believe in the hereafter, and that 75 percent believe that religion is important. . . .

It is true that our forefathers meant this nation to be free from religious domination. The men who built America were primarily victims of oppression. They felt that the terrors of the wilderness were as nothing to that of government oppression of religious faith. But the founding fathers in their determination to have freedom "of" religion never meant to have freedom "from" religion. Separation of church and state in no way implies separation of religion and state affairs. They are spiritually inseparable. . . .

The tremendous prosperity, power and blessing which America has enjoyed through the years came because we as a nation have honored God. . . .

American democracy rests on the belief in the reality of God and His respect for the individual. Ours is a freedom under law, but it is also a freedom that will evaporate if the religious foundations upon which it has been built are taken away. I'm not so sure we would continue to be free if our men in public life had no faith in God. I'm not sure that atheists and agnostics would be quite so zealous to preserve the Bill of Rights or the writ of habeas corpus or the two-party system or the right to trial by jury or the legal innocence of a man before he is proved guilty.

[Cuban leader Fidel] Castro has shown us all over again how easy it is to rationalize, to postpone elections, to justify tyranny in the name of land reform or some other benevolence. A dictator convinced that destiny lies in his own hands is bound to be proud, ruthless and ultimately destructive. . . . If a political leader fears God and believes that God is in control of the universe, that certain moral laws are operating, then his faith will be reflected in his conduct. Our beliefs make us what we are. This faith in God is the source of our liberty.

We are living in the most critical period in American history. We are faced with the possible destruction of our entire civilization. With a militant, atheistic Communism threatening to bury us, we need to rediscover national goals, to reexamine our national destiny. Whether he intends to, the American atheist administering a public office has essentially conceded the battle to Communism. By his atheism he underwrites in principle the Communist, materialistic, nonspiritual concept of life. He has surrendered spiritual, moral and rational arguments against Communism. The kind of moral conduct American life has historically demanded has grown on a religious soil which recognizes the moral laws of God. The morality of justice, the claims of honesty, the regard for and respect of the rights of others have grown on Judeo-Christian soil.

For a generation we have been emphasizing material things. We have been "living it up," reaching for that extra status symbol, milking an affluent society for all we can get. Now we are discovering, in the age of the fifty-megaton bombs, what Haggai, the prophet, wrote: "Ye have sown much, and bring in little; ye eat, but ye have not enough; ye drink, but ye are not filled with drink; ye clothe you, but there is none warm; and he that earneth wages earneth wages to put it into a bag with holes. . . . Ye looked for much, and, lo, it came to little and when ye brought it home, I did blow upon it." . . . As I travel throughout the country, I find that people are suffering from the neurosis of fear. A leading psychiatrist told me recently, "Seventy percent of the people that come to my office are afraid, and they don't know what they're afraid of." There is a jaded, banal and empty feeling on the part of millions. People are searching for a creed to believe, a song to sing and a flag to follow. In Moscow's Red Square some time ago thousands of young Russians were stamping their feet and shouting, "We're going to change the world, we're going to change the world." I could not help contrasting them with some of the young Americans we meet so often, drifting aimlessly from one pleasure spot to another, wondering what to do with themselves. Many of our young people are uncommitted. Their superficial goals do not satisfy them.

It is clearly evident that America needs a renewal of faith in God. But this renewal will have to start with the individual. The Bible teaches that "all have sinned and come short of the glory of God." We must confess our spiritual failure. There must be deep, genuine repentance. In our faith we must turn to Christ, Who died for our sins and arose again for our justification. If we are humble enough to make this deep and honest confession and commitment, God will forgive our sins and lead us to greater national heights.

READING AND DISCUSSION QUESTIONS

1. How does Graham define the crisis facing America? What solution to the crisis does he urge upon his readers?

2. What assumptions does Graham make about the relationship between democracy in America and Christianity?

25-4 | Journalist Parodies Dr. Spock

DAN GILLMOR, *"The Care and Feeding of Spock-Marked Fathers"* (1954)

The dominant postwar domestic ideology lavished attention on the family and the healthy rearing of children. Dr. Benjamin Spock was one of the most prominent pediatricians of the period, and his best-selling book *Dr. Spock's Baby and Child Care* soothed an audience of nervous mothers who sought the opinion of experts on such things as feeding habits, toilet training, and discipline. Spock offered advice to mothers that contradicted the conventional wisdom practiced by earlier generations of parents, but his ultimate message to mothers was to trust their instincts. By the time Dan Gillmor wrote his tongue-in-cheek article almost a decade later, Spock's baby advice had come to define a largely middle-class approach to parenting. In this article, Gillmor humorously attempts to apply some of Spock's famous tips for raising babies to the proper care of husbands and fathers.

Though I swear by, and never at, Dr. Benjamin Spock's "Baby and Child Care," I must admit he has left out an important section in his famous Baby Bible. You see, he said very little about fathers, practically nothing, in fact. Yet any woman could have told him that men are just overgrown boys. It follows that Dr. Spock should have included a section called "Care of Husbands."

The good doctor needn't bother, however, because, between feedings, I have solved the problem and right out of the authentic, original Spock pages, too. All I have done is to borrow a good deal of what he has already said in his book on baby and child care. Only a few of the words of wisdom have been changed. But I have substituted the word "husband" wherever the word "baby" appears in Dr. Spock's original text. Take section 89, for instance. It is called "Being companionable with your baby."

Being companionable with your husband. Be quietly friendly with your husband whenever you are with him. He's getting a sense of how much you mean to each other all the time you're feeding him. . . holding him, or just sitting in the room with him. When you hug him or make noises at him, when you show him that you think he's the most wonderful husband in the world, it makes his spirit grow. . . .

Naturally, I don't mean that you should be talking a blue streak at him all the time he's awake, or constantly joggling him or tickling him. That would tire him out, and in the long run would make him tense. You can be quiet nine tenths of the time you are with him. It's the gently easy-going kind of companionship that's good for him and good for you. It's the comfortable

Dan Gillmor, *"The Care and Feeding of Spock-Marked Fathers,"* Parents' Magazine & Family Home Guide 29 (July 1954): 36–37, 92–93. Used with permission from Meredith Corporation. Originally published in Parents® magazine. All Rights Reserved.

feeling that goes into your arms when you hold him, the fond, peaceful expression on your face when you look at him and the gentle tone in your voice. . . .

Can you spoil a husband? Not by feeding him when he's hungry, comforting him when he's especially miserable, being sociable with him in an easygoing way. Generally speaking, a husband who gets extra attention when he's uncomfortable is perfectly willing to do without it when he feels well. . . Spoiling mostly comes if an older husband is fussed over when he doesn't need any attention. . . .

He isn't a schemer. He needs loving. You'd think from all you hear about husband's demanding attention that they come into the world determined to get their wives under their thumbs by hook or by crook. This is not true at all. Your husband is born to be a reasonable, friendly human being. If you treat him nicely he won't take advantage of you. Don't be afraid to love him or respond to his needs. Every husband needs to be smiled at, talked to gently and lovingly—just as he needs vitamins and calories, and the husband who doesn't get any loving will grow cold and unresponsive. . . .

Much of what Dr. Spock has said regarding jealousy would be handy as applied to husbands as follows:

It is good for a husband to know ahead of time that he is going to have a baby. . . so that he can get used to the idea gradually. . . .

The arrival of the baby should change a husband's life as little as possible, especially if he has been the only husband up to that time. It is better to make all possible changes well ahead of time. . . .

Jealousy takes many forms. If a husband picks up a large shoe and swats the baby with it, the mother knows well enough that it's jealousy. But another husband is more polite. He admires the baby for a couple of days without enthusiasm and then says, "I have to work late at the office tonight, dear."

Helping a first husband to be outgoing. Most first husbands grow up happy and well adjusted. . . but a few of them have a harder time adjusting to the outside world. . . .

What makes the difference? One trouble is that the first husband. . . gets more fussing over than is good for him. . . This gives him too little chance to develop his own interests. . . He may be shown off to others too much. A little of this is harmless; a steady diet of it makes him self-conscious. . . .

Of course, the answer is not to ignore a first husband. He needs affection and responsiveness in good measure. But let him play at his own games as long as he is interested and happy, with the least possible interference, bossing, scolding and anxious concern. Give him a chance to start the conversation sometimes. When visitors come, let him make up to them himself. When he comes to you for play or for affection, be warm and friendly, but let him go when he turns back to his own pursuits. . . .

Temper tantrums. Almost any husband will have a few temper tantrums after one to three years of marriage. He's gotten a sense of his own desires and individuality. When he's thwarted he knows it and feels angry. Yet he doesn't usually attack the wife who has interfered with him. Perhaps she is too important and too big.

A temper tantrum once in a while doesn't mean anything: there are bound to be some frustrations. If they are happening regularly, several times a day, it may mean that the husband is getting overtired, or isn't eating enough, or has some chronic physical trouble. Frequent tantrums are more often due to the fact that the wife hasn't learned the knack of handling the husband tactfully. There are several questions to ask. . . Is the house arranged so that his wife doesn't have to keep forbidding him to touch many things? Is she, without realizing it, arousing his balkiness by telling him to come and wash for dinner? When she sees she has to interrupt him. . . does she frustrate him, or get his mind on something pleasant? When she sees a storm brewing, does she meet it head on, grimly, or does she distract him to something else?

You can be both firm and friendly. It's probably a good idea, after I have been emphasizing how you handle a young husband by distraction and consideration, to point out that there are limits. Some gentle, unselfish wives devote so much effort to being tactful and generous to a husband, that they give him the feeling that he's the crown prince, or rather the king. . . This isn't good for him or for her. . . .

Conscientious wives often let a husband take advantage of them for a while. . . until their patience is exhausted. . . and then turn on him crossly. But neither of these stages is really necessary. If wives have a healthy self-respect, they can stand up for themselves while they are still feeling friendly. For instance, if your husband is insisting that you continue to watch television after you are exhausted, don't be afraid to say cheerfully but definitely, "I'm all tired out. I'm going to read a book now and you can read *your* book, too."

Yes, indeed. Spock, revisited, turns out to be an excellent guide to husband handling, but before you try applying it, read the rewritten version of Dr. Spock's original section one, as follows:

You know more than you think you do. Soon you're going to have a husband. Maybe you have him already. You're happy and excited, but, if you haven't had much experience, you wonder whether you are going to know how to do a good job. Lately you have been listening more carefully to your friends and relatives when they talk about handling a husband. You've begun to read articles by experts in the magazines and newspapers. . . Sometimes it sounds like a very complicated business. You find out all the vitamins a husband needs. . . You hear that a husband must be cuddled plenty. . . .

Don't take too seriously all that the neighbors say. Don't be overawed by what the experts say. Don't be afraid to trust your own common sense. Taking care of your husband won't be a complicated job if you take it easy, trust your own instincts and follow the directions that your doctor gives you. We know for a fact that the natural loving care that kindly wives give to their husbands is a hundred times more valuable than their knowing how to iron a shirt just right, or making pie expertly. Every time you. . . smile at him, he's getting a feeling that he belongs to you and that you belong to him. Nobody else in the world, no matter how skillful, can give that to him.

Come to think of it, you could apply all this excellent advice to the benefit of wives, too. In fact, I think I'll try it.

READING AND DISCUSSION QUESTIONS

1. Gillmor borrows liberally from Dr. Spock's *Baby and Child Care* book. What can you infer about the advice Dr. Spock gave to new parents?

2. What conclusion about gender relations in the 1950s can you draw from the way Gillmor talks about husbands and wives?

3. Gillmor intended his article to be funny. What do you think made it funny in the context of the period? Do you think husbands read his article the same way wives did?

25-5 | National Concerns About the Corruptions of Youth
Crimes by Women (1948)

The 1950s postwar affluence affirmed conventional values of middle-class morality and idealized the nuclear family with a working father and stay-at-home mother. At the same time, the economic comforts provided opportunities for consumer indulgence and a relaxation of social and moral constraints. Concerns about immorality haunted the middle class. Reformers began defining a crisis among America's youth that they attributed to the explicit sexual and violent themes appearing in comic books. Even the U.S. Congress held hearings on the link between children reading comic books and the increase in juvenile delinquency. Parents and politicians worried about the subversive messages in comics that valorized crime, indulged violent and sadistic fantasies, and titillated with revealing images of women's bodies. In an updated Bonnie and Clyde story issued by Fox Feature Syndicate in its "Crimes by Women" series, this Bonnie is a bored waitress who sees an opportunity for quick cash and some thrills when Clyde and his crime partner, Ray Hamilton, come into her restaurant. The three of them begin a spree of robberies, and Bonnie is quick with the gun, killing bank tellers, ticket agents, and innocent women bystanders. Eventually Ray splits, saying: "This is gettin' too much for me. I can't cope with no crazy dame." Their criminal career ends when their car crashes into a tree during a police pursuit. The following are two pages from the June 1948 issue, which sets up the story and shows Bonnie in action.

Crimes by women/Fox Feature Syndicate/published June 1948

Crimes by women/Fox Feature Syndicate/published June 1948

READING AND DISCUSSION QUESTIONS

1. As you examine these images, consider what critics at the time might have found subversive in the comic book's art and story.

2. Why do you think children in the 1950s might have been drawn to gangster-style comic books?

3. What does the anxiety of juvenile delinquency expressed by some parents and politicians at the time suggest about Cold War American culture in general?

25-6 | The Pros and Cons of Suburbia

J. R. EYERMAN, *Photograph of Los Angeles Development Boom* (1952) and MALVINA REYNOLDS, *"Little Boxes"* (1962)

One feature of the postwar boom was a reinvigorated American Dream defined by the nuclear family with its own home in the suburbs. The affluence and stability of middle-class living appealed to the generation reared in the shadows of depression and war. But not everyone felt the same way. Beat poets, folk singers, and social critics bemoaned the suburban ideals depicted in this *Life* magazine photograph. Malvina Reynolds, a popular folk singer and activist, wrote "Little Boxes" in 1962 in response to the housing developments springing up in her native California. Her song became something of an anthem for the generation of 1960s activists, including Pete Seeger, whose recording of the song made it popular.

J. R. Eyerman/Getty Images

Little boxes on the hillside,
Little boxes made of ticky tacky[1]
Little boxes on the hillside,
Little boxes all the same,
There's a green one and a pink one
And a blue one and a yellow one
And they're all made out of ticky tacky
And they all look just the same.

And the people in the houses
All went to the university
Where they were put in boxes
And they came out all the same
And there's doctors and there's lawyers
And business executives
And they're all made out of ticky tacky
And they all look just the same.

And they all play on the golf course
And drink their martinis dry
And they all have pretty children
And the children go to school,
And the children go to summer camp
And then to the university
Where they are put in boxes
And they come out all the same.

And the boys go into business
And marry and raise a family
In boxes made of ticky tacky
And they all look just the same.

READING AND DISCUSSION QUESTIONS

1. Examine what is going on in this *Life* magazine photograph. What does it suggest about the middle-class American Dream in postwar America?

2. To what extent do you think the photographer used this image to celebrate or criticize the suburbanization of America? Do you think the photographer felt the same way as Malvina Reynolds? Do you think the photograph was staged? If so, does it change the way historians use the source?

3. What is the nature of Reynolds's critique? What elements of postwar America does she single out for criticism and why?

---

[1]**Ticky tacky:** Low quality and inexpensive building materials.

▪ COMPARATIVE QUESTIONS ▪

1. Parents' anxiety over comic books (Document 25-5) and Malvina Reynolds's song about suburbia (Document 25-6) both speak to problems facing America in the postwar era. Did critics see comic books and suburbia as part of the same problem? Explain.

2. Based on your analysis and evaluation of the historical evidence presented in this chapter, what conclusion could you make about the significance of middle-class values to Cold War America?

3. Explain and evaluate the 1950s and the 1920s as two eras of cultural conservatism. To what degree do you see these periods as conservative? What apparent social norms lead you to this conclusion?

4. Compare Cold War evangelicalism with earlier periods of religious enthusiasm by identifying similarities and differences in the perspectives of Billy Graham (Document 25-3) and W. B. Riley (Document P7-4). Did these evangelists identify a common foe to American religiosity? If so, what was it?

26

The Civil Rights Movement
1941–1973

Three years after Martin Luther King Jr. shared his dream at the Lincoln Memorial in 1963, a young civil rights activist preached: "I am black and I am beautiful! I am Somebody." Jesse Jackson's boast hinted at the extraordinary impact of the civil rights movement, which had restored a sense of self-worth to millions of people who faced discrimination. The African American civil rights movement targeted racial discrimination in its legal, social, and economic guises by embracing tactics ranging from interracial alliances to Black Power militancy. Its important victories, including the Civil Rights Act of 1964 and the Voting Rights Act of 1965, pressed forward significant changes in the lives of African Americans, who had long found themselves relegated to the margins of American society. The movement spoke to others as well, including members of many other groups who had similarly faced jeers and taunts as they struggled for political, social, and economic acceptance. The social revolution for rights mobilized America's lesbian, gay, bisexual, and transgender community, ethnic minorities, and Native Americans who saw in the struggle of African Americans some hope that the sound of their voices could also lift freedom's chorus. While the achievements of the civil rights movement were too modest for some, they were to others a hint of America's real promise.

26-1 | Southern Congressmen Issue Manifesto Against *Brown v. Board* Decision

Declaration of Constitutional Principles (1956)

In 1954, the Supreme Court ruled in *Brown v. Board of Education* that the long-standing "separate but equal" doctrine, affirmed in the 1896 case *Plessy v. Ferguson*, was unconstitutional. The *Brown* decision required the racial integration of public schools by arguing that separate institutions were "inherently" unequal. One hundred and one congressmen from southern states, outraged by the Court's decision, signed their names to the "Declaration of Constitutional Principles," often referred to as the "Southern Manifesto."

We regard the decision of the Supreme Court in the school cases as clear abuse of judicial power. It climaxes a trend in the Federal judiciary undertaking to legislate, in derogation of the authority of Congress, and to encroach upon the reserved rights of the states and the people.

The original Constitution does not mention education. Neither does the Fourteenth Amendment nor any other amendment. The debates preceding the submission of the Fourteenth Amendment clearly show that there was no intent that it should affect the systems of education maintained by the states.

The very Congress which proposed the amendment subsequently provided for segregated schools in the District of Columbia.

When the amendment was adopted in 1868, there were thirty-seven states of the Union. Every one of the twenty-six states that had any substantial racial differences among its people either approved the operation of segregated schools already in existence or subsequently established such schools by action of the same law-making body which considered the Fourteenth Amendment.

As admitted by the Supreme Court in the public school case (*Brown v. Board of Education*), the doctrine of separate but equal schools "apparently originated in *Roberts v. City of Boston* (1849), upholding school segregation against attack as being violative of a state constitutional guarantee of equality." This constitutional doctrine began in the North—not in the South—and it was followed not only in Massachusetts but in Connecticut, New York, Illinois, Indiana, Michigan, Minnesota, New Jersey, Ohio, Pennsylvania and other northern states until they, exercising their rights as states through the constitutional processes of local self-government, changed their school systems.

In the case of *Plessy v. Ferguson* in 1896 the Supreme Court expressly declared that under the Fourteenth Amendment no person was denied any of his rights if the states provided separate but equal public facilities. This decision has been followed in many other cases. It is notable that the Supreme Court, speaking

Congressional Record, 84th Cong., 2d Sess., vol. 102, part 4 (Washington, DC: Government Printing Office, 1956), 4460.

through Chief Justice Taft, a former President of the United States, unanimously declared in 1927 in *Lum v. Rice* that the "separate but equal" principle is "within the discretion of the state in regulating its public schools and does not conflict with the Fourteenth Amendment."

This interpretation, restated time and again, became a part of the life of the people of many of the states and confirmed their habits, customs, traditions and way of life. It is founded on elemental humanity and common sense, for parents should not be deprived by Government of the right to direct the lives and education of their own children.

Though there has been no constitutional amendment or act of Congress changing this established legal principle almost a century old, the Supreme Court of the United States, with no legal basis for such action, undertook to exercise their naked judicial power and substituted their personal political and social ideas for the established law of the land.

This unwarranted exercise of power by the court, contrary to the Constitution, is creating chaos and confusion in the states principally affected. It is destroying the amicable relations between the white and Negro races that have been created through ninety years of patient effort by the good people of both races. It has planted hatred and suspicion where there has been heretofore friendship and understanding.

Without regard to the consent of the governed, outside agitators are threatening immediate and revolutionary changes in our public school systems. If done, this is certain to destroy the system of public education in some of the states.

With the gravest concern for the explosive and dangerous condition created by this decision and inflamed by outside meddlers:

We reaffirm our reliance on the Constitution as the fundamental law of the land.

We decry the Supreme Court's encroachments on rights reserved to the states and to the people, contrary to established law and to the Constitution.

We commend the motives of those states which have declared the intention to resist forced integration by any lawful means.

We appeal to the states and people who are not directly affected by these decisions to consider the constitutional principles involved against the time when they too, on issues vital to them, may be the victims of judicial encroachment.

Even though we constitute a minority in the present congress, we have full faith that a majority of the American people believe in the dual system of government which has enabled us to achieve our greatness and will in time demand that the reserved rights of the states and of the people be made secure against judicial usurpation.

We pledge ourselves to use all lawful means to bring about a reversal of this decision which is contrary to the Constitution and to prevent the use of force in its implementation.

READING AND DISCUSSION QUESTIONS

1. How did the congressmen frame their opposition to the Supreme Court's decision in *Brown v. Board*? What specifically did they say they were objecting to?

2. What conclusions can you draw from the Southern Manifesto about the challenges that faced the civil rights movement in the 1950s and 1960s?

26-2 | Civil Rights Activist Challenges Racial Discrimination

FANNIE LOU HAMER, *Testimony Before the Credentials Committee of the Democratic National Convention* (1964)

The foot soldiers of the civil rights movement included women like Fannie Lou Hamer, an African American activist born in 1917 in Mississippi, where racial oppression often took violent form, as she recounts in this testimony. In 1964, Hamer's Mississippi Freedom Democratic Party (MFDP) sought delegate seats at the Democratic National Convention, but President Johnson, seeking reelection, wanted to avoid a convention split over civil rights. Johnson won, and neither Hamer nor any other MFDP delegates were seated, but her compelling story, aired on national television, brought visible attention to the movement's cause.

Mr. Chairman, and to the Credentials Committee, my name is Mrs. Fannie Lou Hamer, and I live at 626 East Lafayette Street, Ruleville, Mississippi, Sunflower County, the home of Senator James O. Eastland, and Senator Stennis.

It was the 31st of August in 1962 that eighteen of us traveled twenty-six miles to the county courthouse in Indianola to try to register to become first-class citizens. We was met in Indianola by policemen, Highway Patrolmen, and they only allowed two of us in to take the literacy test at the time. After we had taken this test and started back to Ruleville, we was held up by the City Police and the State Highway Patrolmen and carried back to Indianola where the bus driver was charged that day with driving a bus the wrong color.

After we paid the fine among us, we continued on to Ruleville, and Reverend Jeff Sunny carried me four miles in the rural area where I had worked as a timekeeper and sharecropper for eighteen years. I was met there by my children, who told me the plantation owner was angry because I had gone down—tried to register.

After they told me, my husband came, and said the plantation owner was raising Cain because I had tried to register. And before he quit talking the plantation owner came and said, "Fannie Lou, do you know—did Pap tell you what I said?"

And I said, "Yes, sir."

He said, "Well I mean that."

Fannie Lou Hamer Speech before DNC, August 22, 1964. Used by permission of Vergie Hamer Faulkner.

Said, "If you don't go down and withdraw your registration, you will have to leave." Said, "Then if you go down and withdraw," said, "you still might have to go because we're not ready for that in Mississippi."

And I addressed him and told him and said, "I didn't try to register for you. I tried to register for myself."

I had to leave that same night.

On the 10th of September 1962, sixteen bullets was fired into the home of Mr. and Mrs. Robert Tucker for me. That same night two girls were shot in Ruleville, Mississippi. Also, Mr. Joe McDonald's house was shot in.

And June the 9th, 1963, I had attended a voter registration workshop; was returning back to Mississippi. Ten of us was traveling by the Continental Trailway bus. When we got to Winona, Mississippi, which is Montgomery County, four of the people got off to use the washroom, and two of the people — to use the restaurant — two of the people wanted to use the washroom.

The four people that had gone in to use the restaurant was ordered out. During this time I was on the bus. But when I looked through the window and saw they had rushed out I got off of the bus to see what had happened. And one of the ladies said, "It was a State Highway Patrolman and a Chief of Police ordered us out."

I got back on the bus and one of the persons had used the washroom got back on the bus, too.

As soon as I was seated on the bus, I saw when they began to get the five people in a highway patrolman's car. I stepped off of the bus to see what was happening and somebody screamed from the car that the five workers was in and said, "Get that one there." And when I went to get in the car, when the man told me I was under arrest, he kicked me.

I was carried to the county jail and put in the booking room. They left some of the people in the booking room and began to place us in cells. I was placed in a cell with a young woman called Miss Ivesta Simpson. After I was placed in the cell I began to hear sounds of licks and screams. I could hear the sounds of licks and horrible screams. And I could hear somebody say, "Can you say, 'yes, sir,' nigger? Can you say 'yes, sir'?"

And they would say other horrible names.

She would say, "Yes, I can say 'yes, sir.' "

"So, well, say it."

She said, "I don't know you well enough."

They beat her, I don't know how long. And after a while she began to pray, and asked God to have mercy on those people.

And it wasn't too long before three white men came to my cell. One of these men was a State Highway Patrolman and he asked me where I was from. And I told him Ruleville. He said, "We are going to check this." And they left my cell and it wasn't too long before they came back. He said, "You are from Ruleville all right," and he used a curse word. And he said, "We're going to make you wish you was dead."

I was carried out of that cell into another cell where they had two Negro prisoners. The State Highway Patrolmen ordered the first Negro to take the blackjack. The first Negro prisoner ordered me, by orders from the State Highway Patrolman, for me to lay down on a bunk bed on my face. And I laid on my face, the first Negro began to beat me.

And I was beat by the first Negro until he was exhausted. I was holding my hands behind me at that time on my left side, because I suffered from polio when I was six years old.

After the first Negro had beat until he was exhausted, the State Highway Patrolman ordered the second Negro to take the blackjack.

The second Negro began to beat and I began to work my feet, and the State Highway Patrolman ordered the first Negro who had beat to sit on my feet—to keep me from working my feet. I began to scream and one white man got up and began to beat me in my head and tell me to hush.

One white man—my dress had worked up high—he walked over and pulled my dress—I pulled my dress down and he pulled my dress back up.

I was in jail when Medgar Evers was murdered.

All of this is on account of we want to register, to become first-class citizens. And if the Freedom Democratic Party is not seated now, I question America. Is this America, the land of the free and the home of the brave, where we have to sleep with our telephones off of the hooks because our lives be threatened daily, because we want to live as decent human beings, in America?

READING AND DISCUSSION QUESTIONS

1. What argument about African American civil rights does Hamer make in her speech to the credentials committee? What is the nature of her appeal?

2. What evidence does her testimony provide for your understanding of the obstacles African Americans endured in seeking their civil rights? From her story, what can you infer about the peculiar vulnerabilities facing black women activists?

26-3 | Civil Rights Movement Takes a More Militant Turn
MALCOLM X, *The Ballot or the Bullet* (1964)

Martin Luther King Jr.'s nonviolent approach to civil rights frustrated some, like Malcolm X, who demanded more direct and immediate action against the system of racial oppression that faced African Americans. Malcolm X, who preached an alternative, Black Nationalist message, gave this 1964 speech to a symposium on the theme of "The Negro Revolt." His public break with the Nation of Islam precipitated his assassination in February 1965.

The question tonight, as I understand it, is "The Negro Revolt, and Where Do We Go From Here?" or "What Next?" In my little humble way of understanding it, it points toward either the ballot or the bullet. . . .

Although I'm still a Muslim, I'm not here tonight to discuss my religion. I'm not here to try and change your religion. I'm not here to argue or discuss anything that we differ about, because it's time for us to submerge our differences and realize that it is best for us to first see that we have the same problem, a common problem—a problem that will make you catch hell whether you're a Baptist, or a Methodist, or a Muslim, or a nationalist. Whether you're educated or illiterate, whether you live on the boulevard or in the alley, you're going to catch hell just like I am. We're all in the same boat and we all are going to catch the same hell from the same man. He just happens to be a white man. All of us have suffered here, in this country, political oppression at the hands of the white man, economic exploitation at the hands of the white man, and social degradation at the hands of the white man.

Now in speaking like this, it doesn't mean that we're anti-white, but it does mean we're anti-exploitation, we're anti-degradation, we're anti-oppression. And if the white man doesn't want us to be anti-him, let him stop oppressing and exploiting and degrading us. . . .

If we don't do something real soon, I think you'll have to agree that we're going to be forced either to use the ballot or the bullet. It's one or the other in 1964. It isn't that time is running out—time has run out! 1964 threatens to be the most explosive year America has ever witnessed. The most explosive year. Why? It's also a political year. It's the year when all of the white politicians will be back in the so-called Negro community jiving you and me for some votes. The year when all of the white political crooks will be right back in your and my community with their false promises, building up our hopes for a letdown, with their trickery and their treachery, with their false promises which they don't intend to keep. As they nourish these dissatisfactions, it can only lead to one thing, an explosion; and now we have the type of black man on the scene in America today—I'm sorry, Brother Lomax[1]—who just doesn't intend to turn the other cheek any longer. . . .

I'm not a politician, not even a student of politics; in fact, I'm not a student of much of anything. I'm not a Democrat. I'm not a Republican, and I don't even consider myself an American. If you and I were Americans, there'd be no problem. Those Hunkies that just got off the boat, they're already Americans; Polacks are already Americans; the Italian refugees are already Americans. Everything that came out of Europe, every blue-eyed thing, is already an American. And as long as you and I have been over here, we aren't Americans yet.

Well, I am one who doesn't believe in deluding myself. I'm not going to sit at your table and watch you eat, with nothing on my plate, and call myself a diner. Sitting at the table doesn't make you a diner, unless you eat some of what's

---

[1]**Brother Lomax**: Louis Lomax, an African American journalist and civil rights activist who spoke before Malcolm X at the 1964 symposium.

on that plate. Being here in America doesn't make you an American. Being born here in America doesn't make you an American. Why, if birth made you American, you wouldn't need any legislation; you wouldn't need any amendments to the Constitution, you wouldn't be faced with civil-rights filibustering in Washington, D.C., right now. They don't have to pass civil-rights legislation to make a Polack an American.

No, I'm not an American. I'm one of the 22 million black people who are the victims of Americanism. One of the 22 million black people who are the victims of democracy, nothing but disguised hypocrisy. So, I'm not standing here speaking to you as an American, or a patriot, or a flag-saluter, or a flag-waver—no, not I. I'm speaking as a victim of this American system. And I see America through the eyes of the victim. I don't see any American dream; I see an American nightmare. . . .

The same government that you go abroad to fight for and die for is the government that is in a conspiracy to deprive you of your voting rights, deprive you of your economic opportunities, deprive you of decent housing, deprive you of decent education. You don't need to go to the employer alone, it is the government itself, the government of America, that is responsible for the oppression and exploitation and degradation of black people in this country. And you should drop it in their lap. This government has failed the Negro. This so-called democracy has failed the Negro. And all these white liberals have definitely failed the Negro.

So, where do we go from here? . . . To those of us whose philosophy is black nationalism, the only way you can get involved in the civil-rights struggle is give it a new interpretation[,] . . . an interpretation that will enable us to come into it, take part in it. And these handkerchief-heads who have been dillydallying and pussyfooting and compromising—we don't intend to let them pussyfoot and dillydally and compromise any longer. . . .

The black nationalists, those whose philosophy is black nationalism, in bringing about this new interpretation of the entire meaning of civil rights, look upon it as meaning . . . equality of opportunity. Well, we're justified in seeking civil rights, if it means equality of opportunity, because all we're doing there is trying to collect for our investment. Our mothers and fathers invested sweat and blood. Three hundred and ten years we worked in this country without a dime in return—I mean without a dime in return. You let the white man walk around here talking about how rich this country is, but you never stop to think how it got rich so quick. It got rich because you made it rich. . . .

Whenever you demonstrate against segregation, whether it is segregated education, segregated housing, or anything else, the law is on your side, and anyone who stands in the way is not the law any longer. They are breaking the law; they are not representatives of the law. Any time you demonstrate against segregation and a man has the audacity to put a police dog on you, kill that dog, kill him, I'm telling you, kill that dog. I say it, if they put me in jail tomorrow, kill—that—dog. Then you'll put a stop to it. Now, if these white people in here don't want to see that kind of action, get down and tell the mayor to tell the police department to pull the dogs in. That's all you have to do. If you don't do it, someone else will. . . .

Any time you know you're within the law, within your legal rights, within your moral rights, in accord with justice, then die for what you believe in. But don't die alone. Let your dying be reciprocal. This is what is meant by equality. What's good for the goose is good for the gander.

. . . You may wonder why all of the atrocities that have been committed in Africa and in Hungary and in Asia, and in Latin America are brought before the UN [United Nations], and the Negro problem is never brought before the UN. This is part of the conspiracy. This old, tricky blue eyed liberal who is supposed to be your and my friend, supposed to be in our corner, supposed to be subsidizing our struggle, and supposed to be acting in the capacity of an adviser, never tells you anything about human rights. They keep you wrapped up in civil rights. And you spend so much time barking up the civil-rights tree, you don't even know there's a human-rights tree on the same floor.

When you expand the civil-rights struggle to the level of human rights, you can then take the case of the black man in this country before the nations in the UN. . . . You can take Uncle Sam before a world court. . . . Human rights are something you were born with. Human rights are your God-given rights. Human rights are the rights that are recognized by all nations of this earth. And any time any one violates your human rights, you can take them to the world court. Uncle Sam's hands are dripping with blood, dripping with the blood of the black man in this country. He's the earth's number-one hypocrite. He has the audacity — yes, he has — imagine him posing as the leader of the free world. The free world! And you over here singing "We Shall Overcome." Expand the civil-rights struggle to the level of human rights. Take it into the United Nations, where our African brothers can throw their weight on our side, where our Asian brothers can throw their weight on our side, where our Latin-American brothers can throw their weight on our side, and where 800 million Chinamen are sitting there waiting to throw their weight on our side.

Let the world know how bloody his hands are. Let the world know the hypocrisy that's practiced over here. Let it be the ballot or the bullet. Let him know that it must be the ballot or the bullet.

READING AND DISCUSSION QUESTIONS

1. To what degree does Malcolm X see possibilities for interracial cooperation in the civil rights movement? Does he welcome such cooperation? Why or why not?

2. What was the nature of the choice implied in his title? Of what use to the civil rights movement were the ballot and the bullet?

26-4 | Stonewall Riot and Gay Power

EDMUND WHITE, *Letter to Alfred and Ann Corn* (1969)

The civil rights movement is studded with iconic moments: the Selma march, the Montgomery bus boycott, King's "I Have a Dream" speech. For the gay rights movement, that iconic moment is the Stonewall riots. In late June 1969, police raided the Stonewall Inn, a popular gay bar located in the Greenwich Village neighborhood of New York City. While members of the LGBTQ community and their allies had pressed for their civil rights before Stonewall, this event crystalized the movement for gay pride. In this letter written a few days after the Stonewall riots, Edmund White describes for friends what happened. His claim that "we're part of a vast rebellion of all the repressed" speaks to White's sense in that moment that gay power was linked with the other civil rights movements taking place. White, who was thirty at the time of Stonewall and just beginning his literary career, went on to become one of the celebrated writers of the twentieth century with countless books and memoirs that explored gay life in America.

Dear Ann and Alfred,

Well, the big news here is Gay Power. It's the most extraordinary thing. It all began two weeks ago on a Friday night. The cops raided the <SW>, that mighty Bastille which you know has remained impregnable for three years, so brazen and so conspicuous that one could only surmise that the Mafia was paying off the pigs[2] handsomely. Apparently, however, a new public official, Sergeant Smith, has taken over the Village, and he's a peculiarly diligent lawman. In any event, a mammoth paddy wagon, as big as a school bus, pulled up to the Wall and about ten cops raided the joint. The kids were all shooed into the street; soon other gay kids and straight spectators swelled the ranks to, I'd say, about a thousand people. Christopher Street was completely blocked off and the crowds swarmed from the Voice office[3] down to the Civil War hospital.

As the Mafia owners were dragged out one by one and shoved into the wagon, the crowd would let out Bronx cheers and jeers and clapping. Someone shouted "Gay Power," others took up the cry—and then it dissolved into giggles. A few more gay prisoners—bartenders, hatcheck boys—a few more cheers, someone starts singing "We Shall Overcome"—and then they started camping on it. A drag queen is shoved into the wagon; she hits the cop over the head with her purse. The cop clubs her. Angry stirring in the crowd. The cops, used to the cringing and disorganization of the gay crowds, snort off. But the crowd doesn't disperse. Everyone is restless, angry and high-spirited. No one has a slogan, no one even has an attitude, but something's brewing.

Some adorable butch hustler boy pulls up a parking meter, mind you, out of the pavement, and uses it as a battering ram (a few cops are still inside the Wall, locked in). The boys begin to pound at the heavy wooden double doors and windows; glass shatters all over the street. Cries of "Liberate the Bar."

White, Edmund, Letter to Alfred and Ann Corn. July 8 1969. In *The Violet Quill Reader: The Emergence of Gay Writing After Stonewall.* ed. David Bergman, pp. 1–4. New York: St. Martin's Press. 1994. Reprinted by permission of Edmund White.

[2] **Pigs**: pejorative name for police officers

[3] *Voice* **office**: *The Village Voice*, an alternative weekly newspaper that began in 1955 and whose editorial office in 1969 was located on Christopher Street, just down the block from the Stonewall Inn.

Bottles (from hostile straights?) rain down from the apartment windows. Cries of "We're the Pink Panthers."[4] A mad Negro queen whirls like a dervish with a twisted piece of metal in her hand and breaks the remaining windows. The door begins to give. The cop turns a hose on the crowd (they're still within the Wall). But they can't aim it properly, and the crowd sticks. Finally the door is broken down and the kids, as though working to a prior plan, systematically dump refuse from the waste cans into the Wall, squirting it with lighter fluid, and ignite it. Huge flashes of flame and billows of smoke.

Now the cops in the paddy wagon return, and two fire engines pull up. Clubs fly. The crowd retreats.

Saturday night, the pink panthers are back full force. The cops form a flying wedge at the Greenwich Avenue end of Christopher and drive the kids down towards Sheridan Square. The panthers, however, run down Waverly, up Gay Street, and come out behind the cops, kicking in a chorus line, taunting, screaming. Dreary middle-class East Side queens stand around disapproving but fascinated, unable to go home, as though torn between their class loyalties, their desire to be respectable, and their longing for freedom. Sheridan Square is cordoned off by the cops. The United Cigar store closes, Riker's closes, the deli closes. No one can pass through the square; to walk up Seventh Avenue, you must detour all the way to Bleeker.

A mad left-wing group of straight kids called the Crazies is trying to organize gay kids, point out that Lindsay[5] is to blame (the Crazies want us to vote for Procaccino, or "Prosciutto," as we call him). A Crazy girl launches into a tirade against Governor Rockefeller, "Whose Empire," she cries, "Must Be Destroyed." Straight Negro boys put their arms around me and say we're comrades (it's okay with me — in fact, great, the first camaraderie I've felt with blacks in years). Mattachine[6] (our NAACP) hands out leaflets about "what to do if arrested." Some man from the Oscar Wilde bookstore hands out a leaflet describing to newcomers what's going on. I give a stump speech about the need to radicalize, how we must recognize we're part of a vast rebellion of all the repressed. Some jeers, some cheers. Charles Burch[7] plans to make a plastique to hurl at cops.

Sunday night, the Stonewall, now reopened — though one room is charred and blasted, all lights are smashed, and only a few dim bulbs are burning, no bad liquor being sold — the management posts an announcement: "We appreciate all of you and your efforts to help, but the Stonewall believes in peace. Please end the riots. We believe in peace." Some kids, nonetheless, try to turn over a cop car. Twelve are arrested. Some straight toughs rough up some queens. The queens beat them up. Sheridan Square is again blocked off by the pigs. That same night a group of about seventy-five vigilantes in Queens chops down a wooded part of a park as vengeance against the perverts who are cruising in bushes. "They're

---

[4]**Pink Panthers**: A play on the African American Black Panther group, the Pink Panther Patrol of New York was a gay-rights group just then organizing to defend LGBTQ people.

[5]**Lindsay**: John Lindsay, mayor of New York from 1966 to 1973.

[6]**Mattachine**: Mattachine Society, a gay and lesbian–rights group founded in Los Angeles in 1950 that worked to fight police persecution.

[7]**Charles Burch**: A friend of White's. He and White were walking by the Stonewall Inn when the raid began.

endangering our women and children." The Times, which has scarcely mentioned the Sheridan Square riots (a half column, very tame) is now so aroused by the conservation issue that it blasts the "vigs" for their malice toward nature.

Wednesday. The Voice runs two front-page stories on the riots, both snide, both devoted primarily to assuring readers that the authors are straight.

This last weekend, nothing much happened because it was the Fourth of July and everyone was away. Charles Burch has decided it's all a drag. When he hears that gay kids are picketing Independence Hall in Philly because they're being denied their constitutional rights, he says: "But of course, the Founding Fathers didn't intend to protect perverts and criminals. "Who knows what will happen this weekend, or this week? I'll keep you posted.

Otherwise, nothing much. I've been going out with a mad boy who tried to kill me last Friday. He's very cute, and I'm sure it'd be a kick, but I think I'll take a rain check on the death scene.

Finished the first act of my play and outlined the second. My sister has a new boyfriend who's got $30 million, two doctorates, working on a third. She met him in the bughouse (shows the advantages of sending your daughter to the best bughouse in town). I'm going out to Chicago in two weeks to help her move.

I miss you both frightfully. No more fun dinners, no endless telephone conversations, no sharing of exquisite sensations, gad, it's awful.

Love, Ed

READING AND DISCUSSION QUESTIONS

1. While White's letter reports the events at the Stonewall Inn, he is also shaping a narrative that helps him make sense of that weekend. What does he choose to describe? How is he making meaning from the events of that moment?

2. What does his letter suggest about his understanding of who was part of America's gay culture at the time? Does he see the variety of groups and individuals ("butch hustler boy," "Pink Panthers," "middle-class East Side queens") a source of strength for the movement?

3. What does White's letter suggest about the effect of the African American struggle for civil rights on the gay rights movement?

26-5 | Native Americans Claim Alcatraz Island

INDIANS OF ALL TRIBES, *Proclamation: To the Great White Father and All His People* (1970)

In November 1969, a small group of Native Americans began a nineteen-month occupation of San Francisco Bay's Alcatraz Island, which had been the site of the notorious federal penitentiary until 1963. These occupiers, members of a group calling themselves Indians of

Indians of All Tribes, "Proclamation: To the Great White Father and All His People," Museum Collections at Alcatraz Island, Golden Gate National Recreation Area, National Park Service, https://www.nps.gov/museum/exhibits/alca/exb/Indian/documents/Goga-35158bSS.html.

All Tribes, claimed the island, citing the 1868 Treaty of Fort Laramie, wherein the federal government pledged to return abandoned land to native peoples. The occupation failed in its immediate goal of gaining ownership of the island to establish a Native American cultural and educational center and museum, but the publicity it generated forced greater accommodation of federal Indian policy.

We, the native Americans, re-claim the land known as Alcatraz Island in the name of all American Indians by right of discovery.

We wish to be fair and honorable in our dealings with the Caucasian inhabitants of this land, and hereby offer the following treaty:

We will purchase said Alcatraz Island for twenty-four dollars (24) in glass beads and red cloth, a precedent set by the white man's purchase of a similar island about 300 years ago. We know that $24 in trade goods for these 16 acres is more than was paid when Manhattan Island was sold, but we know that land values have risen over the years. Our offer of $1.24 per acre is greater than the 47 cents per acre the white men are now paying the California Indians for their land.

We will give to the inhabitants of this island a portion of the land for their own to be held in trust by the American Indian Affairs and by the bureaus of Caucasian Affairs to hold in perpetuity — for as long as the sun shall rise and the rivers go down to the sea. We will further guide the inhabitants in the proper way of living. We will offer them our religion, our education, our life-ways, in order to help them achieve our level of civilization and thus raise them and all their white brothers up from their savage and unhappy state. We offer this treaty in good faith and wish to be fair and honorable in our dealings with all white men.

We feel that this so-called Alcatraz Island is more than suitable for an Indian reservation, as determined by the white man's own standards. By this we mean that this place resembles most Indian reservations in that:

1. It is isolated from modern facilities, and without adequate means of transportation.
2. It has no fresh running water.
3. It has inadequate sanitation facilities.
4. There are no oil or mineral rights.
5. There is no industry and so unemployment is very great.
6. There are no health care facilities.
7. The soil is rocky and non-productive; and the land does not support game.
8. There are no educational facilities.
9. The population has always exceeded the land base.
10. The population has always been held as prisoners and kept dependent upon others.

Further, it would be fitting and symbolic that ships from all over the world, entering the Golden Gate, would first see Indian land, and thus be reminded of the true history of this nation. This tiny island would be a symbol of the great lands once ruled by free and noble Indians.

What use will we make of this land?

Since the San Francisco Indian Center burned down, there is no place for Indians to assemble and carry on tribal life here in the white man's city. Therefore, we plan to develop on this island several Indian institutions:

1. A CENTER FOR NATIVE AMERICAN STUDIES will be developed which will educate them to the skills and knowledge relevant to improve the lives and spirits of all Indian peoples. Attached to this center will be traveling universities, managed by Indians, which will go to the Indian Reservations, learning those necessary and relevant materials now about.

2. AN AMERICAN INDIAN SPIRITUAL CENTER which will practice our ancient tribal religious and sacred healing ceremonies. Our cultural arts will be featured and our young people trained in music, dance, and healing rituals.

3. AN INDIAN CENTER OF ECOLOGY which will train and support our young people in scientific research and practice to restore our lands and waters to their pure and natural state. We will work to de-pollute the air and water of the Bay Area. We will seek to restore fish and animal life to the area and to revitalize sea life which has been threatened by the white man's way. We will set up facilities to desalt sea water for human benefit.

4. A GREAT INDIAN TRAINING SCHOOL will be developed to teach our people how to make a living in the world, improve our standard of living, and to end hunger and unemployment among our people. This training school will include a center for Indian arts and crafts, and an Indian restaurant serving native foods, which will restore Indian culinary arts. This center will display Indian arts and offer Indian foods to the public, so that all may know of the beauty and spirit of the traditional INDIAN ways.

Some of the present buildings will be taken over to develop an AMERICAN INDIAN MUSEUM, which will depict our native food & other cultural contributions we have given to the world. Another part of the museum will present some of the things the white man has given to the Indians in return for the land and life he took: disease, alcohol, poverty and cultural decimation (As symbolized by old tin cans, barbed wire, rubber tires, plastic containers, etc.). Part of this museum will remain a dungeon to symbolize both those Indian captives who were incarcerated for challenging white authority, and those who were imprisoned on reservations. The museum will show the noble and the tragic events of Indian history, including the broken treaties, the documentary of the Trail of Tears, the Massacre of Wounded Knee, as well as the victory over Yellow Hair Custer and his army.

In the name of all Indians, therefore, we re-claim this island for our Indian nations, for all these reasons. We feel this claim is just and proper, and that this land should rightfully be granted to us for as long as the rivers shall run and the sun shall shine.

READING AND DISCUSSION QUESTIONS

1. How do the Indians of All Tribes define their objectives in occupying Alcatraz Island? To what extent do they link their efforts to the wider civil rights movement?

2. What rhetorical point are the occupiers making in their proclamation by offering to hold in trust a portion of the island to be administered by a "Bureau of Caucasian Affairs"? What historical references do they expect the audience to catch?

26-6 | Chicano Civil Rights
La Raza Peace Moratorium Flyer (1970)

In the 1960s, Mexican Americans were one of many groups mobilized in the hopes of righting long-standing wrongs regarding their civil liberties. As the United States deepened its involvement in the Vietnam War, a new urgency spurred their activism as Chicanos were drafted to fight a war against communist oppression overseas while they faced discrimination at home. The National Chicano Moratorium Committee organized to sponsor antiwar demonstrations, including one in East Los Angeles in August 1970. That protest resulted in the police shooting of reporter Rubén Salazar. Subsequent marches against the war occurred, including one two weeks later in Oxnard, California. This flyer, with notes from one of the participants, advertises the march on September 19.

Flyer of La Raza Moratorium Peace March, Oxnard, California, September 19, 1970. Courtesy of the Dr. Luis H. Moreno Family Collection.

READING AND DISCUSSION QUESTIONS

1. *La raza* means "the people." What are the people protesting? What do you think "Our Struggle is in the Barrios" means?

2. What are some of the concerns identified by the handwritten notes? What is significant about the numbers written on the back of the flyer?

▪ COMPARATIVE QUESTIONS ▪

1. Compare the civil rights philosophy of someone like Martin Luther King Jr. with the approach advocated by Fannie Lou Hamer (Document 26-2) and Malcolm X (Document 26-3) to identify similarities and differences in their approach to reform. To what extent do their differences reveal the fractures in the movement during the 1960s?

2. What continuities across time can you identify by analyzing and comparing La Raza's Peace Moratorium flyer (Document 26-6) with the *LULAC News* editorial (Document 23-4)? How are the approaches to Mexican American civil rights similar or different in these periods?

3. What comparison can you draw between the issues raised in the civil rights movement of the late nineteenth and early twentieth centuries and the movement during the 1960s? Compare the views of Booker T. Washington (Document 17-5) and W. E. B. Du Bois (Document 19-6) with those of Fannie Lou Hamer (Document 26-2) and Malcolm X (Document 26-3).

4. Analyze and evaluate the advantages and disadvantages to historical understanding of the periodization of the civil rights movement offered here. What alternatives to this periodization could you suggest and why?

27

Liberal Crisis and Conservative Rebirth

1961–1972

Triumph and tragedy define the sixties, two bold and conflicting themes marking a period that witnessed both man's landing on the moon and man's inhumanity to man. Americans entered this era inspired by President John Kennedy's call to serve and lifted by the dreams of a better society described by Martin Luther King Jr. and President Lyndon Johnson. This liberal current, sustained by a New Deal coalition, moved men and women to levels of political and social engagement focused on redeeming the founders' promise of liberty and equality for all. Their agenda envisioned new federal programs to right wrongs, feed and house the poor, school the children, and protect the land. The Vietnam War dashed these hopes and radicalized political and generational opposition that tore the liberal movement apart. Into this vortex stepped a resurgent conservative movement that questioned the fundamentals of the liberal state. Harking back to traditional values, conservatives offered Middle America an alternative to the chaos they claimed was undermining America's strength at home and abroad. They pointed to the demonstrations, riots, and rebellions in America's streets carried out by those demanding recognition of their rights, and they appealed to law and order. These liberal and conservative tensions defined the era's political mood, establishing patterns of political conflict persisting into the twenty-first century.

27-1 | President's Vision for America

LYNDON BAINES JOHNSON, *The Great Society* (1964)

Lyndon Johnson's shining moment may have come on the campus of the University of Michigan. There, in 1964, he delivered a rallying commencement address mobilizing the graduates to help him mend the fractious society over which he presided. Born in poverty, Johnson possessed determination that helped him navigate the political world of Texas, becoming the Senate majority leader, then vice president, until John F. Kennedy's assassination brought him to the presidency exactly six months before giving this speech. Here, President Johnson harnesses his rhetorical powers to define the Great Society he hoped to bequeath as his legacy.

I have come today from the turmoil of your Capital to the tranquility of your campus to speak about the future of your country. . . .

Your imagination, your initiative, and your indignation will determine whether we build a society where progress is the servant of our needs, or a society where old values and new visions are buried under unbridled growth. For in your time we have the opportunity to move not only toward the rich society and the powerful society, but upward to the Great Society.

The Great Society rests on abundance and liberty for all. It demands an end to poverty and racial injustice, to which we are totally committed in our time. But that is just the beginning.

The Great Society is a place where every child can find knowledge to enrich his mind and to enlarge his talents. It is a place where leisure is a welcome chance to build and reflect, not a feared cause of boredom and restlessness. It is a place where the city of man serves not only the needs of the body and the demands of commerce but the desire for beauty and the hunger for community.

It is a place where man can renew contact with nature. It is a place which honors creation for its own sake and for what it adds to the understanding of the race. It is a place where men are more concerned with the quality of their goals than the quantity of their goods.

But most of all, the Great Society is not a safe harbor, a resting place, a final objective, a finished work. It is a challenge constantly renewed, beckoning us toward a destiny where the meaning of our lives matches the marvelous products of our labor.

So I want to talk to you today about three places where we begin to build the Great Society — in our cities, in our countryside, and in our classrooms.

Many of you will live to see the day, perhaps 50 years from now, when there will be 400 million Americans — four-fifths of them in urban areas. In the remainder of this century urban population will double, city land will double, and we will have to build homes, high-ways, and facilities equal to all those

Lyndon B. Johnson, "Remarks at the University of Michigan," May 22, 1964. Online by Gerhard Peters and John T. Woolley, *The American Presidency Project*, https://www.presidency.ucsb .edu/node/239689.

built since this country was first settled. So in the next 40 years we must rebuild the entire urban United States. . . .

Our society will never be great until our cities are great. Today the frontier of imagination and innovation is inside those cities and not beyond their borders. New experiments are already going on. It will be the task of your generation to make the American city a place where future generations will come, not only to live but to live the good life. . . .

A second place where we begin to build the Great Society is in our countryside. We have always prided ourselves on being not only America the strong and America the free, but America the beautiful. Today that beauty is in danger. The water we drink, the food we eat, the very air that we breathe, are threatened with pollution. Our parks are overcrowded, our seashores overburdened. Green fields and dense forests are disappearing.

A few years ago we were greatly concerned about the "Ugly American." Today we must act to prevent an ugly America. . . .

A third place to build the Great Society is in the classrooms of America. There your children's lives will be shaped. Our society will not be great until every young mind is set free to scan the farthest reaches of thought and imagination. We are still far from that goal.

Today, 8 million adult Americans, more than the entire population of Michigan, have not finished 5 years of school. Nearly 20 million have not finished 8 years of school. Nearly 54 million—more than one-quarter of all America—have not even finished high school.

Each year more than 100,000 high school graduates, with proved ability, do not enter college because they cannot afford it. And if we cannot educate today's youth, what will we do in 1970 when elementary school enrollment will be 5 million greater than 1960? And high school enrollment will rise by 5 million. College enrollment will increase by more than 3 million.

In many places, classrooms are overcrowded and curricula are outdated. Most of our qualified teachers are underpaid, and many of our paid teachers are unqualified. So we must give every child a place to sit and a teacher to learn from. Poverty must not be a bar to learning, and learning must offer an escape from poverty. . . .

These are three of the central issues of the Great Society. While our Government has many programs directed at those issues, I do not pretend that we have the full answer to those problems.

But I do promise this: We are going to assemble the best thought and the broadest knowledge from all over the world to find those answers for America. I intend to establish working groups to prepare a series of White House conferences and meetings—on the cities, on natural beauty, on the quality of education, and on other emerging challenges. And from these meetings and from this inspiration and from these studies we will begin to set our course toward the Great Society.

The solution to these problems does not rest on a massive program in Washington, nor can it rely solely on the strained resources of local authority. They require us to create new concepts of cooperation, a creative federalism, between the National Capital and the leaders of local communities. . . .

For better or for worse, your generation has been appointed by history to deal with those problems and to lead America toward a new age. You have the chance never before afforded to any people in any age. You can help build a society where the demands of morality, and the needs of the spirit, can be realized in the life of the Nation.

So, will you join in the battle to give every citizen the full equality which God enjoins and the law requires, whatever his belief, or race, or the color of his skin? Will you join in the battle to give every citizen an escape from the crushing weight of poverty?

Will you join in the battle to make it possible for all nations to live in enduring peace—as neighbors and not as mortal enemies?

Will you join in the battle to build the Great Society, to prove that our material progress is only the foundation on which we will build a richer life of mind and spirit?

There are those timid souls who say this battle cannot be won; that we are condemned to a soulless wealth. I do not agree. We have the power to shape the civilization that we want. But we need your will, your labor, your hearts, if we are to build that kind of society.

Those who came to this land sought to build more than just a new country.

They sought a new world. So I have come here today to your campus to say that you can make their vision our reality. So let us from this moment begin our work so that in the future men will look back and say: It was then, after a long and weary way, that man turned the exploits of his genius to the full enrichment of his life.

READING AND DISCUSSION QUESTIONS

1. To what extent do you see Johnson's vision for the Great Society as something new or as a continuation of Franklin Roosevelt's New Deal efforts?

2. From his speech, what do you infer about Johnson's assessment of the challenges facing America? What obstacles stood in the way, and how were they to be overcome?

27-2 | Conservative Rebirth of the Republican Party

BARRY GOLDWATER, *Acceptance Speech at the Republican National Convention* (1964)

By midcentury, both Democrats and Republicans agreed on the federal government's active role in the nation's economy. By the mid-1960s, however, dissenting conservative voices rebuffed this consensus and powered their way into presidential politics. With the nomination

Barry Goldwater, "The Republican National Convention Acceptance Speech," *Vital Speeches of the Day*, vol. 30 (August 15, 1964): 642–644.

of Arizona senator Barry Goldwater in 1964, conservatives hoped to turn back the creeping socialism they feared from the New Deal legacy. President Johnson crushed Goldwater in the November election, but conservatives scored an ideological victory, setting the stage for a conservative resurgence in the years to follow.

Now, my fellow Americans, the tide has been running against freedom. Our people have followed false prophets. We must, and we shall, return to proven ways—not because they are old, but because they are true.

We must, and we shall, set the tide running again in the cause of freedom. And this party, with its every action, every word, every breath and every heart beat, has but a single resolve, and that is freedom.

Freedom made orderly for this nation by our constitutional government. Freedom under a government limited by laws of nature and of nature's God. Freedom balanced so that order lacking liberty will not become the slavery of the prison cell; balanced so that liberty lacking order will not become the license of the mob and of the jungle.

Now, we Americans understand freedom, we have earned it; we have lived for it, and we have died for it. This nation and its people are freedom's model in a searching world. We can be freedom's missionaries in a doubting world.

But, ladies and gentlemen, first we must renew freedom's mission in our own hearts and in our own homes.

During four futile years the Administration which we shall replace has distorted and lost that faith. It has talked and talked and talked and talked the words of freedom but it has failed and failed and failed in the works of freedom.

Now failure cements the wall of shame in Berlin; failures blot the sands of shame at the Bay of Pigs; failures marked the slow death of freedom in Laos; failures infest the jungles of Vietnam; and failures haunt the houses of our once great alliances and undermine the greatest bulwark ever erected by free nations, the NATO community.

Failures proclaim lost leadership, obscure purpose, weakening wills and the risk of inciting our sworn enemies to new aggressions and to new excesses.

And because of this Administration we are tonight a world divided. We are a Nation becalmed. We have lost the brisk pace of diversity and the genius of individual creativity. We are plodding at a pace set by centralized planning, red tape, rules without responsibility and regimentation without recourse.

Rather than useful jobs in our country, people have been offered bureaucratic make-work; rather than moral leadership, they have been given bread and circuses; they have been given spectacles, and, yes, they have even been given scandals.

Tonight there is violence in our streets, corruption in our highest offices, aimlessness among our youth, anxiety among our elderly, and there's a virtual despair among the many who look beyond material success toward the inner meaning of their lives. And where examples of morality should be set, the opposite is seen. Small men seeking great wealth or power have too often and too long turned even the highest levels of public service into mere personal opportunity. . . .

The growing menace in our country tonight, to personal safety, to life, to limb and property, in homes, in churches, on the playgrounds and places of business, particularly in our great cities, is the mounting concern or should be of every thoughtful citizen in the United States. Security from domestic violence, no less than from foreign aggression, is the most elementary and fundamental purpose of any government, and a government that cannot fulfill that purpose is one that cannot long command the loyalty of its citizens. . . .

Those who seek to live your lives for you, to take your liberties in return for relieving you of yours; those who elevate the state and downgrade the citizen must see ultimately a world in which earthly power can be substituted for Divine Will. And this nation was founded upon the rejection of that notion and upon the acceptance of God as the author of freedom.

Now those who seek absolute power, even though they seek it to do what they regard as good, are simply demanding the right to enforce their own version of heaven on earth, and let me remind you they are the very ones who always create the most hellish tyranny.

Absolute power does corrupt, and those who seek it must be suspect and must be opposed. Their mistaken course stems from false notions, ladies and gentlemen, of equality. Equality, rightly understood, as our founding fathers understood it, leads to liberty and to the emancipation of creative differences; wrongly understood, as it has been so tragically in our time, it leads first to conformity and then to despotism.

Fellow Republicans, it is the cause of Republicanism to resist concentrations of power, private or public, which enforce such conformity and inflict such despotism.

It is the cause of Republicanism to insure that power remains in the hands of the people. . . .

It is further the cause of Republicanism to restore a clear understanding of the tyranny of man over man in the world at large. It is our cause to dispel the foggy thinking which avoids hard decisions in the delusion that a world of conflict will somehow resolve itself into a world of harmony, if we just don't rock the boat or irritate the forces of aggression—and this is hogwash.

It is, further, the cause of Republicanism to remind ourselves, and the world, that only the strong can remain free; that only the strong can keep the peace. . . .

It has been during Democratic years that we have weakly stumbled into conflicts, timidly refusing to draw our own lines against aggression, deceitfully refusing to tell even our own people of our full participation and tragically letting our finest men die on battlefields unmarked by purpose, unmarked by pride or the prospect of victory.

Yesterday it was Korea; tonight it is Vietnam. Make no bones of this. Don't try to sweep this under the rug. We are at war in Vietnam. And yet the President, who is the Commander of Chief of our forces, refuses to say, refuses to say, mind you, whether or not the objective over there is victory, and his Secretary of Defense continues to mislead and misinform the American people, and enough of it has gone by.

And I needn't remind you, but I will, it has been during Democratic years that a billion persons were cast into communist captivity and their fate cynically sealed.

Today — today in our beloved country we have an Administration which seems eager to deal with Communism in every coin known — from gold to wheat; from consulates to confidence, and even human freedom itself.

Now the Republican cause demands that we brand Communism as a principal disturber of peace in the world today. Indeed, we should brand it as the only significant disturber of the peace. And we must make clear that until its goals of conquest are absolutely renounced, and its relations with all nations tempered, Communism and the governments it now controls are enemies of every man on earth who is or wants to be free. . . .

I believe that the Communism which boasts it will bury us will instead give way to the forces of freedom. And I can see in the distant and yet recognizable future the outlines of a world worthy of our dedication, our every risk, our every effort, our every sacrifice along the way. Yes, a world that will redeem the suffering of those who will be liberated from tyranny. . . .

My fellow Republicans, we do no man a service by hiding freedom's light under a bushel of mistaken humility.

I seek an America proud of its past, proud of its ways, proud of its dreams and determined actively to proclaim them. But our example to the world must, like charity, begin at home.

In our vision of a good and decent future, free and peaceful, there must be room, room for the liberation of the energy and the talent of the individual, otherwise our vision is blind at the outset.

We must assure a society here which while never abandoning the needy or forsaking the helpless, nurtures incentives and opportunity for the creative and the productive. . . .

During Republican years, this again will be a nation of men and women, of families proud of their role, jealous of their responsibilities, unlimited in their aspirations — a nation where all who can will be self-reliant.

We Republicans see in our constitutional form of government the great framework which assures the orderly but dynamic fulfillment of the whole man, and we see the whole man as the great reason for instituting orderly government in the first place.

We can see in private property and in economy based upon and fostering private property the one way to make government a durable ally of the whole man, rather than his determined enemy.

We see in the sanctity of private property the only durable foundation for constitutional government in a free society.

And beyond that we see and cherish diversity of ways, diversity of thoughts, of motives, and accomplishments. We don't seek to lead anyone's life for him. We only seek to secure his rights, guarantee him opportunity, guarantee him opportunity to strive with government performing only those needed and constitutionally sanctioned tasks which cannot otherwise be performed.

We, Republicans, seek a government that attends to its inherent responsibilities of maintaining a stable monetary and fiscal climate, encouraging a free and a competitive economy and enforcing law and order.

Thus do we seek inventiveness, diversity, and creative difference within a stable order, for we Republicans define government's role where needed at many, many levels, preferably though the one closest to the people involved: our towns and our cities, then our counties, then our states, then our regional contacts and only then, the national government.

That, let me remind you, is the land of liberty built by decentralized power. On it also we must have balance between the branches of government at every level.

Balance, diversity, creative difference — these are the elements of Republican equation. Republicans agree, Republicans agree heartily to disagree on many, many of their applications. But we have never disagreed on the basic fundamental issues of why you and I are Republicans. . . .

[T]he task of preserving and enlarging freedom at home and safeguarding it from the forces of tyranny abroad is great enough to challenge all our resources and to require all our strength.

Anyone who joins us in all sincerity we welcome. Those who do not care for our cause, we don't expect to enter our ranks in any case. And let our Republicanism so focused and so dedicated not be made fuzzy and futile by unthinking and stupid labels.

I would remind you that extremism in the defense of liberty is no vice.

And let me remind you also that moderation in the pursuit of justice is no virtue.

READING AND DISCUSSION QUESTIONS

1. Analyze Goldwater's acceptance speech to identify the conservative themes he highlights in contrasting Republican political views with those of his Democratic opponent. What themes does he believe would best resonate with his audience of conservative Americans?

2. The most famous line of Goldwater's speech was his reminder that "extremism in the defense of liberty is no vice" and "moderation in the pursuit of justice is no virtue." Why do you think that line rallied conservatives and inflamed his liberal opponents?

27-3 | Protesting Vietnam

ERIK FALKENSTEEN, *NYC: Peace Demonstration* (1966) and JAMES JOHNSON, *Speech* (1966)

By the end of 1966, the year this photograph was taken, there were already more than 380,000 U.S. troops in Vietnam. The escalation was rapid. President Johnson had ordered the first large-scale deployment in 1965 and those U.S. Marines arrived on the beaches of South Vietnam on March 8, coincidentally, at the same time police were beating civil rights activists trying to cross the Edmund Pettus Bridge in Selma, Alabama. The escalation of the war in Vietnam provoked marches and demonstrations like the International Days of Protest organized for New York City on March 25 and 26, 1966. This photograph shows women and children protesting the war while carrying signs reading: "No Vietnamese Ever Called Me Nigger" and "Defend the Fort Hood Three." The Fort Hood Three refers to three soldiers who refused to deploy to Vietnam. Pvt. Dennis Mora, a Puerto Rican immigrant who grew up in Spanish Harlem; Pvt. David Samas, a Chicago resident of Lithuanian and Italian heritage; and PFC James Johnson, an African American from East Harlem, all came from working-class families. Their resistance generated press coverage and led to a widening of protests and additional soldier defections. Ultimately, however, they were court-martialed and sentenced to prison. As their protest began, James Johnson intended to give this speech, reproduced here, at a July 7 press conference. It was read instead by his brother Darwin because James had been arrested earlier that day.

Erik Falkensteen/GRANGER

The Fort Hood Three: The Case of the Three G.I.'s Who Said "No" to the War in Vietnam (New York: Fort Hood Three Defense Committee, 1966), 19–20.

I was with Jimmy when he got arrested today. Just like Dave and Dennis he didn't finish his speech either, so this is just a rough draft of his speech but I'll do my best to see how it comes out. Okay?

"On December 6, 1965, I entered the Army reluctantly. Although I did not voice my opposition I was opposed to the war in Vietnam. But like most of the other G.I's I was inducted and went along with the program. After basic training I began to seriously consider the prospect of Vietnam. I devoted much of my free time to reading, listening, and discussing America's role in Vietnam. I felt that I had been following blindly too long in the Army. A soldier is taught not to question, not to think, just to do what he is told. Are your convictions and your conscience supposed to be left at home, or on the block? I had to take a stand.

I once told a Colonel about my opposition to the war. I was told that I was being paid to be a soldier not a politician. Should I let the Pentagon decide whether I should live or die? After studying the situation in Vietnam, I learned that the government was not being honest with the American people. The government tells us that the United States is in Vietnam at the request of the Vietnamese government in Saigon. They fail to tell us, though, that the Saigon government was not elected by the people. There have never been free elections there. In fact the U.S. government installed a regime of its own choosing, headed by Diem[1], in 1954. Since then there has been a succession of military dictators. All supported at our expense. Not one of these governments was worth the support of the people. They were supported by our army.

The government also tells us that we are spending our men and money to preserve freedom in Vietnam. Yet the current dictator, General Ky[2], declared that Adolf Hitler is his hero. Like Hitler he uses extreme brutality to crush any opposition that may arise. President Johnson tells us that he is trying to bring about discussions for peace in Vietnam. Yet peace offers were made by North Vietnam last spring. But they were rejected by our government and the American people were not told about them.

Is the U.S. afraid of losing Asia to the Communists? I read a statement by Senator Church[3] which said, "We cannot lose what we never owned. We cannot force everyone to adopt our way of life. We must escape the trap of becoming so preoccupied with communism that we dissipate our strength in a vain attempt to force local quarantine against it."

Now there is a direct relationship between the peace movement and the civil rights movement. The South Vietnamese are fighting for representation, like we ourselves. The South Vietnamese just want a voice in the government, nothing else. Therefore the Negro in Vietnam is just helping to defeat what his black

---

[1]**Diem**: Ngo Dinh Diem, President of South Vietnam from 1955 to his assassination by a military coup in 1963.

[2]**General Ky**: Nguyen Cao Ky, Prime Minister of South Vietnam from 1965 to 1967 and Vice President from 1967 to 1971. He participated in the 1963 coup.

[3]**Senator Church**: Frank Church, (D-Idaho) served in the U.S. Senate from 1957 to 1981 and was an early congressional opponent of the war in Vietnam.

brother is fighting for in the United States. When the Negro soldier returns, he still will not be able to ride in Mississippi or walk down a certain street in Alabama. There will still be proportionately twice as many Negroes as whites in Vietnam. Those Negroes that die for their country still cannot be assured of a burial place which their family feels is suitable for them. His children will still receive an inferior education and he will still live in a ghetto. Although he bears the brunt of the war he will reap no benefits.

It is time that the Negro realizes that his strength can be put to much better use right here at home. This is where his strength lies. We can gain absolutely nothing in Vietnam. All this is lending to the decision I have made. I know it is my right to make this decision.

This is what my brother was going to say, but they wouldn't let him speak. They just wouldn't give him a chance.

READING AND DISCUSSION QUESTIONS

1. Photographs, like any other source, have points of view. What is the point of view of this image? What do you think the photographer was trying to accomplish?

2. Examine the elements within the photograph. Who is marching? How are they dressed? What is significant about the signs they carry? How does this image compare with other images of Vietnam-era protests you may have seen?

3. What argument about the civil rights movement and the anti-war movement does Johnson make? How does Johnson frame his opposition to the war?

27-4 | Saving the Earth

KEEP AMERICA BEAUTIFUL, *Magazine Advertisement* (1971)

In 1962 naturalist and science writer Rachel Carson published *Silent Spring*, a powerful exposé of the environmental consequences of the excessive use of chemical pesticides. Her evocation of spring made silent by the killing of songbirds popularized a growing environmental movement. Two years later, President Johnson made addressing the threats to "America the beautiful" a priority in his Great Society speech. Activists pointed to two examples of environmental disasters in 1969 alone: the Santa Barbara oil spill that killed thousands of birds and marine animals and Ohio's Cuyahoga River fire caused by the profligate dumping of industrial waste. Such environmental disasters led to the creation of the Environmental Protection Agency and the organization of the first Earth Day celebration in 1970. Public relations campaigns also helped to promote environmental activism. One of the most famous was what came to be called the "crying Indian" advertisement. Despite being one of the most successful ad campaigns in American history, critics noted that Keep America Beautiful, Inc., the organization responsible for the ad, was a national non-profit funded by corporate giants in the bottling, packaging, and tobacco industries. These corporate backers often emphasized the individual's responsibility for ending pollution while opposing legislation that would mitigate the harmful environmental impacts of their industries.

Keep America Beautiful/ADVERTISING ARCHIVES ('B' IMAGES)/Bridgeman Images

READING AND DISCUSSION QUESTIONS

1. What is the message of this advertisement? Explain why you think the advertisement uses the tag line, "People start pollution. People can stop it"

2. Why did the advertisement use the image of an "Indian" who was in reality Italian-American actor Espera de Corti? What does it suggest about the cultural role Native Americans were thought to play in America's national consciousness?

27-5 | *Ms.* Magazine Provides Platform for Feminism
First Cover of Ms. *Magazine* (1972)

Though women secured the right to vote in 1920 with the ratification of the Nineteenth Amendment, inequalities between men and women persisted. During the 1960s, a "second wave" of feminism emerged inspired by such works as Betty Friedan's *Feminine Mystique*, a book she wrote in 1963 that gave voice to the dissatisfaction many, primarily middle-class and white, women had with postwar gender roles. Friedan co-founded the National Organization for Women (NOW) in 1966 to push for equality of opportunity by targeting such issues as gender discrimination in employment practices. Feminists exposed systems of power they said disadvantaged women, including within the institution of marriage, government policy, and education. One of the most visible platforms for these discussions was Gloria Steinem and Patricia Carbine's *Ms.* magazine, whose first issue appeared in early 1972. The first cover of their magazine is reproduced here. Among the articles in the first issue was one by Johnnie Tillmon who argued that "Welfare is a Women's Issue" because poverty disproportionately affected them. Other articles advocated for legalized abortions (written before the Supreme Court decision in *Roe v. Wade*) and sex-neutral language. This second-wave feminism did not satisfy everyone, however. Many opponents of feminism pushed back, but even within the movement there was friction regarding tactics and emphases. For instance, some lesbian, African American, Latina, and working poor women pointed out that the movement gave too little attention to issues of race and class.

The Granger Collection, New York

READING AND DISCUSSION QUESTIONS

1. Examine the cover of the Spring 1972 issue of *Ms.* magazine. What are some issues that feminists considered important?

2. What is the significance of the cover illustration, which relates to Jane O'Reilly's article on the role of the housewife included in this first issue? What can you infer about O'Reilly's argument based on the cover image? What do you think the housewife's "moment of truth" is?

27-6 | Mexican American Labor Leader Defends Farm Worker Activism

DOLORES HUERTA, *Testimony Before U.S. Senate Subcommittee on Migratory Labor* (1969)

Co-founder of the United Farm Workers union, labor activist Dolores Huerta organized nonviolent strikes and boycotts, including the famous strike against Delano, California grape growers that lasted a remarkable five years, from 1965 to 1970. The economic impact of the long strike and boycott of California and Arizona-grown grapes led to grower concessions, including recognition of farmers' collective bargaining rights. When Huerta testified before the U.S. Senate's Subcommittee on Migratory Labor nearly four years into the strike, she reported on the persistent efforts by government and the grape growers to undermine the boycott and fight unionization efforts.

Mr. Chairman and members of the committee, we are again glad to be here and present our long, sad story of trying to organize the farmworkers. . . .

The horrible state in which farmworkers find themselves, faced with such extreme poverty and discrimination, has taught us that the only way we can change our situation is by organization of a union. . . .

As you know, UFWOC[4] has undertaken an international boycott of all California-Arizona table grapes in order to gain union recognition for striking farmworkers. We did not take up the burden of the boycott willingly. It is expensive. It is a hardship on the farmworkers' families who have left the small valley towns to travel across the country to boycott grapes.

But, because of the table grape growers' refusal to bargain with their workers, the boycott is our major weapon and I might say a nonviolent weapon, and our last line of defense against the growers who use foreign labor to break our strikes.

It is only through the pressure of the boycott that UFWOC has won contracts with major California wine grape growers. At this point, the major obstacles to our efforts to organize farmworkers are obstacles to our boycott.

Our boycott has been met with well-organized and well-financed opposition by the growers and their sympathizers. Most recently, several major California grape growers joined with other agribusiness interests members of the John Birch Society to form an employer-dominated "union," the Agricultural Workers Freedom To Work Association (AWFWA), for the sole purpose of destroying UFWOC. . . .

In spite of this type of antiunion activity, our boycott of California-Arizona table grapes has been successful. It is being successful for the simple reason that

---

United Farm Workers Organizing Committee

[4]**UFWOC**: Dolores Huerta, "Testimony before the U.S. Senate Subcommittee on Migratory Labor," U.S. Senate, 91st Congress, 1st sess., (Washington, DC: Government Printing Office, 1970), 551–556, 559, 562.

millions of Americans are supporting the grape workers' strike by not buying table grapes. . . .

However, the. U.S. Department of Defense table grape purchases have been very detrimental to our effort.

Now that the boycott has brought us so close to a negotiated settlement of this 3-year-old dispute, we learn that the U.S. Department of Defense (DOD) has doubled its purchases of table grapes. We appear to be witnessing an all-out effort by the military to bail out the growers and break our boycott. Let me review the facts behind this imposing Federal obstacle to farmworker organizing. . . .

DOD table grape shipments to South Vietnam this year have increased by 400 percent. . . .

Commercial shipments of fresh table grapes to South Vietnam in 1968 have risen nine times since 1966, according to U.S. Department of Commerce statistics. . . .

"This could not have occurred," states the AFLCIO News of June 14, 1969, "without both DOD and Agriculture Department encouragement."

These are the facts as to how the grapes of wrath are being converted into the grapes of war by the world's richest government in order to stop farmworkers from waging a successful boycott and organizing campaign against grape growers. . . .

Table grape prices, like those of other fruits and vegetables, are extremely susceptible to minor fluctuations in supply. DOD purchases of some table grapes are probably shoring up the price of all table grapes and, at a critical point in the UFWOC boycott, are permitting many growers to stand firm in their refusal to negotiate with their workers.

It is obvious that the DOD is taking sides with the growers in this dispute. . . .

DOD table grape purchases are a national outrage. The history of our struggle against agribusiness is punctuated by the continued violations of health and safety codes by growers, including many table grape growers. Much of this documentation has already been submitted to the Senate Subcommittee on Migratory Labor. Such violations are so well documented that Superior Judge Irving Perluss, of California, recently ruled that a jobless worker was within his rights when he refused to accept farm labor work offered him through the California Department of Employment on grounds that most of such jobs are in violation of State health and sanitation codes. . . .

If the Federal Government and the DOD is not concerned about the welfare of farmworkers, they must be concerned with protecting our servicemen from contamination and disease carried by grapes picked in fields without toilets or washstands.

Recent laboratory tests have found DDT residues on California grapes. Economic poisons have killed and injured farmworkers. Will they also prove dangerous to U.S. military personnel? . . . .

The Department of Defense increasing purchases of table grapes is nothing short of a national outrage. It is an outrage to the millions of American taxpayers who are supporting the farmworkers' struggle for justice by boycotting table grapes. How can any American believe that the U.S. Government is sincere in its efforts to eradicate poverty when the military uses its immense purchasing power to subvert the farmworkers' nonviolent struggle for a decent, living wage and a better future?

Many farmworkers are members of minority groups. They are Filipino and Mexican and black Americans. These same minority people are on the frontlines of battle in Vietnam. It is a cruel and ironic slap in the face to these men who have left the fields to fulfill their military obligation to find increasing amounts of boycotted grapes in their messkits. . . .

So, now can the Department of Defense explain or justify the intervention into the grape boycott, while we are supposedly fighting for freedom in Vietnam, and yet we are trying to destroy the farmworkers' struggle for economic freedom in our own country?

While it seems like the Department of Defense is doing everything to break our boycott, the Congress voted a $3.9 billion subsidy for the growers of this country so that they can further fight the unions and use Government funds to help the farmer avoid improving conditions. . . .

I don't see that we are going to get any kind of a relief from the courts at all. Even under the national labor relations law, even though we are not covered by the law, the growers are constantly filing unfair labor practices against us, and although they know they can't win them, this takes up the time of our attorneys.

When we try to go to the Government for any kind of help, even for the enforcement of the sanitation laws, the Government turns its head. . . .

This is all the way from the Governor down to the local agencies. . . .

We are not afraid, and we will continue, but we do need some help, and we hope that the committee here will be able to furnish some of it.

READING AND DISCUSSION QUESTIONS

1. How does Huerta hope to rally support among senators for the unionization efforts of migrant workers?

2. What does Huerta identify as some of the obstacles facing America's farm workers? Who does she say is complicit in their struggle for economic justice?

3. Huerta is testifying before a subcommittee of the U.S. Senate. In addition to that audience of senators, who else do you think she and the striking workers she represented were speaking to?

■ COMPARATIVE QUESTIONS ■

1. Do you think Barry Goldwater (Document 27-2) and Billy Graham (Document 25-3) appealed to the same audience of Americans? What point of view about human nature, God, and the role of government did they share? Who was excluded by their ideology?

2. To what extent did the American experience in Southeast Asia refute Goldwater's boast that the defense of liberty at home and abroad justified "extremism"?

3. Compare the contrasting visions of American society as articulated by Lyndon Johnson (Document 27-1) and Barry Goldwater (Document 27-2), the major party candidates for president in 1964. What choice did they present to the American people? Does Johnson's victory tell you anything about the mood of the American people?

4. Several sources in this chapter refer directly to the civil rights movement. From your analysis and comparison of this chapter's documents with those by Fannie Lou Hamer (Document 26-2) and Malcolm X (Document 26-3), what conclusions can you draw about the evolution, goals, and strategies of the broadly defined civil rights movement?

5. Compare the 1920s and the 1960s as two eras of reform. Do their similarities (in goals and effects) outweigh the differences you see? Which era speaks more directly to the issues we face today?

28

The Search for Order in an Era of Limits

1973–1980

The succession of crises in the 1970s — including the ongoing war in Vietnam, antiwar protests on campuses, the Watergate scandal, and the economic recession — strained that quintessential American characteristic: optimism. It was hard for Americans to be hopeful when the indicators pointed to America's declining influence in an increasingly globalized economy. Though still the leading superpower, the United States suffered a humiliating defeat in Vietnam. The crisis between Israel and its Arab neighbors pulled America into the quagmire of the Middle East with devastating effects on oil imports that hastened the economic recession and stalled the postwar economic boom Americans had begun to take for granted. The period ended with another humiliation: Iranian revolutionaries attacked the U.S. embassy and held Americans hostage for 444 days. These international defeats occurred in the context of a political and cultural referendum on the 1960s, as conservatives tried to curb what they saw as liberalism's excesses. The polarized politics of the decade defined the electoral map for the next generation as Americans grappled with this new era of limits.

28-1 | Taxpayer Revolt

TONY KORODY, *Demonstration on Support of Proposition 13* (1978)

By the 1970s, America's postwar economic boom had slowed and the nation faced a serious recession that demoralized and angered working and middle-class families. Policymakers, economists, pundits, and the press started using a new word to describe the economic crisis: stagflation, a condition of high unemployment paired with rising prices for consumer goods (inflation) within a relatively stagnant economic environment. Economist Arthur Okun created the "Misery Index" to measure the effects of stagflation on average Americans. In California, misery inspired a suburban-based tax revolt. Inflation raised the price of consumer goods but it also led to higher property values, which in turn meant higher property tax bills. This photograph shows Californians rallying in support of Proposition 13, a proposed amendment to the state's constitution that would reduce the assessed value of homes (to 1 percent of the home's purchase price) and limit future increases in assessed value to a maximum of two percent per year. This revolt was spearheaded by Howard Jarvis, a Republican businessman and frequent candidate for public office. "Prop 13" struck a chord. More than 62 percent of California voters in 1978 supported the measure. In later years, some critics argued that Proposition 13 led localities to impose other taxes and fees to replace the lost revenue from property taxes and forced reductions in government spending, including for public schools. Jarvis's success led to similar measures in other states and focused voter attention on limited taxation, an issue that became a central plank in Republican politics in the 1980s and beyond.

Tony Korody/Sygma/Sygma via Getty Images

READING AND DISCUSSION QUESTIONS

1. What does this photograph suggest about the impact of economic conditions in the 1970s on American families? What do you notice about the people in this photograph? How would you describe them?

2. Proposition 13 was especially popular among residents in California's suburbs. What might that suggest about the postwar relationship between America's cities and suburban neighborhoods? How might you assess the impact of suburbanization on American politics?

3. Why do you think this photograph was taken? It is clearly a staged, not a candid, shot, so who do you think this image was for? What does this photograph suggest about the strategies used by those encouraging this "taxpayer revolt"?

28-2 | Steel Town Faces Challenge of Deindustrialization

ROBERT HOWARD, *Youngstown Fights Back* (1979)

The effects of the global economy were felt across the country in the 1970s as American industry faced low-wage competition from overseas, leading to an erosion of the manufacturing base. Youngstown, Ohio, long a center of steel production, lost its competitive edge to lower-priced Japanese steel and corporate buyouts. In this excerpt, *The New Republic* chronicles efforts by steelworkers to reverse the effects of deindustrialization.

Studies rate Youngstown as the most economically depressed metropolitan area in the state of Ohio (where the competition is stiff). The local economy suffers from an extreme version of the general problems affecting the entire American steel industry. Youngstown is representative of urban areas throughout the northeast—a working-class city burdened with an outmoded industrial plant and victimized by the flight of badly needed capital to more profitable climates in the south and southwest.

. . . During the past year a group of about 200 local religious leaders calling itself the Ecumenical Coalition of the Mahoning Valley has led a sustained community effort to combat economic decline. After the closing of a major steel mill in the Youngstown area, the Mahoning Ecumenical Coalition and its supporters—an unusual mixture of church groups, veterans of the new left and local activists in the steelworkers' union—have devised a plan for a community and worker-owned corporation to purchase the mill and its operation.

In September 1977, the Youngstown Sheet and Tube company announced the closing of major portions of its Campbell Works mill. Sheet and Tube had been a locally-owned company since its establishment in 1902, but in 1969 it was swallowed up by a sunbelt conglomerate, the Lykes Corporation from

New Orleans. Lykes's occupation of Sheet and Tube is a history of neglect. Lykes put in only about one-fourth of the capital investment necessary to keep the plant from deteriorating, let alone attempting to modernize it. Sheet and Tube's substantial cash-flow was diverted to other Lykes projects. Finally Lykes decided to write off the Campbell Works. The first of 4,200 workers were laid off days after the closing announcement. In the Youngstown suburb of Campbell, where most of the mill is located, 80 percent of the town's tax base disappeared from the books.

The layoffs shocked Youngstown. Industrial closings were not new to the Mahoning Valley; 10,000 jobs have been lost since 1950. But the size and suddenness of the Campbell layoffs caught everyone by surprise. Traditional business, labor and government circles were paralyzed. Local politicians could do little but point to the same villains that Lykes had cited to excuse the mill closing: foreign steel dumping, federal environmental regulations, etc. Leaders of the United Steelworkers were equally unhelpful. In a meeting in Washington with angry Youngstown steel workers, union president Lloyd McBride urged that the lost jobs be written off, that union locals work to preserve those that still remained.

The Ecumenical Coalition led by Roman Catholic Bishop James Malone, has tried to fill the institutional vacuum with a strange blend of old-time community capitalism and 1960s participatory democracy. Two months after the layoffs, the Coalition produced a manifesto entitled "A Religious Response to the Mahoning Valley Steel Crisis," arguing that large corporations must be accountable to the individuals they employ and the communities where they are located. The Coalition statement found ready supporters among certain officials of the affected United Steelworkers' locals. Caught between the anger and disillusion of their members and the apparent indifference of the international union leadership, these union activists were the first to suggest the idea of community ownership. The Coalition then contacted experts outside the immediate community whose legacy is largely that of the new left. Economist Gar Alperovitz, director of the Washington-based National Center for Economic Alternatives, proposed that the Youngstown people risk something big—a massive project to buy the Campbell Works and to run it through a corporation owned by the workers employed at the mill, members of the Youngstown community and a minority of outside investors. . . .

Critics of the plan see it as the beginning of a permanent federal subsidy to part of the steel industry. Executives of United States Steel and Republic Steel, the two major competitors of a would-be community-owned mill in Youngstown, have condemned the proposal as "socialistic," even "communistic." . . .

Coalition leaders argue that their proposal is a challenge to the federal government to support a new way to confront urban problems. . . . [E]ither the federal government can spend tax dollars on unemployment and welfare, or it can support a project that attempts to solve the central problem. "The value of the Coalition project is as a demonstration of new forms of economic organization," says Coalition lawyer Staughton Lynd. "It's not just another business. It ought to be viewed as a kind of TVA for the '70s—socially desirable for its own sake."

. . . The real target of the Coalition's campaign has been the Carter administration. The tactic has been to appeal to the president's favorite theme of self-reliance. A full-page ad in *The Washington Post* signed by 2000 Ohio religious and community leaders announced "Mr. President, Youngstown's job crisis is a moral issue. . . . We need your help to keep self-help alive there and in the rest of Ohio."

So far the federal response has been contradictory, positive enough to suggest active interest, guarded enough to avoid any real commitment. . . .

The steelworkers of the Mahoning Valley face a crisis that is not only economic but also political and cultural. The economic changes symbolized by the Campbell layoffs threaten an entire way of life. That life was shaped by the growth of the American steel industry, the labor struggles of the 1930s, and the subsequent partnership of big business and big labor forged in the Second World War.

"Since I been two or three years old, I seen that mill," one Youngstown worker said. "Then all of a sudden, you see the place dead. I worked there for years, still go by every day. 'Course you're not allowed in there now; you're out. Living here all my life I see these things, just like sand castles washed away. And I can't understand why." The same thing happened to Appalachian miners of the 1950s. "We've got guys in the mill who were run out of West Virginia and Pennsylvania when the coal mines went bust," Ed Mann said. "And now it's happening here."

These men see clearly that their needs are not being met by conventional agencies of power . . . not by government, certainly not by business, not even by labor. They make up an available constituency: disoriented, angry, increasingly willing to move toward organizations that will meet those needs—or appear to do so. . . .

As the political system attempts to respond to citizens' distress about the economic realities of the 1970s, a social movement has developed in a direction quite opposed to America's much touted "move to the right." The Youngstown experiment may be the harbinger of a progressive movement aimed at that very group conservatives have proclaimed to be the bedrock of the silent majority, the traditional white ethnic working class.

READING AND DISCUSSION QUESTIONS

1. What conclusions can you draw about the short- and long-term effects of globalization on Youngstown, Ohio, as its steel mill closed? What happened to Youngstown's community identity?

2. How hopeful is Robert Howard that the workers' plans for community and employee ownership would reverse the ill effects of globalization? What challenge to the existing economy is implicit in the workers' plans?

3. What does Howard imply about the electoral significance of the Youngstown experiment? If you were in the leadership of the Republican Party in 1979, what lessons would you take away from Howard's reporting?

28-3 | Abortion Case Highlights Divisions
Supreme Court Decision in Roe v. Wade (1973)

The Supreme Court's decision in the controversial case of *Roe v. Wade* was both a cause and a consequence of America's cultural unrest. The decision legalized abortion, reversing state-level restrictions that had banned the procedure. Justice Harry Blackmun wrote the Court's opinion. The other excerpts are *amicus curiae*, or "friend of the court," briefs. One is from Nancy Stearns on behalf of the Women's Health and Abortion Project supporting Jane Roe (the pseudonymous name of the woman bringing the appeal). The second, from the National Right to Life Committee, challenged the constitutional arguments supporting abortion rights.

Edited Decision of Justice Harry Blackmun in *Roe v. Wade*

The Constitution does not explicitly mention any right of privacy.... [H]owever, ... the Court has recognized that a right of personal privacy, or a guarantee of certain areas or zones of privacy, does exist under the Constitution. . . .

This right of privacy, whether it be founded in the Fourteenth Amendment's concept of personal liberty and restrictions upon state action . . . or . . . in the Ninth Amendment's reservation of rights to the people, is broad enough to encompass a woman's decision whether or not to terminate her pregnancy. The detriment that the State would impose upon the pregnant woman by denying this choice altogether is apparent. Specific and direct harm medically diagnosable even in early pregnancy may be involved. Maternity, or additional offspring, may force upon the woman a distressful life and future. Psychological harm may be imminent. Mental and physical health may be taxed by child care. There is also the distress, for all concerned, associated with the unwanted child, and there is the problem of bringing a child into a family already unable, psychologically and otherwise, to care for it. In other cases, as in this one, the additional difficulties and continuing stigma of unwed motherhood may be involved. All these are factors the woman and her responsible physician necessarily will consider in consultation.

On the basis of elements such as these, appellant and some *amici* argue that the woman's right is absolute and that she is entitled to terminate her pregnancy at whatever time, in whatever way, and for whatever reason she alone chooses. With this we do not agree. At some point in pregnancy, these respective interests become sufficiently compelling to sustain regulation of the factors that govern the abortion decision. The privacy right involved, therefore, cannot be said to be absolute. . . .

We, therefore, conclude that the right of personal privacy includes the abortion decision, but that this right is not unqualified and must be considered against important state interests in regulation. . . .

Roe v. Wade 410 U.S. 113 (1973). For *amicus curiae* briefs, see Linda Greenhouse and Reva B. Siegel, *Before* Roe v. Wade: *Voices That Shaped the Abortion Debate Before the Supreme Court's Ruling* (New York: Kaplan Publishing, 2011), 329–337, 352–359.

Where certain "fundamental rights" are involved, the Court has held that regulation limiting these rights may be justified only by a "compelling state interest," and that legislative enactments must be narrowly drawn to express only the legitimate state interests at stake. . . .

We repeat . . . that the State does have an important and legitimate interest in preserving and protecting the health of the pregnant woman . . . and that it has still *another* important and legitimate interest in protecting the potentiality of human life. These interests are separate and distinct. Each grows in substantiality as the woman approaches term and, at a point during pregnancy, each becomes "compelling." . . .

To summarize and to repeat: A state criminal abortion statute of the current Texas type, that excepts from criminality only a *lifesaving* procedure on behalf of the mother, without regard to pregnancy state and without recognition of the other interests involved, is inviolate of the Due Process Clause of the Fourteenth Amendment. . . .

The decision leaves the State free to place increasing restrictions on abortion as the period of pregnancy lengthens, so long as those restrictions are tailored to the recognized state interests. The decision vindicates the right of the physician to administer medical treatment according to his professional judgment up to the points where important state interests provide compelling justifications for intervention. Up to those points, the abortion decision in all its aspects is inherently, and primarily, a medical decision, and basic responsibility for it must rest with the physician. If an individual practitioner abuses the privilege of exercising proper medical judgment, the usual remedies, judicial and intra-professional, are available. *It is so ordered.*

Amicus Curiae Brief in Support of Jane Roe, New Women's Lawyers; Women's Health and Abortion Project, Inc.; and National Abortion Action Coalition

Under the Fourteenth Amendment to the Constitution, no state shall ". . . deprive any person of life, liberty, or property without due process of law." The courts have not yet, however, begun to come to grips with the fact that approximately one half of our citizenry is systematically being denied those guarantees of the Fourteenth Amendment. That is exactly the effect of the abortion laws of Texas and Georgia, and nearly every other state in the United States. Amici urge this Court not to shrink from redressing the constitutional wrongs perpetrated on women. . . .

The decision by a woman of whether and when she will bear children may be the most fundamental decision of her life because of its far-reaching significance, affecting almost every aspect of her life from the earliest days of her pregnancy. . . .

Persons seeking to uphold restrictive abortion laws argue that the State has a compelling interest in protecting human life. Amici could not agree more. But, we argue that the responsibility of the State runs to persons who are living and that the State may not maintain laws which effect the most serious invasions of the constitutional rights of its citizens. . . .

[W]hile governments profess their overwhelming concern for human life, they force their female citizens into the intolerable dilemma of choosing between what in many instances would be a totally irresponsible act of bearing and casting off, or even "raising" an unwanted child or jeopardizing their life and health, both physical and mental, by obtaining an illegal abortion or attempting to self-abort. . . .

Pregnancy, from the moment of conception, severely limits a woman's liberty. In many cases of both public and private employment women are forced to temporarily or permanently leave their employment when they become pregnant. The employer has no duty to transfer a pregnant woman to a less arduous job during any stage of pregnancy (should the woman or her doctor consider this advisable); nor is there any statutory duty to rehire the woman after she gives birth. . . . [R]egardless of whether the woman wishes and/or needs to continue working, regardless of whether she is physically capable of working, she may nonetheless be required to stop working solely because of her pregnancy. In many if not most states women who are public employees are compelled to terminate their employment at some arbitrary date during pregnancy regardless of whether they are capable of continuing work. . . .

Under these circumstances, a case can well be made that the anti-abortion law, in compelling a pregnant woman to continue this condition against her wishes, is not merely a denial of liberty, but also an imposition of cruel and unusual punishment on the woman. . . .

Here we see inextricably the rights to life and liberty are mixed and even more how laws restricting abortion deny women both. . . .

For a woman perhaps the most critical aspect of liberty is the right to decide when and whether she will have a child—with all the burdens and limitations on her freedom which that entails. But that has been robbed from her by men who make the laws which govern her. . . .

Restrictive laws governing abortion such as those of Texas and Georgia are a manifestation of the fact that men are unable to see women in any role other than that of mother and wife. . . .

The statutes of Georgia, Texas and nearly every other state in the nation similarly deny to women throughout the country their most precious right to control their lives and bodies. . . .

Millions of women are now becoming truly conscious of the manifold forms of oppression and discrimination of their sex in our society. They are beginning to publicly express their outrage at what they have always known—that bearing and raising a child that they do not want is indeed cruel and unusual punishment. Such punishment involves not only an indeterminate sentence and a loss of citizenship rights as an independent person . . . great physical hardship and emotional damage disproportionate to the crime of participating equally in sexual activity with a man . . . but is punishment for her status as a woman and a potential child-bearer. . . . Abortion laws reinforce the legally legitimized indignities that women have already suffered under for too long and bear witness to the inferior position to which women are relegated. The total destruction of a woman's status in society results from compelling her to take sole responsibility for having the illegal abortion or bear the unwanted child, and suffer the physical hardship and mental anguish whichever she chooses. . . .

Men (of whom the legislature and courts are almost exclusively composed) must now learn that they may not constitutionally impose the cruel penalties of unwanted pregnancy and motherhood on women, where the penalties fall solely on them.

Amicus Curiae Brief in Support of Henry Wade, National Right to Life Committee

The National Right to Life Committee is a non-sectarian, interdisciplinary organization that is committed to informing and educating the general public on questions related to the sanctity of human life. Protecting the right to life of the unborn child is of central concern for NRLC. The Committee believes that proposals for total repeal or relaxation of present abortion laws represent a regressive approach to serious human problems. NRLC is in favor of a legal system that protects the life of the unborn child, while recognizing the dignity of the child's mother, the rights of its father, and the responsibility of society to provide support and assistance to both the mother and child. . . .

. . . NRLC sees no point in belaboring the scientifically obvious. Life begins at conception and for practical medical purposes can be scientifically verified within 14 days. . . .

Let us then address ourselves specifically to the question of balancing the two rights which may appear to be in conflict in these cases. That question must be: To what extent can the State protect the right of an unborn infant to continue its existence as a living being in the face of a claim of right of privacy on the part of a woman to decide whether or not she wishes to remain with child?

This Court has decided that the Constitution protects certain rights of privacy on the part of a woman arising from the marital relationship which cannot be unjustifiably interfered with by the State. NRLC believes that the genesis of such rights, to the extent such rights may exist, must be found among the "penumbral" personal liberties protected by the Due Process Clause of the Fifth Amendment. Yet equally unchallengeable is the proposition that an unborn child's right not to "be deprived of life," to quote the words of the Due Process Clause itself, is also a fundamental personal right or liberty protected by that same amendment and entitled to the traditional searching judicial scrutiny and review afforded when basic personal liberties are threatened by state action, whether legislative or judicial in character. Therefore, it is very clear that this case is not one, as the appellants would portray it, which involves merely the balancing of a right of personal liberty (i.e., a married woman's privacy) against some competing, generalized state interest of lower priority or concern in an enlightened scheme of constitutional values, such as the state's police power. Here, the Court must choose between a nebulous and undefined legal "right" of privacy on the part of a woman with respect to the use of her body and the State's right to prevent the destruction of a human life. That election involves the determination as to whether the State's judgment that human life is to be preferred is a prohibited exercise of legislative power.

There would be no question of the answer, of course, if the choice were between a woman's "right to privacy" and the destruction of an unwanted after-born child. Yet abortion is distinguishable from infanticide only by the event of birth. . . . Now the separate, early and independent existence of fetal life has been conclusively proven by medical science. While it may be impossible for the State to insist on maintaining such a life under all circumstances, can it seriously be maintained that the Government is powerless to insist on protecting it from intentional destruction, absent danger to the mother's life? . . .

[I]n the amicus brief filed by the American Association of University Women and other women's organizations, the "sovereignty of the body" argument is made in a disguised and superficially more plausible form. These amici assert a woman's right of "reproductive autonomy." This they define as the "personal, constitutional right of a woman to determine the number and spacing of her children, and thus to determine whether to bear a particular child. . . ." Such a right, those amici argue, evolves inevitably from the recognition which this Court has afforded to those human interests "which relate to marriage, sex, the family and the raising of children." . . . Parents may have a constitutional right to plan for the number and spacing of children. Still, that right cannot be extended to permit the destruction of a living human being absent a threat to the life of the mother carrying the unborn baby. Family planning, including the contraceptive relationship, is a matter between a man and a woman alone. The abortion relationship, on the other hand, is between the parents and the unborn child. . . .

. . . NRLC disputes the assertion that a woman enjoys any right of privacy, as yet undefined in American law, which vests in her alone the absolute authority to terminate a pregnancy for any reason whatsoever. No precedents of this Court have gone so far. . . .

The suggestion that abortion laws are peculiarly the product of a male-dominated government is especially inapposite in the case of Georgia, which enacted the abortion statute involved in this litigation in 1968. This amicus applauds the continuing process by which illegal discriminations against women have been removed. However, the claim that a woman should be free to destroy a human being whom she has conceived by voluntarily having sexual intercourse can only make sense if that human being be regarded as part of herself, a part which she may discard for her own good. However, at this point, the evolution of social doctrine favoring freedom for women collides squarely with modern scientific knowledge and with the medical and judicial recognition that the fetus in the womb is a living person. A woman should be left free to practice contraception; she should not be left free to commit feticide.

READING AND DISCUSSION QUESTIONS

1. What arguments does the Court rely on in making its ruling in *Roe v. Wade*? How does the Court accept or reject the arguments in the *amicus curiae* briefs?

2. What conclusions about the political culture of the early 1970s can you draw from the evidence of the Court's decision and friend-of-the-court briefs? How do these sources reflect a range of views?

3. How do you assess the historical significance of this Court decision in the early 1970s and its legacy in the decades after? What impact did the decision have on the era's political culture?

28-4 | Conservative Response to Equal Rights Amendment

PHYLLIS SCHLAFLY, *Statement Opposing the ERA* (1977)

The proposed Equal Rights Amendment to the Constitution became a lightning-rod issue during the 1970s. Feminists rallied behind the amendment, claiming that its provisions barring discrimination on the basis of sex were the culmination of nearly two centuries of efforts to advance the cause of women's rights. Opponents, including the national chairman of Stop ERA, Phyllis Schlafly, mobilized conservatives to prevent ratification. The amendment failed to win ratification before the June 1982 deadline imposed by Congress.

The Equal Rights Amendment pretends to be an advance for women, but actually it will do nothing at all for women. It will not give women equal pay for equal work or any new employment advantages, rights or benefits. There is no way it can extend the rights already guaranteed by the Equal Employment Opportunity Act of 1972. Under this act and the commission it created women have already won multi-million-dollar back-pay settlements against the largest companies in our land.

The Education Amendments of 1972 have already given women full equal rights in education at every level, from kindergarten through graduate schools. The Equal Credit Opportunity Act of 1974 has already given women equal rights and ended all discrimination in credit. There is no law that discriminates against women.

What ERA will do is to require us to "neuterize" all Federal and state laws, removing the "sexist" words such as male, female, man, woman, husband and wife, and replacing them with the sex-neutral words such as person and spouse. Every change this requires will deprive women of a right, benefit or exemption that they now enjoy.

At the federal level the most obvious result would be on the draft and military combat. ERA will take away a young girl's exemption from the draft in all future wars and force her to register for the draft just like men. The Selective Service Act would have to read "all persons" instead of "all male citizens."

Statement Opposing the ERA (1977). From "Statement on the ERA," by Phyllis Schlafly, in *Congressional Digest* 56 (June–July 1977), pp. 189, 191. Used by permission of Phyllis Schlafly.

Likewise, ERA will require the military to assign women to all jobs in the armed services, including combat duty. Present federal laws that exempt women from combat duty will become unconstitutional under ERA because the U.S. Constitution is "the supreme law of the land."

Last month's newspapers featured headlines such as "Draft is Inevitable, Arms Chairman Says" and "Pentagon Urges Standby Draft." You have to be kidding to call it an advance for women to make our girls subject to military induction and combat duty in all our country's future wars!

When the laws pertaining to family support are neuterized, this will void the husband's obligation to support his wife, to provide her with a home, and to support their minor children. Those present obligations are not sex equal, and they could not survive under ERA.

When I debated the leading pro-ERA legal authority, Professor Thomas I. Emerson, he stated that ERA will change the family support law so that the financial obligation will be "reciprocal" or "mutual," and husband and wife will be obliged to support each other only if he or she is incapacitated. That would be a tremendous ripoff of the legal rights of homemakers.

The neuterization of our laws under ERA would have a great effect on the legal definition of marriage. Most people do not think a union of a person and a person is the same thing as a union of a man and a woman. No wonder Senator Sam J. Ervin, Jr., stated on Feb. 22, 1977: "I don't know but one group of people in the United States the ERA would do any good for. That's homosexuals."

Since it is the law of our land that "separate but equal is not equal" and the elimination of discrimination requires full integration, every aspect of our school system would have to be fully coed, whether our citizens want it or not. Private schools and colleges that admit only girls or only boys would be constitutionally required to go fully coed; otherwise they would be in violation of the constitutional mandate against sex discrimination.

In other words, ERA will deprive you of your freedom of choice to attend an all-girls' or all-boys' school or college. All sports, including contact sports, would have to be coed for practice and competition. If you thought the department of Health, Education and Welfare was behaving foolishly and arrogantly when it tried to outlaw mother-daughter and father-son events, that's nothing to the mischief it will do under ERA!

Probably the greatest danger in ERA is Section Two, the provision that Congress will have the power of enforcement. This means that the executive branch will administer ERA and the federal courts will adjudicate it. Section Two will transfer into the hands of the federal government the last remaining aspects of our life that the feds haven't yet got their meddling fingers into, including marriage, divorce, child custody, prison regulations, protective labor legislation, and insurance rates.

Why anyone would want to give the federal politicians, bureaucrats, and judges more power, when they can't solve the problems they have now, is difficult to understand. Yet, ERA will, in the words of former Sen. Sam J. Ervin, Jr., "virtually reduce the states of the union to meaningless zeroes on the nation's map."

While we all want equality of treatment in many aspects of life, such as freedom of speech, press, and religion, trial by jury, and due process, in other aspects, equal treatment of all our citizens would be a grievous injustice. Do you think it would be just to make everyone pay the same income tax regardless of his or her income?

Reasonable people do want differences of treatment between men and women based on their obvious factual differences, namely that women have babies (and men do not) and that women do not have the same physical strength as men. These differences vitally affect the draft, combat duty, family support, factory work, and manual labor. If ERA is permitted to deprive us of options to make the reasonable differences that reasonable men and women want, it will be the most grievous injustice ever perpetrated.

The ERA would be dead today if it were not for the unconstitutional White House pressure and illegal expenditure of Federal funds used to try to force the state legislators to ratify ERA. Article V of the U.S. Constitution gives the ratification power exclusively to state legislatures, and it is shocking the way Big Brother in the Executive Branch of the Federal Government is telling state legislators how to vote.

Nevertheless, the momentum is all going against ERA, and nine states have already defeated it this year.

READING AND DISCUSSION QUESTIONS

1. What arguments does Schlafly use to mobilize opposition to the proposed Equal Rights Amendment? What does she mean when she says the ERA will "neuterize" laws? What impact does she predict for women?

2. What does opposition to the ERA suggest about the political context of the 1970s civil rights movement?

28-5 | Diagnosing the "National Malaise"

JIMMY CARTER, *The Crisis of Confidence* (1979)

The political and economic crises of the 1970s, which included Watergate, Vietnam, and the recession and energy crisis, led Jimmy Carter to conclude that Americans suffered from a national "malaise." In a national address to Americans in the summer of 1979, Carter spoke directly to their shaken faith in American progress. He focused on the energy crunch to involve Americans in the effort to restore their faith in themselves while also solving the country's problems. The despair deepened only months later when Iranians stormed the U.S. embassy, beginning a hostage crisis that doomed his presidency.

Jimmy Carter, "Address to the Nation on Energy and National Goals: 'The Malaise Speech,' " July 15, 1979. Online by Gerhard Peters and John T. Woolley, *The American Presidency Project*, https://www.presidency.ucsb.edu/node/249458.

I want to talk to you right now about a fundamental threat to American democracy.

I do not mean our political and civil liberties. They will endure. And I do not refer to the outward strength of America, a nation that is at peace tonight everywhere in the world, with unmatched economic power and military might.

The threat is nearly invisible in ordinary ways. It is a crisis of confidence. It is a crisis that strikes at the very heart and soul and spirit of our national will. We can see this crisis in the growing doubt about the meaning of our own lives and in the loss of a unity of purpose for our Nation.

The erosion of our confidence in the future is threatening to destroy the social and the political fabric of America. . . .

In a nation that was proud of hard work, strong families, close-knit communities, and our faith in God, too many of us now tend to worship self-indulgence and consumption. Human identity is no longer defined by what one does, but by what one owns. But we've discovered that owning things and consuming things does not satisfy our longing for meaning. We've learned that piling up material goods cannot fill the emptiness of lives which have no confidence or purpose. . . .

These changes did not happen overnight. They've come upon us gradually over the last generation, years that were filled with shocks and tragedy.

We were sure that ours was a nation of the ballot, not the bullet, until the murders of John Kennedy and Robert Kennedy and Martin Luther King, Jr. We were taught that our armies were always invincible and our causes were always just, only to suffer the agony of Vietnam. We respected the Presidency as a place of honor until the shock of Watergate.

We remember when the phrase "sound as a dollar" was an expression of absolute dependability, until 10 years of inflation began to shrink our dollar and our savings. We believed that our Nation's resources were limitless until 1973, when we had to face a growing dependence on foreign oil.

These wounds are still very deep. They have never been healed. . . .

What you see too often in Washington and elsewhere around the country is a system of government that seems incapable of action. You see a Congress twisted and pulled in every direction by hundreds of well-financed and powerful special interests. You see every extreme position defended to the last vote, almost to the last breath by one unyielding group or another. You often see a balanced and a fair approach that demands sacrifice, a little sacrifice from everyone, abandoned like an orphan without support and without friends.

Often you see paralysis and stagnation and drift. You don't like it, and neither do I. What can we do?

First of all, we must face the truth, and then we can change our course. We simply must have faith in each other, faith in our ability to govern ourselves, and faith in the future of this Nation. Restoring that faith and that confidence to America is now the most important task we face. It is a true challenge of this generation of Americans. . . .

We are at a turning point in our history. There are two paths to choose. One is a path I've warned about tonight, the path that leads to fragmentation and self-interest. Down that road lies a mistaken idea of freedom, the right to grasp for ourselves some advantage over others. That path would be one of constant conflict between narrow interests ending in chaos and immobility. It is a certain route to failure.

All the traditions of our past, all the lessons of our heritage, all the promises of our future point to another path, the path of common purpose and the restoration of American values. That path leads to true freedom for our Nation and ourselves. We can take the first steps down that path as we begin to solve our energy problem.

Energy will be the immediate test of our ability to unite this Nation, and it can also be the standard around which we rally. On the battlefield of energy we can win for our Nation a new confidence, and we can seize control again of our common destiny.

In little more than two decades we've gone from a position of energy independence to one in which almost half the oil we use comes from foreign countries, at prices that are going through the roof. Our excessive dependence on OPEC has already taken a tremendous toll on our economy and our people. This is the direct cause of the long lines which have made millions of you spend aggravating hours waiting for gasoline. It's a cause of the increased inflation and unemployment that we now face. This intolerable dependence on foreign oil threatens our economic independence and the very security of our Nation.

The energy crisis is real. It is worldwide. It is a clear and present danger to our Nation. These are facts and we simply must face them:

What I have to say to you now about energy is simple and vitally important.

Point one: I am tonight setting a clear goal for the energy policy of the United States. Beginning this moment, this Nation will never use more foreign oil than we did in 1977; never. . . . The generation-long growth in our dependence on foreign oil will be stopped dead in its tracks. . . . I am tonight setting the further goal of cutting our dependence on foreign oil by one-half by the end of the next decade; a saving of over 4½ million barrels of imported oil per day.

Point two: To ensure that we meet these targets, I will use my Presidential authority to set import quotas. I'm announcing tonight that for 1979 and 1980, I will forbid the entry into this country of one drop of foreign oil more than these goals allow. These quotas will ensure a reduction in imports even below the ambitious levels we set at the recent Tokyo summit.

Point three: To give us energy security, I am asking for the most massive peacetime commitment of funds and resources in our Nation's history to develop America's own alternative sources of fuel; from coal, from oil shale, from plant products for gasohol, from unconventional gas, from the Sun.

I propose the creation of an energy security corporation to lead this effort to replace 2½ million barrels of imported oil per day by 1990. The corporation will issue up to $5 billion in energy bonds, and I especially want them to be in small denominations so that average Americans can invest directly in America's energy security.

. . . I will soon submit legislation to Congress calling for the creation of this Nation's first solar bank, which will help us achieve the crucial goal of 20 percent of our energy coming from solar power by the year 2000. . . .

Point four: I'm asking Congress to mandate, to require as a matter of law, that our Nation's utility companies cut their massive use of oil by 50 percent within the next decade and switch to other fuels, especially coal, our most abundant energy source.

Point five: . . . I will urge Congress to create an energy mobilization board which, like the War Production Board in World War II, will have the responsibility and authority to cut through the redtape, the delays, and the endless roadblocks to completing key energy projects.

We will protect our environment. But when this Nation critically needs a refinery or a pipeline, we will build it.

Point six: I'm proposing a bold conservation program to involve every State, county, and city and every average American in our energy battle. This effort will permit you to build conservation into your homes and your lives at a cost you can afford.

I ask Congress to give me authority for mandatory conservation and for standby gasoline rationing. To further conserve energy, I'm proposing tonight an extra $10 billion over the next decade to strengthen our public transportation systems. And I'm asking you for your good and for your Nation's security to take no unnecessary trips, to use carpools or public transportation whenever you can, to park your car one extra day per week, to obey the speed limit, and to set your thermostats to save fuel. Every act of energy conservation like this is more than just common sense; I tell you it is an act of patriotism.

Our Nation must be fair to the poorest among us, so we will increase aid to needy Americans to cope with rising energy prices. We often think of conservation only in terms of sacrifice. In fact, it is the most painless and immediate way of rebuilding our Nation's strength. Every gallon of oil each one of us saves is a new form of production. It gives us more freedom, more confidence, that much more control over our own lives.

So, the solution of our energy crisis can also help us to conquer the crisis of the spirit in our country. It can rekindle our sense of unity, our confidence in the future, and give our Nation and all of us individually a new sense of purpose.

You know we can do it. We have the natural resources. We have more oil in our shale alone than several Saudi Arabias. We have more coal than any nation on Earth. We have the world's highest level of technology. We have the most skilled work force, with innovative genius, and I firmly believe that we have the national will to win this war.

I do not promise you that this struggle for freedom will be easy. I do not promise a quick way out of our Nation's problems, when the truth is that the only way out is an all-out effort. What I do promise you is that I will lead our fight, and I will enforce fairness in our struggle, and I will ensure honesty. And above all, I will act.

We can manage the short-term shortages more effectively and we will, but there are no short-term solutions to our long-range problems. There is simply no way to avoid sacrifice. . . .

Little by little we can and we must rebuild our confidence. We can spend until we empty our treasuries, and we may summon all the wonders of science. But we can succeed only if we tap our greatest resources; America's people, America's values, and America's confidence.

READING AND DISCUSSION QUESTIONS

1. How does Carter account for the sense of crisis many Americans felt during the late 1970s? What factors does he cite as evidence of this crisis?

2. What solution to the nation's energy crisis does Carter recommend? How does he think these solutions would impact the crisis of confidence he describes?

3. From Carter's tone, what conclusions can you draw about the mood of the nation in the 1970s? What reaction might his speech have had on Americans?

28-6 | Evangelicals on the Rise

CHRISTIANITY TODAY, *An Interview with the Lone Ranger of American Fundamentalism* (1981)

The 1960s cultural wars between conservatives and liberals continued into the 1970s, focused around flashpoint issues like abortion, homosexuality, and feminism. To evangelical conservatives like the Reverend Jerry Falwell, pastor of the Thomas Road Baptist Church in Lynchburg, Virginia, *Roe v. Wade*, gay pride, and the Equal Rights Amendment were evidence of America's unmooring from traditional values. He was a founder of the Moral Majority, a nondenominational political organization promoting what he described as pro-family issues. In this interview with *Christianity Today*, a leading evangelical Christian magazine, Falwell explains the goals of the Moral Majority.

What are your really deep spiritual goals for the Moral Majority? What would you like to see happen?

I would like to see Moral Majority become a very powerful and positive movement for morality in this country. And I would hope that in this decade we will be able to bring the nation back to an appreciation of the traditional values and moral principles that really have been the American way for 200 years. I'd like to see the family become prominent in our society again. I would like to see television featuring united families rather than broken and distorted families. I would like to see language on the television screen again assume some dignity

"An Interview with the Lone Ranger of American Fundamentalism," *Christianity Today* (September 4, 1981): 22–27. Used with permission.

and gravity, and not be seasoned with profanity. I would like to see the country become more sensitive. I can see Moral Majority creating a sensitivity among the American people for the needs of the unfortunate, the poor, and the disenfranchised that will cause the private sector, particularly the churches, to fill the vacuum that is going to be created by the government's necessary withdrawal from that sphere. I would like to see us remaining nonpartisan, within the two-party system. . . .

What is your relationship with fundamentalist pastors who probably don't see eye to eye with you on many of your involvements?

The most aggressive leaders in Moral Majority are fundamentalist pastors. That isn't necessary, because Moral Majority is not a religious organization; it's political. There is no theological agreement in Moral Majority. At the same time, fundamentalists like me were taught to fight before we were taught to read and write. There is no lack of courage among fundamentalists. Fortunately, fundamentalists like me have been growing up over the past 20 years. We have been finding we can fellowship only in truth, but that we can have friendship in many other affinities.

How would you define a fundamentalist?

Well, there are differences. Definitions change every decade. My definition of a fundamentalist is one who, first, believes in the inerrancy of Scripture, and second, is committed to biblical separation in the world and to the lordship of Christ. For me, the definition of separation from the world may be different from some others'. I don't use alcoholic beverages and I preach teetotalism. That would be the practice of 18,000 members of this church. I don't think it has anything to do with salvation. But when I talk about separation, I mean separation from the rock music culture, separation from immorality, separation from the Hollywood culture. . . .

. . . I'm a Bible-believing, Christ-exalting, soul-winning preacher. I know that the "Old Time Gospel Hour" and Thomas Road church are committed to winning people to Jesus, planting local churches, building Christian schools, and witnessing to everybody, everywhere. At the same time, I think America is great, but not because it is a Christian nation: it is *not* a Christian nation, it has never been a Christian nation, it is never going to be a Christian nation. It is not a Jewish nation. It is a nation *under God*, and a nation in which for 200 years there has been absolute freedom to preach whatever religious conviction one might have, without ever impinging on the liberties and freedom of others. Madalyn Murray O'Hair[1] has every right to preach her venomous message.

---

[1]**Madalyn Murray O'Hair**: Controversial founder and president of American Atheists, an organization defending the civil liberties of atheists, who won notoriety for bringing suit against the Baltimore Public School system, resulting in a 1963 Supreme Court ruling banning prayer in the public schools.

America has become the greatest nation on earth because of what Solomon said in Proverbs 14 (in paraphrase): "Living by God's principles promotes a nation to greatness; violating God's principles brings a nation to shame."

If a nation or a society lives by divine principles, even though the people personally don't know the One who taught and lived those principles, that society will be blessed. An unsaved person in business will be blessed by tithing to the work of God. He'll still go to hell a tither, but God blesses the principle.

I feel that the dignity of life is a principle we protected in this country until 1973. I think the traditional family, the monogamous husband-wife relationship, is a principle that America has honored until lately. Now we have a 40 percent divorce rate and we accept homosexual marriage, so we are beginning to violate that principle. The principle of moral decency has been honored in this country until lately; pornography is a recent phenomenon. All these principles and many others have been honored in this country, and for that reason God has honored the United States. That has nothing to do with whether people go to heaven or hell. It is a personal relationship with Christ that determines that.

In order for the churches in America to evangelize the world, we need the environment of freedom in America that will permit us to do it. If we, through Moral Majority and other such organizations, can protect and preserve those principles, America will stay free, so that the ultimate goal of the gospel—world evangelization—can be pursued by the churches.

You grew up during a time when patriotism went down rather sharply. How did you come by your rather intense patriotism?

There are lots of paradoxes in my development. I grew up in a home where my father did not believe in religious values. He was never inside a church in his life. My mother was a *very* religious woman. Dad would not allow her to force us to go to church, so we were home on Sunday mornings. My mother would leave the radio on when she left for church, and that is how I heard Charles E. Fuller and became a Christian. I was an 18-year-old college sophomore studying mechanical engineering at the time I was converted. Two months later, in 1952, I felt the call of God to full-time Christian service.

When I was a boy in Virginia, in a redneck society, patriotism was just a part of life. Whatever was for America was right, whether it was right or not. I had an overdose of patriotism as a boy. I also grew up in a segregated society. I was a segregationist, and Thomas Road church was five years old before God flushed that out of my system. I thought segregation and spirituality were the same. I would have fought you over saying that I was prejudiced; I would say it was scriptural. When I first baptized a black man in this church, it caused quite a ripple.

A number of years after that, Thomas Road Baptist Church, which had always been patriotic in a redneck way, really became patriotic in the Christian way. It was through an osmosis by which the Spirit of God, through the Word of God, taught me that I was wrong and made me willing to say it publicly.

It cost me a lot of friends for a while. That's not an issue any more, but it was a big issue in this town 20 years ago. We still have that to overcome with the older black people in this community who remember Jerry Falwell in that context.

But patriotism was just a way of life as a boy. I realized later that one could be committed to his country and still be an internationalist in world missions without compromising either.

God has raised up America in these last days for the cause of world evangelization and for the protection of his people, the Jews. I don't think America has any other right or reason for existence other than those two purposes.

Speaking of your outspoken support for the Jews, and particularly the Zionists, do you not see a parallel between your former redneck segregationist views and your rather uncritical, enthusiastic support now of the Zionists?

I don't think so. I have personally examined that possibility in my own heart. I support the Jews, first, for biblical reasons; I take the Abrahamic covenant literally. God has blessed America because we have blessed the Jews. God has also blessed America because we have done more for the cause of world evangelization than any other nation. I also support the Jews because I think, historically, the evidence is on their side that Palestine belongs to them. Legally, they have had the right to be in the land since 1948. I also support the Jews because from the humanitarian perspective, they have the right to exist, and there are a hundred million neighbors who are committed to their extinction. I also support the Jews because they are the only true friends America has in the Middle East. . . .

Some political leaders are fearful of right-wing "hit lists." They say these are unfair to our traditional political process. Does Moral Majority have a hit list of congressmen or senators you are trying to defeat?

We have no hit lists. We are not attacking candidates; we are not endorsing or supporting candidates. We did not put Ronald Reagan in office; the perception of that is much greater than the reality. We are committed to issues and principles that the liberal leaders of our nation don't have on their agenda. We look on abortion as murder. That's a strong statement and I realize it runs counter to the grain of liberal sociologists and educators. In our reaction against the social gospel, we have ignored the social implications of the gospel in conservative Christianity. In the past five years we became aware of that, and we acknowledged our wrong attitude. We must now make it a priority in the 1980s. . . .

Are you too much of a showman? Do you spend too much time on TV raising money?

I am fully expecting between now and the coming of the Lord that this world is going to experience a spiritual awakening unlike anything in the past. There is going to be an invasion of God on this planet, and changing of lives: real biblical evangelism. There is going to be a terrific harvest of souls somewhere between here and the Rapture. I believe that God's role for America is as catalyst, that he wants to set the spiritual time bomb off right here. If that is the case, America must stay free. And for America to stay free we must come back to the only principles that God can honor: the dignity of life, the traditional family, decency, morality, and so on. I just see myself as one to stand in the gap and, under God, with the help of millions of others, to bring the nation back to a moral standard so we can stay free in order that we can evangelize the world. And protect the Jews.

If you have to go on TV and be a showman, a money raiser, a promoter, it is because everything feeds into that overriding purpose.

It does indeed.

READING AND DISCUSSION QUESTIONS

1. To what extent did the success of the Moral Majority depend on a sense of cultural crisis? Could the organization have developed as rapidly as it did without the cultural wars in which Falwell was engaged?

2. How do you assess the impact of evangelical Christians on the political culture of the 1970s? What does Falwell's ministry at Thomas Road Baptist Church and the Moral Majority tell you about the intersection of faith and politics in this period?

■ COMPARATIVE QUESTIONS ■

1. From the sources in this chapter, what conclusion can you draw about the political culture of the era? How do you assess the mood of the 1970s?

2. Do you think Americans' perspective in the 1970s was shaped more by the economic crises they endured or by the cultural conflict over values? How might a historian assess the historical significance of these factors?

3. Compare Phyllis Schlafly's ERA statement (Document 28-4) to the cover of *Ms.* magazine (Document 27-5) and Carrie Chapman Catt's 1918 statement (Document 21-2) to understand historical patterns of change and continuity on the issue of women's rights. What differences can you identify in how individuals framed the issues at different times and for different audiences?

4. To what extent is presidential rhetoric — the language presidents use in speeches — reflective of the period? Compare, for example, Jimmy Carter's national address (Document 28-5) to Woodrow Wilson's Fourteen Points (Document 20-6), Franklin Roosevelt's inaugural address (Document 22-1), and Lyndon Johnson's Great Society speech (Document 27-1).

PART

8

DOCUMENT SET

The Modern State and the Age of Liberalism

(1945–1980)

In a 1941 editorial in *Time* magazine, publisher Henry Luce proclaimed the dawning of what he termed the "American Century." With a missionary's optimism, Luce's expansive vision of America's role in the world included global leadership in political, military, economic, and cultural affairs. It is hard to dispute Luce's powers of prophecy. The half century since World War II witnessed America's rise to global dominance fueled by its economic and military resources. America's foreign policy, however, was shaped by contradictory impulses. Policymakers were not only confident—critics would say arrogant—from their World War II victory but also anxious to stem the tide of communism's growing subversive influence. This marriage of confidence and anxiety led to the creation of a "national security state" with enormous and far-reaching power to defend American interests at home and abroad. Those national interests, however, were defined by policymakers wearing red-tinted glasses. They saw world events everywhere within the paradigm of the Cold War conflict between a God-fearing, capitalist, democratic America and an atheistic, communist, authoritarian regime in the Soviet Union. Americans believed they could meet the advances of communism and feared the consequences of not doing so. So they did. Luce was right. This became the American Century, but critics wisely asked: At what cost?

P8-1 | Creating the National Security State to Fight the Cold War
NSC-68 (1950)

As President Truman's national security team was assessing the comparative strength of the United States and the Soviet Union, the latter detonated an atomic bomb. Nine months later, on June 25, 1950, the North Korean military pushed across the 38th parallel, the geographical boundary separating it from South Korea, launching the Korean War. These events focused American policymakers' attention on the need to operationalize Truman's containment policy more aggressively and with greater resources than originally thought necessary. Truman's National Security Council issued its secret report (NSC-68) with recommendations for waging a global war against the communist threat.

Within the past thirty-five years the world has experienced two global wars of tremendous violence. It has witnessed two revolutions—the Russian and the Chinese—of extreme scope and intensity. It has also seen the collapse of five empires—the Ottoman, the Austro-Hungarian, German, Italian, and Japanese—and the drastic decline of two major imperial systems, the British and the French. During the span of one generation, the international distribution of power has been fundamentally altered. For several centuries it has proved impossible for any one nation to gain such preponderant strength that a coalition of other nations could not in time face it with greater strength. The international scene was marked by recurring periods of violence and war, but a system of sovereign and independent states was maintained, over which no state was able to achieve hegemony.

Two complex sets of factors have now basically altered this historical distribution of power. First, the defeat of Germany and Japan and the decline of the British and French Empires have interacted with the development of the United

"A Report to the National Security Council by the Executive Secretary on the United States Objectives and Programs for National Security," April 12, 1950, President's Secretary's File, Truman Papers.

States and the Soviet Union in such a way that power has increasingly gravi-
tated to these two centers. Second, the Soviet Union, unlike previous aspirants
to hegemony, is animated by a new fanatic faith, antithetical to our own, and
seeks to impose its absolute authority over the rest of the world. Conflict has,
therefore, become endemic and is waged, on the part of the Soviet Union, by
violent or non-violent methods in accordance with the dictates of expediency.
With the development of increasingly terrifying weapons of mass destruction,
every individual faces the ever-present possibility of annihilation should the
conflict enter the phase of total war. . . .

The fundamental design of those who control the Soviet Union and the
international communist movement is to retain and solidify their absolute
power, first in the Soviet Union and second in the areas now under their control.
In the minds of the Soviet leaders, however, achievement of this design requires
the dynamic extension of their authority and the ultimate elimination of any
effective opposition to their authority.

The design, therefore, calls for the complete subversion or forcible destruction of the machinery of government and structure of society in the countries of
the non-Soviet world and their replacement by an apparatus and structure sub-
servient to and controlled from the Kremlin. To that end Soviet efforts are now
directed toward the domination of the Eurasian land mass. The United States, as
the principal center of power in the non-Soviet world and the bulwark of opposition to Soviet expansion, is the principal enemy whose integrity and vitality
must be subverted or destroyed by one means or another if the Kremlin is to
achieve its fundamental design. . . .

It is quite clear from Soviet theory and practice that the Kremlin seeks to bring
the free world under its dominion by the methods of the cold war. The preferred
technique is to subvert by infiltration and intimidation. Every institution of our
society is an instrument which it is sought to stultify and turn against our purposes. Those that touch most closely our material and moral strength are obviously the prime targets, labor unions, civic enterprises, schools, churches, and
all media for influencing opinion. The effort is not so much to make them serve
obvious Soviet ends as to prevent them from serving our ends, and thus to make
them sources of confusion in our economy, our culture, and our body politic.
The doubts and diversities that in terms of our values are part of the merit of a
free system, the weaknesses and the problems that are peculiar to it, the rights
and privileges that free men enjoy, and the disorganization and destruction left
in the wake of the last attack on our freedoms, all are but opportunities for the
Kremlin to do its evil work. Every advantage is taken of the fact that our means
of prevention and retaliation are limited by those principles and scruples which
are precisely the ones that give our freedom and democracy its meaning for us.
None of our scruples deter those whose only code is, "morality is that which
serves the revolution." . . .

But there are risks in making ourselves strong. A large measure of sacrifice
and discipline will be demanded of the American people. . . . A program for rapidly building up strength and improving political and economic conditions will

place heavy demands on our courage and intelligence; it will be costly; it will be dangerous. But half-measures will be more costly and more dangerous, for they will be inadequate to prevent and may actually invite war. Budgetary considerations will need to be subordinated to the stark fact that our very independence as a nation may be at stake.

A comprehensive and decisive program to win the peace and frustrate the Kremlin design should be so designed that it can be sustained for as long as necessary to achieve our national objectives. It would probably involve:

(1) The development of an adequate political and economic framework for the achievement of our long-range objectives.

(2) A substantial increase in expenditures for military purposes adequate to meet the requirements for the tasks listed in Section D-1.

(3) A substantial increase in military assistance programs designed to foster cooperative efforts, which will adequately and efficiently meet the requirements of our allies for the tasks referred to in Section D-1-e.

(4) Some increase in economic assistance programs and recognition of the need to continue these programs until their purposes have been accomplished.

(5) A concerted attack on the problem of the United States balance of payments, along the lines already approved by the President.

(6) Development of programs designed to build and maintain confidence among other peoples in our strength and resolution, and to wage overt psychological warfare calculated to encourage mass defections from Soviet allegiance and to frustrate the Kremlin design in other ways.

(7) Intensification of affirmative and timely measures and operations by covert means in the fields of economic warfare and political and psychological warfare with a view to fomenting and supporting unrest and revolt in selected strategic satellite countries.

(8) Development of internal security and civilian defense programs.

(9) Improvement and intensification of intelligence activities.

(10) Reduction of Federal expenditures for purposes other than defense and foreign assistance, if necessary by the deferment of certain desirable programs.

(11) Increased taxes. . . .

The threat to the free world involved in the development of the Soviet Union's atomic and other capabilities will rise steadily and rather rapidly. For the time being, the United States possesses a marked atomic superiority over the Soviet Union which . . . inhibits aggressive Soviet action. This provides an opportunity for the United States, in cooperation with other free countries, to launch a build-up of strength which will support a firm policy directed to the frustration of the Kremlin design. The immediate goal of our efforts to build a successfully functioning political and economic system in the free world backed by adequate military strength is to postpone and avert the disastrous situation which, in light of the Soviet Union's probable fission bomb capability and possible thermonuclear bomb capability, might arise in 1954 on a continuation of our present programs. By acting promptly and vigorously in such a way that this date is, so to speak, pushed into the future, we would permit time for the process of accommodation, withdrawal, and frustration to produce the necessary changes in the Soviet system. Time is short, however, and the risks of war attendant upon a decision to build up strength will steadily increase the longer we defer it.

READING AND DISCUSSION QUESTIONS

1. Analyze the language policymakers used in describing the Soviet Union. What does their choice of words and phrases reveal to you about their perspective on the Soviet threat?

2. To what extent did the national security state envisioned by NSC-68 establish national defense priorities for the next twenty years? What political, social, and economic impact do you think its recommendations had in shaping U.S. foreign policy goals since the mid-twentieth century?

3. How does NSC-68 help explain U.S. military and economic involvement in the latter half of the twentieth century?

P8-2 | Nixon's Goodwill Tour Turns Violent in Venezuela

PAUL SCHUTZER, *Cover of Life Magazine* (1958)

U.S.–Latin American relations have been defined by several key moments. The 1823 Monroe Doctrine and the 1906 Roosevelt Corollary established a U.S. interest in Latin American affairs, the latter even claiming the U.S. had a right to intervene within Latin American states to preserve order. During the Cold War era, that claim was exercised a number of times as American policymakers framed Latin America as a sphere of influence to keep free of communist aggression. In 1954, the CIA orchestrated the overthrow of the democratically elected president of Guatemala, Jacobo Arbenz, because his government threatened to nationalize the lands of the United Fruit Company, a U.S.-based corporation. American policymakers saw Arbenz's policies as evidence of communist influence. Such high-handed actions by the United States in the 1950s fueled anti-American feelings in Latin America. It was this distrust of the United States that inspired Vice President Richard Nixon's "Goodwill Tour" of Latin America, an effort to rebuild U.S.–Latin American relations. In May 1958, Nixon and his wife visited Uruguay, Peru, and Venezuela. Months before his visit to Venezuela, the country's military dictator, General Marcos Perez Jiminez, was overthrown. Jiminez was friendly to the United States and its business interests, and in 1954 the United States awarded him the Legion of Merit, an award given to foreign military personnel. By the time Nixon arrived, anti-American sentiment surged. This photograph on the cover of *Life* magazine shows a secret service agent chasing Nixon's limousine as two Venezuelan protesters kick the side of the car. At one point, protesters blocked its passage and rocked the car in an attempt to flip it over. Nixon narrowly escaped but not before the car's windows were smashed.

Paul Schutzer/Getty Images

READING AND DISCUSSION QUESTIONS

1. What does this photograph reveal about the standing of the United States in places like Venezuela during the Cold War era?

2. How might you use evidence such as this magazine cover to discuss the limits of U.S. foreign policy during the Cold War?

P8-3 | A "Peace Race" Proposal for Nuclear Disarmament

JOHN F. KENNEDY, *Address to the United Nations General Assembly* (1961)

When President Kennedy addressed the United Nations in September 1961, the prospects for peace seemed elusive and remote. An ill-fated U.S.-supported invasion at the Bay of Pigs in Cuba dealt Kennedy a humiliating foreign policy blow just three months into his term. In August, the Soviet-backed East German government erected the Berlin Wall. Shadowing these crises was a civil war in the Asian nation of Laos, which triggered American and Soviet responses, another in a series of proxy wars between the two superpowers. Kennedy's assessment of the grave threats to world peace included his bold proposal for the complete disarmament of nuclear weapons.

Today, every inhabitant of this planet must contemplate the day when this planet may no longer be habitable. Every man, woman, and child lives under a nuclear sword of Damocles, hanging by the slenderest of threads, capable of being cut at any moment by accident or miscalculation or by madness. The weapons of war must be abolished before they abolish us.

Men no longer debate whether armaments are a symptom or a cause of tension. The mere existence of modern weapons — ten million times more powerful than anything the world has ever seen, and only minutes away from any target on Earth — is a source of horror, and discord and distrust. . . .

For 15 years this organization has sought the reduction and destruction of arms. Now that goal is no longer a dream — it is a practical matter of life or death. The risks inherent in disarmament pale in comparison to the risks inherent in an unlimited arms race.

It is in this spirit that the recent Belgrade Conference — recognizing that this is no longer a Soviet problem or an American problem, but a human problem — endorsed a program of "general, complete, and strictly an internationally controlled disarmament." It is in this same spirit that we in the United States have labored this year, with a new urgency, and with a new, now-statutory agency fully endorsed by the Congress, to find an approach to disarmament which would be so far-reaching yet realistic, so mutually balanced and beneficial, that it could be accepted by every nation. And it is in this spirit that we have presented with the agreement of the Soviet Union — under the label both nations now accept of "general and complete disarmament" — a new statement of newly-agreed principles for negotiation.

But we are well aware that all issues of principle are not settled — and that principles alone are not enough. It is therefore our intention to challenge the Soviet Union, not to an arms race, but to a peace race — to advance together

---

John F. Kennedy, "Address to the United Nations General Assembly, September 25, 1961," papers of John F. Kennedy: President's Office Files, January 20, 1961 to November 22, 1963, ARC Identifier 193907, National Archives.

step by step, stage by stage, until general and complete disarmament has been achieved. We invite them now to go beyond agreement in principle to reach agreement on actual plans. . . .

Such a plan would not bring a world free from conflict or greed—but it would bring a world free from the terrors of mass destruction. It would not usher in the era of the super state—but it would usher in an era in which no state could annihilate or be annihilated by another. . . .

The logical place to begin is a treaty assuring the end of nuclear tests of all kinds, in every environment, under workable controls. The United States and the United Kingdom have proposed such a treaty that is both reasonable, effective, and ready for signature. We are still prepared to sign that treaty today.

We also proposed a mutual ban on atmospheric testing, without inspection or controls, in order to save the human race from the poison of radioactive fall-out. We regret that that offer was not accepted. . . .

But to halt the spread of these terrible weapons, to halt the contamination of the air, to halt the spiraling nuclear arms race, we remain ready to seek new avenues of agreement, our new Disarmament Program thus includes the following proposals:

—First, signing the Test-Ban Treaty by all Nations. This can be done now. Test ban negotiations need not and should not await general disarmament.

—Second, stopping the production of fissionable materials for use in weapons, and preventing their transfer to any nation now lacking in nuclear weapons.

—Third, prohibiting the transfer of control over nuclear weapons to states that do not own them.

—Fourth, keeping nuclear weapons from seeding new battlegrounds in outer space.

—Fifth, gradually destroying existing nuclear weapons and converting their materials to peaceful uses; and

—Finally, halting the unlimited testing and production of strategic nuclear delivery vehicles, and gradually destroying them as well. . . .

As we extend the rule of law on earth, so must we also extend it to man's new domain: outer space.

All of us salute the brave cosmonauts of the Soviet Union. The new horizons of outer space must not be driven by the old bitter concepts of imperialism and sovereign claims. The cold reaches of the universe must not become the new arena of an even colder war.

To this end, we shall urge proposals extending the United Nations Charter to the limits of man's exploration in the Universe, reserving outer space for peaceful use, prohibiting weapons of mass destruction in space or on celestial bodies, and opening the mysteries and benefits of space to every nation. . . .

My Country favors a world of free and equal states. We agree with those who say that colonialism is a key issue in this Assembly. . . .

But colonialism in its harshest forms is not only the exploitation of new nations by old, of dark skins by light—or the subjugation of the poor by the rich. My Nation was once a colony—and we know what colonialism means; the exploitation and subjugation of the weak by the powerful, of the many by the few, of the governed who have given no consent to be governed, whatever their continent, their class, or their color.

And that is why there is no ignoring the fact that the tide of self-determination has not reached the communist empire where a population far larger than that officially termed "dependent" lives under governments installed by foreign troops instead of free institutions—under a system which knows only one party and one belief—which suppresses free debate, and free elections, and free newspapers, and free books, and free trade unions—and which builds a wall to keep truth a stranger and its own citizens prisoners. Let us debate colonialism in full—and apply the principle of free choice and the practice of free plebiscites in every corner of the globe.

Finally, as President of the United States, I consider it my duty to report to this Assembly on two threats to the peace which are not on your crowded agenda, but which cause us, and most of you, the deepest concern.

The first threat on which I wish to report is widely misunderstood: the smoldering coals of war in Southeast Asia. South Vietnam is already under attack—sometimes by a single assassin, sometimes by a band of guerrillas, recently by full battalions. The peaceful borders of Burma, Cambodia, and India have been repeatedly violated. And the peaceful people of Laos are in danger of losing the independence they gained not so long ago.

No one can call these "wars of liberation." For these are free countries living under governments. Nor are these aggressions any less real because men are knifed in their homes and not shot in the fields of battle.

The very simple question confronting the world community is whether measures can be devised to protect the small and weak from such tactics. For if they are successful in Laos and South Vietnam, the gates will be opened wide. . . .

Secondly, . . . if there is a dangerous crisis in Berlin—and there is—it is because of threats against the vital interests and the deep commitments of the Western Powers, and the freedom of West Berlin. We cannot yield these interests. We cannot fail these commitments. We cannot surrender the freedom of these people for whom we are responsible. . . . [E]very nation today should know, be he friend or foe, that the United States has both the will and the weapons to join free men in standing up to their responsibilities. . . .

Never have the nations of the world had so much to lose—or so much to gain. Together we shall save our planet—or together we shall perish in its flames. Save it we can—and save it we must—and then shall we earn the eternal thanks of mankind and, as peace makers, the eternal blessing of God.

READING AND DISCUSSION QUESTIONS

1. How does Kennedy assess the multiple threats to peace in 1961? What role does he envision for America in the world, and what role does he hope the United Nations might play in addressing these crises?

2. What conclusion can you draw regarding Kennedy's foreign policy priorities? To what extent were his priorities in line with Cold War policies since the end of World War II?

P8-4 | Diplomatic Impasse in Vietnam

Letters Between Lyndon Johnson and Ho Chi Minh (1967)

America's involvement in Vietnam exacerbated domestic turmoil and compromised its standing in many parts of the world, especially in developing nations, which often found themselves pawns in the Cold War conflict between the United States and the Soviet Union. The United States' first steps in Vietnam began during the Truman administration but reached a crisis point during the presidencies of Johnson and Nixon. Through five presidencies, U.S. policy-makers considered the defense of South Vietnam an essential element of America's strategy to defeat communist expansion. This exchange of letters between Johnson and North Vietnamese leader Ho Chi Minh reveals the conflicting perspectives on the calamity in Vietnam.

His Excellency
Ho Chi Minh
President, Democratic Republic of Vietnam

DEAR MR. PRESIDENT: I am writing to you in the hope that the conflict in Vietnam can be brought to an end. This conflict has already taken a heavy toll—in lives lost, in wounds inflicted, in property destroyed, and in simple human misery. If we fail to find a just and peaceful solution, history will judge us harshly.

Therefore, I believe that we both have a heavy obligation to seek earnestly the path to peace. It is in response to that obligation that I am writing directly to you.

We have tried over the past several years, in a variety of ways and through a number of channels, to convey to you and your colleagues our desire to achieve a peaceful settlement. For whatever reasons, these efforts have not achieved any results.

It may be that our thoughts and yours, our attitudes and yours, have been distorted or misinterpreted as they passed through these various channels. Certainly that is always a danger in indirect communication.

There is one good way to overcome this problem and to move forward in the search for a peaceful settlement. That is for us to arrange for direct talks between trusted representatives in a secure setting and away from the glare of publicity. Such talks should not be used as a propaganda exercise but should be a serious effort to find a workable and mutually acceptable solution.

In the past two weeks, I have noted public statements by representatives of your government suggesting that you would be prepared to enter into direct bilateral talks with representatives of the U.S. Government, provided that we ceased "unconditionally" and permanently our bombing operations

"President Johnson's Proposal for Negotiations on Viet-Nam Rejected by Ho Chi Minh," *Department of State Bulletin*, vol. 56 (April 10, 1967): 595–597.

against your country and all military actions against it. In the last day, serious and responsible parties have assured us indirectly that this is in fact your proposal.

Let me frankly state that I see two great difficulties with this proposal. In view of your public position, such action on our part would inevitably produce worldwide speculation that discussions were under way and would impair the privacy and secrecy of these discussions. Secondly, there would inevitably be grave concern on our part whether your government would make use of such action by us to improve its military position.

With these problems in mind, I am prepared to move even further towards an ending of hostilities than your Government has proposed in either public statements or through private diplomatic channels. I am prepared to order a cessation of bombing against your country and the stopping of further augmentation of U.S. forces in South Viet-Nam as soon as I am assured that infiltration into South Viet-Nam by land and by sea has stopped. These acts of restraint on both sides would, I believe, make it possible for us to conduct serious and private discussions leading toward an early peace.

I make this proposal to you now with a specific sense of urgency arising from the imminent New Year holidays in Viet-Nam. If you are able to accept this proposal I see no reason why it could not take effect at the end of the New Year, or Tet, holidays. The proposal I have made would be greatly strengthened if your military authorities and those of the Government of South Viet-Nam could promptly negotiate an extension of the Tet truce.

As to the site of the bilateral discussions I propose, there are several possibilities. We could, for example, have our representatives meet in Moscow where contacts have already occurred. They could meet in some other country such as Burma. You may have other arrangements or sites in mind, and I would try to meet your suggestions.

The important thing is to end a conflict that has brought burdens to both our peoples, and above all to the people of South Viet-Nam. If you have any thoughts about the actions I propose, it would be most important that I receive them as soon as possible.

Sincerely,

LYNDON B. JOHNSON

His Excellency
Lyndon B. Johnson
President of the United States

Excellency, on February 10, 1967, I received your message. Here is my response.

Viet-Nam is situated thousands of miles from the United States. The Vietnamese people have never done any harm to the United States. But, contrary to the commitments made by its representative at the Geneva Conference of 1954, the United States Government has constantly intervened in Viet-Nam, it has launched and intensified the war of aggression in South Viet-Nam for the purpose of prolonging the division of Viet-Nam and of transforming

South Viet-Nam into an American neo-colony and an American military base. For more than two years now, the American Government, with its military aviation and its navy, has been waging war against the Democratic Republic of Viet-Nam, an independent and sovereign country.

The United States Government has committed war crimes, crimes against peace and against humanity. In South Viet-Nam a half-million American soldiers and soldiers from the satellite countries have resorted to the most inhumane arms and the most barbarous methods of warfare, such as napalm, chemicals, and poison gases in order to massacre our fellow countrymen, destroy the crops, and wipe out the villages. In North Viet-Nam thousands of American planes have rained down hundreds of thousands of tons of bombs, destroying cities, villages, mills, roads, bridges, dikes, dams and even churches, pagodas, hospitals, and schools. In your message you appear to deplore the suffering and the destruction in Viet-Nam. Permit me to ask you: Who perpetrated these monstrous crimes? It was the American soldiers and the soldiers of the satellite countries. The United States Government is entirely responsible for the extremely grave situation in Viet-Nam.

The American war of aggression against the Vietnamese people constitutes a challenge to the countries of the socialist camp, a threat to the peoples' independent movement, and a grave danger to peace in Asia and in the world.

The Vietnamese people deeply love independence, liberty, and peace. But in the face of the American aggression they have risen up as one man, without fearing the sacrifices and the privations. They are determined to continue their resistance until they have won real independence and liberty and true peace. Our just cause enjoys the approval and the powerful support of peoples throughout the world and of large segments of the American people.

The United States Government provoked the war of aggression in Viet-Nam. It must cease that aggression, it is the only road leading to the re-establishment of peace. The United States Government must halt definitely and unconditionally the bombings and all other acts of war against the Democratic Republic of Viet-Nam, withdraw from South Viet-Nam all American troops and all troops from the satellite countries, recognize the National Front of the Liberation of South Viet-Nam, and let the Vietnamese people settle their problems themselves. Such is the basic content of the four-point position of the Government of the Democratic Republic of Viet-Nam, such is the statement of the essential principles and essential arrangements of the Geneva agreements of 1954 on Viet-Nam. It is the basis for a correct political solution of the Vietnamese problem. In your message you suggested direct talks between the Democratic Republic of Viet-Nam and the United States. If the United States Government really wants talks, it must first halt unconditionally the bombings and all other acts of war against the Democratic Republic of Viet-Nam. It is only after the unconditional halting of the American bombings and of all other American acts of war against the Democratic Republic of Viet-Nam that the Democratic Republic of Viet-Nam and the United States could begin talks and discuss questions affecting the two parties.

The Vietnamese people will never give way to force, it will never accept conversation under the clear threat of bombs.

Our cause is absolutely just. It is desirable that the Government of the United States act in conformity to reason.

Sincerely,
HO CHI MINH

READING AND DISCUSSION QUESTIONS

1. What conflicting points of view regarding the Vietnam War are revealed by Johnson's letter and Ho Chi Minh's response? How does each understand the cause and significance of the war?

2. From Ho's letter, what conclusion can you draw about the effect of American foreign policy in the developing world? How did Ho assess its impact? What influence do you think Vietnam had on shaping subsequent U.S. policy?

P8-5 | Africa on America's Cold War Radar

CHARLES SANDERS, *Kissinger in Africa* (1976)

The United States' interest in Africa took a backseat to other global hot spots, including Vietnam and the Middle East, but in the mid-1970s Africa became another Cold War battleground. As reported in *Ebony*, an African American magazine, Secretary of State Henry Kissinger's 1976 diplomatic tour of key African nations highlighted a renewed attention to the continent's issues, motivated by the presence of military and economic support by Soviet and Chinese communist governments. These factors within the Cold War context influenced U.S. involvement in African affairs.

Upon his arrival in Dar es Salaam, one of the first stops on his tour of Africa in the spring, U.S. Secretary of State Henry A. Kissinger stood beside his plane exchanging pleasantries with Tanzanian diplomats. Suddenly, a swarm of bees appeared above his head. They hovered for a while then flew away.

"If he had come as an enemy," said one of the African journalists at the airport, "he'd have been stung right away."

The story of the bees would be printed in The Tanzania Daily News, and mixed with the praise that Kissinger would receive for his "new program for Africa" would be a great deal of criticism and more than one comment that the bees might have made a mistake.

While in Africa, Kissinger met with six presidents—Jomo Kenyatta of Kenya, Julius Nyerere of Tanzania, Kenneth Kaunda of Zambia, Mobutu Sese Seko of Zaire, William R. Tolbert Jr. of Liberia and Léopold Sédar Senghor of Senegal.

He explained details of his "new program" to African experts on international politics and economics, and held closely guarded talks with Joshua Nkomo, a leader of the African National Council, and with representatives of Mozambique, Botswana, Zambia and Tanzania, the militant "front-line" countries in the campaign to overthrow white governments in Rhodesia and South Africa.

In a long, detailed policy speech in Lusaka, Zambia, Kissinger made promises which, if implemented, will mark a radical turning point in American-African relations. He pledged U.S. support for black majority rule in Rhodesia (Zimbabwe), said that the present white regime will "face our unrelenting opposition," and warned American citizens to get out of the country because the U.S. could offer them no protection there. He said the Ford Administration would urge Congress to repeal the Byrd Amendment which permits the U.S. to import Rhodesian chromium ($43 million worth last year) in defiance of United Nations sanctions against Rhodesia. He pledged $12.5 million in aid to Mozambique, which has suffered economic hardship since closing its borders with Rhodesia in an effort to block shipment of Rhodesian products. He said the U.S. would provide a black-ruled Zimbabwe with economic, technical, and educational assistance. He said that the U.S. would urge South Africa to grant independence to South-West Africa (Namibia) and to end "institutional racism" —*apartheid*—and bring about "peaceful change" in the country's racial policies. He said the U.S. would step up its various aid projects in Africa in an effort to speed development, and would give special attention to manpower training, rural development, advanced technology, and transportation problems. For the black-ruled states of southern Africa, he said he would triple financial assistance to about $85 million during the next three years.

While President Kaunda embraced Kissinger at the end of the speech and said the U.S. would find him and "my colleagues, the Presidents of Tanzania, Mozambique and Botswana, cooperative, cooperative," most other African leaders seemed to prefer a wait-and-see approach. President Nyerere, for example, responded to Kissinger's call for a "negotiated settlement" in Rhodesia by declaring: "Negotiated settlement? In Zimbabwe, the war of liberation has already begun!" Nigeria, black Africa's richest and most populous country, refused to allow Kissinger to visit it, and Ghana withdrew its invitation because of the "ill health" of the head of state, Gen. Ignatius K. Acheampong. U.S. officials blamed Nigeria and the Soviet Union for Ghana's action and said they had learned of "Soviet agitation" of students in Accra.

One of Kissinger's purposes for visiting Africa was to bolster the morale and polish the image of those heads of state—especially Mobutu of Zaire and Kaunda of Zambia—who are considered to be "friends of the United States." President Mobutu has been in serious political trouble and his country has grappled with economic crises since backing—with U.S. and South African support—the losing side in the Angolan civil war. President Mobutu's worries involve not only his political and economic problems but also the SAM-7 missiles and the estimated 350 heavy Russian tanks just across the border in the hands of his old foes. In Zambia, President Kaunda's action in closing his borders with Rhodesia caused a loss of vital revenue in the face of declining world prices for Zambian copper ore. Zambia must make decisions about whether to cast its fortunes with the U.S. and other Western powers or with the powerful Soviet bloc. Kissinger's visits to Kinshasa and Lusaka and the assurances were very well-timed.

Growing concern about Soviet influence on the African continent was one other reason for the visit. Soviet weaponry can be found in many African nations and Soviet technicians and military experts are living in Africa and lending expertise. A number of Chinese have arrived, too, especially in Tanzania, and are engaged in work ranging from teaching to building highways and railroads. Soviet and Chinese ships are the most prominent ones in the harbor at Dar es Salaam and trucks and heavy equipment built in Eastern bloc nations are seen on many roads. "For years, we begged the United States to pay some attention to us and help us, but we didn't even exist as far as the Americans were concerned," said a Tanzanian student sipping tea in the Kilimanjaro hotel. "Now that we have found friends elsewhere, Kissinger comes dashing over trying to stem the tide. Where has he been during the last 8 or 10 years?"

Kissinger was keenly aware of his Johnny-come-lately status and admitted publicly that Africa has had "low priority" in U.S. foreign policy schemes. He pleaded: "you have to remember that we've been preoccupied with a whole range of things — Vietnam, East-West relations, the Middle East, the oil crisis, our domestic problems. But my trip to Africa represents the beginning of a policy, not the end of one, so we ought to forget the mistakes of the past."

In a commentary on the Kissinger visit, the influential Kenyan magazine, The Weekly Review, reminded its readers of the lucrative trade relations the U.S. has with Rhodesia and South Africa, and of the hundreds of millions of dollars worth of U.S. investments in the two countries. This reality, coupled with that of the traditional rivalry between the U.S. and the Soviet Union, prompted this analysis by the Review: ". . . it is only by a very elastic stretch of the imagination that southern African liberation problems can be included within [U.S. foreign policy objectives] . . . it is going to take a good deal of double talking on the part of the American secretary of state to convince his African hosts with any 'ambiguous clarity,' as he puts it, that Africa means more to Washington than a mere pawn in the great global power game."

The Kissinger trip has raised a number of questions for which Africans — those whose hopes were buoyed, those whose frustrations were assuaged, those who have had no reason to believe in promises from Washington — will be waiting for answers: Is the U.S. really prepared to give meaningful help to Africa in its continuing struggle for liberation, development, and eventual self-sufficiency? Has a deal been struck between the U.S. and South Africa to "sacrifice" Rhodesia in order for South Africa to "buy time" and continue *apartheid*? In the face of escalating activity by Soviet-backed guerillas against white regimes in southern Africa, would the U.S. risk war to "stop communism" and protect American investments there?

Then there is the bottom-line question: Did those bees in Dar es Salaam make a mistake?

READING AND DISCUSSION QUESTIONS

1. Examine *Ebony*'s coverage of Kissinger's trip for evidence of the magazine's perspective on U.S. policy toward Africa. What factors does the article suggest motivated changes in American policy?

2. What conclusion can you draw about Africa's strategic significance to the United States? How does Kissinger's visit reflect the challenges of Cold War diplomacy?

P8-6 | America's Crisis in Iran

Iranian Demonstrators Burn an Effigy of Uncle Sam (1979)

In 1953, the United States helped topple Iranian prime minister Mohammad Mosaddegh, installing the pro-U.S. shah of Iran, Mohammad Reza Pahlavi, in his place. Despite the shah's autocratic rule, the United States supported him for decades until he was deposed during the 1979 Iranian Revolution, which brought Ayatollah Khomeini back from exile. Relations with the United States rapidly deteriorated, culminating in the Iranian seizure of the U.S. embassy in Tehran on November 4, 1979, where fifty-two Americans were held hostage for more than a year. This image shows Iranian demonstrators burning an effigy of Uncle Sam outside the American embassy.

AP Photo

READING AND DISCUSSION QUESTIONS

1. Analyze the photograph, taken nine days after the seizure of the U.S. embassy in the Iranian capital of Tehran. What is the significance of the "Down with Carter and Imperialism" sign? Why does the effigy of Uncle Sam have "CIA" on his right arm?

2. From the Iranian hostage crisis, what can you conclude about the Cold War history of America's foreign policy? How did America's economic and military involvement in the Middle East impact U.S. foreign policy goals and the country's relationship with Iran?

3. What effect do you think the hostage crisis had on domestic affairs within the United States?

▪ COMPARATIVE QUESTIONS ▪

1. Compare NSC-68 (Document P8-1) with George Kennan's telegram (Document 24-1) to form an argument about the point of view of American policymakers at the start of the Cold War. What did they see as the stakes involved in this global war with the Soviet Union? What strategies did they embrace in countering the Soviet threat?

2. Assess the consequences of the Cold War for the United States and the world. To what extent did the Cold War promote or hinder American interests? What effect did the Cold War have on America's domestic politics?

3. Analyze the goals of U.S. policymakers over the course of the Cold War. To what extent were their goals achieved? How did U.S. internationalism affect America's role in global affairs?

4. Was ideology or economics the driving force shaping America's foreign policy in the decades following World War II? Explain.

5. Compare the two images in this chapter (Documents P8-2 and P8-6). What do these photographs suggest about U.S. foreign policy during the Cold War era? Do the protesters share a common perspective on United States power?

29

Conservative America in the Ascent
1980–1991

For many conservatives, the 1980s dawned bright with the election of Ronald Reagan, whose charismatic personality and boundless optimism became a powerful vessel for spreading their political philosophy. Following the economic and political crises of the 1970s, Reagan's unrelenting message was a well-timed antidote to the despair that had seized so many. His decisive elections in 1980 and 1984 confirmed for conservatives the power of their ideas as a repudiation of the liberal excesses of the 1960s generation. Republicans targeted fiscal policy, cut taxes, and stripped regulations they claimed hampered free enterprise. With the support of evangelicals at his back, Reagan waged a social and cultural war to restore what conservatives described as traditional American values. Conservatives targeted pornography and drugs, supported the appointment of conservative judges to the federal bench, and opposed *Roe v. Wade*, the flashpoint case from 1973 that focused attention on abortion. Reagan's Cold War rhetoric spurred a costly arms race that his supporters claimed led to the dissolution of the Soviet Union. Despite his popularity, Reagan and the conservatives he rallied were polarizing figures, and opponents chipped away at his legacy, waiting for opportunities to turn back the conservative tide.

29-1 | Reagan Lays Out the Conservative Challenge

RONALD REAGAN, *Remarks at the Conservative Political Action Conference Dinner* (1981)

Ronald Reagan debuted as a leading conservative figure in the Republican Party when he delivered a keynote speech endorsing Barry Goldwater for president at the party's 1964 nominating convention. As governor of California, Reagan resisted Johnson's Great Society programs and condemned student protests against the Vietnam War. He quickly became a powerful voice for conservative ideas, culminating in his 1980 election as president. In this speech, just weeks after his inauguration, Reagan addresses his fellow conservatives by reminding them of the challenges and opportunities ahead.

Who can forget that July night in San Francisco when Barry Goldwater told us that we must set the tides running again in the cause of freedom, and he said, "until our cause has won the day, inspired the world, and shown the way to a tomorrow worthy of all our yesteryears"? And had there not been a Barry Goldwater willing to take that lonely walk, we wouldn't be here talking of a celebration tonight.

But our memories are not just political ones. I like to think back about a small, artfully written magazine named *National Review*, founded in 1955 and ridiculed by the intellectual establishment because it published an editorial that said it would stand athwart the course of history yelling, "Stop!" And then there was a spritely written newsweekly coming out of Washington named *Human Events* that many said would never be taken seriously, but it would become later "must reading" not only for Capitol Hill insiders but for all of those in public life.

How many of us were there who used to go home from meetings like this with no thought of giving up, but still find ourselves wondering in the dark of night whether this much-loved land might go the way of other great nations that lost a sense of mission and a passion for freedom? . . .

Our goals complement each other. We're not cutting the budget simply for the sake of sounder financial management. This is only a first step toward returning power to the States and communities, only a first step toward reordering the relationship between citizen and government. We can make government again responsive to people not only by cutting its size and scope and thereby ensuring that its legitimate functions are performed efficiently and justly.

Because ours is a consistent philosophy of government, we can be very clear: We do not have a social agenda, separate economic agenda, and a separate foreign agenda. We have one agenda. Just as surely as we seek to put our financial house in order and rebuild our nation's defenses, so too we seek to

Ronald Reagan, "Remarks at the Conservative Political Action Conference Dinner," March 20, 1981. Online by Gerhard Peters and John T. Woolley, *The American Presidency Project*, https://www.presidency.ucsb.edu/node/247522.

protect the unborn, to end the manipulation of schoolchildren by utopian planners, and permit the acknowledgement of a Supreme Being in our classrooms just as we allow such acknowledgements in other public institutions. . . .

Now, during our political efforts, we were the subject of much indifference and often times intolerance, and that's why I hope our political victory will be remembered as a generous one and our time in power will be recalled for the tolerance we showed for those with whom we disagree.

But beyond this, we have to offer America and the world a larger vision. We must remove government's smothering hand from where it does harm; we must seek to revitalize the proper functions of government. But we do these things to set loose again the energy and the ingenuity of the American people. We do these things to reinvigorate those social and economic institutions which serve as a buffer and a bridge between the individual and the state—and which remain the real source of our progress as a people.

And we must hold out this exciting prospect of an orderly, compassionate, pluralistic society—an archipelago of prospering communities and divergent institutions—a place where a free and energetic people can work out their own destiny under God.

I know that some will think about the perilous world we live in and the dangerous decade before us and ask what practical effect this conservative vision can have today. When Prime Minister Thatcher[1] was here recently . . . I told [her] that everywhere we look in the world the cult of the state is dying. And I held out hope that it wouldn't be long before those of our adversaries who preach the supremacy of the state were remembered only for their role in a sad, rather bizarre chapter in human history. The largest planned economy in the world has to buy food elsewhere or its people would starve.

We've heard in our century far too much of the sounds of anguish from those who live under totalitarian rule. We've seen too many monuments made not out of marble or stone but out of barbed wire and terror. But from these terrible places have come survivors, witnesses to the triumph of the human spirit over the mystique of state power, prisoners whose spiritual values made them the rulers of their guards. With their survival, they brought us "the secret of the camps," a lesson for our time and for any age: Evil is powerless if the good are unafraid.

That's why the Marxist vision of man without God must eventually be seen as an empty and a false faith—the second oldest in the world—first proclaimed in the Garden of Eden with whispered words of temptation: "Ye shall be as gods." The crisis of the Western world, Whittaker Chambers[2] reminded us,

---

[1] **Prime Minister Thatcher:** Margaret Thatcher, British Conservative Party leader and prime minister from 1979 to 1990, was a strong ally of Ronald Reagan.

[2] **Whittaker Chambers:** Author of *Witness* (1952), Chambers renounced his membership in the Communist Party and became a hero among conservatives, implicating State Department official Alger Hiss in the famous espionage trial that brought notoriety to Richard Nixon, then a young member of Congress.

exists to the degree in which it is indifferent to God. "The Western world does not know it," he said about our struggle, "but it already possesses the answer to this problem—but only provided that its faith in God and the freedom He enjoins is as great as communism's faith in man."

This is the real task before us: to reassert our commitment as a nation to a law higher than our own, to renew our spiritual strength. Only by building a wall of such spiritual resolve can we, as a free people, hope to protect our own heritage and make it someday the birthright of all men.

There is, in America, a greatness and a tremendous heritage of idealism which is a reservoir of strength and goodness. It is ours if we will but tap it. And, because of this—because that greatness is there—there is need in America today for a reaffirmation of that goodness and a reformation of our greatness.

The dialog and the deeds of the past few decades are not sufficient to the day in which we live. They cannot keep the promise of tomorrow. The encrusted bureaucracies and the engrained procedures which have developed of late respond neither to the minority or the majority. We've come to a turning point. We have a decision to make. Will we continue with yesterday's agenda and yesterday's failures, or will we reassert our ideals and our standards, will we reaffirm our faith, and renew our purpose? This is a time for choosing. . . .

I made a speech by that title in 1964. I said, "We've been told increasingly that we must choose between left or right." But we're still using those terms—left or right. And I'll repeat what I said then in '64. "There is no left or right. There's only an up or down": up to the ultimate in individual freedom, man's age old dream, the ultimate in individual freedom consistent with an orderly society—or down to the totalitarianism of the ant heap. And those today who, however good their intentions, tell us that we should trade freedom for security are on that downward path.

Those of us who call ourselves conservative have pointed out what's wrong with government policy for more than a quarter of a century. Now we have an opportunity to make policy and to change our national direction. All of us in government—in the House, in the Senate, in the executive branch—and in private life can now stand together. We can stop the drain on the economy by the public sector. We can restore our national prosperity. We can replace the overregulated society with the creative society. We can appoint to the bench distinguished judges who understand the first responsibility of any legal system is to punish the guilty and protect the innocent. We can restore to their rightful place in our national consciousness the values of family, work, neighborhood, and religion. And, finally, we can see to it that the nations of the world clearly understand America's intentions and respect for resolve.

Now we have the opportunity—yes, and the necessity—to prove that the American promise is equal to the task of redressing our grievances and equal to the challenge of inventing a great tomorrow.

This reformation, this renaissance will not be achieved or will it be served, by those who engage in political claptrap or false promises. It will not be achieved by those who set people against people, class against class, or institution against institution. So, while we celebrate our recent political victory we must understand there's much work before us: to gain control again of government, to reward personal initiative and risk-taking in the marketplace, to revitalize our system of federalism, to strengthen the private institutions that make up the independent sector of our society, and to make our own spiritual affirmation in the face of those who would deny man has a place before God. Not easy tasks perhaps. But I would remind you as I did on January 20th, they're not impossible, because, after all, we're Americans. . . .

Fellow citizens, fellow conservatives, our time is now. Our moment has arrived. We stand together shoulder to shoulder in the thickest of the fight. If we carry the day and turn the tide, we can hope that as long as men speak of freedom and those who have protected it, they will remember us, and they will say, "Here were the brave and here their place of honor."

READING AND DISCUSSION QUESTIONS

1. How does Reagan define the conservative agenda? What ideas influenced his thinking and the policy choices he supported?

2. What were Reagan and his conservative supporters reacting against? What sort of voters do you think his program appealed to and why? What can you infer from his speech about his political opponents?

29-2 | AIDS Activism

CATHERINE McGANN, *ACT UP Protest at FDA* (1988)

In June 1981, medical professionals began reporting cases of a mysterious infection that weakened the immune system of their gay male patients. The press called it "gay cancer" but by September 1982 the Center for Disease Control named it AIDS, or Acquired Immune Deficiency Syndrome. The number of reported cases climbed rapidly, and in July 1985 actor Rock Hudson acknowledged publicly that he had AIDS, the first high profile public figure to do so. Two months later, President Ronald Reagan mentioned AIDS publicly for the first time during a news conference where he responded to critics calling for more government spending to fight the disease. The president noted that nearly half a billion dollars in federal money had been directed to AIDS research since he took office. It was not enough, said his critics, including American playwright Larry Kramer who in 1987 created AIDS Coalition to Unleash Power, or ACT UP, a direct-action political organization targeting government, public health agencies, and pharmaceutical companies. This photograph records one of ACT UP's political rallies in 1988. Protesters hold signs with images of leading Republicans, including that of Jesse Helms, a U.S. Senator from North Carolina. The year before, he sponsored the Helms Amendment, which aimed to limit federal funding for health education to classes that only taught abstinence. Helms, like some other conservatives, worried that access to educational materials promoting condom use and clean needles would encourage reckless behavior and increase the spread of AIDS.

Catherine McGann/Getty Images

READING AND DISCUSSION QUESTIONS

1. Besides Reagan and Helms, who are the individuals singled out by ACT UP protestors? What are they "guilty" of, according to ACT UP?

2. What do you think made AIDS activism particularly challenging during the 1980s, an era when conservatism and the religious right had gained significant political influence?

29-3 | Exposing Reagan's Latin American Policies

ROBERT J. HENLE, *The Great Deception: What We Are Told About Central America* (1986)

The Reagan administration opposed Nicaragua's leftist Sandinista regime, led by Daniel Ortega, on the grounds that its Marxist ideology threatened the stability of neighboring Latin American countries. Early in his term, Reagan authorized support for a group of rebels known as the Contras, aiding them in the attempt to oust Ortega's government. Congress banned such aid in 1982, but the administration secretly continued its supply of money and arms by selling weapons to Iran and diverting proceeds to the Contras. This illegal covert operation was ultimately exposed in November 1986, months after Robert Henle's article condemning Reagan's Latin American policies.

From "The Great Deception: What We are Told About Central America," by Robert J. Henle, in *America* 154 (May 24, 1986), pp. 432–434. Reprinted from America May 24, 1986 with Permission of America Press, Inc. 2013. All rights reserved. For subscription information, call 1-800-627-9533 or visit www.americamagazine.org.

To anyone who has been following the developments in Central America, the credibility of the White House and the State Department with regard to Central America has reached absolute zero. I now believe nothing they say about Central America, unless there is clear, independent verification.

A few instances selected from many: Early on, President Reagan and then Secretary of State Alexander M. Haig jubilantly displayed photos as proof positive that the Sandinistas were committing atrocities. These photos were subsequently identified as showing Somoza's[3] National Guardsmen committing atrocities.

I was in the live audience in the Old Executive Office Building when Mr. Reagan firmly stated that he "had just received a verbal message from the Pope approving our policies in Central America." I immediately dismissed this as absurd. A few days later, the Vatican twice flatly denied the assertion.

When Nicaragua instituted a draft, President Reagan distorted this by saying, "They are forcing their [the people's] children to fight." All modern states use a draft in time of war: it is the only just means of raising a national army. It was new in Central America, since traditionally only the sons of the poor were impressed into the army. President José Napoleón Duarte has been trying to get a draft in El Salvador.

Some 150,000 families have been forced from their homes near the border by the contras. The Nicaraguan Government established camps to protect them and to provide temporary shelter until they could be relocated. President Reagan distorted this by saying, "They are putting people in concentration camps!" There are no "concentration" camps in Nicaragua.

President Reagan has consistently asserted that the Sandinistas are committing atrocities and the contras are not. While there have been some atrocities committed by Sandinistas, there is universal independent agreement (Americas Watch, Amnesty International, various on-the-spot documentaries, grass-roots verification, e.g., the testimony of Lisa Fitzgerald [*The Washington Post*, 6/18/83], various U.S. and European reporters, many personal grass-roots contacts of my own, etc.) that these very few cases pale into insignificance beside the continual, deliberate, and atrocious actions of the contras. . . . Massive evidence shows that the contras regularly torture their victims.

President Reagan has asserted that Nicaragua is exporting terrorism. . . . The charge has no ground. President Reagan also linked Nicaragua to terrorism in Colombia. But the Colombian Government, after an investigation, completely exonerated Nicaragua. What happened in Ecuador was not terrorism. It was simply an indigenous rebellion of a dissatisfied "General." President Reagan asserted a Nicaraguan connection with the murder of four U.S. Marines in San Salvador. No evidence for this has been advanced.

Another piece of propaganda is that the Latin Americans support aid to the contras and that the neighboring countries fear a Nicaraguan invasion and an exported

---

[3] **Somoza**: The Somoza family ruled Nicaragua as a dictatorship from 1939 until the Sandinista National Liberation Front overthrew them in 1979.

insurgency. Not a single Latin American leader (with the obvious exception of those in El Salvador and in the military of Guatemala) supports President Reagan. . . .

The civilian Government of Honduras has displayed increasing concern about the presence of the contras in its country. That Government is in the absurd position of officially denying that contra bases exist in its territory, since their presence violates both the laws of Honduras and international law. But the Honduran Government has opposed transport of supplies through its territory to the contras. It has even returned shipments to the United States. Information from my grass-roots contacts in Honduras indicates that the Hondurans are not worried about an invasion from Nicaragua but are afraid of the contras (who have already committed crimes, including theft and rape, against local Hondurans) and also of the Salvadoran army. The Hondurans are ambiguous about the American military subjection of their country, but the American presence brings dollars into their almost ruined economy. . . .

The Honduran Government, however, is under terrible pressure from the Reagan Administration. In fact, certain analysts doubt whether Honduras can be considered an independent sovereign state. In Latin America, Honduras is now laughingly referred to as "U.S.A. Honduras."

Finally, there is the Cecil B. De Mille vision of a red tide sweeping through Central America, overwhelming the Canal Zone and roaring up through Mexico to the Texas border. The only thing this is based on is President Reagan's imagination. . . .

This tale of deception could be extended. It is, however, quite clear that, in regard to Central America, the White House and the Departments of State and Defense have been trying to deceive both the Congress and the American people.

READING AND DISCUSSION QUESTIONS

1. To what extent does Henle imply that Reagan's foreign policy was trapped in a Cold War paradigm?

2. How does Henle explain Reagan's support for the Contras and his opposition to the democratically elected Sandinista government? According to Henle, what is motivating Reagan's policies? What does he imply will be the long-term effect on America's interests in the region?

29-4 | Feminist Urges Referendum on Reagan Years

BELLA ABZUG, *Gender Gap* (1984)

Unapologetic radical and feminist, Bella Abzug spent a lifetime in New York city and national politics, fighting for liberal causes while happily playing the role of political gadfly and irritant to entrenched power. She served in Congress for three terms, during which she called for President Nixon's resignation and the withdrawal of troops from Vietnam. Though she never again

---

held public office after she left Congress in 1977, she remained a national figure into the 1990s, promoting women's rights and environmental justice issues. In her co-authored 1984 book, *The Gender Gap*, Abzug identified what was at stake for women under a Reagan presidency.

On November 9, 1982, top aides to President Ronald Reagan held an emergency session in the White House. The topic was an alarming trend that had been confirmed in the congressional and gubernatorial elections a week earlier: women were voting differently than men, and they were voting *against* the President's policies and candidates.

The phenomenon had a name: the Gender Gap.

It had been observed in the 1980 election, in which Reagan had won the presidency with eight percentage points' less support from women than from men. After two years of Reagan rule, public opinion polls and electoral results both showed that, if anything, the gap was widening. Women were becoming more opposed to Reagan's handling of the economy, foreign policy, environmental protection, and issues touching on equality of the sexes. . . .

As polls continued to show eroding support, the White House clean-up squad began to work on changing the President's fading image among women voters. Female staff members were shuffled about, and some cosmetic reshaping of the Reagan persona was evident when he appointed two women to his cabinet and went so far as to devote a whole paragraph to women in his State of the Union message. Reagan's quick-change act turned out to be one of his most unconvincing performances. . . .

In alarmed tones, Edward J. Rollins, the President's chief political adviser, told a meeting of the Republican Women's Leadership Forum, "The gender gap is part of an enormous wave of demographic change sweeping the country that threatens to swamp the Republican Party." He warned that "the political party that gets the women's vote will be the majority party, while the party of men will be the minority."

Meanwhile, Democratic Party officials were celebrating — perhaps prematurely — the new electoral development. Analyses of the gender gap showed that the Democrats could not take the women's vote for granted, even though women were now a majority of the party's supporters. The new women's vote is thoughtful, reflecting the values of the organized women's movement that has become a permanent part of the American landscape. It is based largely on a candidate's position on important public policy matters, not on party affiliation of whether the candidate has charm or smiles a lot. . . .

As Republican and Democratic political strategists ponder the long-term meaning of the newly emerging electoral gender gap, another gender gap remains firmly entrenched in the political structure of our nation. It is, in fact, more than a gap. It is a wide and deep chasm that separates two contradictory realities. Women are a majority of the population, yet they hold only a pathetically small percentage of elective and appointive offices. Women may vote for what they hope will be compassionate and peaceful government policies, but they do not occupy the seats of power where the real decisions — about how we are to live, and how we may die — are made.

There is, too, yet another entrenched gender gap, one that keeps women locked up in an economic ghetto and enriches American industry and business by billions of dollars a year. For almost thirty years, working women have averaged only fifty-nine cents an hour in pay for every dollar men earn. Despite all the efforts of the women's movement to achieve equal pay for work of comparable value, that wage gap remains unchanged. True, more women are breaking past age-old barriers into male job territory, earning higher salaries, and winning pay-discrimination lawsuits, but women as a whole are a majority of the poor, and their numbers are multiplying. The widely noted "feminization of poverty" development means that the poor increasingly consist of white women, black, Hispanic, and other minority women, single women heads of households, and elderly women. The one hopeful sign is that thanks to rising feminist consciousness, women are organizing to demand their economic rights. Their new voting behavior is a product of their desire to win equality in the pay envelope as well as in the Constitutions. . . .

Women are a majority of Americans, and for the first time in our history they are at odds with their government on almost every important issue of foreign and domestic policy. They are constantly confronted with government actions that ignore their needs, deny their aspirations, and threaten the peace of their families and the entire world. Each day's scary headlines make them more worried and angry about the enormous gulf between what they believe should be done and what an unrepresentative government of white upper-middle-class and rich men is doing in the name of all Americans. . . .

The Reagan Record; Unfair to Women and Children

If what Ronald Reagan pretended to *do for* women was a sham, what he did *against* women and children was only too real and hurtful. It was nothing less than a massive, across-the-board attack on every government program affecting women and children that had been laboriously won over a period of decades. For years Reagan had earned an easy living as a General Electric spokesman, peddling his "free enterprise" ideology on the banquet circuit and telling his favorite "welfare cheat" horror stories, which usually featured a mythical woman who drove in her limousine to pick up a welfare check. His audience of expense-account, tax-finagling businessmen with their three-martini luncheons loved that story. Inside Reagan's packaged "nice guy" exterior was a tough reactionary who, unlike Scrooge, was not a candidate for repentance. Instead, once in the White House, Reagan set about trying to enact the entire right-wing agenda, regardless of the human suffering it would and did bring. . . .

Reagan's anti-inflation program was based on an induced depression and mass layoffs. His unprecedented increase in military spending was accompanied by a staggering federal budget deficit of more than $200 billion and high interest rates that threatened to bring an international economic collapse.

Millions of women and male members of their families lost their jobs, and even after economic recovery had been proclaimed, more than 10 million Americans were officially unemployed. More than $300 billion in national income was lost as a result of the deepest depression the economy had suffered since the 1930s. Reduced inflation did not bring down prices, but simply slowed the rate at which they rose. The costs of food, clothing, and shelter—major components of middle-class and poor-family budgets—were still too high for millions of Americans; many lost their homes through mortgage foreclosures, and small-business failures were widespread. For working women, Reagan's statement in his 1983 State of the Union address that he would "not tolerate wage discrimination based on sex" had a hypocritical ring because his administration was busily removing government protections that offered women and minorities their only hope of a fair break in the job market.

After Reagan took office, two and a half million more women sank into poverty, and the national poverty rate increased to 15 percent, the highest level in seventeen years, with the traditional have-nots—women and minorities—the prime victims. Hunger, soup kitchens, and breadlines again became part of the American scene, and doctors reported the reappearance of malnutrition and other hunger-induced illnesses in children. Reagan professed to be "perplexed" at reports of mass hunger and ordered a study of the problem which his own policies had brought about. . . .

Federal funds for food assistance were among the major targets of Reagan's initial budget cuts. Child-nutrition programs were cut by $1.46 billion. Of the 26 million children who were getting free or subsidized school lunches before Reagan took office, 3.2 million were dropped from the program because of the changes he effected. In 1982 an estimated twenty-seven hundred schools stopped participating in the lunch program because the new Reagan rules made it impracticable for them to continue. . . .

Although women account for approximately 33 percent of the federal work force, in 1981, after Reagan ordered mass firings of government employees, women constituted 45 percent of those who lost their jobs. According to a congressional study of federal agencies, minority personnel were dismissed at a rate 50 percent greater than whites in 1981. In 1982, in proportion to their percentages in the federal work force, two minority workers were laid off for every white worker.

Reagan's Justice Department virtually abandoned the affirmative action policies of the past twenty years, stating that it would no longer advocate hiring goals and timetables even in cases in which courts had identified blatant discrimination. The scope and effectiveness of the Office of Federal Contract Compliance was drastically limited by a new policy that exempted about 76 percent of all companies doing business with the government from having to file affirmative action plans, and by reducing back-pay awards to victims of discrimination.

The Equal Employment Opportunity Commission, which had worked effectively under Eleanor Holmes Norton in the Carter administration, became significantly less active after Reagan's election. In the first three quarters of 1982, only seventy-two equal employment opportunity lawsuits were filed—73.9 percent fewer than in 1981. In fiscal 1982, only 761 backpay awards were made, compared to 4336 in Carter's 1980 fiscal year. . . .

Reagan's opposition to the ERA and abortion rights came as no surprise; he encouraged the Republican opposition to the reintroduced ERA, which was defeated in the House, and used his office to encourage attempts to win congressional approval of a constitutional amendment restricting or outlawing women's access to safe, legal abortions. He also sought regulations making it more difficult for young women to obtain contraceptives and family planning services. His 1982 budget had slashed by more than 25 percent funding for federal family planning services.

With the President's approval, the Department of Health and Human Services announced a "squeal rule" regulation, requiring federally funded family planning clinics to notify parents when teen-agers received prescriptions for contraceptives. This rule applied only to female teen-agers because male contraceptive devices are over-the-counter, nonprescription items. . . .

All Reagan's blundering attempts to overcome the gender gap foundered on the solid rock of his anti-woman actions as President. On every national issue on which a majority of American women had expressed their opinions—whether they touched on women's rights or domestic or foreign policy—Reagan took a contrary view, which he backed up with the full might of his governmental power. He succeeded in further angering the nation's large feminist constituency and alienated women from every social, economic, racial, and age group, including large numbers of women in his own party.

In 1984 the cave men were still in control of the government, but millions of angry women were waiting to go to the polls to vote them out of power.

READING AND DISCUSSION QUESTIONS

1. How does Abzug define the dimensions of the gender gap during the Reagan years? Why were Republicans in Reagan's White House worried?

2. What criticism of Reagan's policies did Abzug make? How does she assess the impact of those policies on women and children?

29-5 | America's Family Values Debate

NEW YORK DAILY NEWS, *Front Page—Quayle to Murphy Brown: You Tramp!* (1992)

Family values became a central part of Republican politics in the 1980s. The religious right and Ronald Reagan forged a mutually beneficial relationship during those years, one that his successor George H. W. Bush hoped to maintain. Dan Quayle, who had been a relatively unknown U.S. Senator from Indiana until Bush selected him as running mate, waded into family-values politics during Bush's reelection campaign in 1992. Quayle criticized a character (played by actress Candice Bergen) on the hit TV sitcom *Murphy Brown*. In that show, the title character was a TV journalist who decided to have and raise a baby on her own. "Bearing babies irresponsibly is, simply, wrong," said the Vice President. "It doesn't help matters when prime-time TV has Murphy Brown—a character who supposedly epitomizes today's intelligent, highly paid professional woman—mocking the importance of fathers by bearing a child alone and calling it just another 'life-style choice.'" This front page of the May 20, 1992 issue of the New York *Daily News* brought family values to the front of the election campaign. Ultimately, the Bush-Quayle ticket was defeated in November by Bill Clinton and Al Gore, an election that widened the partisan divide in America.

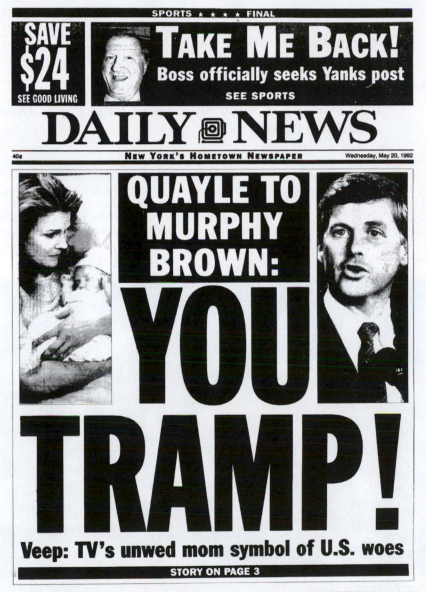

New York Daily News Archive/Getty Images

READING AND DISCUSSION QUESTIONS

1. What were the issues raised by this episode of the 1990s culture war? How did conservatives and liberals interpret the issue of single motherhood?

2. What can you infer about Republican political strategy during the 1992 campaign from Quayle's choice to take aim at this popular TV sitcom? What audience do you think he was addressing with his comments?

3. Quayle did not use the words ("You Tramp!") that the *Daily News* attributed to him on its cover. What can you conclude from this front page about the role of the media in presidential elections?

29-6 | America Reacts to Gulf War Victory

DON EMMERT, *A Navy A-7 Corsair Jet Is Pulled Down Broadway* (1991)

When Iraqi leader Saddam Hussein invaded neighboring Kuwait in August 1990, President George H. W. Bush rallied an international coalition to turn back the invasion, culminating in a decisive victory within days of the ground assault against Iraqi forces. Covered live on television, this quick war appeared to be a complete American victory and a psychological boost to a nation still struggling to forget its loss in Vietnam less than two decades earlier. Returning troops were welcomed home by countless celebrations, including this June 1991 parade down New York City's Broadway.

DON EMMERT/Getty Images

READING AND DISCUSSION QUESTIONS

1. How would you characterize the mood of Americans following the Gulf War as it is depicted in this photograph of a New York City ticker-tape parade?

2. Why do you think the organizers of the parade included a Navy jet?

3. What can you discern about the perspective of the photographer? What story do you think he was trying to tell with this particular shot?

■ COMPARATIVE QUESTIONS ■

1. To what extent does Bella Abzug (Document 29-4) draw upon a liberal tradition extending from the New Deal through the 1960s? Compare her rhetoric with the speeches of Franklin Roosevelt (Documents 22-1 and 23-1) and Lyndon Johnson (Document 27-1). What similarities do you see? Has the focus shifted at all?

2. Using the multiple perspectives gathered in this chapter, summarize both the liberal and conservative agenda during the 1980s. What was the liberal reaction to conservative policies?

3. Assess the historical significance of the Cold War and Vietnam on Reagan-era foreign policy. What evidence of earlier Cold War anxiety do you see in the 1980s?

4. Identify any changes in focus or emphasis that you see in the conservatism of Reagan in the 1980s (Document 29-1) compared to Barry Goldwater in 1964 (Document 27-2). How consistent was the conservative message?

30

National and Global Dilemmas

1989 to the Present

Called the year of revolutions, 1989 marked a transition from the Cold War to a new era of globalization and democracy. In that year, the Berlin Wall came down, Soviet-propped governments in the Eastern bloc fell, Chinese students protested in Tiananmen Square, and racial segregation began to unravel in South Africa. Pundits everywhere heralded the new era as the West's vindication of its long cold war against authoritarianism. The hoped-for peace, however, dissolved as new issues emerged. Without the simplicity of the Cold War divide between the United States (the "good guys") and the Soviet Union (the "bad guys"), Presidents George H. W. Bush and Bill Clinton struggled to articulate America's new role in the world as the only remaining superpower. Domestic politics became increasingly bitter and partisan. The devastating terrorist attacks against the United States on September 11, 2001, provided a brief bipartisan unity and refocused and centered America's foreign policy on what President George W. Bush called a "war on terror." The war continued under Barack Obama, the first African American to win the presidency. During the Obama administration, crippling partisanship stymied efforts to address national problems of war, economic crisis, and globalization. Despite a modest economic recovery and the 2010 passage of his signature health care reform, the Affordable Care Act, President Obama was never able to transcend the deep partisan divisions. A polarized electorate endured an unorthodox 2016 election, which resulted in the electoral college victory of real estate developer Donald Trump over the winner of the popular vote, Democrat Hillary Clinton, the first woman nominated by a major party for president.

30-1 | Protesting the World Trade Organization

ALESHA DAUGHTREY, *Interview by April Eaton* (2000)

In late November 1999, members of the World Trade Organization (WTO) convened in Seattle, Washington, to open negotiations on international trade agreements. The Clinton administration sided with Republicans and supported free-trade negotiations lowering tariffs. Opponents decried globalization's effects on labor and the environment. The Seattle meeting incited antiglobalization protests that ultimately disrupted the WTO talks. Alesha Daughtrey, a field organizer for Global Trade Watch, a division of Ralph Nader's national consumer advocacy organization, Public Citizen, describes her role in the protests.

AD: We do a lot of our field outreach and coalition building through a national fair trade coalition called the Citizens Fair Trade Campaign, which we helped to found a number of years ago. In terms of the mobilization, a lot of that was done through CTC and the CTC partners include a number of different labor unions, mainly the major industrial unions, like the Teamsters and Steel Workers and UAW, as well as UNITE[1], but also the Sierra Club and Friends of the Earth, some additional consumer's organizations, National Family Farm Coalition, the Rural Coalition, some religious groups, including United Methodist Church, Board of Church and Society. So it's fairly broad-based. . . .

AE: How would you summarize the message that your organization was trying to get out during the protest? What was your sound bite? If you wanted to make one thing known, what would that be?

AD: The WTO is an undemocratic and unaccountable organization that works to promote the profit margin over the interests of the people. We feel that international trade is necessary and inevitable. But the rules by which that trade is governed need to have more to do with the interests of citizens than with the back pockets and cash wads of a couple corporate CEOs. And we want to make sure that there is a balance consideration. Obviously people are always going to be concerned with their profits — it's business, we understand that, we accept that. But we think that needs to be balanced with concern for the rights of workers, basic human rights, protecting the environment. . . . [O]ne of the things that I think was really important after the NAFTA fight several years back was

"Interview by April Eaton" (2000). From Alesha Daughtrey, interview by April Eaton, WTO History Project, University of Washington, August 17, 2000. Transcript at http://depts .washington.edu/wtohist/interviews/Daughtrey.pdf. Used by permission.

[1] **CTC . . . UNITE**: Citizens Trade Campaign (CTC) is a coalition group pursuing environmentally just trade policies; the United Auto Workers (UAW) is a labor union; the Union of Needletrades, Industrial and Textile Employees (UNITE) merged with Hotel Employees and Restaurant Employees (HERE) in 2004 to form the union UNITE HERE.

that was the first time, I think, that labor and environmentalists had really been able to dedicate themselves to the same project and begin to see eye to eye. But what happened in Seattle was a deepening of that. . . . I think that a lot of the union leadership was a little bit more hesitant about the direct action than say some of us were, because that wasn't something that they'd had a whole lot of exposure to and experience with, and they weren't sure how that would shake out. We weren't sure how it would shake out either, but we knew it was worth a try. So, that was somewhat of a challenge. . . .

AE: What would you describe as the biggest successes in your experience and the organization's experience in Seattle and, also, things that maybe didn't go so well? . . .

AD: I think that it did quite a lot to sort of re-energize the left a little bit. I think it has been really hard over, especially over the last four years, but really over the last eight, because I think a lot of liberal/progressives sort of saw a Democrat in office and after the Reagan-Bush era figured that their work was done here. And they were willing to sit back, and they figured Clinton was a nice guy, and that was all there was to it. And people got really rather complacent, even though it soon became clear that not that much had changed in the White House or anywhere else. And I think having that magnitude, having a demonstration on that level was something that nobody had really seen in years, in decades actually. And I think it was a big reminder of how much power people actually had. That was good. I wasn't around for the anti-war demonstrations or for the civil rights demonstrations. And I think a lot of younger activists really sort of saw this as something that became their movement. . . . What seems to have happened was, they heard about Seattle in the news and they saw the photos from there, and they thought, there really is something wrong with this WTO thing, and there really is something wrong with the global trade and investment system, and it is very unjust, and it's not democratic, and it's not working well for the people. . . . And I think that contrary to the myth that a lot of younger people are slackers and not politically connected and disinterested in government, in the way society is headed, I think it has really done a lot to bring the student and youth movement alive in the United States, which is good, because it's been asleep for too long. . . .

AE: . . . [H]ow much of this would have been possible without the Internet . . . ?

AD: I have really come to the conclusion that the numbers that were generated in Seattle would have been impossible without the Internet. Because there were so many people literally who arrived on November 30, because on November 29 they saw a live stream video of what was going on in Seattle, and they just decided they had to get in the car and drive up from Portland or San Francisco. And people literally got in the car and drove all night to get there. And it was also really good for sending around calls to action and letting people know what the mobilization points were, what the plans were. So people arrived and they already had some sense of what to expect, what was going on, who to talk to, and how the week would go. I think the level of detail and that information would not have been possible. Ride boards, housing was arranged via the Internet, all of this stuff, it made it logistically a lot easier on that level. But I think what really set the work in Seattle apart from some of the subsequent protests has been that there was a huge amount of local organizing going on and local coalition building and education and outreach. . . . And I think it made for a much more effective message opportunity. . . . [W]e operate about a half dozen list serves here. Some of them are very closed strategy lists that are just for key coalition partners that we work with around the country. Others are far more broad and include thousands of subscribers. And they include the action alerts and updates and things like that. Email on the Internet is really important for a lot of the international work that we do. We do try to have some type of conference call every six to eight weeks at least. . . . And we've tried to have physical meetings once a year. But in terms of day-to-day things, checking up on different projects that each of us has agreed to take on or whatever, it's too hard to mess with the time zones, so definitely it's good for that.

AE: Shifting a little bit to questions about yourself and your own views, first of all, how did you get here? How did you end up doing what you're doing?

AD: . . . I spent the week before the Ministerial [conference] and the week of out there [in Seattle]. I came away with a very, very different take on all of this, because I had believed in all of these things, like I said, but it wasn't personal. And suddenly, when you're standing in the middle of the street, and you're watching somebody half a block down in a wheelchair be beaten by two police in riot gear, and when you're washing tear gas out of the eyes of an eight-year-old child, you start to realize that there is obviously something going on in that Convention Center that they're protecting. What is it that they would fight this hard to protect? And I had always had this theory, simple-minded though it was, that the police were there to serve and protect me, since they were my tax dollars at work, right? Wrong. And I just thought, okay, so what is it that's creating this? And, of course, I knew what the answer was. But for the first time, it became a very personal thing, where these were not just being visited on people via a plant closing, or things that do affect real lives in very real ways. You don't get much more real than this is in your face, than physical conflict on the streets.

READING AND DISCUSSION QUESTIONS

1. How does Daughtrey explain the importance of the issues raised by those groups protesting the WTO meeting in Seattle? What was at stake for the groups Global Trade Watch served?

2. What impact did the internet have on the Seattle protests? How did the organizers use new communications technology to mobilize protesters and broadcast their criticisms of globalization?

3. What evidence does the Seattle WTO protest provide for understanding changes in politics during the late twentieth century?

30-2 | American Ambassador Defines U.S. Interests in Post–Cold War World

MADELEINE ALBRIGHT, *Realism and Idealism in American Foreign Policy Today* (1994)

Speaking at Harvard's Kennedy School of Government commencement in 1994, U.S. ambassador to the United Nations Madeleine Albright addressed the pitfalls of developing a foreign policy in a post–Cold War world without the presence of a Soviet threat. Here she offers criteria guiding U.S. intervention overseas, a policy she would attempt to implement during Clinton's second term when she served as the first female secretary of state.

To be sustainable, American foreign policy must be guided by American interests. But in the wake of the Cold War, a whole category of conflicts has arisen in which the American stake resists precise calculation. . . .

[T]here is no perfect scale or formula for categorizing what is important to our people. Obviously, there remains an inner circle of vital interests related to the defense of our people, territory, allies, and economic well-being. Here, unilateral action, if required, is warranted and would likely have full support from Congress and the American people.

Increasingly, we also recognize an outer circle of important interests that we share with others. Global issues—such as the health of the atmosphere, stabilizing population growth, controlling international crime, and curbing AIDS—fall within this circle. Here, multilateral action is essential because national action alone is not sufficient.

But between and sometimes overlapping these two is a middle circle—a gray area of regional conflicts and potential conflicts that does not fit neatly into any national security framework but which, if left unattended, could erode the foundation of freedom and threaten world peace. Here, the destructive legacy of the Cold War is most evident and the challenge of organizing the peace most complex. Here, regional organizations and regional powers have an important role. Here, the American stake may shift dramatically with changing circumstance and must be evaluated case by case, day by day.

Madeleine Albright, "Realism and Idealism in American Foreign Policy Today," *U.S. Department of State Dispatch* 5, no. 26 (June 27, 1994).

These regional problems do not affect us equally or in the same way . . . [but] . . . if not well-managed, could pose threats to the innermost circle of American concerns. Here, our interests are especially compelling and the risks especially high. . . .

U.S. Engagement: The Need and the Means

. . . The end of the superpower rivalry has made cooperation possible. So peace-keeping and sanctions—little-used previously—have moved to center stage. Each entered to high expectations; each has since received mixed reviews. The Administration's strategy has been to use these tools assertively to supplement diplomatic, political, and military initiatives we have taken on our own. We have sought, at the same time, to hone these tools—to make sanctions a more precise instrument of policy and to make UN peace-keeping more disciplined and more effective.

Although our effort to reform UN peace-keeping has bipartisan support, there are some in Congress who either would pull the plug altogether or so restrict funding as to make the management of peace-keeping impossible. Last month, an amendment was offered in the House of Representatives that . . . would have brought about the virtual collapse of UN peace-keeping. . . . It is sobering that an amendment so contrary to American interests and traditions could have been offered and only narrowly defeated. Our ability to manage the problems . . . in Haiti, Bosnia, and the former Soviet Union would be seriously undermined if UN peace-keeping were no longer an option. And the chances of gaining support from other countries for our policy toward North Korea would also diminish. . . .

If we are going to meet the challenges of this new era, we will need to use every tool available—a strong defense, strong alliances, vigorous diplomacy, better UN peace-keeping, more effective multilateral sanctions, and firm support for the requirements of international law. We need to understand . . . that international peace and security depend not on a parity of power but on a preponderance of power that favors the peacekeepers over the "peace-upsetters." . . .

We have a responsibility in our time . . . to be pathfinders; not to be imprisoned by history but to shape it; to build a world not without conflict but in which conflict is effectively contained; a world, not without repression but in which the sway of freedom is enlarged; a world not without lawless behavior but in which the law-abiding are progressively more secure.

READING AND DISCUSSION QUESTIONS

1. How does Albright prioritize America's foreign policy into "inner circle" and "outer circle" interests? What challenge does she believe the United States faces at the intersection of those circles of interest?

2. What responsibility does she say the United States bears as the world's only remaining superpower? How does her speech deflect critics who might object to America's active engagement in the many international crises threatening peace around the world?

30-3 | America Rallies After 9/11 Attacks

JANETTE BECKMAN, *9/11 Tributes* (2001)

On the morning of September 11, 2001, two planes were flown into the World Trade Center towers in New York City. Another plane was flown into the Pentagon outside the nation's capital. A fourth crashed in Pennsylvania, after actions by passengers averted a probable attack on the White House. More than three thousand people died, including the terrorists who hijacked the planes. President George W. Bush addressed the American people before a joint session of Congress to outline the nation's response, declaring a "war on terror" sequel to the global Cold War won by his father's generation. In the days following the attacks, memorials and tributes to those killed appeared in New York, Pennsylvania, Washington, D.C., and around the world. In a period of political division, this crisis brought Americans together, though the unity of those days began to dissolve as the Bush Administration prosecuted the war on terror, including the war in Iraq.

Janette Beckman/Getty Images

READING AND DISCUSSION QUESTIONS

1. What story do you think the photographer was trying to capture with this image? To what extent do you think she captured the mood in the days following the 9/11 attack?

2. What role do you think tributes such as this one played in the lives of those who witnessed the 9/11 attacks?

30-4 | Tea Party Politics

MATT WUERKER, *Editorial Cartoon* (2010)

Matt Wuerker's editorial cartoon comments on two stories to make a point about the politics of 2010. The first story is the April 20 explosion of the Deepwater Horizon oil rig located in the Gulf of Mexico that released more than three million barrels of oil before it was capped by British Petroleum (BP) in July. This was the largest oil spill in U. S. history, topping the 1989 Exxon Valdez spill in Alaska's Prince William Sound. Investigations revealed that BP's safety record included an earlier refinery explosion in Texas, which cost the lives of 15 workers, and pipeline leaks in Alaska. BP had also been cited for violations of federal environmental standards. Still, critics blamed the disaster on corporate greed, poor government oversight, and ineffective federal regulation. The second story is the rise of the conservative Tea Party movement in 2009, born from a frustration with government spending that shaped their small-government, free-market ideology. The Tea Party's populism played an important role in shaping the politics of the Obama years by pushing the Republican Party to the right. In this cartoon, Wuerker comments on the contradictions inherent in that political moment.

READING AND DISCUSSION QUESTIONS

1. What point about the politics of 2010 is Wuerker making with this cartoon about an environmental disaster?

2. What does the man holding the signs represent? Why does Wuerker draw him the way he does, and what is the significance of the signs and the character's demand that various federal agencies be called?

3. What can you infer about the political significance of the Tea Party movement from this cartoon?

30-5 | Democratic Presidential Candidate Confronts the Issue of Race

BARACK OBAMA, *A More Perfect Union* (2008)

Barack Obama's historic campaign for president in 2008 was nearly derailed when video clips of his former Chicago pastor, the Reverend Jeremiah Wright, surfaced in which Wright implied that the nation's foreign policies had invited the 9/11 terrorist attacks. In another broadly circulated sermon, Wright's litany of America's failings—including its treatment of minority citizens—culminated with: "God Bless America. No . . . not God Bless America. God damn America." Obama's widely praised speech in Philadelphia defanged the issue and rescued his campaign, leading to his fall victory over his rival, Senator John McCain.

[I]t has only been in the last couple of weeks that the discussion of race in this campaign has taken a particularly divisive turn.

On one end of the spectrum, we've heard the implication that my candidacy is somehow an exercise in affirmative action; that it's based solely on the desire of wide-eyed liberals to purchase racial reconciliation on the cheap. On the other end, we've heard my former pastor, Reverend Jeremiah Wright, use incendiary language to express views that have the potential not only to widen the racial divide, but views that denigrate both the greatness and the goodness of our nation; that rightly offend white and black alike.

I have already condemned, in unequivocal terms, the statements of Reverend Wright that have caused such controversy. For some, nagging questions remain. Did I know him to be an occasionally fierce critic of American domestic and foreign policy? Of course. Did I ever hear him make remarks that could be considered controversial while I sat in church? Yes. Did I strongly disagree with many of his political views? Absolutely—just as I'm sure many of you have heard remarks from your pastors, priests, or rabbis with which you strongly disagreed.

But the remarks that have caused this recent firestorm weren't simply controversial. They weren't simply a religious leader's effort to speak out against perceived injustice. Instead, they expressed a profoundly distorted view of this country—a view that sees white racism as endemic, and that elevates what is wrong with America above all that we know is right with America; a view that sees the conflicts in the Middle East as rooted primarily in the actions of stalwart allies like Israel, instead of emanating from the perverse and hateful ideologies of radical Islam.

As such, Reverend Wright's comments were not only wrong but divisive. . . .

Given my background, my politics, and my professed values and ideals, there will no doubt be those for whom my statements of condemnation are not enough. Why associate myself with Reverend Wright in the first place, they may

---

Barack Obama, "A More Perfect Union," March 18, 2008. Online by Gerald Peters and John T. Woolley, *The American Presidency Project*, https://www.presidency.ucsb.edu/node/277610.

ask? Why not join another church? And I confess that if all that I knew of Reverend Wright were the snippets of those sermons that have run in an endless loop on the television and YouTube, or if Trinity United Church of Christ conformed to the caricatures being peddled by some commentators, there is no doubt that I would react in much the same way.

But the truth is, that isn't all that I know of the man. The man I met more than twenty years ago is a man who helped introduce me to my Christian faith, a man who spoke to me about our obligations to love one another; to care for the sick and lift up the poor. . . .

As imperfect as he may be, he has been like family to me. He strengthened my faith, officiated my wedding, and baptized my children. Not once in my conversations with him have I heard him talk about any ethnic group in derogatory terms, or treat whites with whom he interacted with anything but courtesy and respect. He contains within him the contradictions—the good and the bad—of the community that he has served diligently for so many years.

I can no more disown him than I can disown the black community. I can no more disown him than I can my white grandmother—a woman who helped raise me, a woman who sacrificed again and again for me, a woman who loves me as much as she loves anything in this world, but a woman who once confessed her fear of black men who passed by her on the street, and who on more than one occasion has uttered racial or ethnic stereotypes that made me cringe.

These people are a part of me. And they are a part of America, this country that I love. . . .

We do not need to recite here the history of racial injustice in this country. But we do need to remind ourselves that so many of the disparities that exist in the African-American community today can be directly traced to inequalities passed on from an earlier generation that suffered under the brutal legacy of slavery and Jim Crow.

Segregated schools were, and are, inferior schools; we still haven't fixed them, fifty years after *Brown v. Board of Education*, and the inferior education they provided, then and now, helps explain the pervasive achievement gap between today's black and white students.

Legalized discrimination—where blacks were prevented, often through violence, from owning property, or loans were not granted to African-American business owners, or black homeowners could not access FHA mortgages, or blacks were excluded from unions, or the police force, or fire departments . . . helps explain the wealth and income gap between black and white, and the concentrated pockets of poverty that persists in so many of today's urban and rural communities.

A lack of economic opportunity among black men, and the shame and frustration that came from not being able to provide for one's family, contributed to the erosion of black families—a problem that welfare policies for many years may have worsened. And the lack of basic services in so many urban black neighborhoods—parks for kids to play in, police walking the beat, regular garbage pick-up and building code enforcement—all helped create a cycle of violence, blight and neglect that continue to haunt us.

This is the reality in which Reverend Wright and other African-Americans of his generation grew up. . . . That legacy of defeat was passed on to future generations—those young men and increasingly young women who we see standing on street corners or languishing in our prisons, without hope or prospects for the future. . . .

For the men and women of Reverend Wright's generation, the memories of humiliation and doubt and fear have not gone away; nor has the anger and the bitterness of those years. That anger may not get expressed in public, in front of white co-workers or white friends. But it does find voice in the barbershop or around the kitchen table. . . .

And occasionally it finds voice in the church on Sunday morning, in the pulpit and in the pews. The fact that so many people are surprised to hear that anger in some of Reverend Wright's sermons simply reminds us of the old truism that the most segregated hour in American life occurs on Sunday morning. . . .

In fact, a similar anger exists within segments of the white community. Most working- and middle-class white Americans don't feel that they have been particularly privileged by their race. . . . They've worked hard all their lives, many times only to see their jobs shipped overseas or their pension dumped after a lifetime of labor. They are anxious about their futures, and feel their dreams slipping away; in an era of stagnant wages and global competition, opportunity comes to be seen as a zero sum game, in which your dreams come at my expense. So when they are told to bus their children to a school across town; when they hear that an African American is getting an advantage in landing a good job or a spot in a good college because of an injustice that they themselves never committed; when they're told that their fears about crime in urban neighborhoods are somehow prejudiced, resentment builds over time. . . .

But I have asserted a firm conviction—a conviction rooted in my faith in God and my faith in the American people—that working together we can move beyond some of our old racial wounds, and that in fact we have no choice if we are to continue on the path of a more perfect union.

For the African-American community, that path means embracing the burdens of our past without becoming victims of our past. It means continuing to insist on a full measure of justice in every aspect of American life. But it also means binding our particular grievances—for better health care, and better schools, and better jobs—to the larger aspirations of all Americans—the white woman struggling to break the glass ceiling, the white man who's been laid off, the immigrant trying to feed his family. . . .

In the end, then, what is called for is nothing more, and nothing less, than what all the world's great religions demand—that we do unto others as we would have them do unto us. Let us be our brother's keeper, Scripture tells us. Let us be our sister's keeper. Let us find that common stake we all have in one another, and let our politics reflect that spirit as well.

For we have a choice in this country. We can accept a politics that breeds division, and conflict, and cynicism. . . . But if we do, I can tell you that in the next election, we'll be talking about some other distraction. And then another one. And then another one. And nothing will change.

That is one option. Or, at this moment, in this election, we can come together and say, "Not this time." This time we want to talk about the crumbling schools that are stealing the future of black children and white children and Asian children and Hispanic children and Native American children. This time we want to reject the cynicism that tells us that these kids can't learn; that those kids who don't look like us are somebody else's problem. The children of America are not those kids, they are our kids, and we will not let them fall behind in a 21st century economy. Not this time.

This time we want to talk about how the lines in the Emergency Room are filled with whites and blacks and Hispanics who do not have health care; who don't have the power on their own to overcome the special interests in Washington, but who can take them on if we do it together.

This time we want to talk about the shuttered mills that once provided a decent life for men and women of every race, and the homes for sale that once belonged to Americans from every religion, every region, every walk of life. This time we want to talk about the fact that the real problem is not that someone who doesn't look like you might take your job; it's that the corporation you work for will ship it overseas for nothing more than a profit.

This time we want to talk about the men and women of every color and creed who serve together, and fight together, and bleed together under the same proud flag. We want to talk about how to bring them home from a war that never should've been authorized and never should've been waged, and we want to talk about how we'll show our patriotism by caring for them, and their families, and giving them the benefits they have earned.

I would not be running for President if I didn't believe with all my heart that this is what the vast majority of Americans want for this country. This union may never be perfect, but generation after generation has shown that it can always be perfected. And today, whenever I find myself feeling doubtful or cynical about this possibility, what gives me the most hope is the next generation—the young people whose attitudes and beliefs and openness to change have already made history in this election.

READING AND DISCUSSION QUESTIONS

1. How does Obama explain the historical context of Reverend Wright's comments? Though he distanced himself from Wright's more inflammatory language, how does Obama explain to Americans the source and significance of Wright's anger?

2. To what extent do you think historians will interpret Obama's speech as a turning point in the history of America's race relations? How would you assess its short-term effect on the 2008 campaign and its longer-term effect on Americans' discussion of race?

30-6 | President Trump Tweets About Immigration

DONALD TRUMP, *Twitter* (2019)

President Donald Trump disrupted the political scene in 2016 with his unorthodox campaign and America-first rhetoric that often focused on immigration. He began his campaign with attacks on Mexicans and promised to build a wall along the southern border to combat illegal immigration. His message resonated with a base of white, working-class Americans, many of whom attributed their declining fortunes to globalization. Trump's reality-TV background helped his populist message connect with voters, and he used social media to control the political narrative, making an end-run around the mainstream media whom he often characterized as "fake news." Below is a selection of President Trump's tweets from 2019 in which he references immigration and the border wall.

 Donald J. Trump ✔
@realDonaldTrump   ⌄

We must maintain a Strong Southern Border. We cannot allow our Country to be overrun by illegal immigrants as the Democrats tell their phony stories of sadness and grief, hoping it will help them in the elections. Obama and others had the same pictures, and did nothing about it!

9:43 AM · Jun 22, 2018 · Twitter for iPhone

 Donald J. Trump ✔
@realDonaldTrump   ⌄

Fake News Media had me calling Immigrants, or Illegal Immigrants, "Animals." Wrong! They were begrudgingly forced to withdraw their stories. I referred to MS 13 Gang Members as "Animals," a big difference – and so true. Fake News got it purposely wrong, as usual!

6:51 AM · May 18, 2018 · Twitter for iPhone

[1] **MS-13 Gang**: Street gang begun in Los Angeles in the 1980s by El Salvadoran immigrants, whose members have been accused of murder and other violent crimes.

Donald J. Trump ✓
@realDonaldTrump

Four people in Nevada viciously robbed and killed by an illegal immigrant who should not have been in our Country. 26 people killed on the Border in a drug and gang related fight. Two large Caravans from Honduras broke into Mexico and are headed our way. We need a powerful Wall!

6:37 PM · Jan 21, 2019 · Twitter for iPhone

Donald J. Trump ✓
@realDonaldTrump

If Illegal Immigrants are unhappy with the conditions in the quickly built or refitted detentions centers, just tell them not to come. All problems solved!

4:22 PM · Jul 3, 2019 · Twitter for iPhone

59.2K Retweets   **263.2K** Likes

READING AND DISCUSSION QUESTIONS

1. What policy position on immigration can you discern from President Trump's tweets?

2. What audience do you think Trump is attempting to reach with his tweets?

3. How do you evaluate the significance of Trump's use of Twitter? How has his use of social media reshaped the modern American presidency?

▪ COMPARATIVE QUESTIONS ▪

1. Compare Madeleine Albright's speech (Document 30-2) with the foreign policy views expressed by George Kennan (Document 24-1) and Ronald Reagan (Document 29-1). How do their views differ, and what factors account for those differences? Analyze the historical context of the Cold War for clues.

2. What evidence does the Seattle WTO protest (Document 30-1) provide for understanding changes in social protest politics during the late twentieth century? Compare strategies at Seattle with the Indians of All Tribes proclamation (Document 26-5) and the photograph protesting Trump's executive order on immigration (Document P9-6). What comparison could a historian make between them?

3. What historical patterns can you identify in the experience of racial and ethnic minorities in America by comparing the evidence from President Trump's tweets (Document 30-6) to the Citizen Committee letter (Document P7-1), the World War II African American soldier's letter (Document P7-5), Luisa Moreno's speech (Document P7-6), and Dolores Huerta's congressional testimony (Document 27-6)? How were the challenges similar or different in these different periods?

4. What challenges face the historian attempting to write the history of contemporary America? How might personal opinion and memory interfere with the analysis of this chapter's documents more than previous chapters' sources?

5. Compare presidential rhetoric. How have the different occupants of the White House communicated with the American people? To what extent does the form of that communication matter?

PART 9

DOCUMENT SET

Globalization and the End of the American Century

1980 to the Present

CHAPTER 29
Conservative America in the Ascent, 1980–1991

CHAPTER 30
National and Global Dilemmas, 1989 to the Present

The last quarter of the twentieth century revealed the promise and peril of the new era of globalization. Changes in technology and America's economic integration into world markets developed new opportunities for growth on a scale unimaginable to policymakers in the post–World War II era. However, unforeseen side effects demonstrated America's economic and political vulnerabilities. Global markets inspired profit fantasies for corporate America, but blue-collar workers in the traditional manufacturing industries were seized with anxiety as they saw their jobs being exported to lower-wage countries. A period of deindustrialization coincided with the rise of a new labor market in service-sector jobs. The erosion of working-class manufacturing jobs and the rise of sophisticated financial markets widened the income gap, resulting in social and political consequences. Technology pushed globalization by opening information and commercial exchange around the world. Technology companies such as Microsoft and Apple helped popularize personal computing, which in turn, with the introduction of the World Wide Web in the early 1990s, launched an information and consumer revolution. But this, too, came with costs. These seismic changes in work and global exchange created a new economy for the twenty-first century, but they also inspired an ongoing debate over economic values and the role of government that continues to affect America's political culture.

P9-1 | Free-Market Fundamentalism Defines the Conservative Movement

IRVING KRISTOL, *Two Cheers for Capitalism* (1978)

The modern conservative movement traces its origins to the free-market ideology that developed in opposition to Franklin Roosevelt's New Deal, which critics sometimes decried as evidence of creeping socialism. These critics worried that excessive government interference with the economy would strangle free enterprise and lead inevitably to constraints on individual liberty. This ideology captured the Republican party and informed Reagan-era "supply-side economics." Here, the intellectual hero of neoconservatism, Irving Kristol, discusses the effect of government regulation on the national economy.

In all of the recent discussion of our economic condition, there has been controversy over whether tax cuts are really necessary and, if so, what kind would be most beneficial. To the best of my knowledge, no one—not even John Kenneth Galbraith[1]—has dreamed of proposing *a tax increase.* Yet that is what we keep on getting—specifically an increased tax on corporate income—only no one seems to notice.

It is not really as surprising as one might think that our economists, our accountants, even our business executives should be oblivious to the steady increase in corporate taxation that has been taking place. Habitual modes of perception and conventional modes of reckoning are likely to impose themselves on a changing reality rather than go through a painful process of adaptation. And the learned economist or alert executive can fail to observe an important feature of a situation because he wasn't looking for it.

Here is an example of what I mean. Corporation X, in order to meet water pollution standards set by the Environmental Protection Agency, has to install new filtering equipment that costs $2 million. How is this expenditure to be accounted for? Well, at present, it is counted as a "capital investment" and is carried on the books as an "asset" of the corporation. But does that make any sense?

After all, a "capital investment" is supposed to promise an increase in production or productivity, or both. An "asset," similarly, is supposed to represent earning power, actual or potential. But that new filtering equipment may do none of these things. Indeed, it may actually decrease productive capacity and productivity. In short, the $2 million ought properly to be counted as a government-imposed cost—in effect a surtax or effluent tax—and the company's stated after-tax income should be reduced accordingly.

Instead of imposing an actual tax and using the proceeds to purchase and install the equipment, the government mandates that the firm do so. The end result, however, is the same.

Two Cheers for Capitalism (1978). From "The Hidden Costs of Regulation" by Irving Kristol, originally published in the Wall Street Journal January 12, 1977, as it appears in *Two Cheers for Capitalism,* by Irving Kristol, pp. 50–53, 54. Used by permission of Gertrude Kristol.

[1]**John Kenneth Galbraith**: Liberal economist and author of several best-selling books, including *The Affluent Society* (1958).

I am not saying that the new filtering equipment is just money down the drain. It does buy cleaner water, after all. But that cleaner water is a free "social good" and a "social asset" to the population in the neighborhood (and for the fish, too); it represents no economic gain to the corporation, which has only economic assets and knows nothing of "social assets." It also buys governmental "good will," but so do bribes to foreign officials, and I am not aware that anyone has yet thought to capitalize them. On the other hand, the new equipment is unquestionably an *economic cost* to the corporation and, of course, to the economy as a whole.

As things now stand, we render those economic costs invisible. That is both silly and undesirable. Silly, because they are real costs. Undesirable, because we shall never persuade the American people to take the problem of regulation seriously until they appreciate, in the clearest possible way, what it is costing them as stockholders, consumers, and employees.

The costs we are talking about are by no means small, and their impact by no means marginal. In fact, they are far, far larger and more serious than most people realize. Unfortunately, there are no comprehensive, precise estimates available. But one can get a sense of the magnitude of such costs from the following bits and pieces of information.

- In 1977 U.S. Steel signed a seven-year agreement with federal, state, and local environmental agencies that will require it to spend $600 million over that period to eliminate air pollution from its Clairton Coke Works in Pittsburgh.
- The steel industry as a whole will be spending well over $1 billion annually on pollution controls—and that is a conservative estimate. This expenditure amounts to over one quarter of the industry's total annual capital investments.
- Meeting EPA's 1983 waste pollution standards will cost all of American industry, over the next seven years, about $60 billion for capital equipment and another $12 billion annually in operating and maintenance costs.
- Meeting noise pollution standards, as mandated by Congress and enforced by the Occupational Safety and Health Administration (OSHA), will involve expenditures of over $15 billion in capital costs and $2 billion to $3 billion in operating costs in the years immediately ahead. If these noise standards are raised to the level recommended by the U.S. National Institute for Occupational Safety and Health—a recommendation endorsed by the EPA—the capital costs will climb over $30 billion.
- According to the *Wall Street Journal*, new health regulations in the cotton industry will, in the period from 1977 through 1983, cost some $3 billion. It has been estimated by Professor Murray Weidenbaum that American industry's cost to meet OSHA safety standards in 1977 alone were over $4 billion.
- The EPA is on record—for what that is worth—as calculating that industry's total capital investment requirements for all kinds of pollution control equipment will, in the decade 1972–81, add up to $112 billion. . . .

The situation we have gotten ourselves into would be ridiculous if it were not so serious. We have been much exercised—and quite rightly—by the fact that the OPEC monopoly has cost this country well over $30 billion in increased oil prices since 1972. But in that time we have inflicted upon ourselves much larger economic costs through environmental and other regulations and will continue to do so, perhaps at an increasing rate.

Yes, these economic costs do buy real "social goods." But may the prices not be too high? Is the resulting inflation of prices, constriction of productive capacity, and increase in unemployment worth it? Would it not be appropriate for us to ask ourselves this question openly, instead of going along with the environmentalists' pretense—so pleasing to our politicians—that our "social goods" cost us nothing at all? Isn't it time that business stopped bleating in a general way about those costs and showed us what they really mean, all the way down to the bottom line?

READING AND DISCUSSION QUESTIONS

1. How would you summarize the neoconservative contribution to the debates over the value of market capitalism? What was the historical significance of Kristol's economic ideas during the last quarter of the twentieth century?

2. Why does Kristol focus his attention on environmentalists? What does he say has been their impact on the national economy?

P9-2 | Steelworker Explains Industry's Collapse

LEROY McCLELLAND SR., *Interview with Bill Barry* (2006)

The Sparrows Point plant of Bethlehem Steel outside Baltimore, Maryland, typified the effects of twentieth-century globalization. During the 1950s, the steel plant was the industry's largest, employing more than thirty thousand men and women and selling steel domestically and around the world. The United Steelworkers union negotiated contracts that helped pull these workers into middle-class comfort. But factors such as technology enhancements and global competition changed everything for the workers, who consequently witnessed their industry collapse. In 2001, Bethlehem Steel sought bankruptcy protection and eliminated its pension liabilities, destroying retirement security for many workers. Here LeRoy McClelland Sr., who worked at "the Point" for forty-two years, describes his experiences and the factors that caused the industry's decline.

MR. McCLELLAND: Well, now you enter into another part of the change, and that's technology. When we looked at the safety aspect of it we knew that there were certain procedures that could protect certain things from happening,

Interview with LeRoy McClelland Sr., by Bill Barry, May 1, 2006. Transcript in the collection of William Barry.

but with that protection in mind it took technology to put it in place, so that meant a job was no longer necessary. So when you are looking for one issue to resolve another, sometimes you've got to take the outcome of it, too. And in our case with technology being advanced and computers and what have you, we've had operations that would never ever operate unless you had a person there. Now, that's not necessary. In fact, it can have a crew—it used to be six people on a mill reduced to three. Why? Computer, and then it advances further on down the road for technology. When that happened, too, you've got to understand that the idea of the union was to protect jobs, create jobs, not eliminate jobs. Well, I had the unfortunate experience of being the zone committeeman at the time when a lot of this technology was starting to really grow.

MR. BARRY: When was this?

MR. McCLELLAND: Well, it really started in 1975, from '75 on, '80, '90s, biggest part being in the '80s really, the advanced technology. But when these other things started to take place, guys and gals sort of looked at this change coming down, felt hey, that's a God send, not realizing that when that takes place you ain't going to be there to see it because your job is going to be gone. So we would have meetings, I would have department meetings up here trying to make that message as clear as I could I guess to soften the idea that hey, we're going to be losing jobs. That protection that used to be there is not going to be dependable anymore. You can't defend something that's no longer necessary, so we had to take these strong measures, and in my case you could find my name on every bathroom shit house wall in Sparrows Point, because I was wanting these guys to—saw the road coming real fast at me and realized technology is going to replace jobs, and if nothing else, gain something from it. So I was sort of accused of selling people for jobs and jobs for job classes, and all that sort of gets caught up in the big mess in itself, but it's nothing you can do. I mean reality is technology is the future and competitiveness is strong. If you can't deal with competitiveness, if you don't have tons per hour and manpower per hour was the way it was, and that's what had to happen. . . .

MR. BARRY: How difficult was it for you to learn how to use a computer?

MR. McCLELLAND: Well, it was a bit of a challenge because everything we did before was pencil and paper, and it was a challenge, and in fact, I didn't think I would like it, I really didn't. My wife is the one who really got started on it, and she got it basically for games and then it advanced into other things. I happened to go down the cellar here and we've got two computers down there, which I bought one for me, one for her, and I didn't want to tell her I didn't know, so I was trying to just ease my way across to get her to show me what these—God, I can use a typewriter, always can use a typewriter, but the keys are—they do different things and you can screw up very easy if you hit the wrong key or be something on the websites, you can really create a problem. So I got down there a couple times, just watched what she was doing. She said, "Well, do you want to learn this?" I said,

"I don't want to learn nothing, just go ahead and do what you are doing," but I watched her, and one night I went down there by myself and I got on the web and I was so overwhelmed by things that I could get on the web, the web addresses, the e-mail addresses that you can get and the information. I got more information about our politicians, I got more information about what is going on in Annapolis, I got more information on what's going on in the Senate and the Congress right there firsthand. I don't have to wait for the newspaper the next day, it's right there. I can get into every newspaper in this country and get what's going on and whatever is happening in that country that very day. It just engulfs you, and then the fear of the computer doesn't exist anymore. And even at work when the transition of computerization took place, we used to take our scrap buckets, big buckets, big bins I should say, and haul them down there and weigh them. We used to have a scale man there. To show you how advanced that got with technology, they eliminated the scale person and they put a scale there, and all you had to do was hit certain buttons, boom, boom, boom, and it would weigh it, it would give you a card in return of what the weight was and you put the box there and the scrap crane come down and dumped it. You put it back to your place and turned in the weight, and it was all computerized, and they simplified it because they had a red key—a monkey could have done it. That's what they were dealing with, the transition, and with technology also a lot of guys did leave the mill because they were embarrassed, they couldn't make the mental change from using the keyboard to using the hands on.

MR. BARRY: These were people who were eligible to retire and the technology in effect drove them out?

MR. McCLELLAND: Yes, absolutely did. And change is tough for anybody. With me, I'm lucky to be able to experience what I did. . . . [Y]ou and I may not be on this earth, but the generation that does exist, jobs itself, availability, is not going to be here because everything we have done in this country has been an outsourcing and we are outsourcing every day of the week. I mean we're talking about—here, my daughter who worked 12 years at Hecht's, it's no longer a[t] Hecht's, they bought her out. They give her a buyout or she can go to Macy's, but I think it's Macy they are now, she can go there but not where she was originally working at in Whitemarsh. She would be somewhere where they needed her. She is raising a five-year-old. She just can't jump and go. So that change is brought on. Places like Wal-Mart, Sam's, Dollar Stores, I mean people don't realize this is why the economy in this country is going down the tube because we are not exporting anything, we are importing, we are importing more, and when you import, the jobs necessary to make the product isn't needed here because it's done outside. Our own steel industry, our steel industry Mitel, now here is a global giant of steel. He has got operations all around the world. Before it's over with, this person, this family is going to end up absolutely controlling the price of steel, and here America sits when defending this country is going to depend on getting steel from other sorts of the world or other parts of the world. What a challenge that's going to be. Right now Mitel has shut down operations here. Why? Because he has places around the world. Weirton Steel, they shut down the steel side completely. No way down the road are they going to open, reactivate it. It is over. So that's one section. And when that character came here, he made it clear that if productivity becomes a problem, then that place is gone, and he ain't just saying that to threaten them. He said it and meant it, and it's happening. What I see going to come down here again, and this is just me, this isn't standing—this is me, my wave length, my tunnel—sometimes tunnel vision, but it turns out that Weirton Steel produces a better tin plate than Sparrows Point. I say—and my son who works there right now, he's an operator on the halogen lines, I said, "John, don't be surprised if some of your operations here starts shutting down permanently. Do not be surprised." Lo and behold there's no more chrome line down there. Where is it? Weirton. Well, it's just a matter of time before some of the other operations that used to depend on the tin mill to supply them will not be operating there.

READING AND DISCUSSION QUESTIONS

1. How does McClelland explain the effect of changes in technology and the global integration of the steel industry on both the Bethlehem Steel Company and its workers?

2. What can you infer from McClelland's interview about the role of the union in the lives of steelworkers as the company faced the effects of globalization?

P9-3 | President Champions Promise of Free Trade

BILL CLINTON, *Remarks on Signing the North American Free Trade Agreement Implementation Act* (1993)

The North American Free Trade Agreement (NAFTA) eliminated trade barriers between Canada, Mexico, and the United States. Signed into law by Democratic president Bill Clinton, the initial agreements were negotiated under Republican president George H. W. Bush, a sign of the legislation's bipartisan support. Opponents, however, predicted job losses, lowered wages, and the erosion of environmental protections. In his public remarks, President Clinton defended NAFTA from critics' charges. More than two decades later however, NAFTA remained contentious. As the Republican candidate for president, Donald Trump threatened to renegotiate NAFTA as one of the first acts of his presidency. Three years later, he signed a replacement trade agreement known as the United States-Mexico-Canada Agreement (U.S.M.C.A.).

In a few moments, I will sign the North American free trade act into law. NAFTA will tear down trade barriers between our three nations. It will create the

William J. Clinton, "Remarks on Signing the North American Free Trade Agreement Implementation Act," December 8, 1993. Online by Gerhard Peters and John T. Woolley, *The American Presidency Project*, https://www.presidency.ucsb.edu/node/219946.

world's largest trade zone and create 200,000 jobs in this country by 1995 alone. The environmental and labor side agreements negotiated by our administration will make this agreement a force for social progress as well as economic growth. Already the confidence we've displayed by ratifying NAFTA has begun to bear fruit. We are now making real progress toward a worldwide trade agreement so significant that it could make the material gains of NAFTA for our country look small by comparison.

Today we have the chance to do what our parents did before us. We have the opportunity to remake the world. For this new era, our national security we now know will be determined as much by our ability to pull down foreign trade barriers as by our ability to breach distant ramparts. Once again, we are leading. And in so doing, we are rediscovering a fundamental truth about ourselves: When we lead, we build security, we build prosperity for our own people. . . .

Make no mistake, the global economy with all of its promise and perils is now the central fact of life for hard-working Americans. It has enriched the lives of millions of Americans. But for too many those same winds of change have worn away at the basis of their security. For two decades, most people have worked harder for less. Seemingly secure jobs have been lost. And while America once again is the most productive nation on Earth, this productivity itself holds the seeds of further insecurity. After all, productivity means the same people can produce more or, very often, that fewer people can produce more. This is the world we face.

We cannot stop global change. We cannot repeal the international economic competition that is everywhere. We can only harness the energy to our benefit. Now we must recognize that the only way for a wealthy nation to grow richer is to export, to simply find new customers for the products and services it makes. That, my fellow Americans, is the decision the Congress made when they voted to ratify NAFTA. . . .

My fellow Americans, bit by bit all these things are creating the conditions of a sustained global expansion. As significant as they are, our goals must be more ambitious. The United States must seek nothing less than a new trading system that benefits all nations through robust commerce but that protects our middle class and gives other nations a chance to grow one, that lifts workers and the environment up without dragging people down, that seeks to ensure that our policies reflect our values.

Our agenda must, therefore, be far reaching. We are determining that dynamic trade cannot lead to environmental despoliation. We will seek new institutional arrangements to ensure that trade leaves the world cleaner than before. We will press for workers in all countries to secure rights that we now take for granted, to organize and earn a decent living. . . .

Next year, our administration will propose comprehensive legislation to transform our unemployment system into a reemployment and job retraining system for the 21st century. . . . [W]e have an obligation to protect those workers who do bear the brunt of competition by giving them a chance to be retrained and to go on to a new and different and, ultimately, more secure and more rewarding way of work. In recent years, this social contract has been sundered. It cannot continue. . . .

I ask those who opposed NAFTA to work with us to guarantee that the labor and side agreements are enforced, and I call on all of us who believe in NAFTA to join with me to urge the Congress to create the world's best worker training and retraining system. . . . It means greater productivity, lower unemployment, greater worker efficiency, and higher wages and greater security for our people. We have to do that.

We seek a new and more open global trading system not for its own sake but for our own sake. Good jobs, rewarding careers, broadened horizons for the middle-class Americans can only be secured by expanding exports and global growth.

READING AND DISCUSSION QUESTIONS

1. How does Clinton describe the advantages of NAFTA to skeptics? What impact on the American economy does he predict?

2. Analyze Clinton's remarks concerning NAFTA for evidence of the increased importance of globalization in the 1990s. What perspective toward globalization does Clinton embrace?

P9-4 | Retail Giant Dominates Global Marketplace

CHARLES FISHMAN, *The Wal-Mart You Don't Know* (2003)

The success of retailing giant Walmart is indicative of the late-twentieth-century shift in the American economy from an industrial and manufacturing base to a growing service base. As Charles Fishman describes in this profile, Walmart's global supply chains, managed by cutting-edge technology, revolutionized all aspects of the retail industry, leading supporters to praise the company's innovations and causing opponents to lament the economic and social fallout from its relentless quest to shave cents off the price of everyday consumer goods.

A gallon-sized jar of whole pickles is something to behold. The jar is the size of a small aquarium. The fat green pickles, floating in swampy juice, look reptilian, their shapes exaggerated by the glass. It weighs 12 pounds, too big to carry with one hand. The gallon jar of pickles is a display of abundance and excess; it is entrancing, and also vaguely unsettling. This is the product that Wal-Mart fell in love with: Vlasic's gallon jar of pickles.

Wal-Mart priced it at $2.97 — a year's supply of pickles for less than $3! "They were using it as a 'statement' item," says Pat Hunn, who calls himself the "mad scientist" of Vlasic's gallon jar. "Wal-Mart was putting it before consumers,

"The Wal-Mart You Don't Know," (2003). Charles Fishman, "The Wal-Mart You Don't Know," *Fast Company* 77 (December 2003): 68–76. Fast Company by Fast Company, Inc. Reproduced with permission of Fast Company, Inc.

saying, This represents what Wal-Mart's about. You can buy a stinkin' gallon of pickles for $2.97. And it's the nation's number-one brand."

Therein lies the basic conundrum of doing business with the world's largest retailer. By selling a gallon of kosher dills for less than most grocers sell a quart, Wal-Mart may have provided a service for its customers. But what did it do for Vlasic? The pickle maker had spent decades convincing customers that they should pay a premium for its brand. Now Wal-Mart was practically giving them away. And the fevered buying spree that resulted distorted every aspect of Vlasic's operations, from farm field to factory to financial statement.

Indeed, as Vlasic discovered, the real story of Wal-Mart, the story that never gets told, is the story of the pressure the biggest retailer relentlessly applies to its suppliers in the name of bringing us "everyday low prices." It's the story of what that pressure does to the companies Wal-Mart does business with, to U.S. manufacturing, and to the economy as a whole. That story can be found floating in a gallon jar of pickles at Wal-Mart. . . .

Wal-Mart wields its power for just one purpose: to bring the lowest possible prices to its customers. At Wal-Mart, that goal is never reached. The retailer has a clear policy for suppliers: On basic products that don't change, the price Wal-Mart will pay, and will charge shoppers, must drop year after year. But what almost no one outside the world of Wal-Mart and its 21,000 suppliers knows is the high cost of those low prices. Wal-Mart has the power to squeeze profit-killing concessions from vendors. To survive in the face of its pricing demands, makers of everything from bras to bicycles to blue jeans have had to lay off employees and close U.S. plants in favor of outsourcing products from overseas.

Of course, U.S. companies have been moving jobs offshore for decades, long before Wal-Mart was a retailing power. But there is no question that the chain is helping accelerate the loss of American jobs to low-wage countries such as China. Wal-Mart, which in the late 1980s and early 1990s trumpeted its claim to "Buy American," has doubled its imports from China in the past five years alone, buying some $12 billion in merchandise in 2002. That's nearly 10% of all Chinese exports to the United States. . . .

"People ask, 'How can it be bad for things to come into the U.S. cheaply? How can it be bad to have a bargain at Wal-Mart?' Sure, it's held inflation down, and it's great to have bargains," says Dobbins [CEO of Carolina Mills]. "But you can't buy anything if you're not employed. We are shopping ourselves out of jobs."

There is no question that Wal-Mart's relentless drive to squeeze out costs has benefited consumers. . . . There is also no question that doing business with Wal-Mart can give a supplier a fast, heady jolt of sales and market share. But that fix can come with long-term consequences for the health of a brand and a business. . . .

At some point in the late 1990s, a Wal-Mart buyer saw Vlasic's gallon jar and started talking to Pat Hunn about it. Hunn, who has also since left Vlasic, was then head of Vlasic's Wal-Mart sales team, based in Dallas. The gallon intrigued the buyer. In sales tests, priced somewhere over $3, "the gallon sold like crazy," says Hunn, "surprising us all." The Wal-Mart buyer had a brainstorm: What would happen to the gallon if they offered it nationwide and got it below $3? Hunn was skeptical, but his job was to look for ways to sell pickles at Wal-Mart. Why not?

And so Vlasic's gallon jar of pickles went into every Wal-Mart, some 3,000 stores, at $2.97, a price so low that Vlasic and Wal-Mart were making only a penny or two on a jar, if that. It was showcased on big pallets near the front of stores. It was an abundance of abundance. "It was selling 80 jars a week, on average, in every store," says Young. Doesn't sound like much, until you do the math: That's 240,000 gallons of pickles, just in gallon jars, just at Wal-Mart, every week. Whole fields of cucumbers were heading out the door.

For Vlasic, the gallon jar of pickles became what might be called a devastating success. "Quickly, it started cannibalizing our non-Wal-Mart business," says Young. "We saw consumers who used to buy the spears and the chips in supermarkets buying the Wal-Mart gallons. They'd eat a quarter of a jar and throw the thing away when they got moldy. A family can't eat them fast enough."

The gallon jar reshaped Vlasic's pickle business: It chewed up the profit margin of the business with Wal-Mart, and of pickles generally. Procurement had to scramble to find enough pickles to fill the gallons, but the volume gave Vlasic strong sales numbers, strong growth numbers, and a powerful place in the world of pickles at Wal-Mart. Which accounted for 30% of Vlasic's business. But the company's profits from pickles had shriveled 25% or more, Young says—millions of dollars.

The gallon was hoisting Vlasic and hurting it at the same time.

Young remembers begging Wal-Mart for relief. "They said, 'No way,' " says Young. "We said we'll increase the price"—even $3.49 would have helped tremendously—"and they said, 'If you do that, all the other products of yours we buy, we'll stop buying.' It was a clear threat." Hunn recalls things a little differently, if just as ominously: "They said, 'We want the $2.97 gallon of pickles. If you don't do it, we'll see if someone else might.' I knew our competitors were saying to Wal-Mart, 'We'll do the $2.97 gallons if you give us your other business.' " Wal-Mart's business was so indispensable to Vlasic, and the gallon so central to the Wal-Mart relationship, that decisions about the future of the gallon were made at the CEO level.

Finally, Wal-Mart let Vlasic up for air. "The Wal-Mart guy's response was classic," Young recalls. "He said, 'Well, we've done to pickles what we did to orange juice. We've killed it. We can back off.' " Vlasic got to take it down to just over half a gallon of pickles, for $2.79. Not long after that, in January 2001, Vlasic filed for bankruptcy—although the gallon jar of pickles, everyone agrees, wasn't a critical factor. . . .

In the end, of course, it is we as shoppers who have the power, and who have given that power to Wal-Mart. Part of Wal-Mart's dominance, part of its insight, and part of its arrogance, is that it presumes to speak for American shoppers.

If Wal-Mart doesn't like the pricing on something, says Andrew Whitman, who helped service Wal-Mart for years when he worked at General Foods and

Kraft, they simply say, "At that price we no longer think it's a good value to our shopper. Therefore, we don't think we should carry it."

Wal-Mart has also lulled shoppers into ignoring the difference between the price of something and the cost. Its unending focus on price underscores something that Americans are only starting to realize about globalization: Ever-cheaper prices have consequences. Says Steve Dobbins, president of thread maker Carolina Mills: "We want clean air, clear water, good living conditions, the best health care in the world — yet we aren't willing to pay for anything manufactured under those restrictions."

Randall Larrimore, a former CEO of MasterBrand Industries, the parent company of Master Lock, understands that contradiction too well. For years, he says, as manufacturing costs in the United States rose, Master Lock was able to pass them along. But at some point in the 1990s, Asian manufacturers started producing locks for much less. "When the difference is $1, retailers like Wal-Mart would prefer to have the brand-name padlock or faucet or hammer," Larrimore says. "But as the spread becomes greater, when our padlock was $9, and the import was $6, then they can offer the consumer a real discount by carrying two lines. Ultimately, they may only carry one line."

In January 1997, Master Lock announced that, after 75 years making locks in Milwaukee, it would begin importing more products from Asia. Not too long after, Master Lock opened a factory of its own in Nogales, Mexico. Today, it makes just 10% to 15% of its locks in Milwaukee — its 300 employees there mostly make parts that are sent to Nogales, where there are now 800 factory workers.

Larrimore did the first manufacturing layoffs at Master Lock. He negotiated with Master Lock's unions himself. He went to Bentonville. "I loved dealing with Wal-Mart, with Home Depot," he says. "They are all very rational people. There wasn't a whole lot of room for negotiation. And they had a good point. Everyone was willing to pay more for a Master Lock. But how much more can they justify? If they can buy a lock that has arguably similar quality, at a cheaper price, well, they can get their consumers a deal."

It's Wal-Mart in the role of Adam Smith's invisible hand. And the Milwaukee employees of Master Lock who shopped at Wal-Mart to save money helped that hand shove their own jobs right to Nogales. Not consciously, not directly, but inevitably. "Do we as consumers appreciate what we're doing?" Larrimore asks. "I don't think so. But even if we do, I think we say, Here's a Master Lock for $9, here's another lock for $6 — let the other guy pay $9."

READING AND DISCUSSION QUESTIONS

1. What factors does Fishman cite as the leading causes of Walmart's unrivaled success? To what extent do those factors illuminate broader economic trends in America during the early twenty-first century?

2. How does Fishman describe the effects of Walmart's business model on America's labor market? What impact does Walmart have on its workers and the communities in which they live?

P9-5 | Cartoon Highlights Immigration Irony

KHALIL BENDIB, *Help Wanted* (2010)

The NAFTA agreement signed by President Bill Clinton was supposed to lead to economic growth and job creation. Many of its critics, however, pointed out that the free trade zone it created accelerated the movement of American manufacturing to low-wage countries and exacerbated economic uncertainty for vulnerable people in the United States and Mexico. The elimination of tariffs, for example, made it impossible for small-scale Mexican farmers to compete against U.S. agribusiness, which often received federal subsidies. As a consequence, poorer Mexicans sought economic opportunity by crossing the border and taking low-wage jobs in the United States, sometimes in the same industries from which they were displaced in Mexico. Migration and international trade became entwined and these issues created contradictory policy implications, as cartoonist Khalil Bendib captured in his 2010 political cartoon, "Help Wanted." Bendib depicts corporate America and the Immigration and Customs Enforcement agency (ICE) posting "wanted" signs targeting the same population, but for radically different purposes.

Khalil Bendib/OtherWords

READING AND DISCUSSION QUESTIONS

1. What does Bendib see as the core dilemma of the United States' international trade and economic policies? How are the goals of corporate America at odds with the goals of America's immigration policies?

2. To what extent is the issue Bendib highlighted in 2010 still relevant to the politics of today?

P9-6 | Protesting Trump

JAKE GREEN, *Trump Protests—Michigan* (2017)

Republican Donald Trump's electoral college victory stunned political observers, many of whom misjudged the support his unorthodox campaign generated among white working-class Americans who warmed to his "Make America Great Again" message. In a period of rapid globalization, Trump's nationalist rhetoric reversed course from the policies of recent administrations that emphasized engagement with other nations. Within weeks of his inauguration, the president issued executive orders in an attempt to make good on his campaign promises. One order, banning refugees and immigrants from selected Muslim-majority countries, sparked widespread protests. In this February 2017 photograph, women in Kalamazoo, Michigan, protest "Islamophobia" while taking selfies.

Jake Green/Kalamazoo Gazette-MLive Media Group via AP

READING AND DISCUSSION QUESTIONS

1. What political message are the women making with their sign, which reads "Love not hate makes America great"? What is the significance of the sign's image of a Muslim woman wearing an American flag hijab?

2. What can you conclude from this image regarding the issues separating Trump's supporters and opponents? Why do you think immigration dominated the campaign and the early months of Trump's presidency?

3. How might a historian use this image to talk about the role social media played in twenty-first-century America? To what extent do you think social media shaped the 2016 presidential election?

▪ COMPARATIVE QUESTIONS ▪

1. Compare how Irving Kristol (Document P9-1) and Leroy McClelland Sr. (Document P9-2) each would have explained the demise of the steel industry. Which factors would each single out as leading causes? How might you account for the differences you see?

2. Assess the role of organized labor in debates about America's economic policy during the twentieth century by comparing the observations of Leroy McClelland Sr. (Document P9-2) with those of Dolores Huerta (Document 27-6). What similarities or differences can you identify in their assessments of the problems facing workers?

3. Given the information in Charles Fishman's article (Document P9-4), to what extent do you see Walmart as a culmination of trends begun during the late-nineteenth-century industrial and managerial revolution? Did Walmart build on those earlier transformations, or does Walmart represent a new phase in global economics?

4. What conclusions can you draw about capitalism as an economic and social force by comparing Irving Kristol (Document P9-1) with William Graham Sumner (Document P6-1) and Huey Long (Document 22-2)? What changes over time can you identify in their respective assessments of the value of America's market-based economy?

Acknowledgments (*continued from page iv*)

29-4 Excerpts from *Gender Gap: Bella Abzug's Guide to Political Power for America Women* by Bella Abzug and Mimi Kelber. Copyright © 1984 by Bella S. Abzug and Mimi Kelber. Reprinted by permission of Houghton Mifflin Harcourt Publishing Company. All rights reserved.

30-1 "Interview by April Eaton," from Alesha Daughtrey, interview by April Eaton, WTO History Project, University of Washington, August 17, 2000. Transcript at http://depts.washington .edu/wtohist/interviews/Daughtrey.pdf. Used with permission.

28-6 "An Interview with the Lone Ranger of American Fundamentalism," Christianity Today, September 4, 1981, pp. 22–27. Copyright © Christianity Today. All rights reserved. Used with permission.

25-4 Dan Gillmor, "The Care and Feeding of Spock-Marked Fathers" Parents' Magazine & Family Home Guide, 29, July 1954, 36–37, 92–93. Used with permission from Meredith Corporation. Originally published in Parents® magazine. All Rights Reserved.

23-4 "Editorial." From LULAC News Volume 12 (October 1945), pp. 5–6 is reprinted with permission from the publisher of "Testimonio: A Documentary History of the Mexican American Struggle for Civil Rights," edited by F. Arturo Gonzalez (©2000 Arte Publico Press - University of Houston)

25-3 Billy Graham, "Our Right to Require Belief," © SEPS licensed by Curtis Licensing Indianapolis, IN. All rights reserved.

26-2 Fannie Lou Hamer, "Testimony Before the Credentials Committee of the Democratic National Convention," August 22, 1964. Used by permission of Vergie Hamer Faulkner.

29-3 From "The Great Deception: What We are Told About Central America," by Robert J. Henle, in *America* 154 (May 24, 1986), pp. 432–434. Reprinted from *America*, May 24, 1986 with Permission of America Press, Inc. 2013. All rights reserved. For subscription information, call 1-800-627-9533 or visit www.americamagazine.org.

28-2 Robert Howard, "Youngstown Fights Back," The New Republic, 180, January 6, 1979, pp. 19–21. Copyright © 1979 by Robert Howard. All rights reserved. Used with permission.

21-4 Langston Hughes, "The Weary Blues" from THE COLLECTED POEMS OF LANGSTON HUGHES by Langston Hughes, edited by Arnold Rampersad with David Roessel, Associate Editor, copyright © 1994 by the Estate of Langston Hughes. Used by permission of Alfred A. Knopf, an imprint of the Knopf Doubleday Publishing Group, a division of Penguin Random House LLC and Harold Ober Associates. All rights reserved. Copyright 1994 by the Langston Hughes Estate.

24-2 From *The Cold War: A Study in U.S. Foreign Policy* by Walter Lippmann. Copyright 1947 by Walter Lippmann. Copyright renewed © 1975 by Walter Lippmann. Used by permission of HarperCollins Publishers and Harvard Management Company.

15-2 J. Wright Mooar, "The Killing of the White Buffalo," *Buffalo Days: Stories from J. Wright Mooar As Told to James Winford Hunt*, edited by Robert F. Pace, pp. 76–81. Copyright © 2005 by State House Press. All rights reserved. Used with permission.

15-4 Reprinted from *Mourning Dove: A Salishan Autobiography by Mourning Dove*, edited by Jay Miller, by permission of the University of Nebraska Press. Copyright 1990 by the University of Nebraska Press.

25-6 Malvina Reynolds, "Little Boxes." Words & Music by Malvina Records © Copyright 1962 Schroder Music Co. (ASCAP), Renewed 1990. Used by permission. All rights reserved.

28-4 Phyllis Schlafly, "Statement Opposing the ERA," Congressional Digest 56, (June–July 1977, pp. 189, 191. Copyright © 1977 by Phyllis Schlafly. All rights reserved. Used with permission.

26-4 Edmund White, "Letter to Alfred and Ann Corn. July 8 1969," from *The Violet Quill Reader: The Emergence of Gay Writing After Stonewall*. ed. David Bergman, pp. 1–4. New York: St. Martin's Press. Copyright © 1994 by Edmund White. All rights reserved. Used with permission.

23-2 Interview with Claud Woodring, January 2, 2003, from Veterans History Project, American Folklife Center, Library of Congress. http://lcweb2.loc.gov/diglib/vhp-stories/loc.natlib .afc2001001.05288/. Courtesy of Claud Woodring. Interview with Jay S. Adams, July 5, 2001, from Veterans History Project, Americans Folklife Center, Library of Congress. https://memory .loc.gov/diglib/vhp-stories/loc.natlib.afc2001001.00151/transcript?ID=sr0001

26-3 Malcolm X, The Ballot or the Bullet (1964) from Copyright © 1965, 1989 by Betty Shabazz and Pathfinder Press. Reprinted by permission.